Est. SCHIFFER
PUBLISHING *1974*

Inspiring through expert knowledge

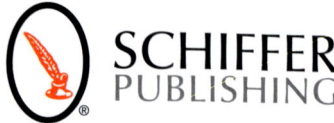
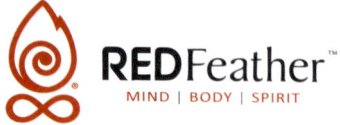
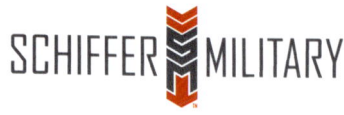
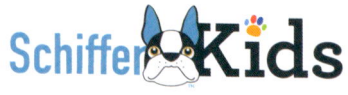

INSIDE THE MOMENT

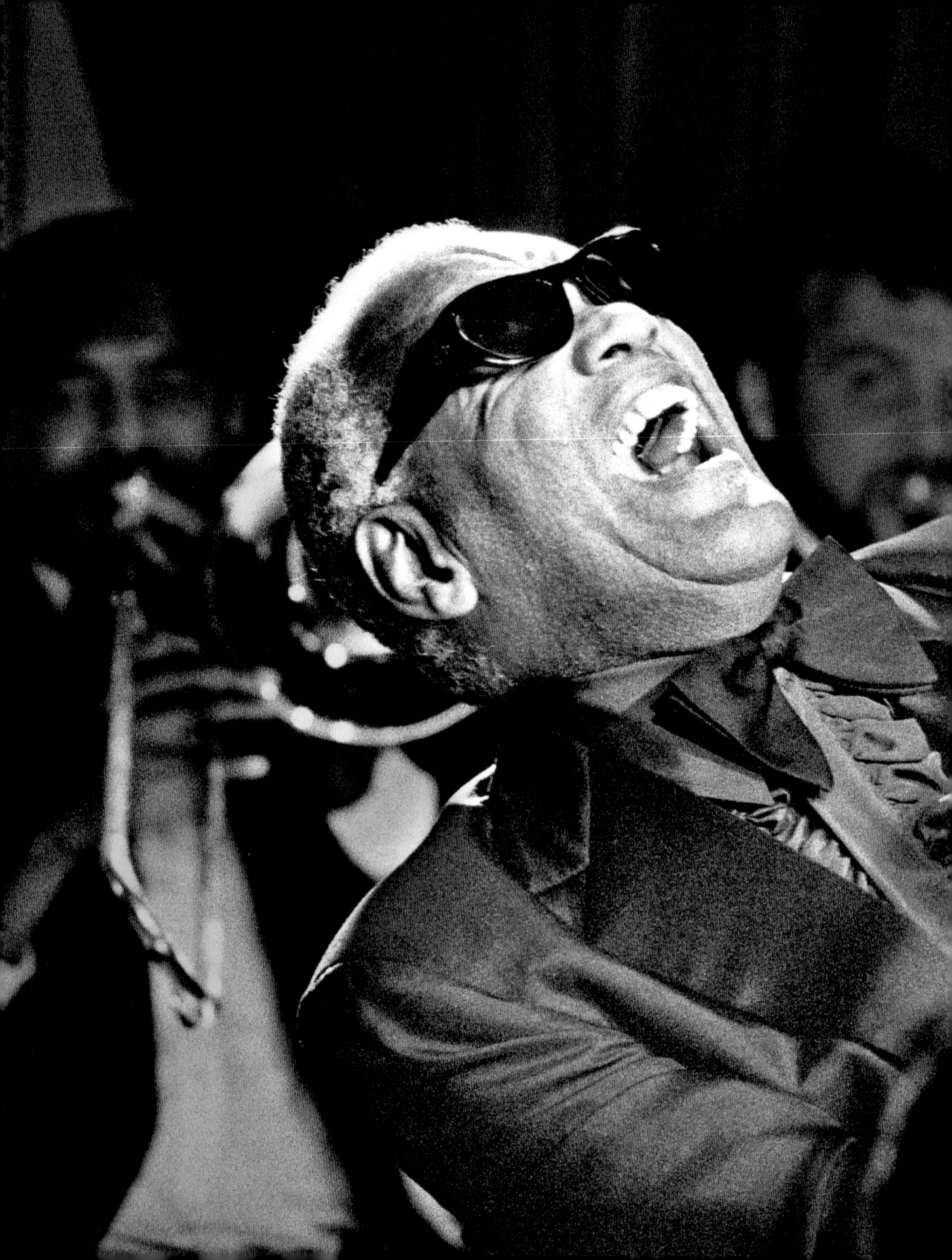

INSIDE THE MOMENT

ICONIC BLUES, SOUL, JAZZ, ROCK & ROLL, AND R&B IMAGES AND HISTORY

Forewords by
Scott Barretta, Steve Berkowitz,
and Dick Shurman

JOSEPH A. ROSEN

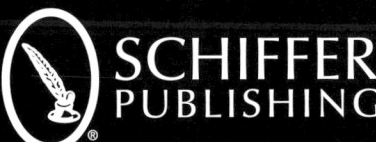

SCHIFFER PUBLISHING

4880 Lower Valley Road • Atglen, PA 19310

Other Schiffer books by the author
Blues Hands
978-0-7643-4963-8

Other Schiffer books on related subjects
Jazz in Available Light: Illuminating the Jazz Greats from the 1960s, '70s, and '80s
Veryl Oakland with foreword by Quincy Jones
978-0-7643-5483-0

The Blues: A Visual History; 100 Years of Music That Changed the World
Mike Evans, edited by Robert Gordon and Scott Barretta, with foreword by Marshall Chess
978-0-7643-5975-0

The Early Years of Rhythm & Blues
Alan Govenar
978-0-7643-1983-9

Designed by Zach Kline
Cover design by Danielle Farmer
Type set in Hackney Bold / Sweet Sans Pro / Freight Display Pro

ISBN: 978-0-7643-7011-3
ePub: 978-1-5073-0611-6

Printed in China
10 9 8 7 6 5 4 3 2 1

Published by Schiffer Publishing, Ltd.
4880 Lower Valley Road
Atglen, PA 19310
Phone: (610) 593-1777; Fax: (610) 593-2002
Email: info@schifferbooks.com
Web: www.schifferbooks.com

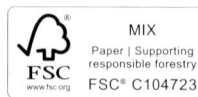

For our complete selection of fine books on this and related subjects, please visit our website at www.schifferbooks.com. You may also write for a free catalog.

Schiffer Publishing's titles are available at special discounts for bulk purchases for sales promotions or premiums. Special editions, including personalized covers, corporate imprints, and excerpts, can be created in large quantities for special needs. For more information, contact the publisher.

We are always looking for people to write books on new and related subjects. If you have an idea for a book, please contact us at proposals@schifferbooks.com.

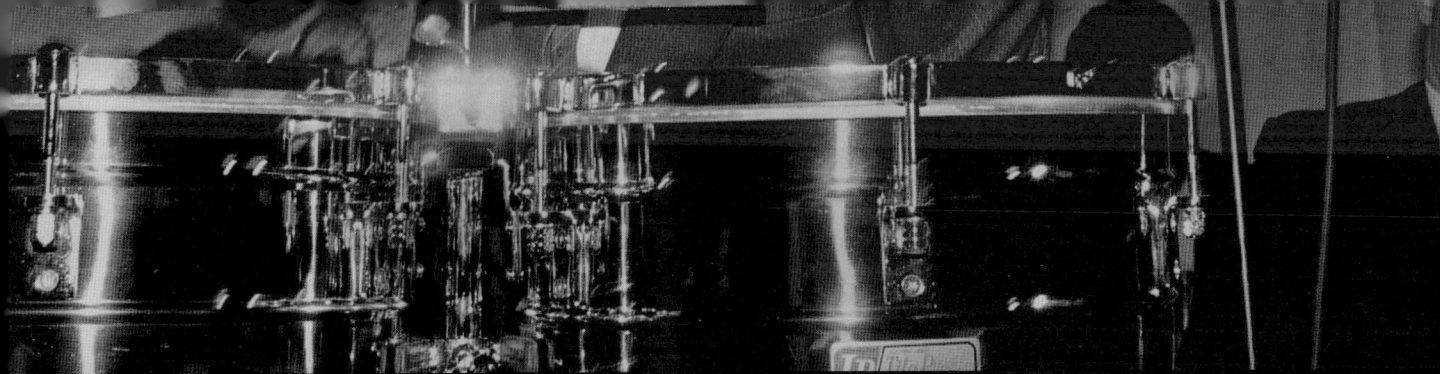

CONTENTS

FOREWORD BY SCOTT BARRETTA   8

FOREWORD BY STEVE BERKOWITZ   10

FOREWORD BY DICK SHURMAN   12

INTRODUCTION   14

CHAPTER 1   MODERN BLUES FOUNDERS   17

CHAPTER 2   SOUL   43

CHAPTER 3   JAZZ   61

CHAPTER 4   LOUISIANA RICHES   87

CHAPTER 5   RHYTHM & BLUES   113

CHAPTER 6   BLUES MOVING FORWARD   127

CHAPTER 7   MISSISSIPPI BLUES   149

CHAPTER 8   ROCK & ROLL   165

NOTES ABOUT THE PHOTOGRAPHS   174

ACKNOWLEDGMENTS   216

INDEX   216

DEDICATION

In making this book of black-and-white music photographs, I cannot think of anyone more fitting to whom to dedicate it than Herman Leonard. Herman was a friend and mentor. I was a fan of his work before I knew it was his. I'd see great photos on albums and in books and magazines, and I was drawn to drama of the figure emerging from dark into the light. It just seemed the right way to take a photograph. When I dug a little deeper, I realized that the photos that most moved me were more often than not Herman's. He was an amazing talent, the dean of the jazz photographers, bringing insight and emotion as well as superb technical skills to his work. When we met, we just hit it off. We would naturally "talk shop," and I might gain some technical insight into his brilliant work, but more important was the friendship. More than in any technical sense, he was a mentor at being and staying creative, open, caring, excited, fresh, and enthusiastic. More that twenty-five years my senior, and a master of older analog photography, he was always exploring, learning, questioning, and sharing. He was an amazing man. He was completely generous of spirit, talent, and wisdom, and the effect he had on me and those who knew him personally, as well as the world in general, is beyond measure.

If I had never touched a camera, I would be proud to call him a friend. His work is part of our culture, and if you're not familiar, I encourage you to seek it out. *Inside the Moment* is dedicated to Herman Leonard.

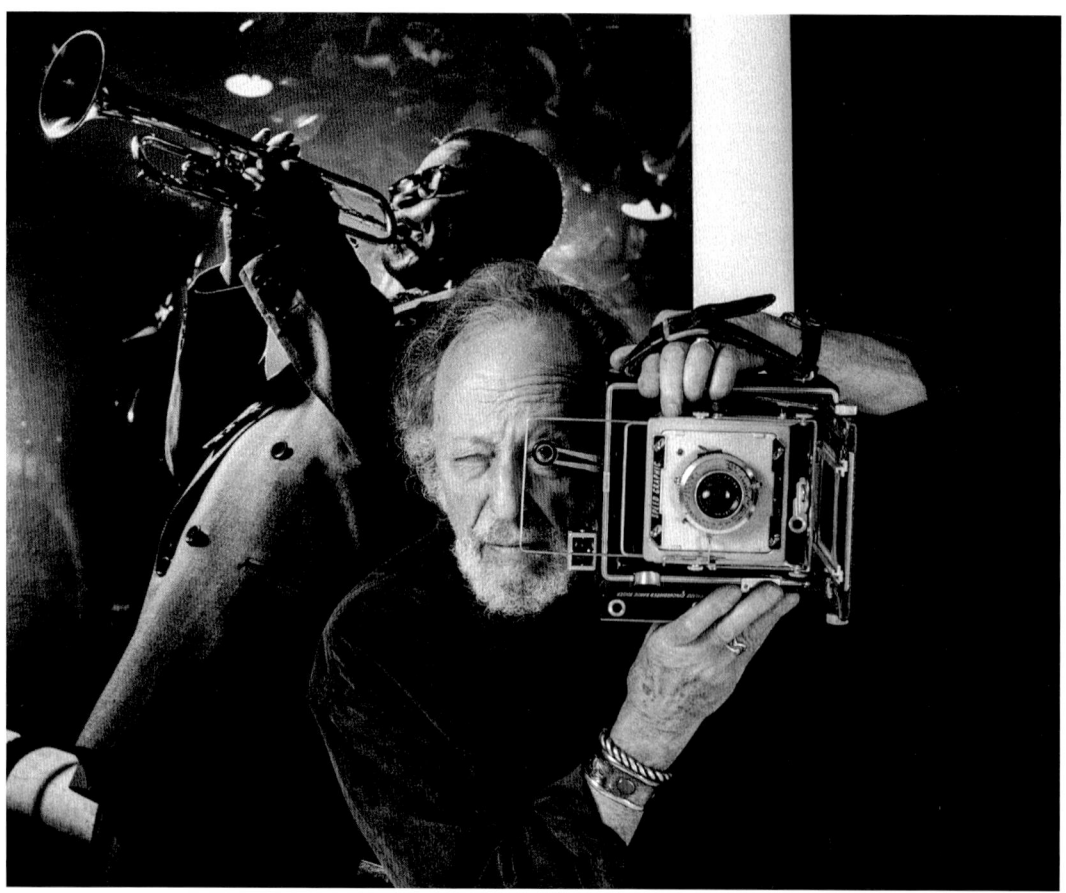

Herman Leonard. © Joseph A. Rosen

There is one thing the photograph must contain, the humanity of the moment.

—ROBERT FRANK

It is an illusion that photos are made with the camera … they are made with the eye, heart, and head.

—HENRI CARTIER-BRESSON

You should have heard just what I seen.

—BO DIDDLEY

I get the camera; it's the rest of the world that confuses me.

—JOSEPH A. ROSEN

Above all, enjoy the music.

—HERMAN LEONARD

FOREWORD

BY SCOTT BARRETTA

Today, photographs of many our favorite musicians are ubiquitous, readily accessible in just seconds on the internet and constantly appropriated to lend a cool vibe to social media profiles. It's a pleasure to have so much at our fingertips, but it's all too seldom that credit, notice, or payment is provided to the photographers who, like Joseph A. Rosen, spent decades honing their skills.

The proliferation of photographs today might be compared to a century ago, when many recording artists were scantily documented. While it's likely we could locate hundreds of photos of now-forgotten million-sellers like Ted Weems or Gene Austin, the dearth of images of artists now considered legendary is striking. Only one photo of Buddy Bolden, the "Father of Jazz," is known to exist, and the 1990 boxed set of the complete recordings of Robert Johnson was delayed for years until the two known, but heretofore unseen, photos of him could be included.

We largely know what many artists from the pre–World War II era or even up through the 1960s look like via publicity shots arranged by labels, or due to the diligence of researchers who located family friends or fellow musicians. While photographers were employed by mainstream media outlets to capture classical performers or New York stage productions, more-vernacular performers tended not to be regarded as "important" enough to be documented.

An exception was specialty magazines such as the jazz bible *DownBeat*, founded in 1934, where pioneering music photographers such as Joe Rosen's friend and mentor, Herman Leonard, published his stunning work of bebop pioneers. The arrival of the LP in the late 1940s provided another important format, resulting in collectible 12" × 12" artwork. The first notable blues photographer was Chicago's Raeburn Flerlage, a fashion industry specialist and record distributor who was recruited by Moe Asch of Folkways Records to shoot album covers.

The burgeoning festival scene in the 1960s allowed unprecedented access to a wide variety of performers, as seen in the work of erstwhile artist manager Dick Waterman, British photographer Valerie Wilmer, and Michael P. Smith, the premier documentarian of New Orleans vernacular musical traditions. David Gahr, a prolific New Yorker who photographed virtually all the Newport Folk and Jazz Festivals, amassed a great body of blues work in addition to his work in other genres. In the jazz realm, men such as Chuck Stewart, Roy DeCarava, and William Claxton are notable for their passion and dedication and also for creating great bodies of work.

Rosen's work can be seen as continuing the legacy of the photographers listed above; we first became acquainted when I began editing *Living Blues* magazine, for which he had been a regular contributor. He's been a dream to work with over the years, quickly providing a wide range of images even with unreasonable deadlines. His live shots "inside the moment" stand out from those of many others, resulting in portraits that have adorned many magazine and record covers, and the depth of his catalog is stunning.

Being based in New York is a plus—I'm perpetually envious when I see his images from long-defunct clubs, including the Lone Star—but Joe's frequently on the move, and I really got to know him through his frequent and extended visits to the music meccas of Chicago, Memphis, New Orleans, southwestern Louisiana, and here in Mississippi, where we've had the pleasure of spending time with many artists who rarely leave the state.

Joe's skills, flexibility, passion, and widely recognized "great guy" qualities have resulted in him becoming a sanctioned and supported photographer at many events, including the Legendary Rhythm & Blues Cruise and the remarkable Ponderosa Stomp festivals in New Orleans, where he captured hundreds of veteran artists from the genres of New Orleans R&B, country, rockabilly, soul, and blues. The Ponderosa Stomp was my favorite event, and, like many others, my memories of it are filtered through Joe's brilliant photography.

SCOTT BARRETTA

Writer/researcher for the Mississippi Blues Trail, instructor of sociology and anthropology at the University of Mississippi

FOREWORD

BY STEVE BERKOWITZ

If you visit Joe Rosen's website, the first photograph you see is of James Brown in full scream, followed by a shot of bejeweled wrists and hands, the backstage wristband of an unidentified pianist … no doubt a blues man, followed by an image of the Great Wall of China, followed by a sparkling photograph of the World Trade Center towers when they were Manhattan's peaks and guidepost. All lasting, iconic, real from their moment in time—shot by Joe Rosen.

The photo sequence is no accident. In addition to his prodigious compositional experience and technical skills as a commercial photographer, Joe Rosen is a music man himself, deeply in focus and in tune with the music, its makers, and their orbits.

Photography is how Joe Rosen makes music.

He has long lived inside the music and arts community, welcomed, accepted, and loved by the musicians, who trust that he will capture their moments and tell their truths. They know he sees, feels, and hears them, that his life is enriched by their efforts to form connections of community, struggle, sorrow, swing, and joy with their audiences.

There is no space between artist, photographer, and audience because, as the title makes clear, Joe Rosen is *inside the moment*, capturing the moment of creation when everything is everything, and the room is unified, fleeting, and abiding.

The book's biographies and captions accompanying those moments provide facts, and maybe a few surprises, from his life's journey. His pictures are illuminations capturing the souls of his subjects, their dignity, their depth of feeling, their individual effort, and their manner of delivery. He joins the union that happens only in that moment that makes music, memories, emotions, and history.

Writing of the great Johnny Otis, Joe reveals his gratitude for "spending a few heartbeats" with the great musician/writer/producer at lunch, after a radio broadcast. Photographs capture one heartbeat at a time, and they can capture the truth; Joe's images do. As the line goes in the song "Every Beat of My Heart" by Johnny Otis: "In every beat of my heart, there's a beat for you."

We get to share that heart and beat *inside the moment*.

Thank you, Joe.

STEVE BERKOWITZ

Musician, producer, former artist manager and Columbia Records / Legacy Recordings / Sony Music executive

FOREWORD

BY DICK SHURMAN

Joe Rosen has been blazing a distinguished path through the world of photography for a half century, earning a degree and parlaying it into a career of high-level commercial and corporate work. Throughout, his passion has been photographing blues, jazz, soul, zydeco, and related vernacular music. His 2002 Keeping the Blues Alive award, exhibitions, countless magazine covers, and accompanying shots, album covers, and calendars reflect his status as he has captured peak musical moments all around the country and the world. He has done mentors and inspirations such as Herman Leonard and Ernest Withers proud and has become a role model and mentor himself.

Joe's previous book, *Blues Hands*, focused on a specific part of the human anatomy and what it reflects. Now, with *Inside the Moment*, the intent is more general: to preserve and perpetuate a remarkable slice of a wondrous but inevitably passing scene. He has collected roughly 125 striking black-and-white photographs of famous and obscure musicians and revelers from venues ranging from South Louisiana dance halls and Mississippi juke joints to Legendary Rhythm and Blues Cruises (Joe has long been an official photographer) and Bluesapalooza in Iraq. The results are organized by genre, geography, and historical context. Each section has a brief but authoritative overview by a knowledgeable contributor to supplement Joe's own observations.

A photographer looks for an eye-catching moment that brings a convergence of factors. Ideally, these factors include expressiveness, authenticity, energy, and a passion not unlike what a great photographer brings to the quest.

Joe offers three special assets in his role in identifying, anticipating, and capturing such moments. First, the ongoing nonmusical work, which has paid most of the bills, reflects obvious chops and skills as a craftsman. His technical prowess is exemplary. Second, Joe brings not only a passion for the music, but a broad and deep knowledge of the contributors and milieus in which they work. So, we get not only Ray Charles and John Lee Hooker, but also L. C. Ulmer and Bud Welch. Of course, the emphasis is on many greats whose musical gifts and captured moments have proven to be timeless. Third, Joe is beloved personally and professionally in the world he inhabits and enriches. He understands and loves the music, the musicians, and the moment, and his subjects appreciate that insight and passion. It's clear that he has soul, and it's recognized and responded to. Joe is not just tolerated as he works—he is welcomed and doubtless inspires the performance in many cases. Anthropologists have long wrestled with the conundrum that the mere act of observation affects that which is observed. Being a positive force sure doesn't hurt.

This foreword is a celebration of Joe and of *Inside the Moment*. But it's not just the welcome appearance of a new book that prompts this praise, and this praise doesn't come just from a longtime fan who is proud to call Joe a friend. At the end of his presentation on the winter 2024 Legendary Rhythm and Blues Cruise, Joe was treated to a richly deserved standing ovation by the overflow audience. That monumental moment was commemorated with a special award during the ritual wrap-up. *Inside the Moment* too deserves such enthusiastic recognition, for the goal of preservation it pursues and for the quality with which it makes remarkable musical moments timeless. A lot of greatness is reflected—on both sides of the camera.

DICK SHURMAN
Producer, writer, historian, Grammy Award recipient, and member
of the Blues Foundation's hall of fame

INTRODUCTION

I am a fan first, who happens to be a professional photographer. Black-and-white photography was my first love. It was my entry to the amazing world of photography.

I'm glad I came of age in an era when the first generation of artists whose work shaped and defined the genres I love were still active, vital, and accessible. I'm also glad that I have been able to experience many artists who, while not widely known, were equally as wonderful as those who had gained great recognition.

There are many active contemporary artists whose music I love and who are carrying the music forward who are not within the scope of this book. With only a few exceptions, this book is composed of earlier photos of those artists whose work is related to those genres and traditions.

As a fan I would attend shows of the music I loved, and it was natural to take photos. Nothing fancy, just a small Leica and maybe a lens or two. When I started, things were very casual. If you were polite, respectful, and unobtrusive, there was never a problem. As time went on, both the equipment and the access became more complex, but the thrill of capturing a moment never changed.

And it's about the moment. With the advances in technology, making sharp, well-exposed photos has become relatively easy, and composition can be learned. For a photograph to succeed, those elements must be present, but it's about more than that. There has to be insight, a humanity, and a connection of the subject to the viewer, and that instant where all three are present and in sync. Then something special is revealed.

That is what I have strived for with these photographs: to render with beauty the spirit, the energy, the music, the artist, and that instant when it all is one. I want to see *inside the moment*.

JOSEPH A. ROSEN

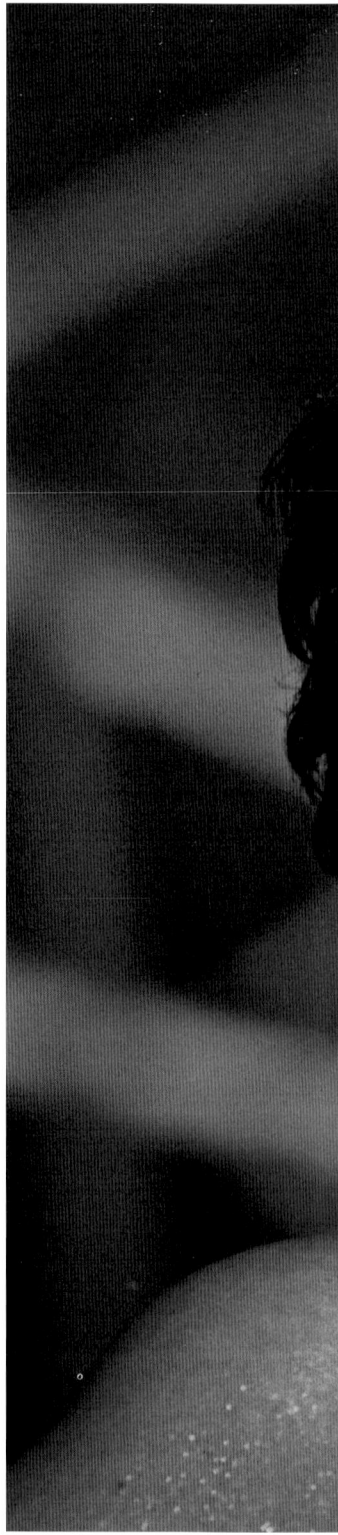

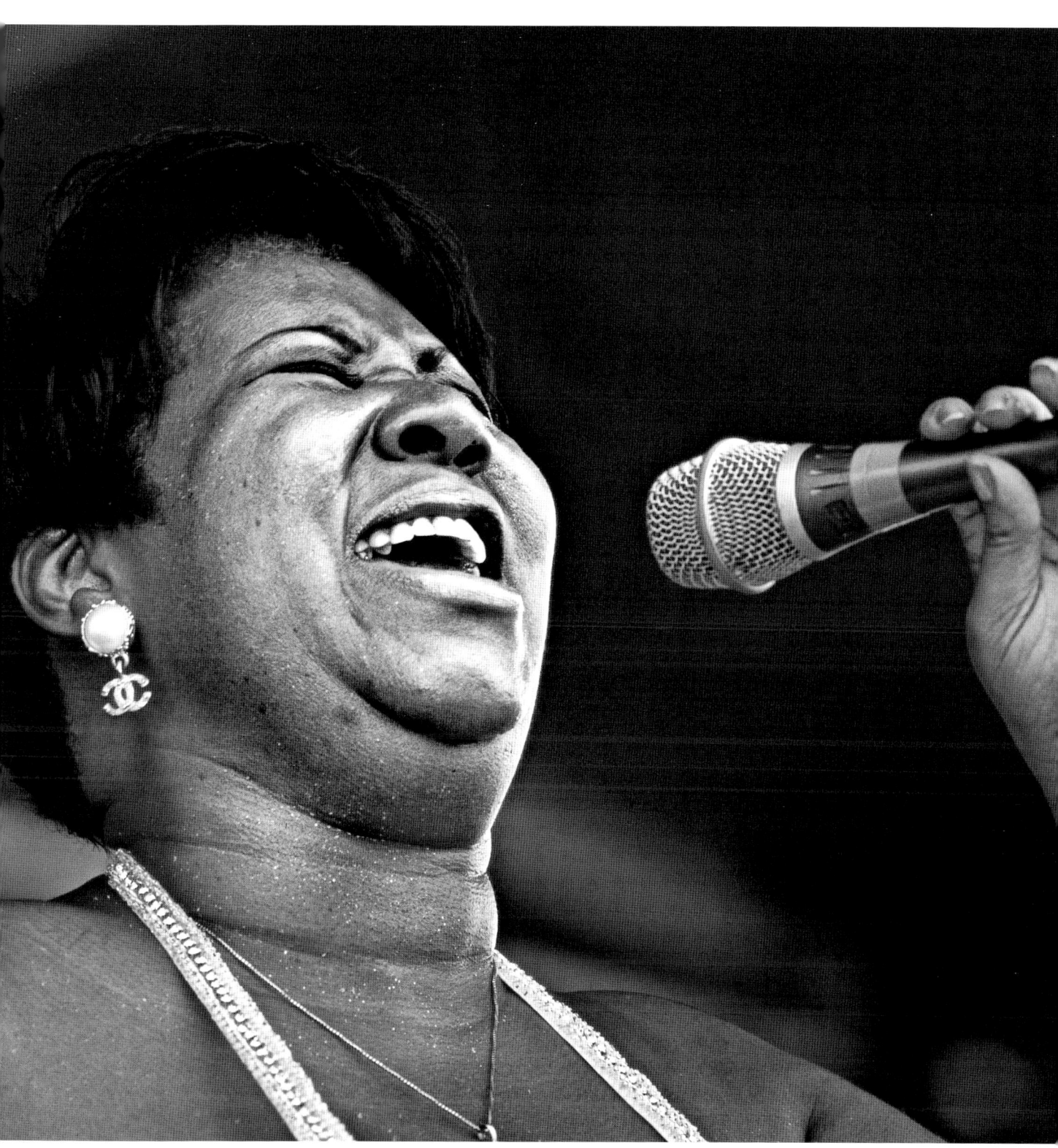

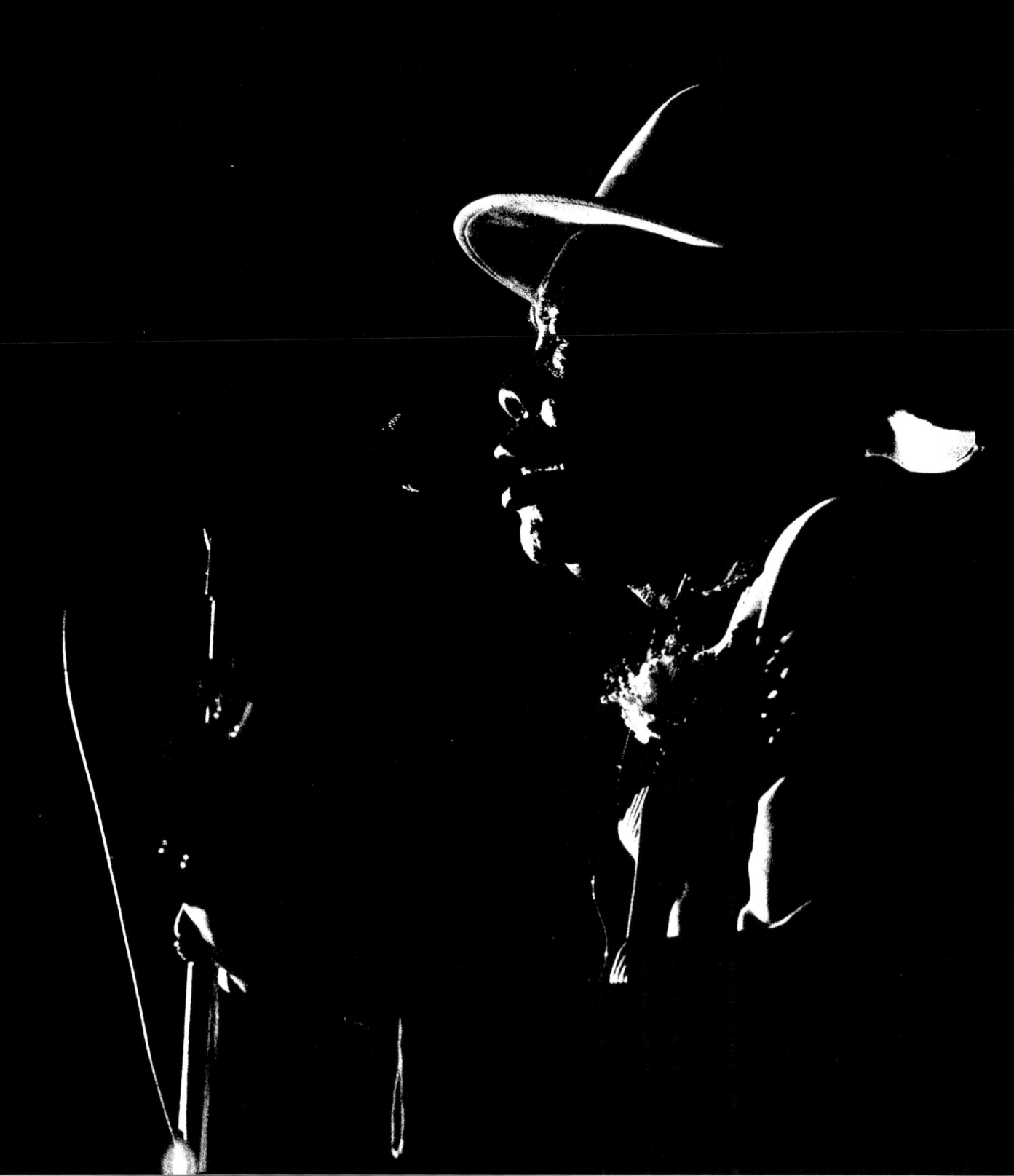

CHAPTER 1

MODERN BLUES FOUNDERS

The introduction of amplification to the guitar transformed the blues genre into a whole new sensation. Prior to World War II, a handful of pioneers led by T-Bone Walker attached pickups to their axes and began adapting what they'd perfected on their trusty acoustic models into something louder and more brash that was tailor-made for all-night juke joint soirees. During the postwar era, electric blues exploded all over the country, from Chicago to Texas, Memphis to Louisiana, and Los Angeles to New York. That groundbreaking movement spawned a set of hallowed heroes that will forever stand as immortal.

In the Windy City, Muddy Waters's slashing slide guitar and gruff Mississippi-bred vocals set a majestic pace, his nonpareil band featuring harmonica genius Little Walter (whose pioneering use of amplification rendered the humble mouth organ truly mammoth in scope), guitarist Jimmy Rogers, and pianist Otis Spann. The feral roar of Howlin' Wolf and laid-back high-end harp wailer Jimmy Reed challenged Muddy for supremacy across the South and West Sides, defining what Chicago blues was all about. During the latter half of the 1950s, a fresh crop of flashy young lead guitarists—Otis Rush, Magic Sam, Buddy Guy, Freddie King, Eddy Clearwater—emerged to offer an up-and-coming generation of British blues rockers an indelible blueprint to follow during the next decade. And follow it they did.

Naturally, T-Bone reigned supreme in the Lone Star State during the postwar era, his impeccable licks and velvet-smooth pipes spawning a small army of accurate imitators. Yet, there was also the ultracool, fleet-fingered Lightnin' Hopkins, as well as Clarence "Gatemouth" Brown, whose dizzying jazz-inflected fretwork expanded wildly on T-Bone's inventions, and later on, the icy, vibrato-laden Telecaster attack of Albert Collins.

John Lee Hooker

Freddie wasn't the only blues guitar titan who happened to sport the regal surname of King. He was preceded by Riley B. King, who adopted the handle of "Blues Boy" when he got his feet wet on Memphis radio, that nickname soon shortened to B.B. No blues guitarist on the planet was more influential over the long haul than B.B.; his immaculate touch on his main axe "Lucille" was as instantly identifiable as his soaring set of pipes. One of his principal competitors also happened to be named King. Albert King was a mountain of a man wielding a southpaw Gibson Flying V, who could bend wire upside down like no one else.

Albert King made a lot of his greatest recordings in Memphis. More than a decade prior to that, Sam Phillips captured some of the roughest, toughest electric blues ever committed to tape there, much of it released on his own Sun Records. Ike Turner and Little Milton made barbed-wire magic on their guitars; harmonica ace Big Walter Horton teamed with engineer Phillips to illustrate just how huge an amplified harp could sound in the right hands.

Nothing lasts forever, and so it was with the first generation of electric-blues legends. The great majority of the postwar giants have proceeded on to blues heaven, but their heirs keep the blues flame alight these many years later, even though the idiom itself has been transformed dramatically in many ways. The advent of blues rock has rendered massive amps and effects racks outfitted with every gizmo imaginable a virtual prerequisite among contemporary blues guitarists, as time inevitably marches on and audience demographics tilt younger.

The electric-blues scene was populated by full-fledged giants when Joe Rosen first picked up his camera to document their singular artistry. He's still doing it today with an unerring eye that few photographers in his field can match, as his stunning portraits of the legends gracing the pages of this book eloquently attest. You can almost hear those electric-blues heroes unleashing their sweet fret fury, so turn the page and dig!

BILL DAHL
Music historian and author

Albert King

18

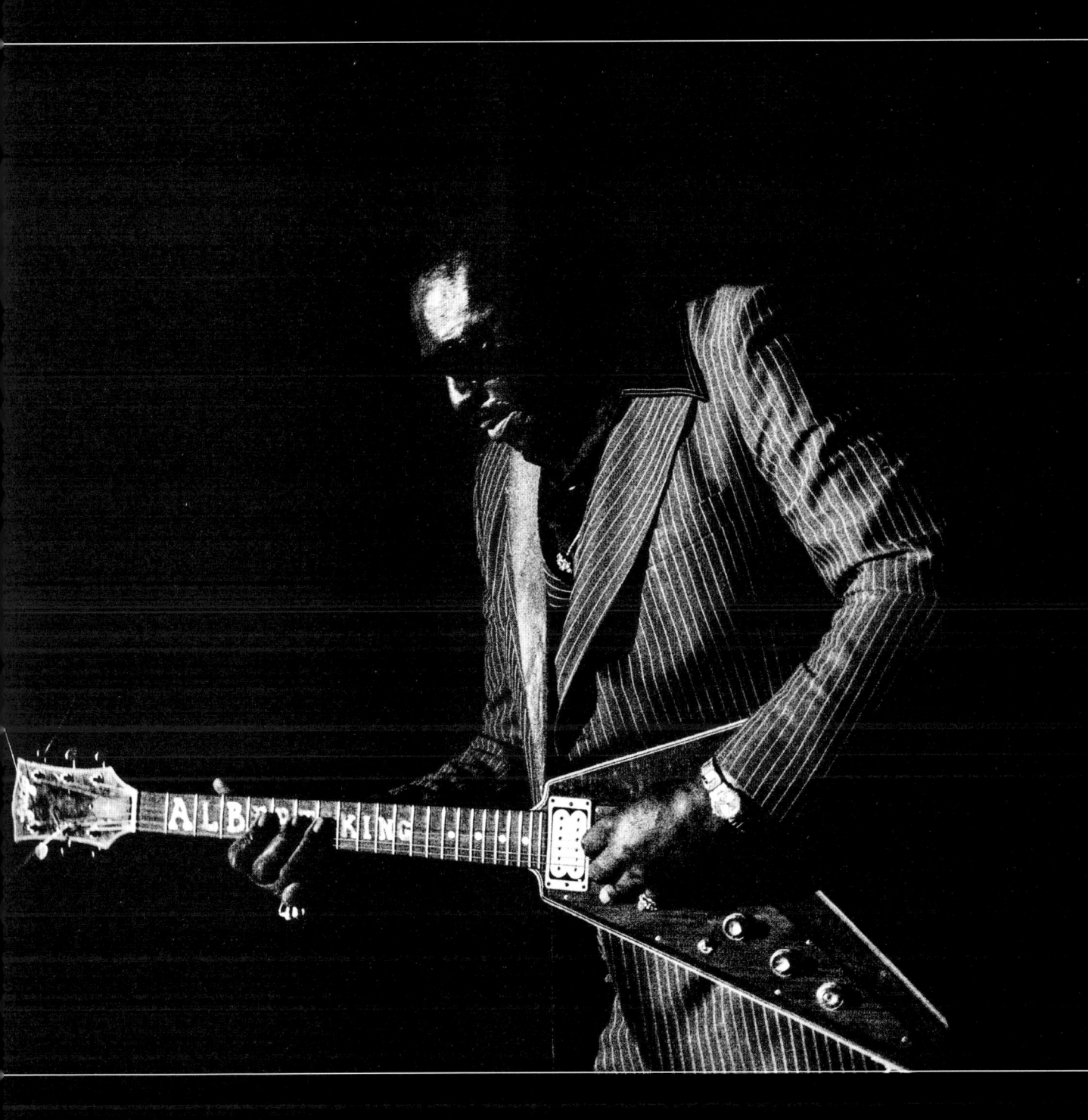

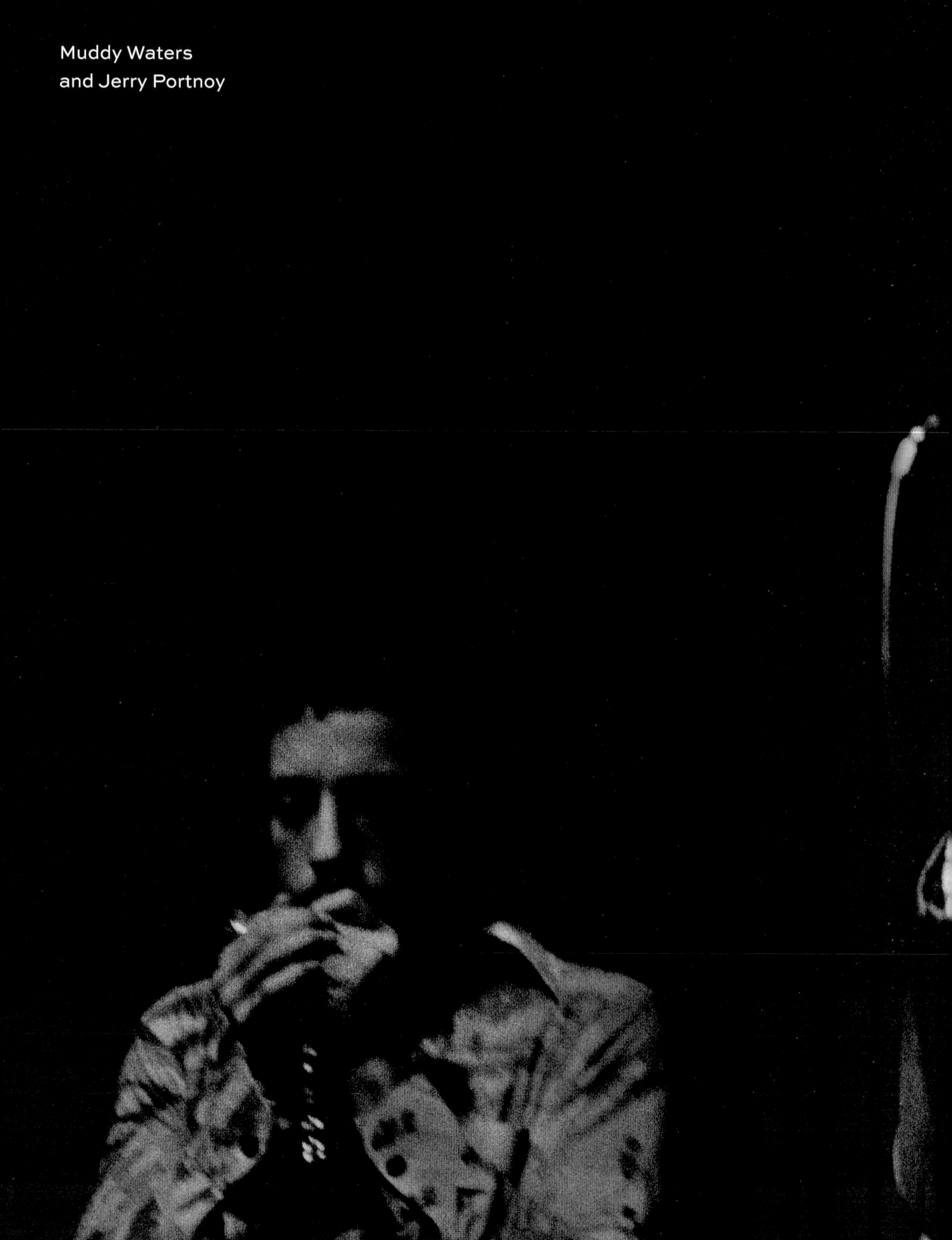

Muddy Waters
and Jerry Portnoy

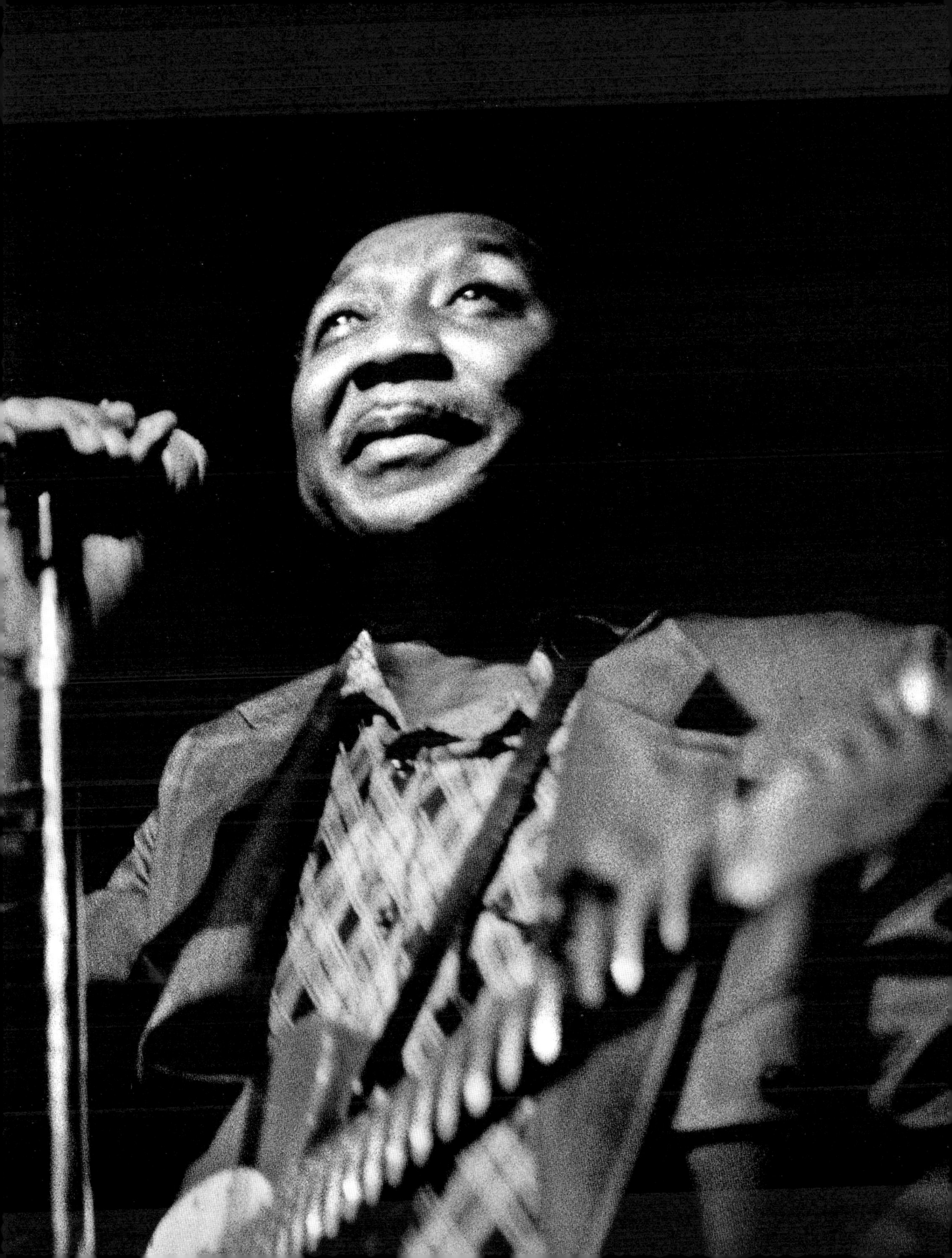

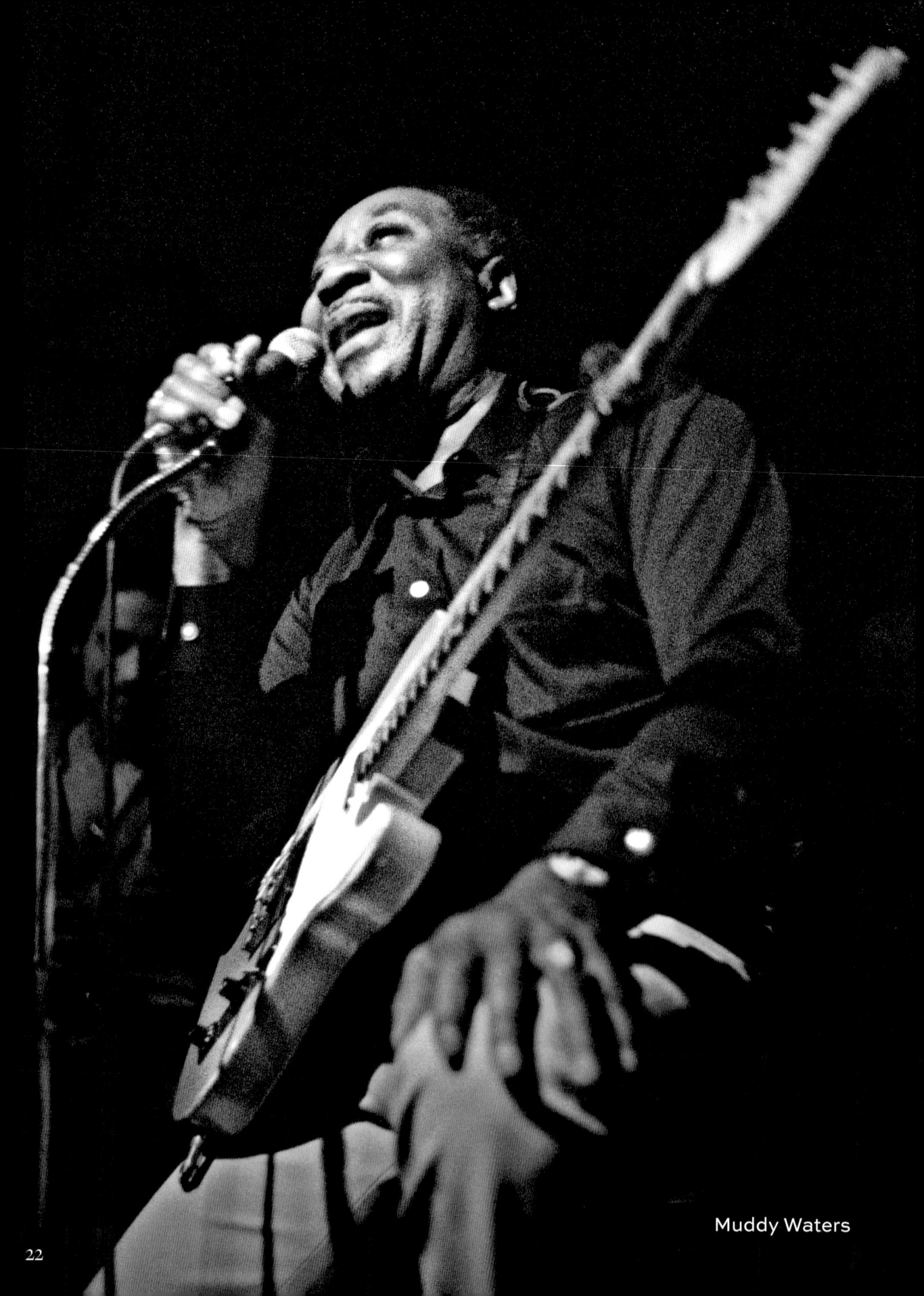

Muddy Waters

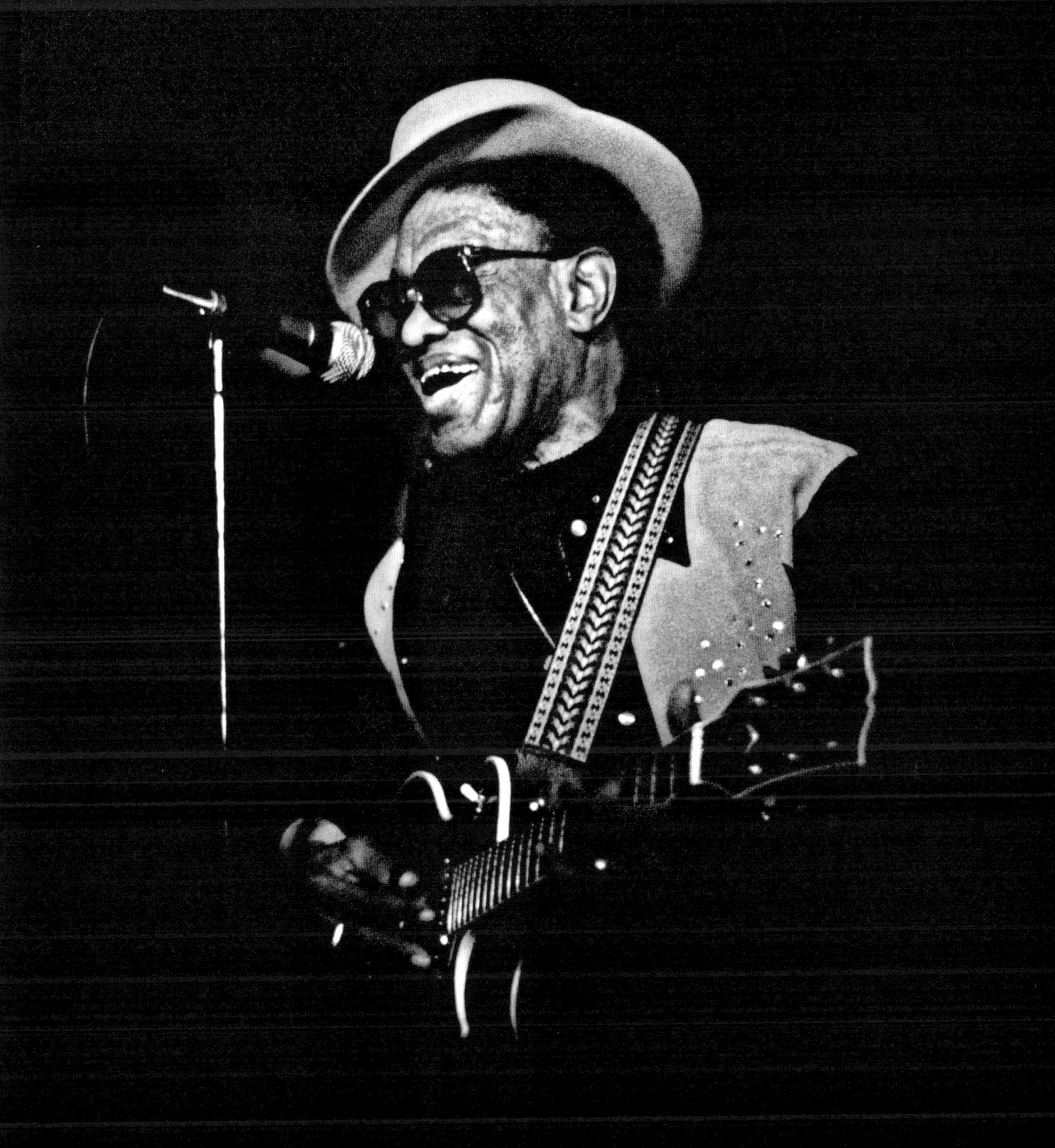

Lightnin' Hopkins

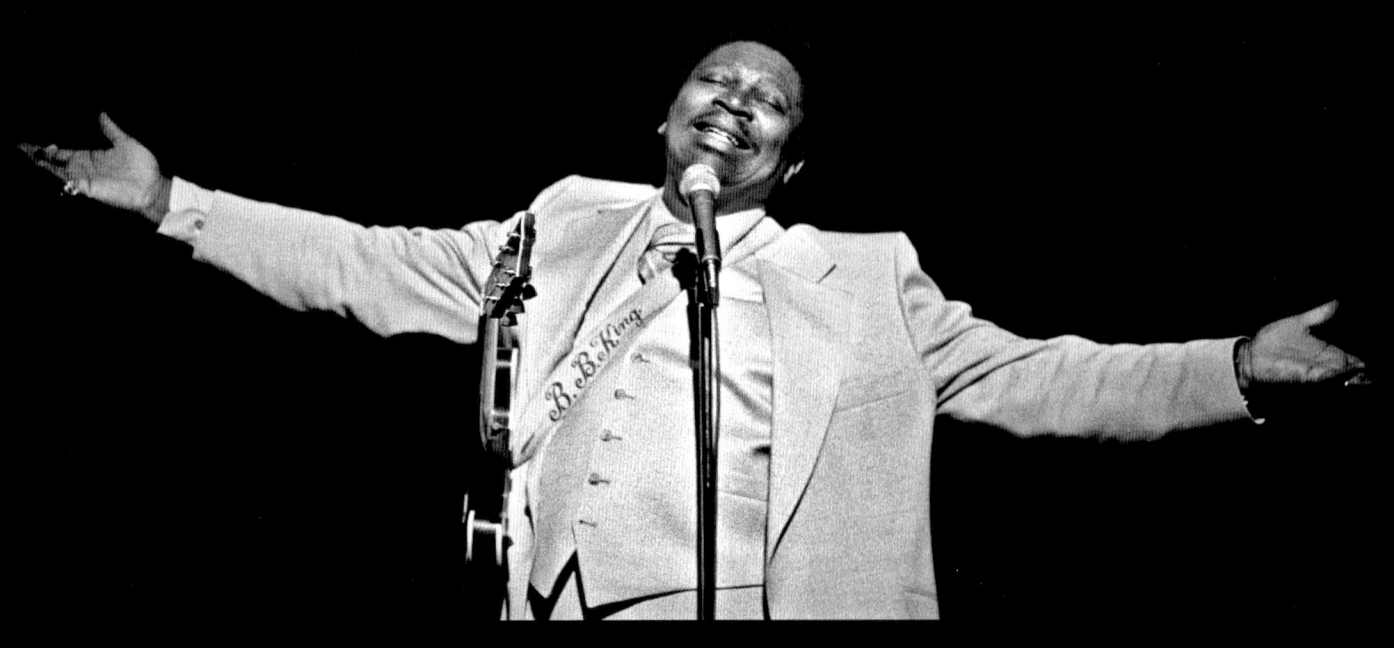

B.B. King

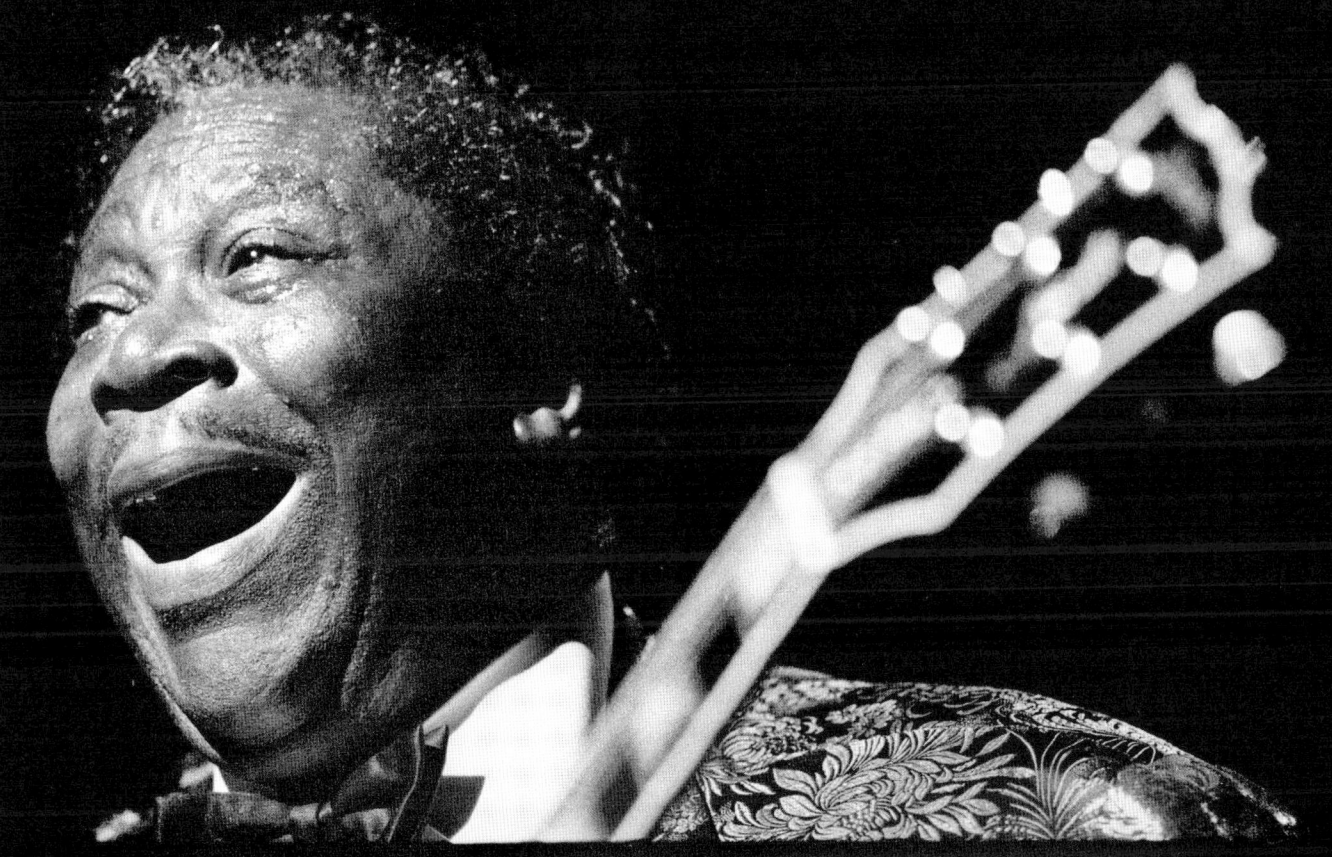

X 5054 TMZ   21   KOD

20A   21

Bobby "Blue" Bland

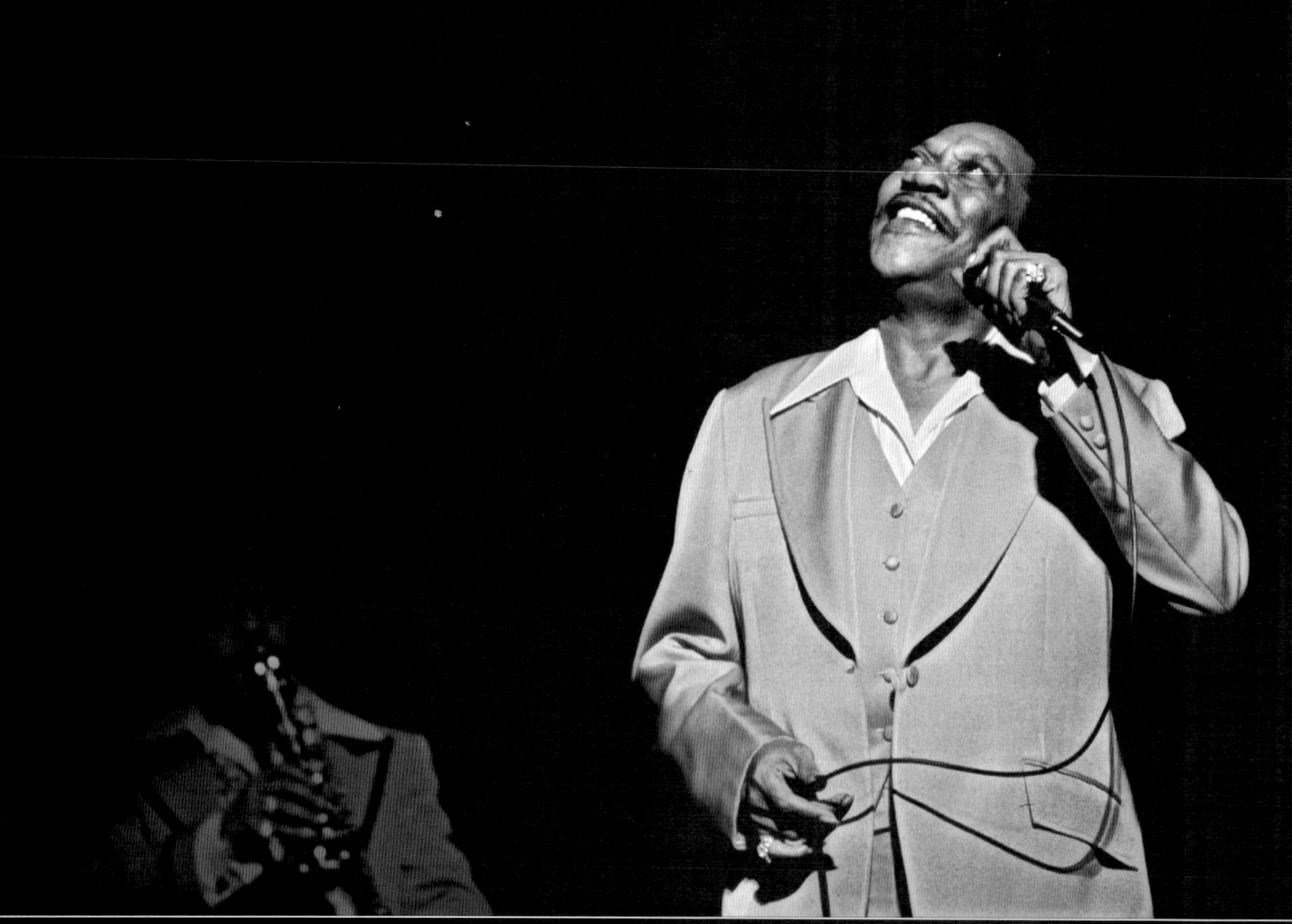

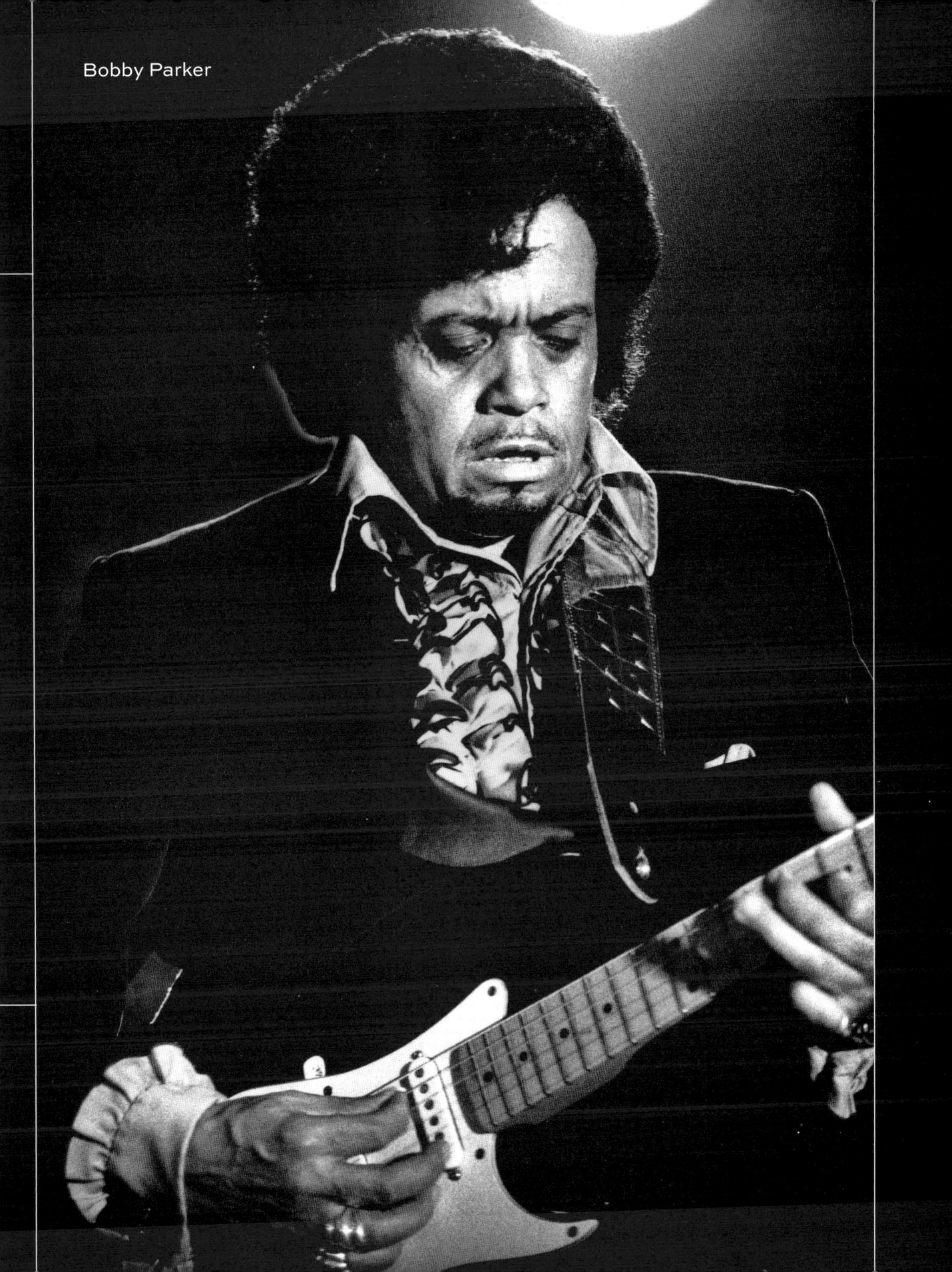

Bobby Parker

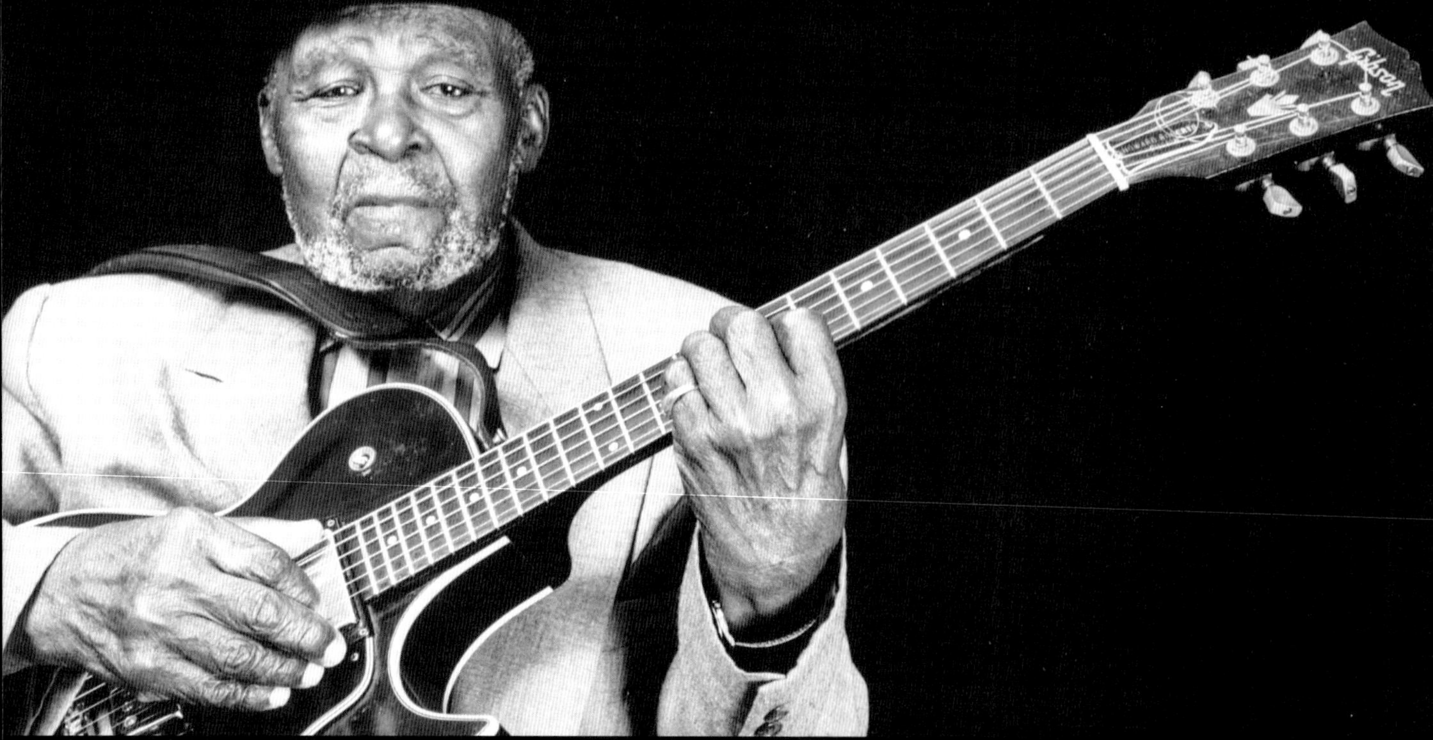

Henry Townsend

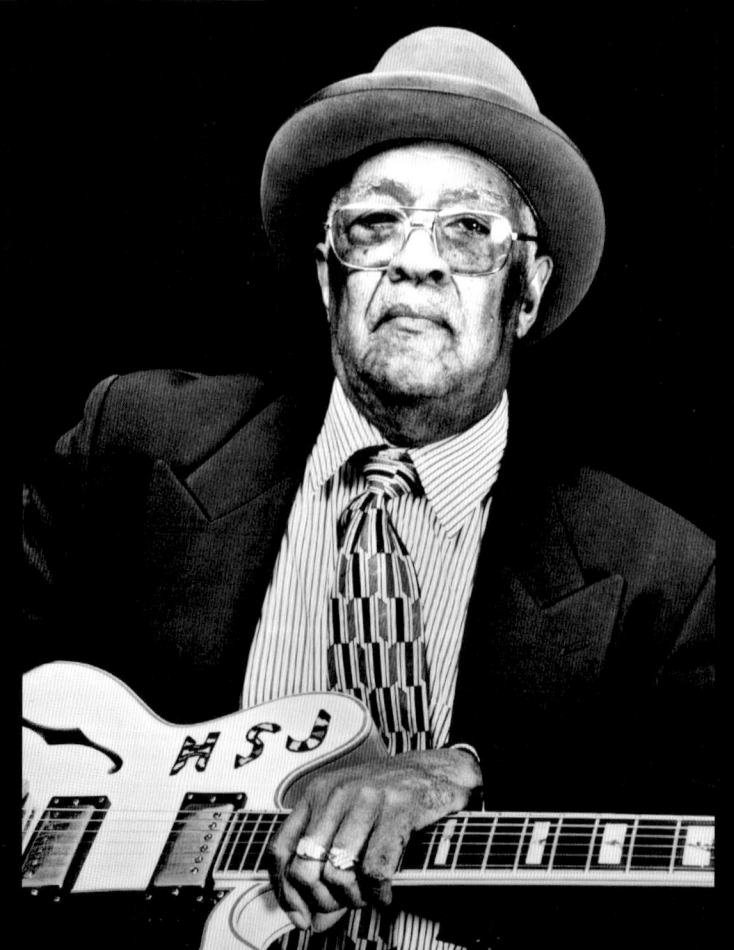

"Homesick" James Williamson

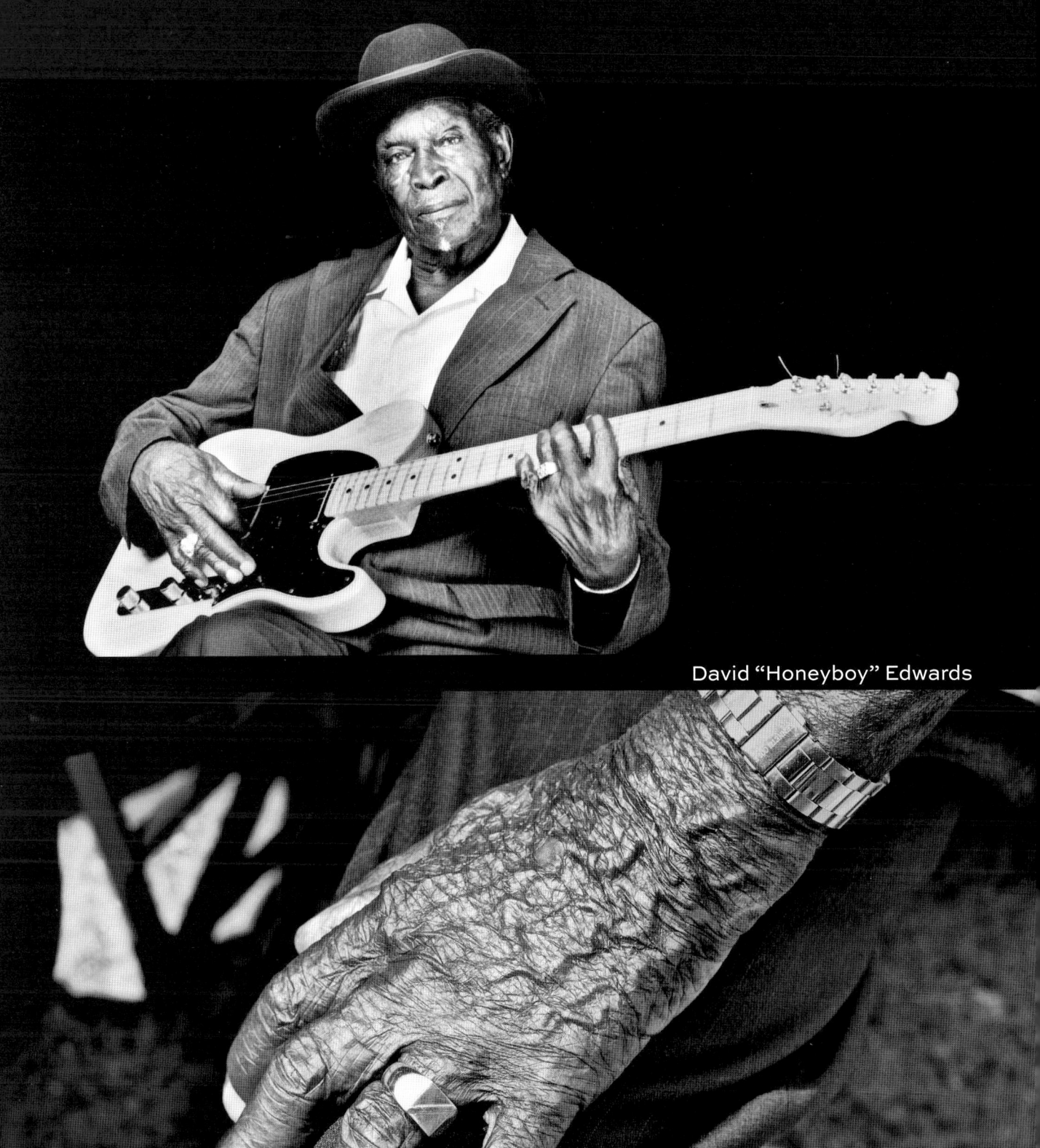

David "Honeyboy" Edwards

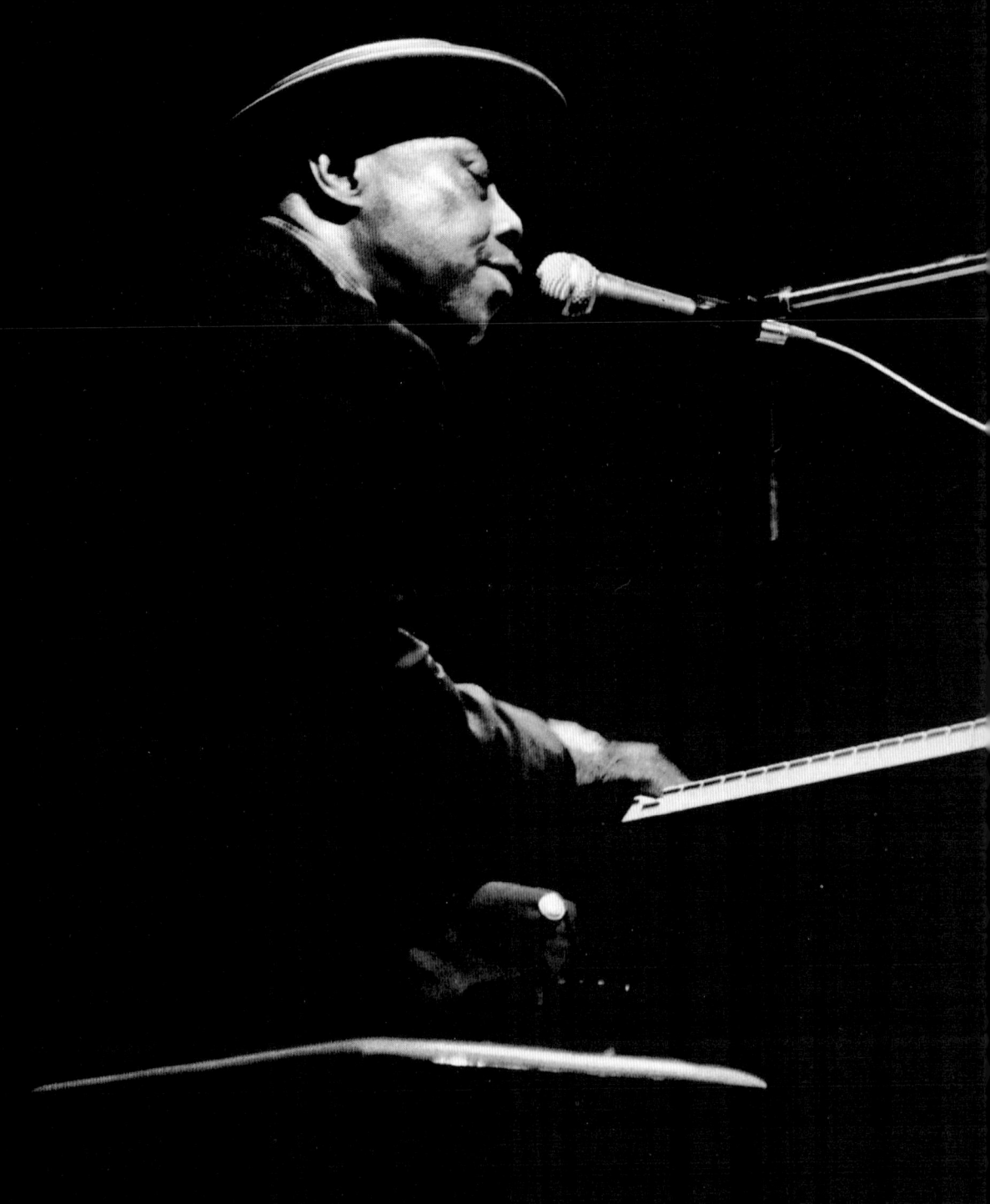

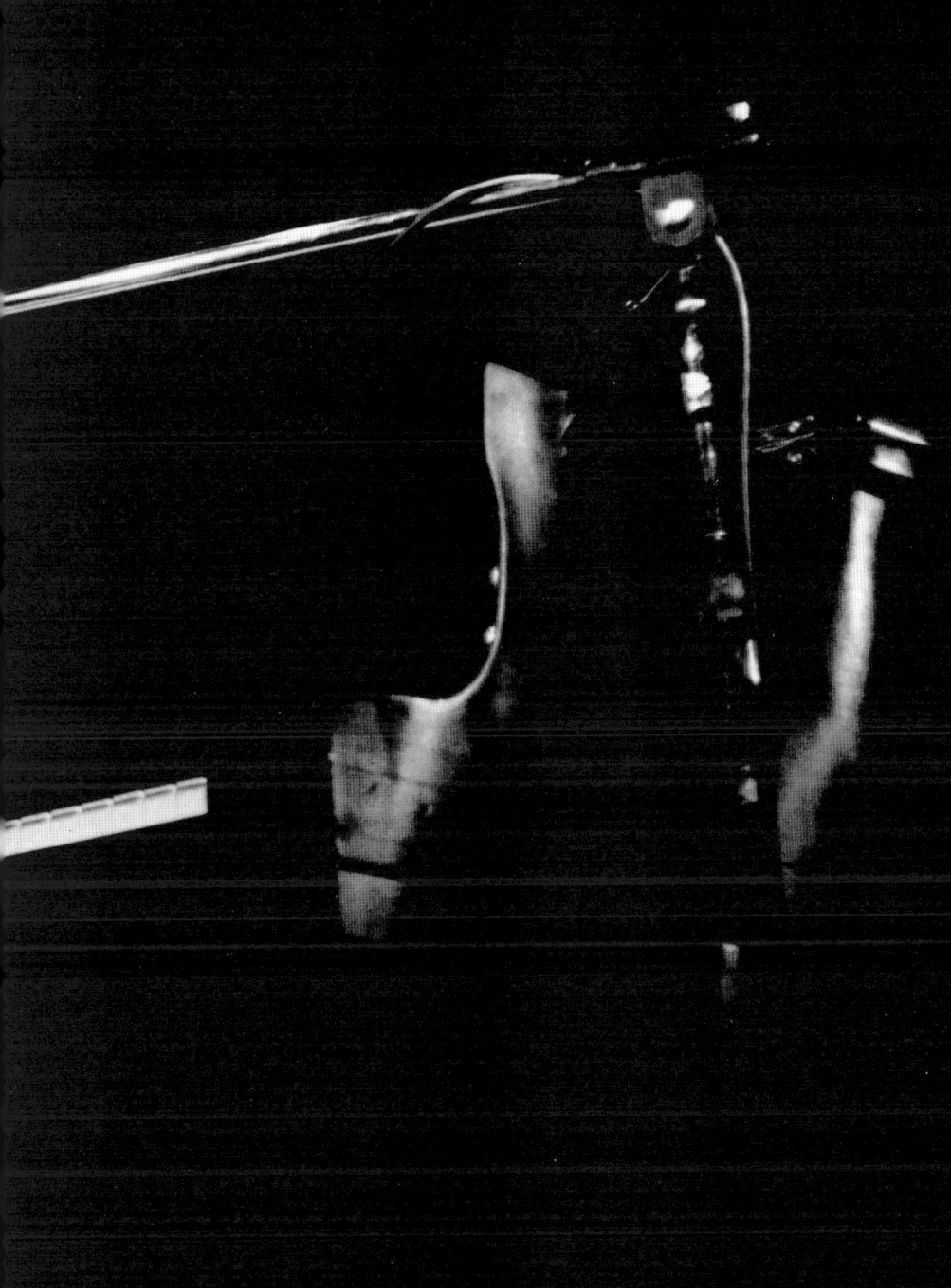

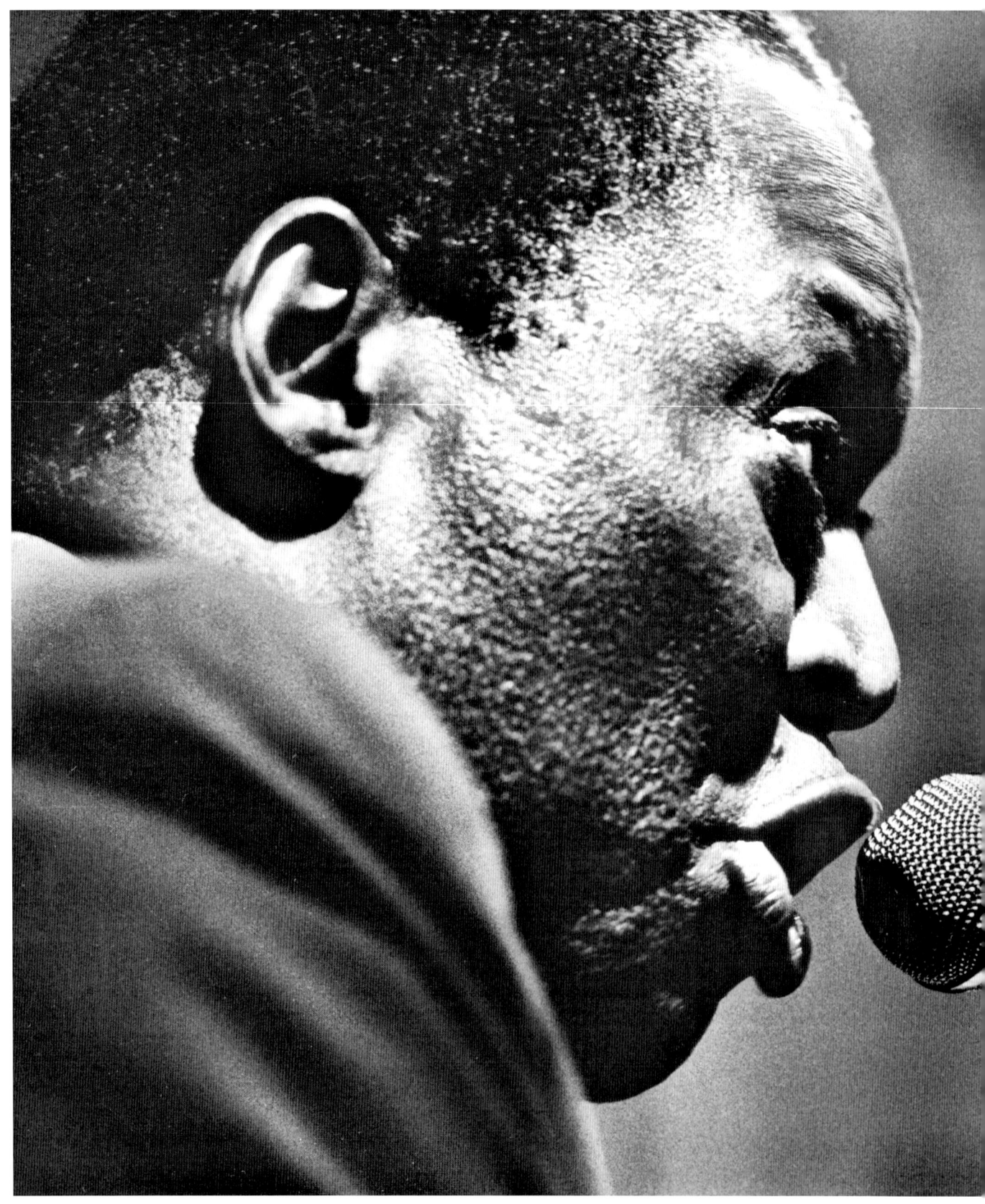

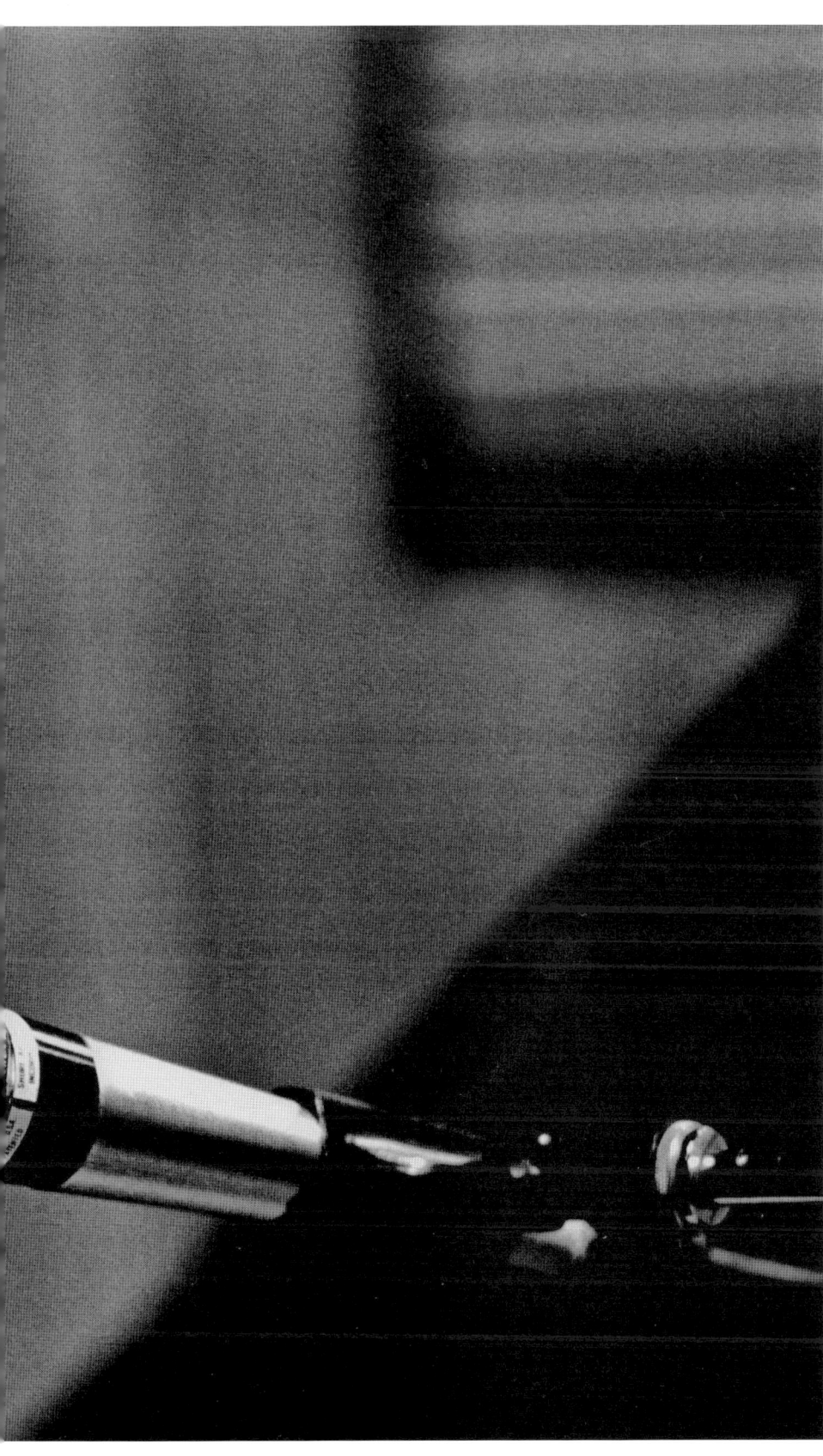

Memphis Slim

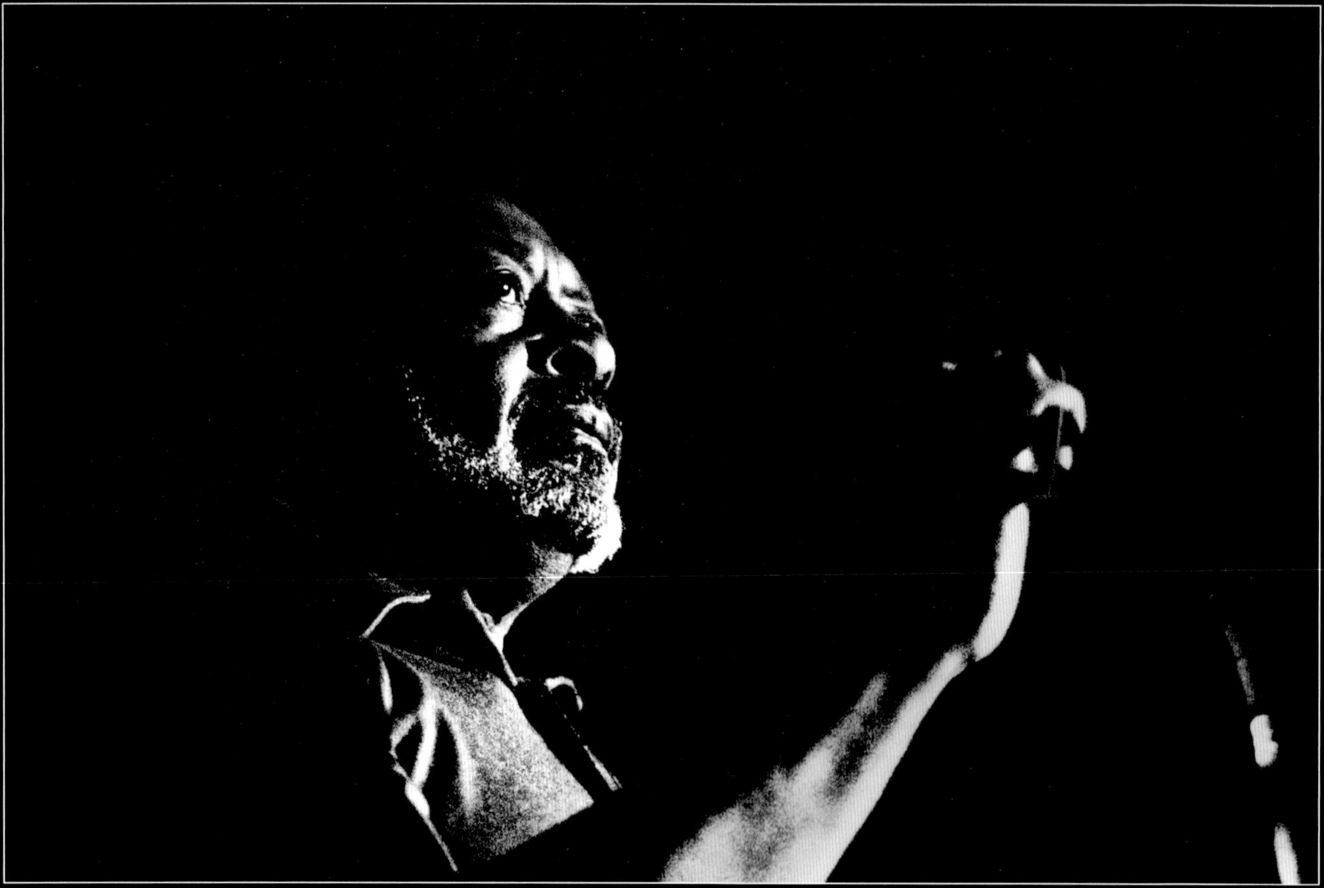

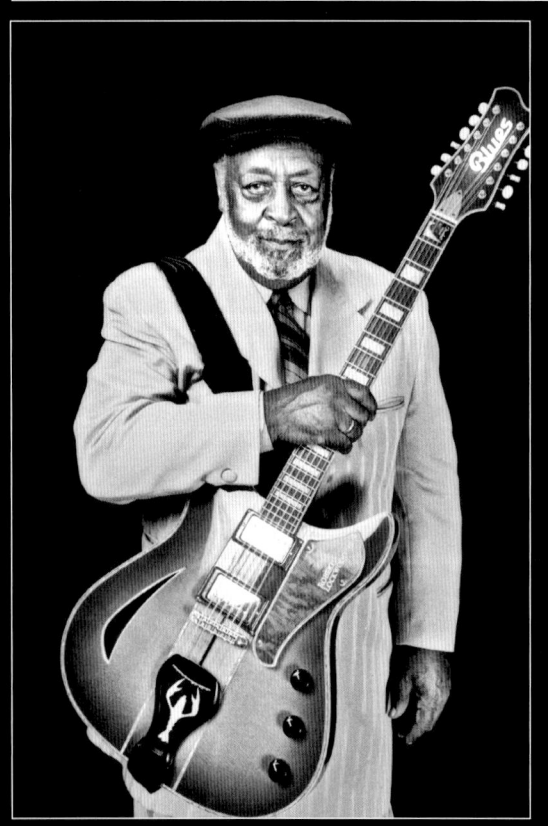

Robert Lockwood Jr.

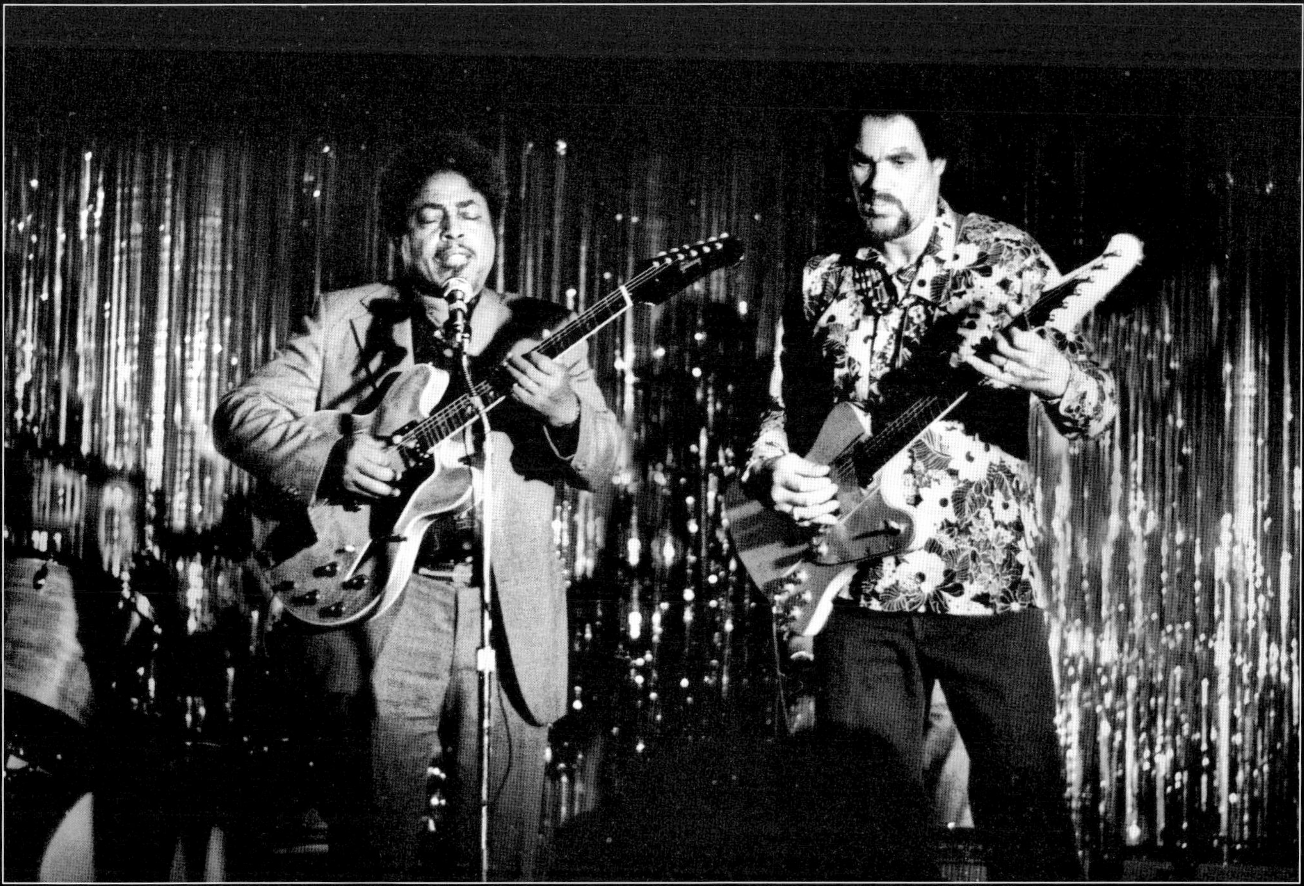

Johnny Shines and Louisiana Red

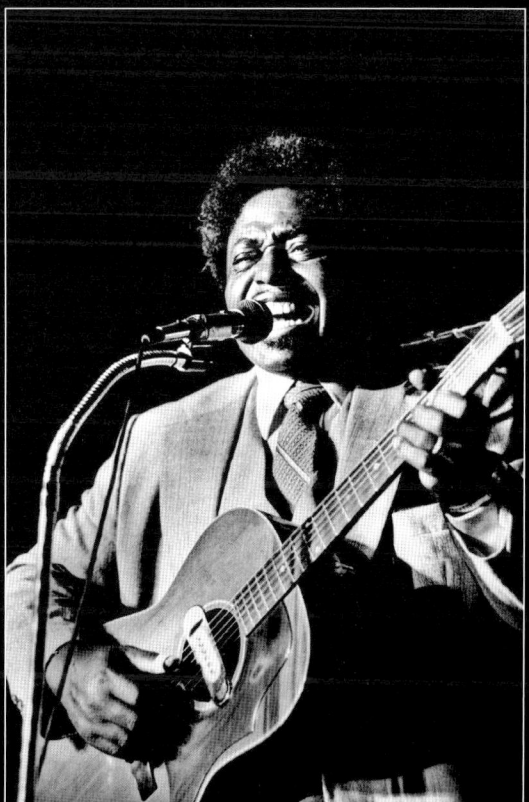

Johnny Shines

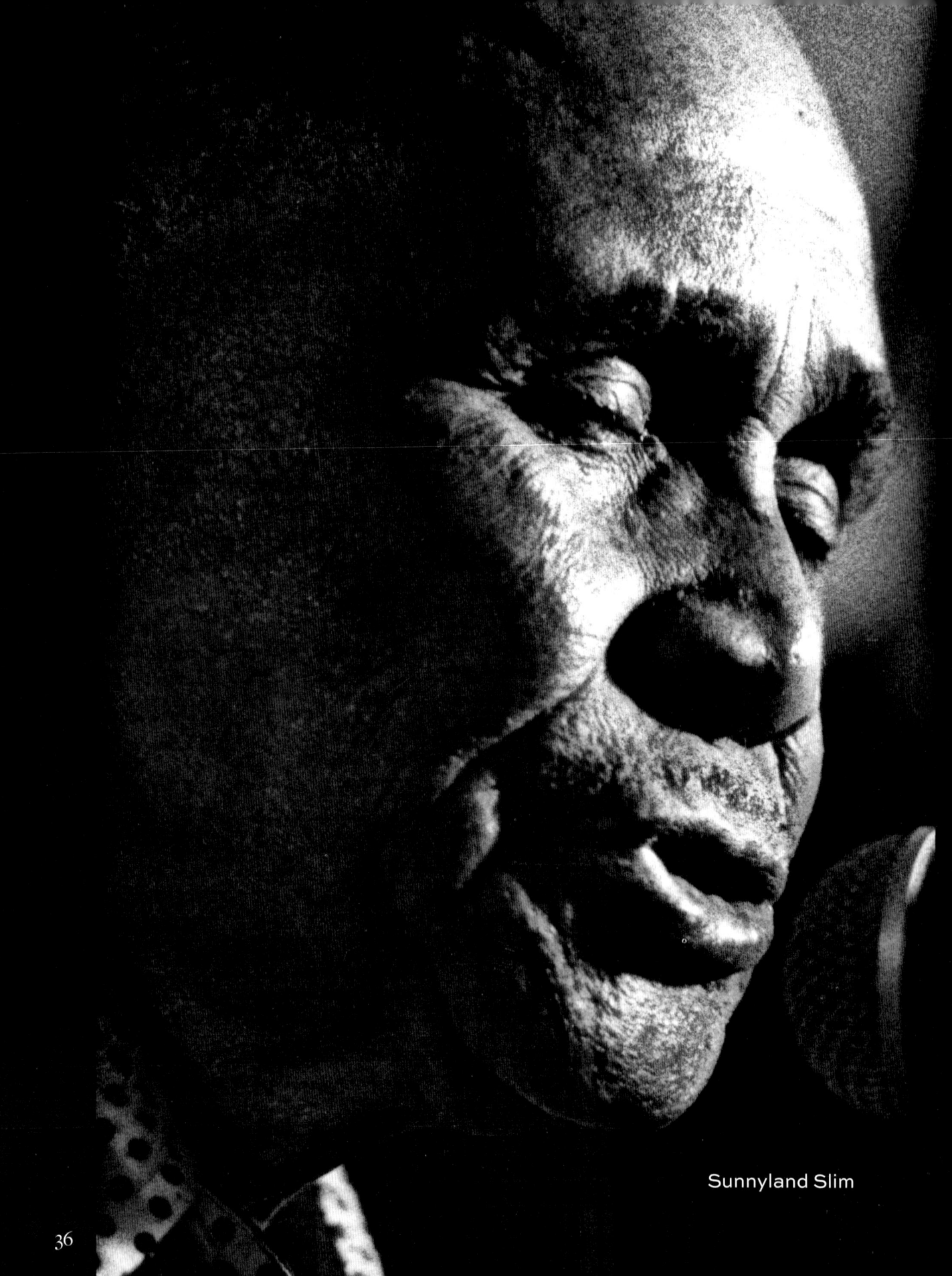

Sunnyland Slim

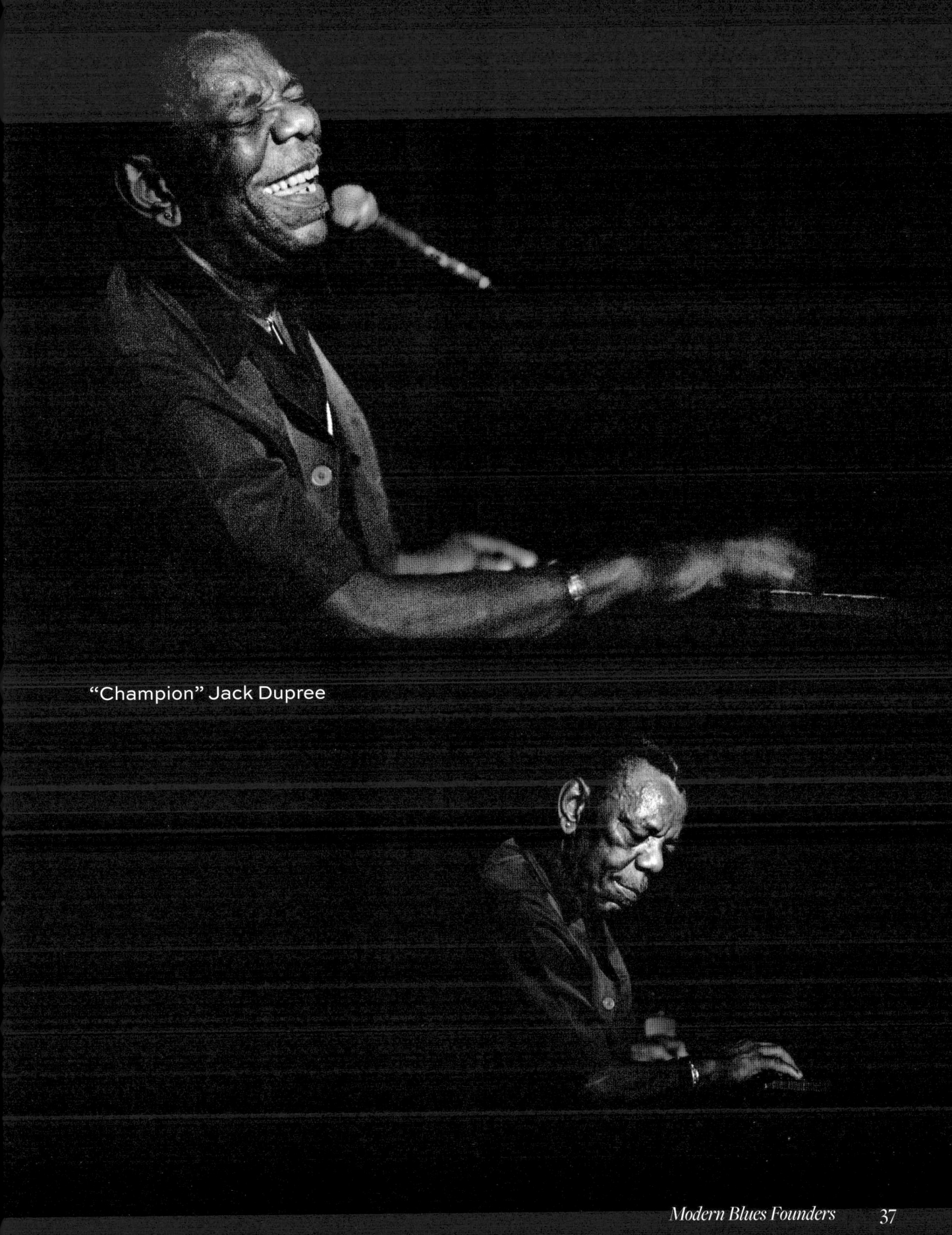

"Champion" Jack Dupree

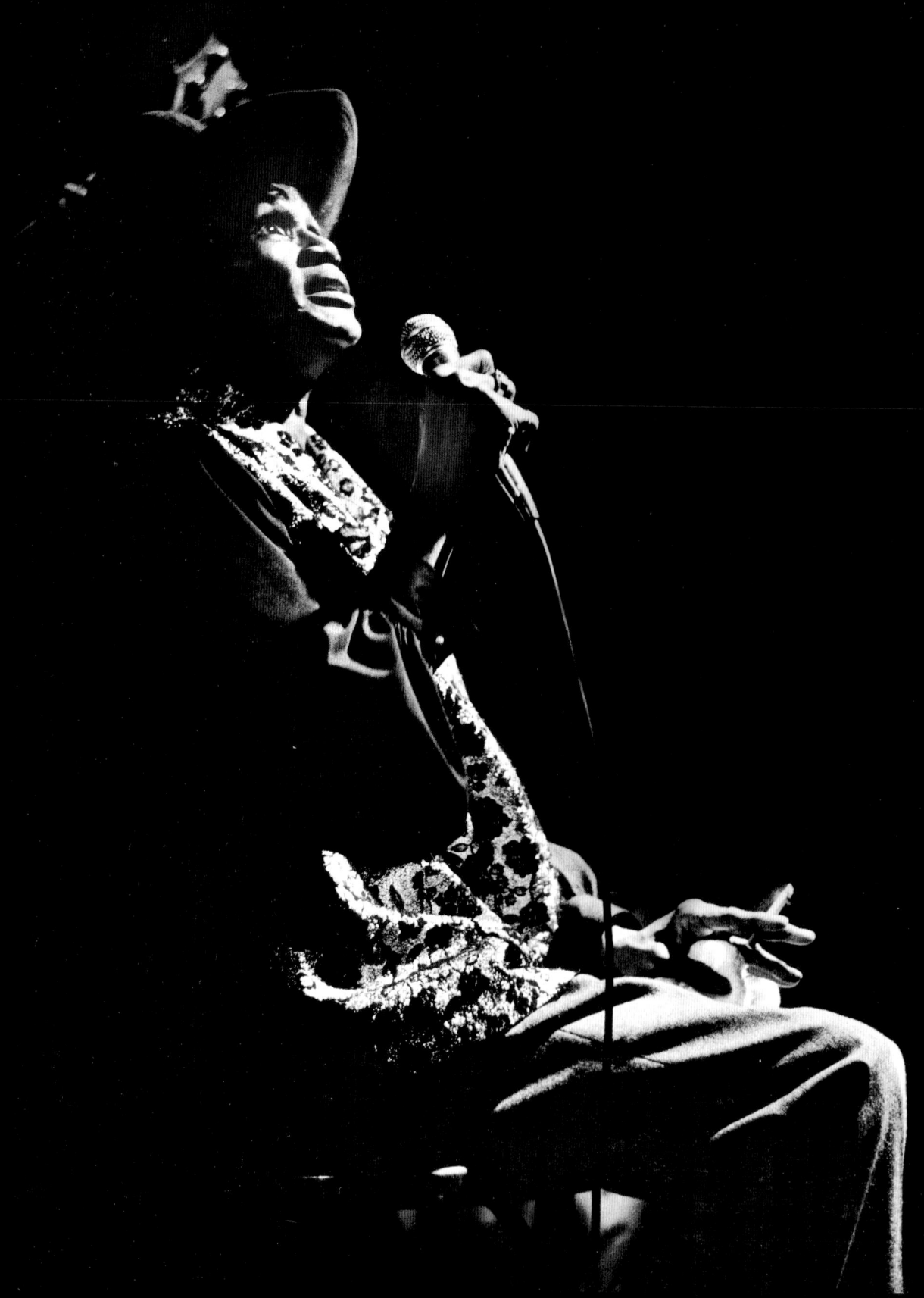

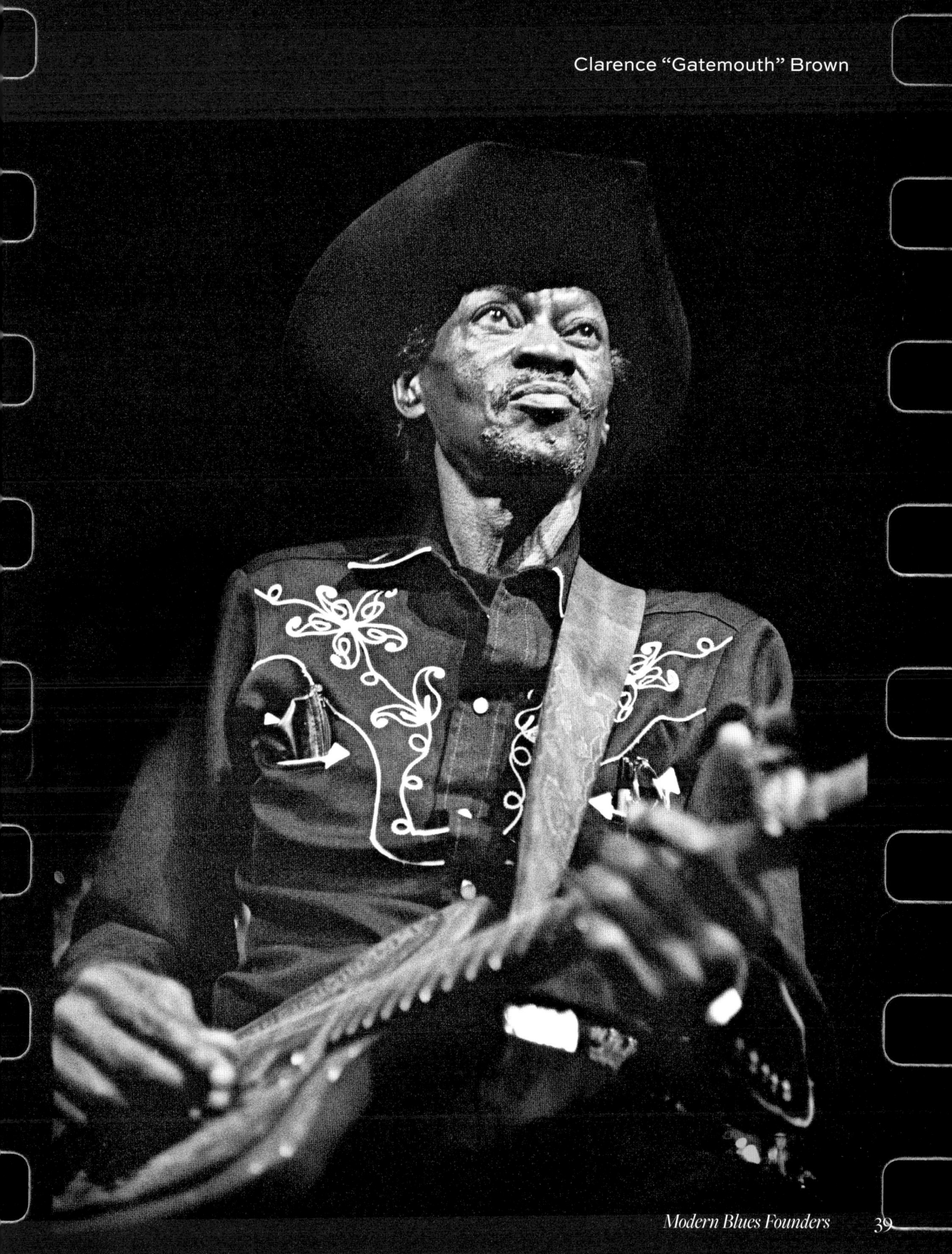

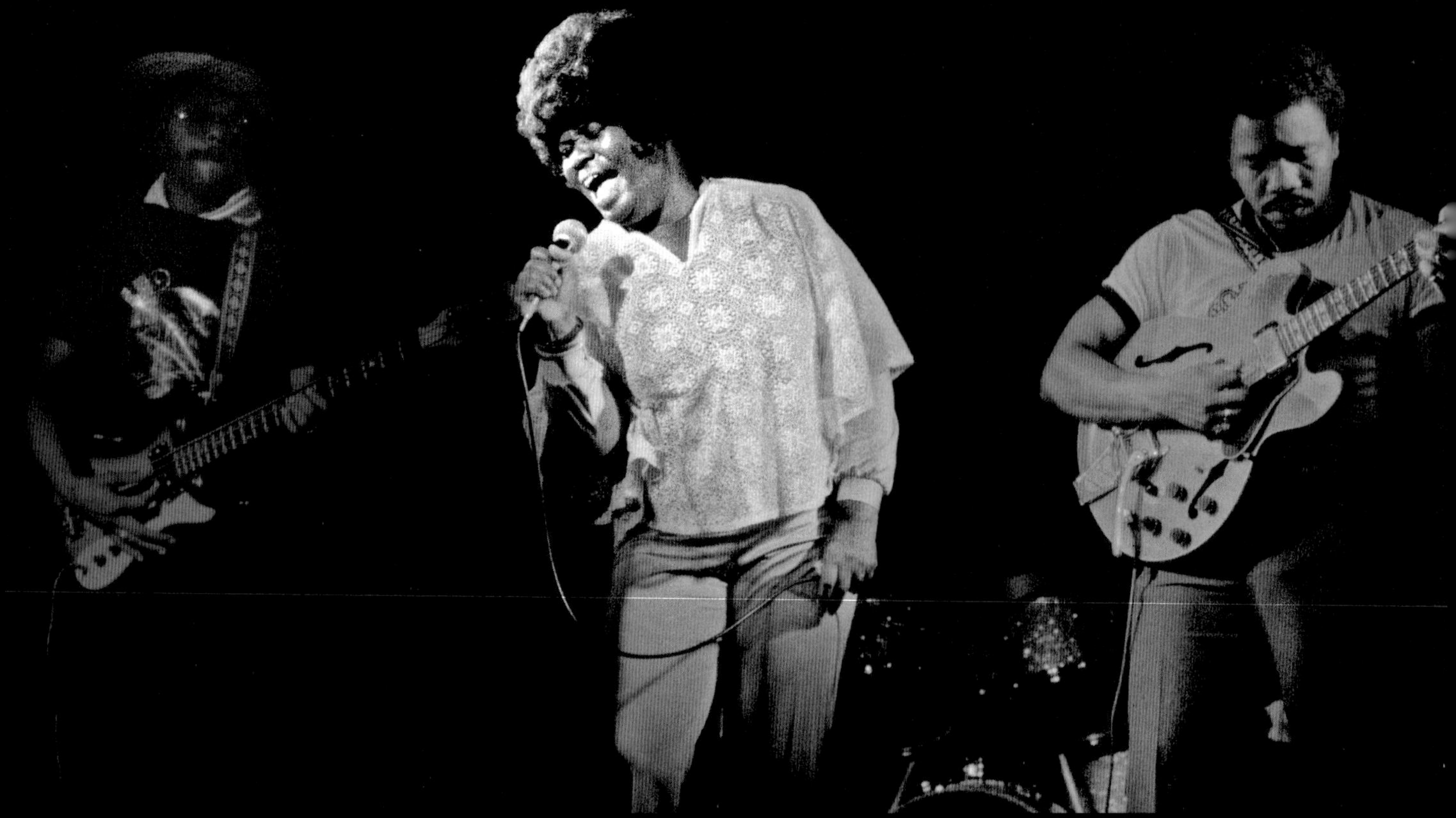

Koko Taylor

Willie Dixon

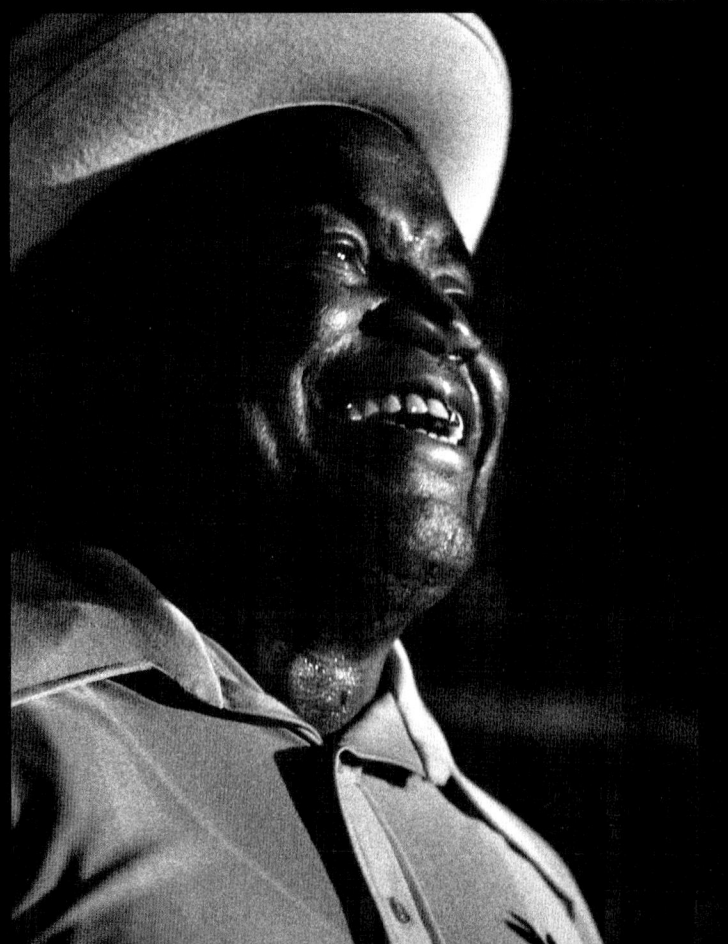

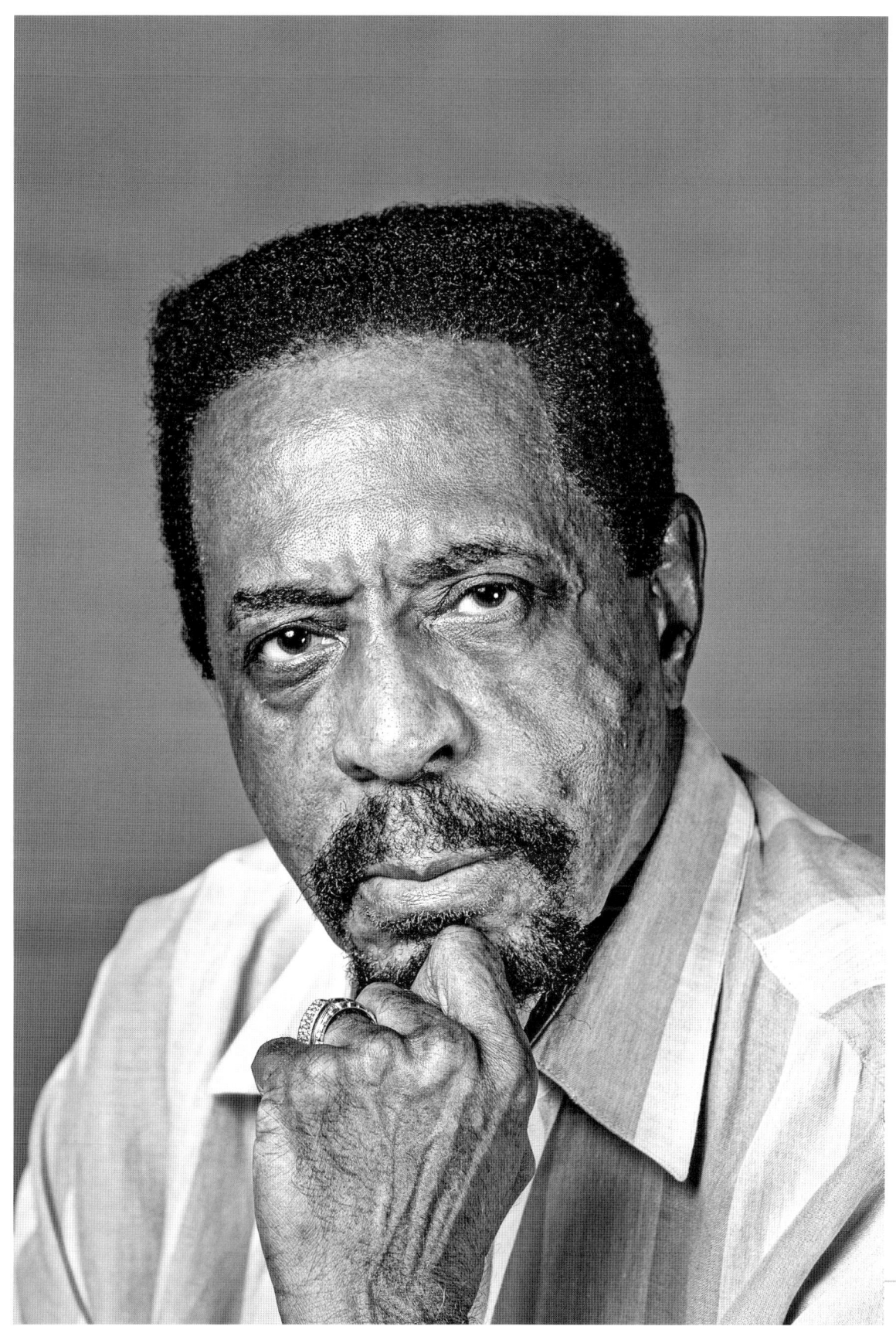

Ike Turner

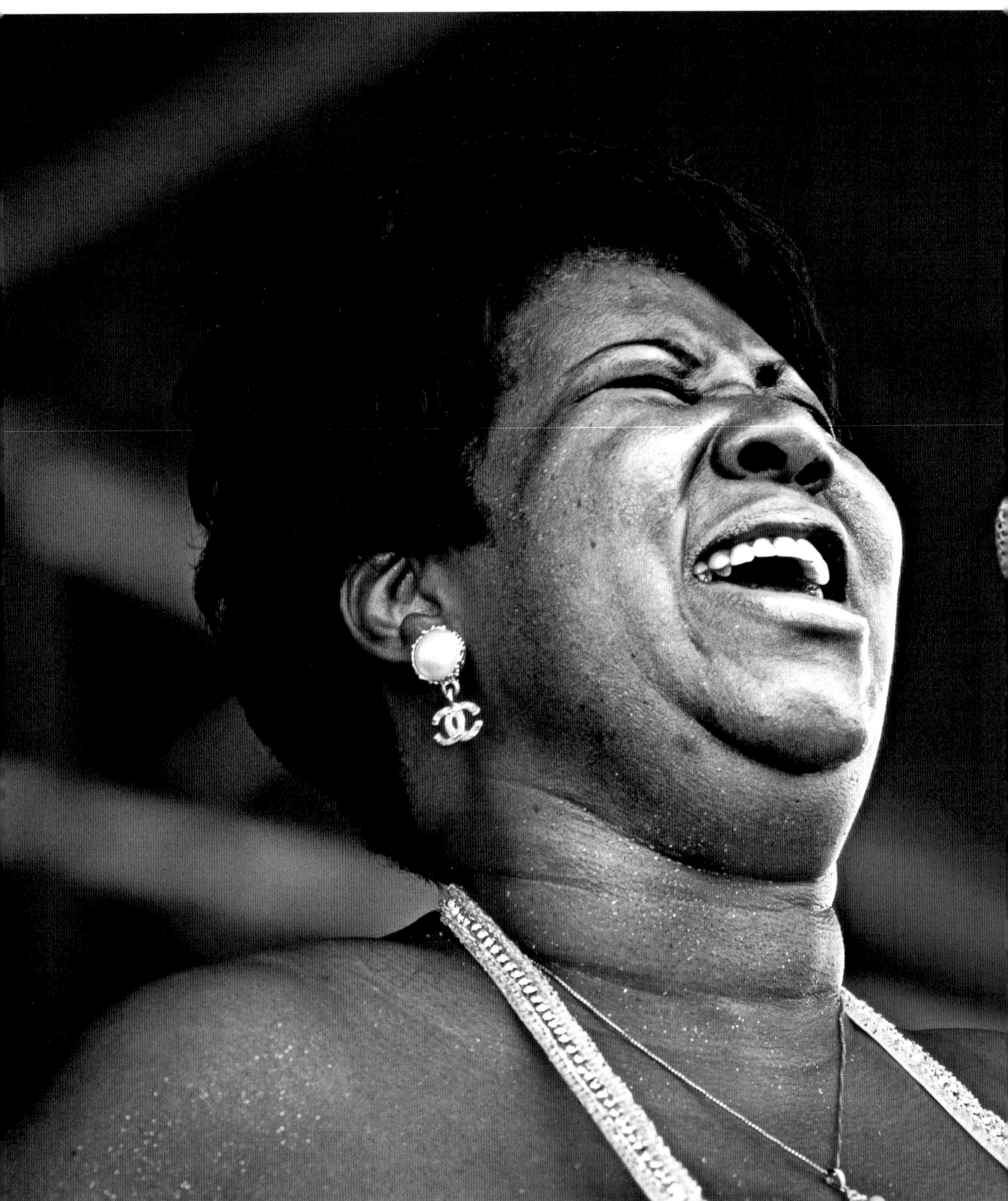

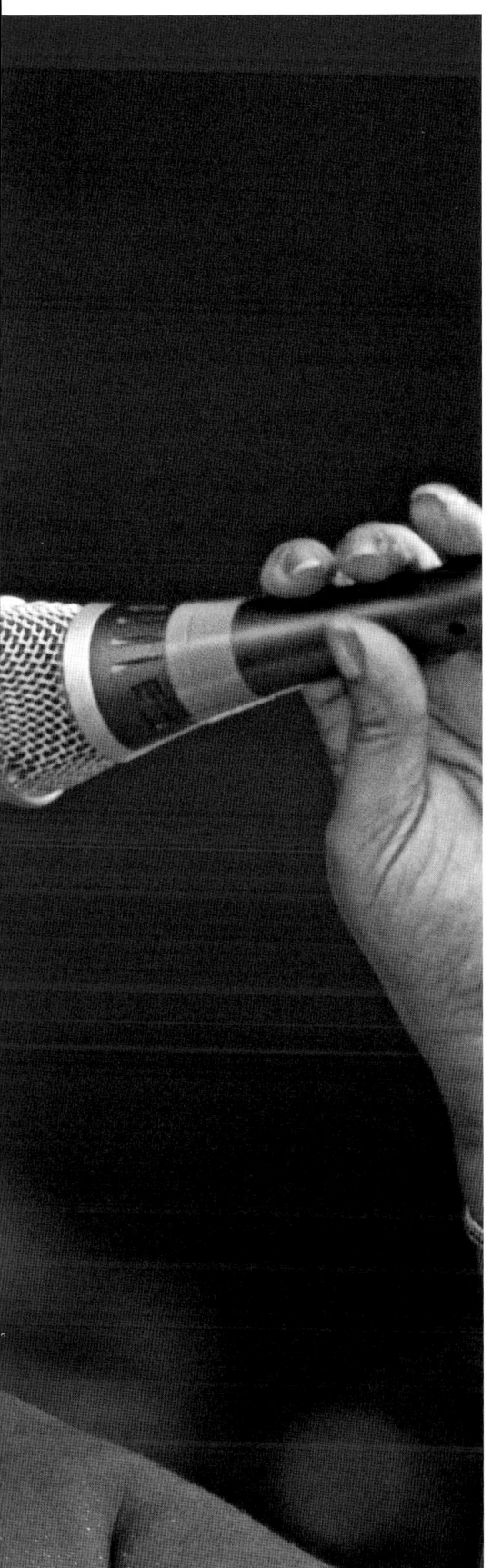

CHAPTER 2

In the liner notes to the seminal 1965 album *Otis Blue: Otis Redding Sings Soul*, Bob Rolontz wrote, "[Soul] usually means an intensely dramatic performance by a singer, projected with such feeling that it ... visibly moves the listener ... the singer is saying something, sometimes even more than the lyrics themselves might normally convey."

Mastery of this extraverbal mode of communication in song is what distinguishes the greatest practitioners of the soul genre. You hear it in the trumpetlike clarity of Otis Redding's voice rising to "you were ti-i-i-i-red" at the end of the first verse of "I've Been Loving You Too Long"; Al Green's astonishing falsetto on the first bridge of "Tired of Being Alone"; O. V. Wright's desolate lament, "You're Gonna Make Me Cry"; James Carr's voice of the ages emerging from the void in response to the tremolo guitar intro of "The Dark End of the Street"; and in the declaration of freedom, independence, and unbridled joy in Aretha Franklin's spelling out of "R-E-S-P-E-C-T" or Philippé Wynne's freestyle vamp on the extended fade of "Mighty Love" by the Spinners. When a tuned-in listener encounters soul singing like this, a physical reaction occurs— hairs stand at attention on the arms or back of the neck, chills run down the spine, tears emerge in the corners of the eyes, throats lock shut, and sweat beads on the forehead.

Soul music derives its inspiration from the African American gospel music that predated it. One of the first artists to apply the musical conventions of gospel music in a pop context was the stylistic boundary spanner Ray Charles, who freely acknowledged his debt to gospel artists such as Alex Bradford and the Five Blind Boys of Mississippi. The echo of Archie Brownlee of the Blind Boys is present in every ecstatic scream in the early Ray Charles recordings. This amalgamation of the spiritual and the secular struck some listeners as disreputable.

Aretha Franklin

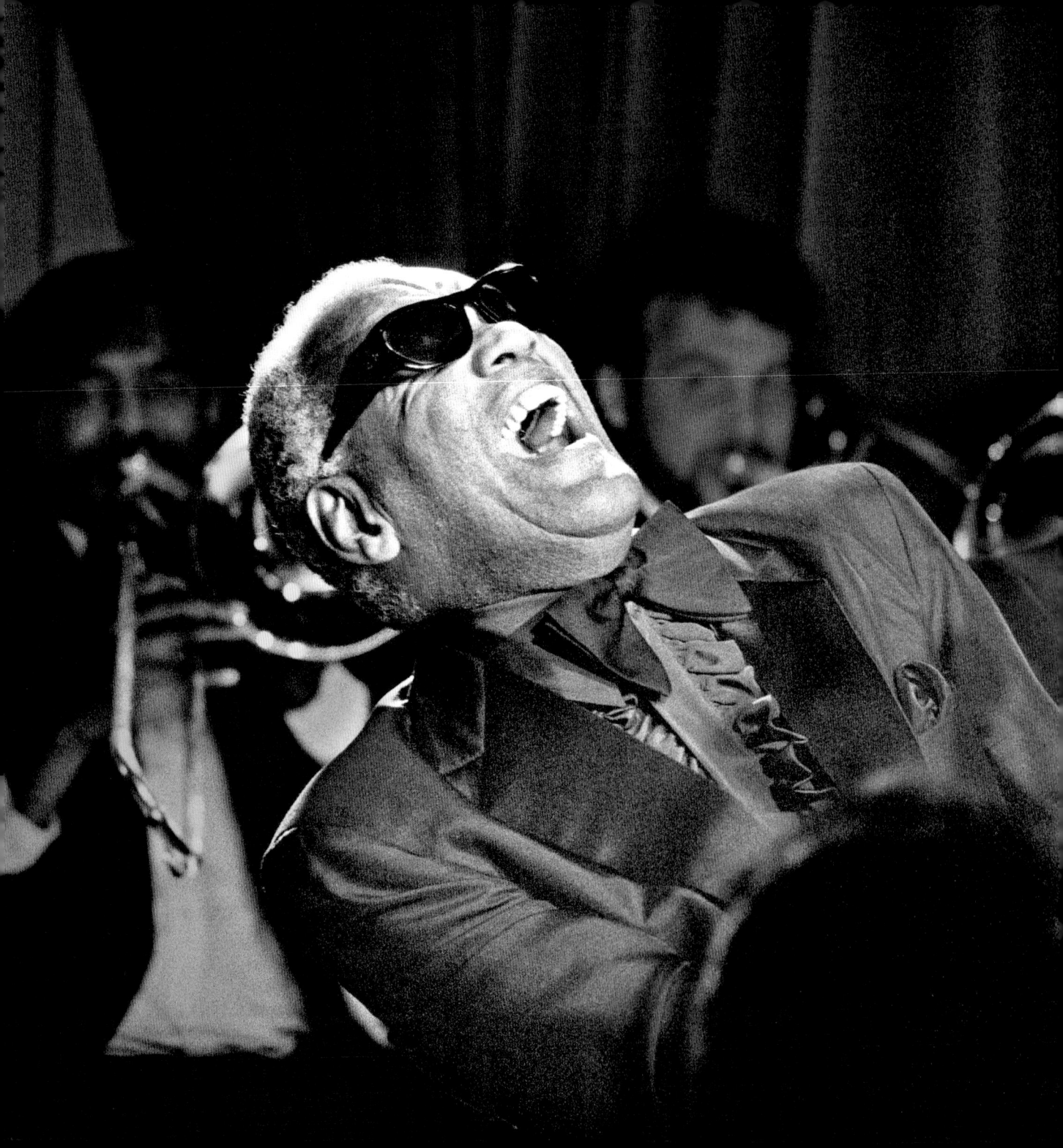

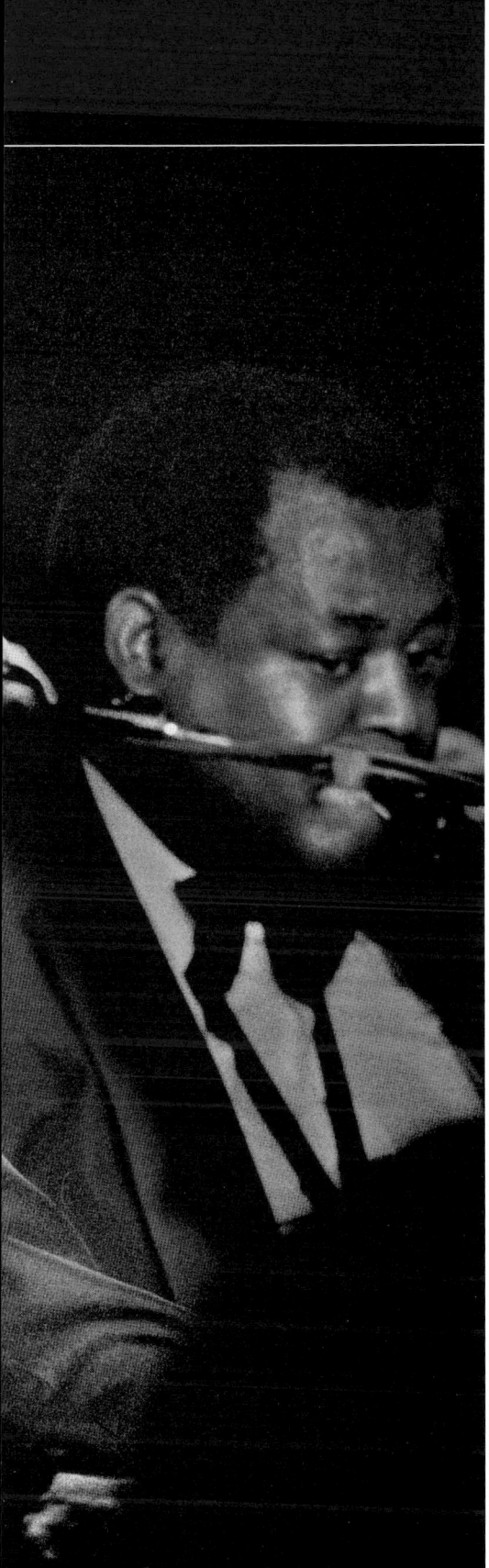

Blues singer Big Bill Broonzy is famously said to have opined, "He's mixing the blues with the spirituals. He should be singing in church."

The great early soul artists always cited their gospel mentors: Aretha Franklin with Clara Ward, Marion Williams, and Mahalia Jackson; Al Green with the Rev. Claude Jeter of the Swan Silvertones; and Wilson Pickett with the Rev. Julius Cheeks of the Sensational Nightingales. And Sam Cooke, one of the earliest and most influential soul singers, transitioned directly from singing lead in the Soul Stirrers gospel quartet, where he replaced his forebear R. H. Harris, to the top of the pop charts, singing in the identical style with only the lyrics altered.

As soul evolved to incorporate elements of pop music, traditional Tin Pan Alley songwriting, and lyrical themes aimed at lonely-hearted teenagers, Detroit-based Motown Records, under the direction of Berry Gordy Jr., could credibly claim the moniker "the Sound of Young America" on the basis of its dominance of pop-music radio and sales charts. Concurrently, more explicitly gospel- and blues-influenced musical styles flourished in the recording studios of the American South, in cities such as Memphis and Nashville, Tennessee; Muscle Shoals, Alabama; and Hialeah, Florida, among others. Meanwhile, from roots in a conventional secular gospel-style quartet, soul singer and bandleader James Brown blazed a path of rhythmic innovation that ran through the creation of funk and hip-hop.

Gospel-inflected soul styles also came to influence the evolution of blues in the work of such hybrid soul-blues artists as Bobby "Blue" Bland, B.B. King, Otis Rush, Magic Sam, Junior Wells, Little Milton, Johnnie Taylor, Tyrone Davis, and Buddy Guy. Soul today is ubiquitous in popular music thanks to the innovations introduced by its pioneers.

BILLY PRICE

Award-winning soul singer, performing artist, writer, and historian

Ray Charles

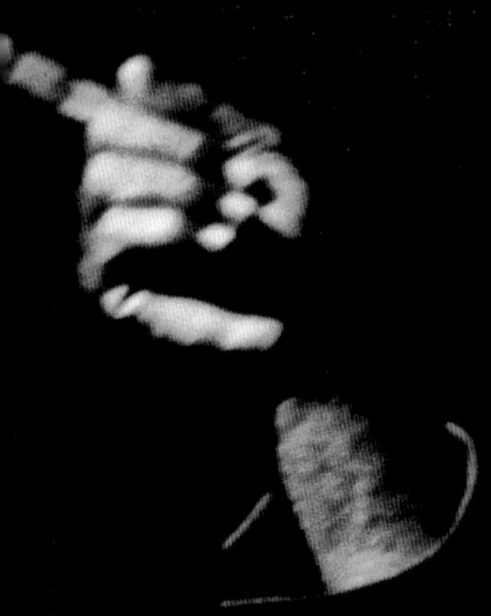

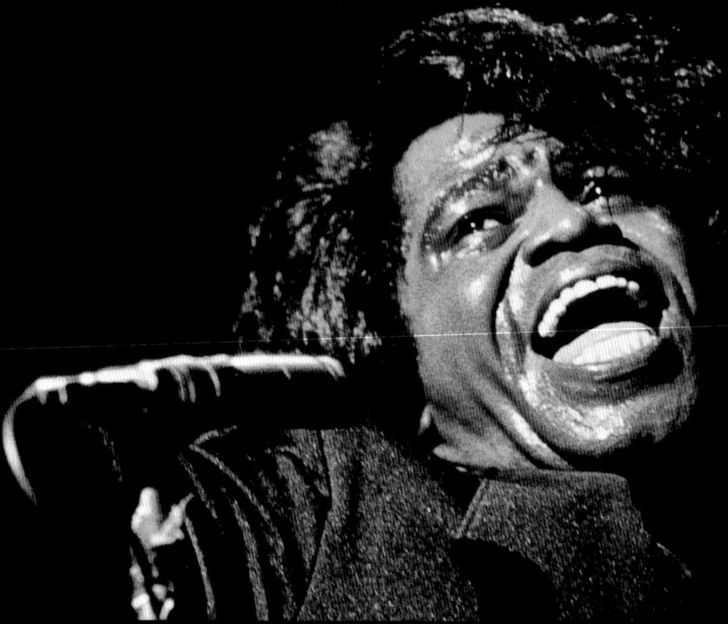

James Brown

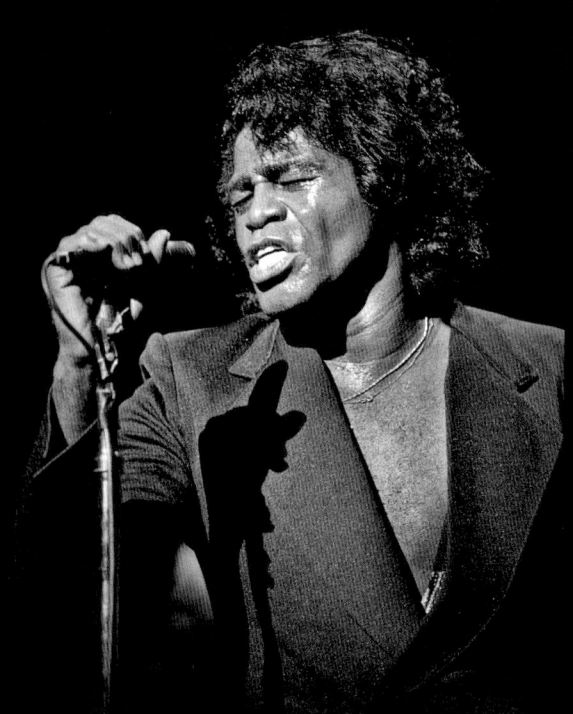

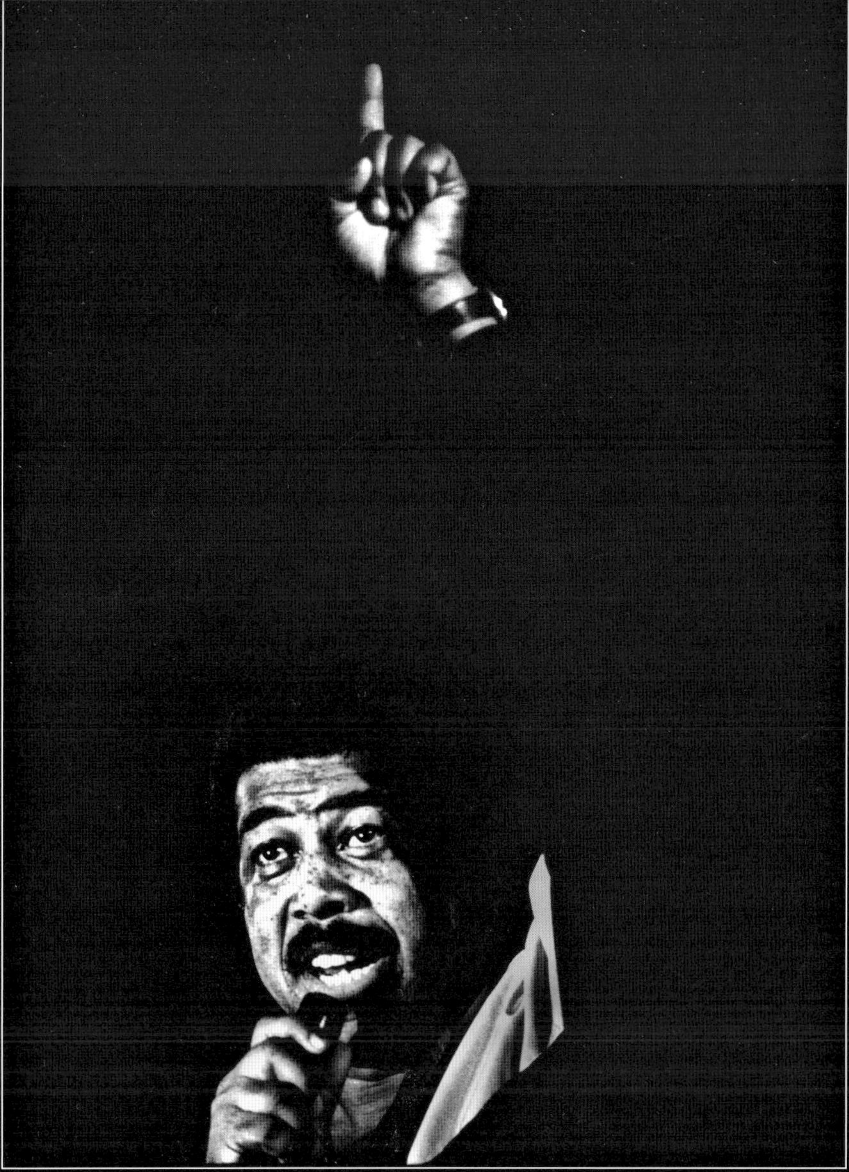

Ben E. King

Jerry Butler

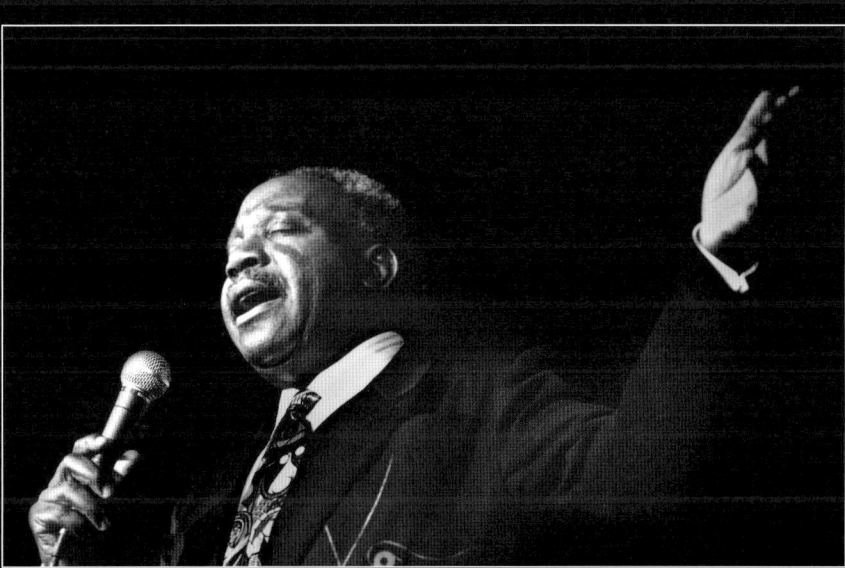

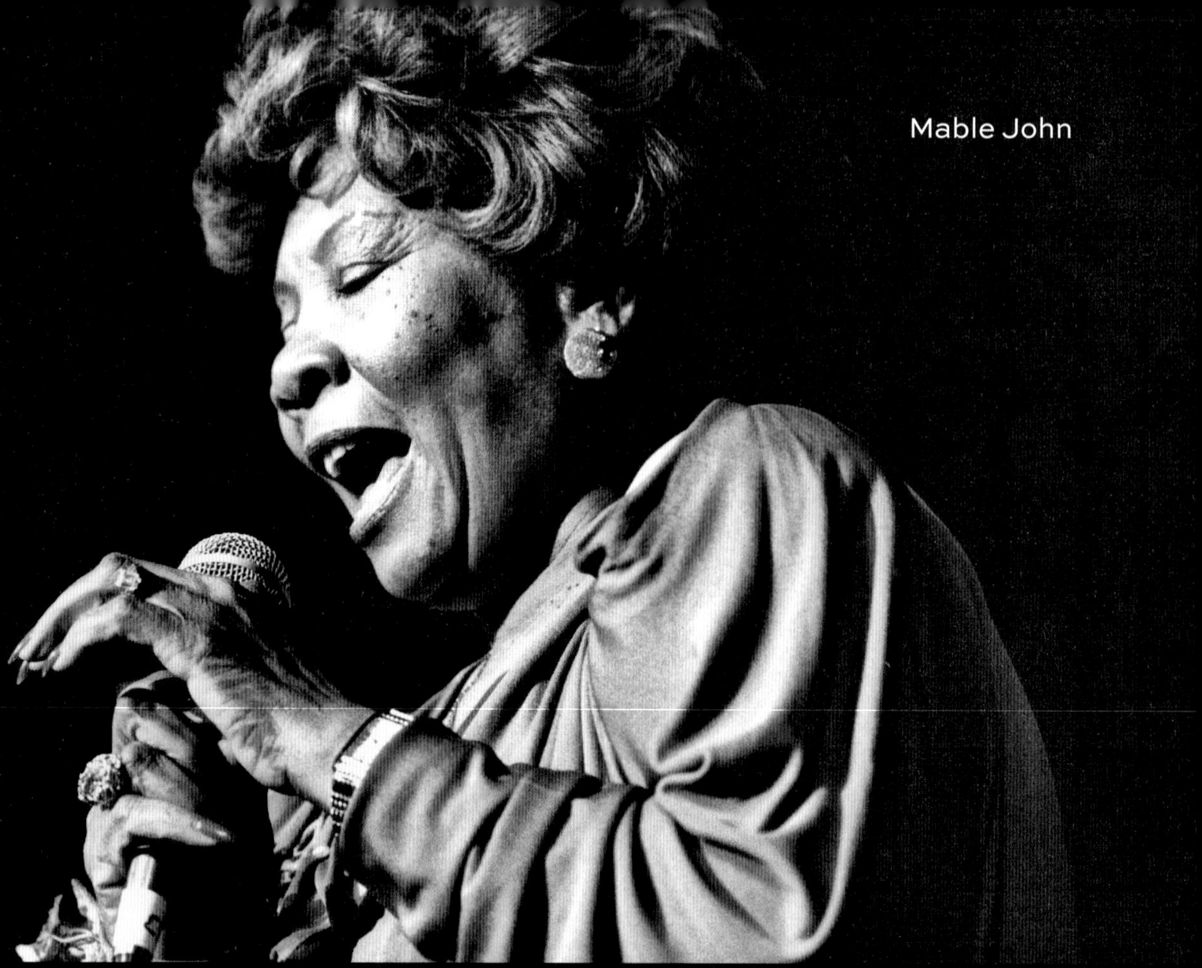

Mable John

Mable John and Booker T. Jones

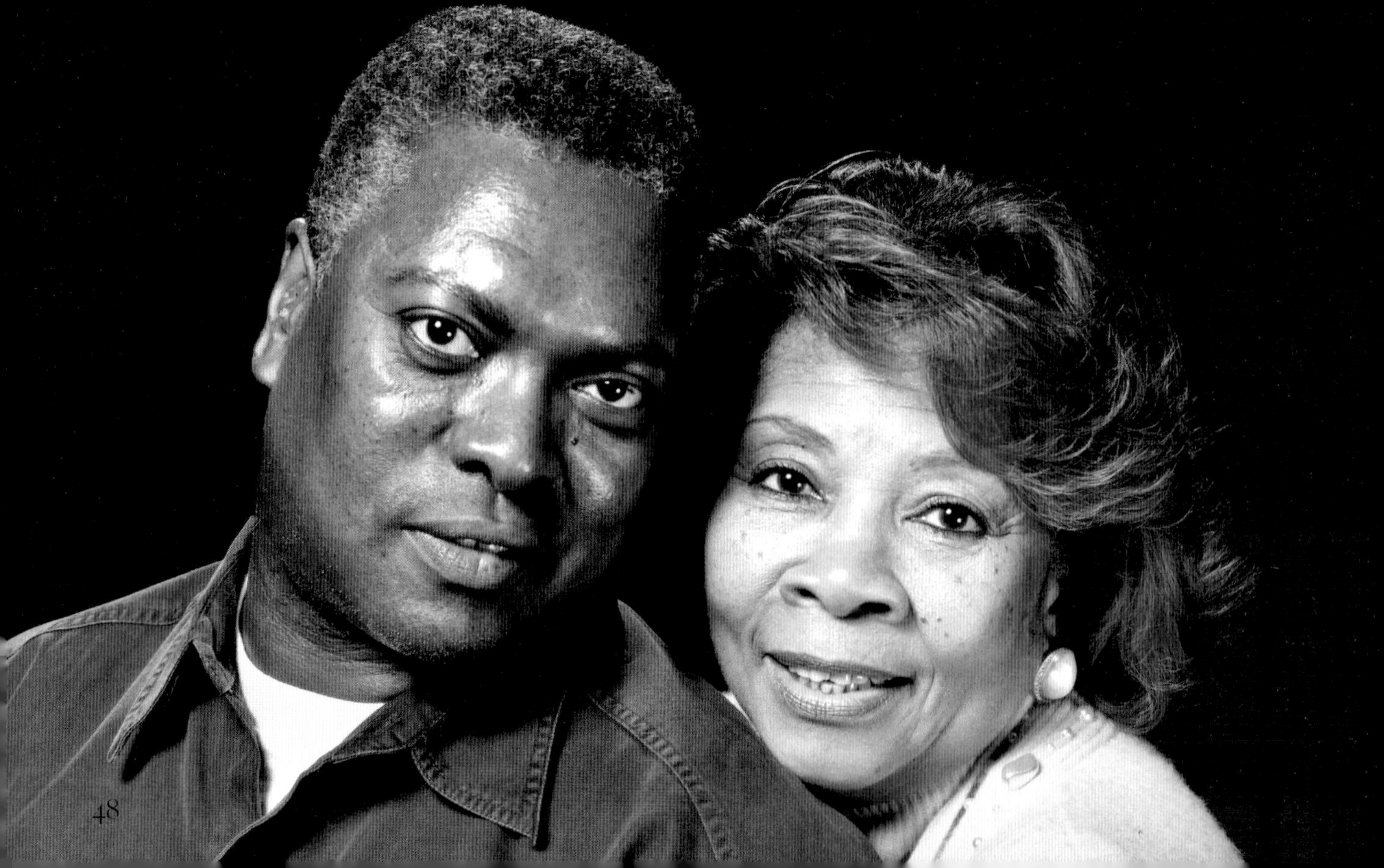

Maxine Brown

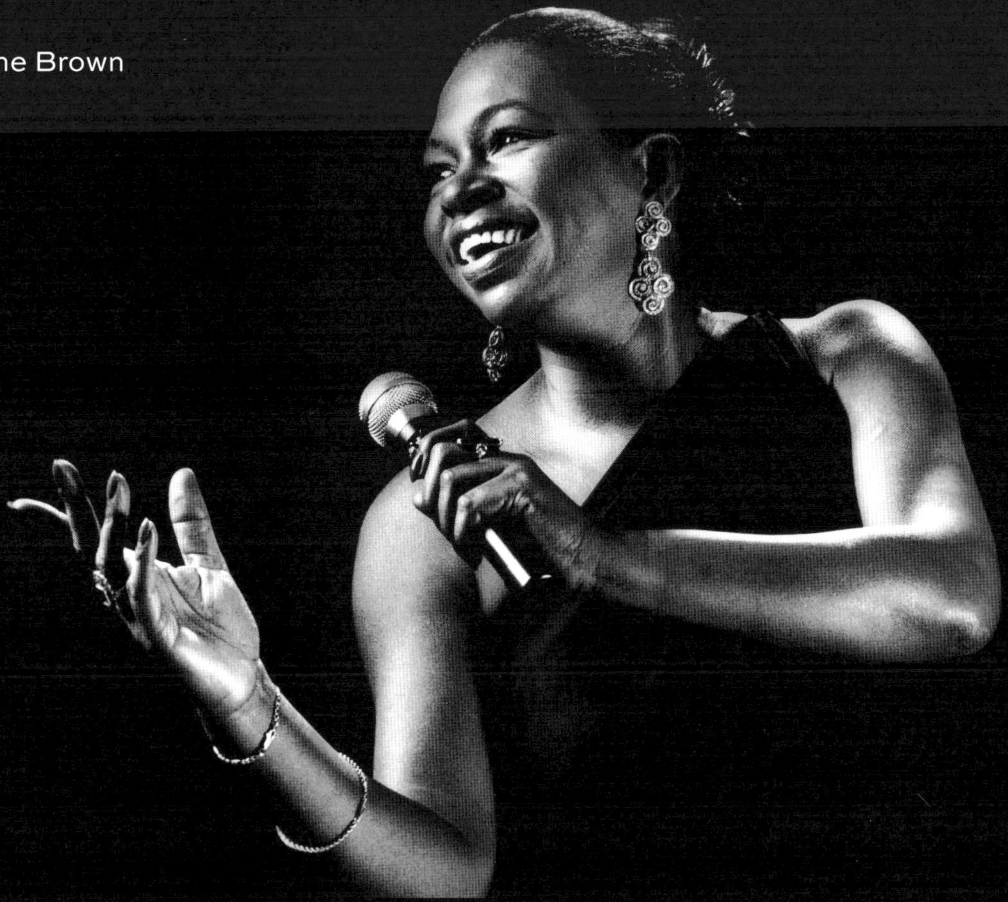

Chuck Jackson

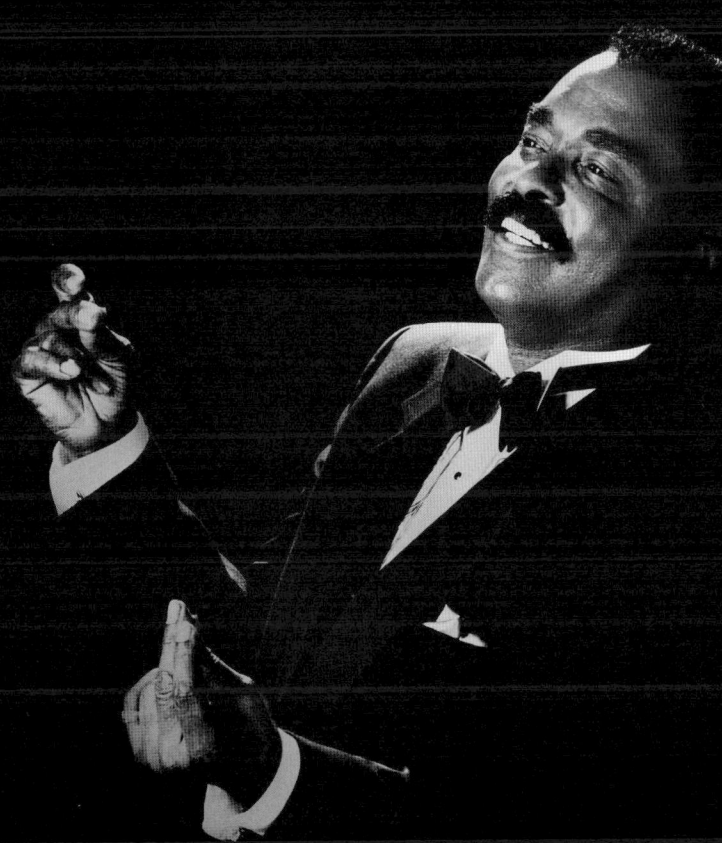

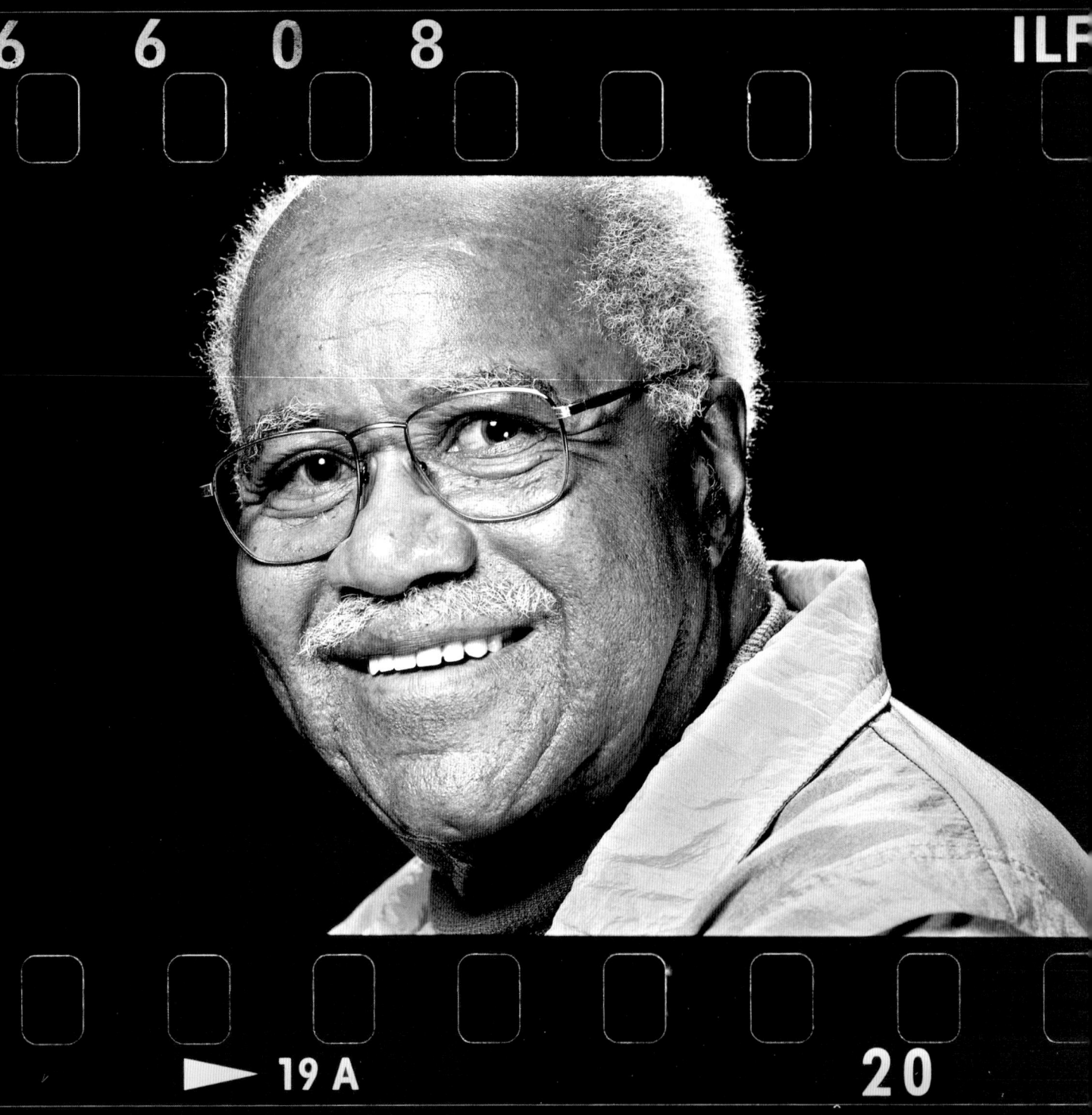

6 6 0 8 ILF

▶ 19 A   20

Roebuck "Pops" Staples

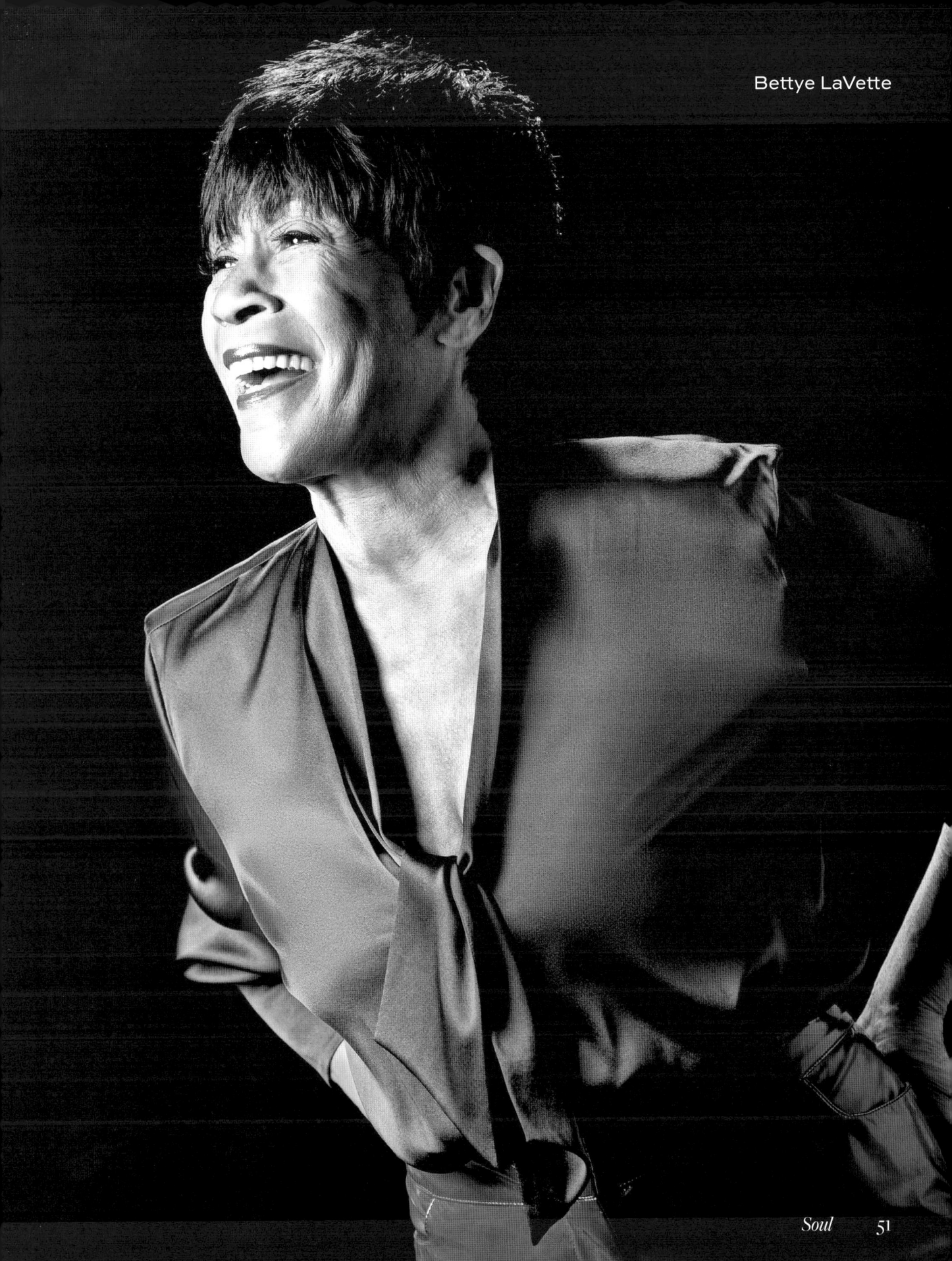

Al Green

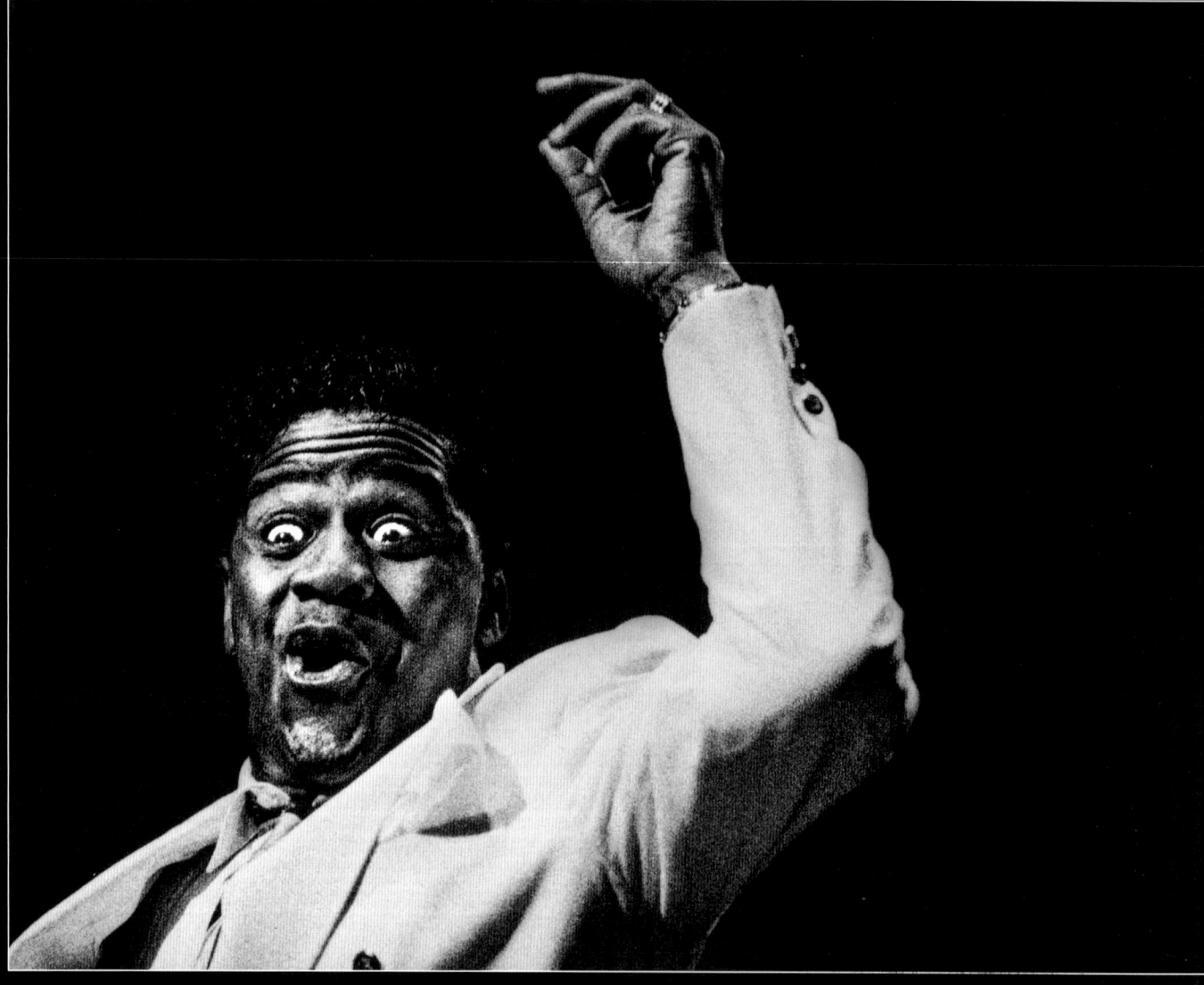

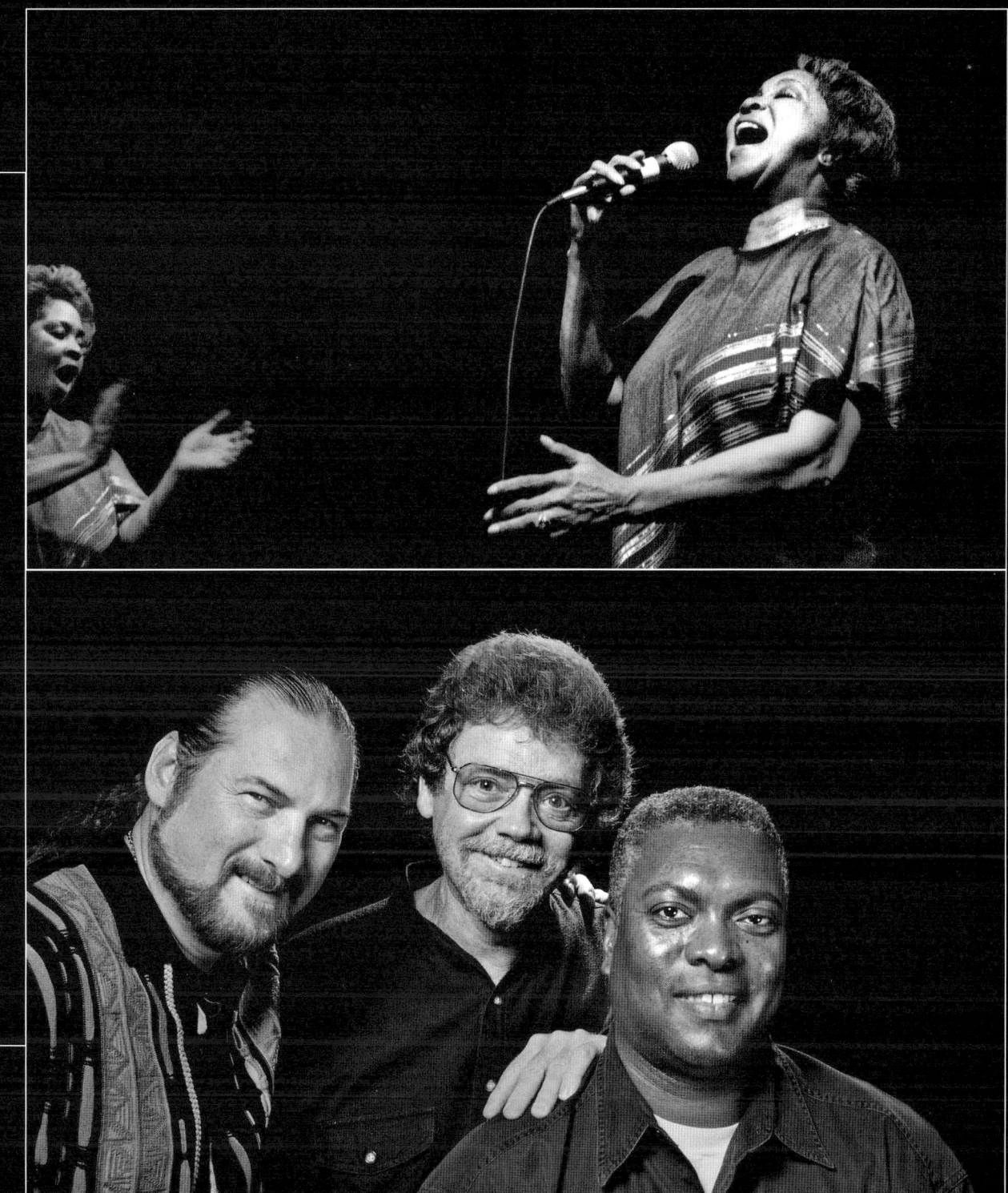

Booker T. & the M.G.s

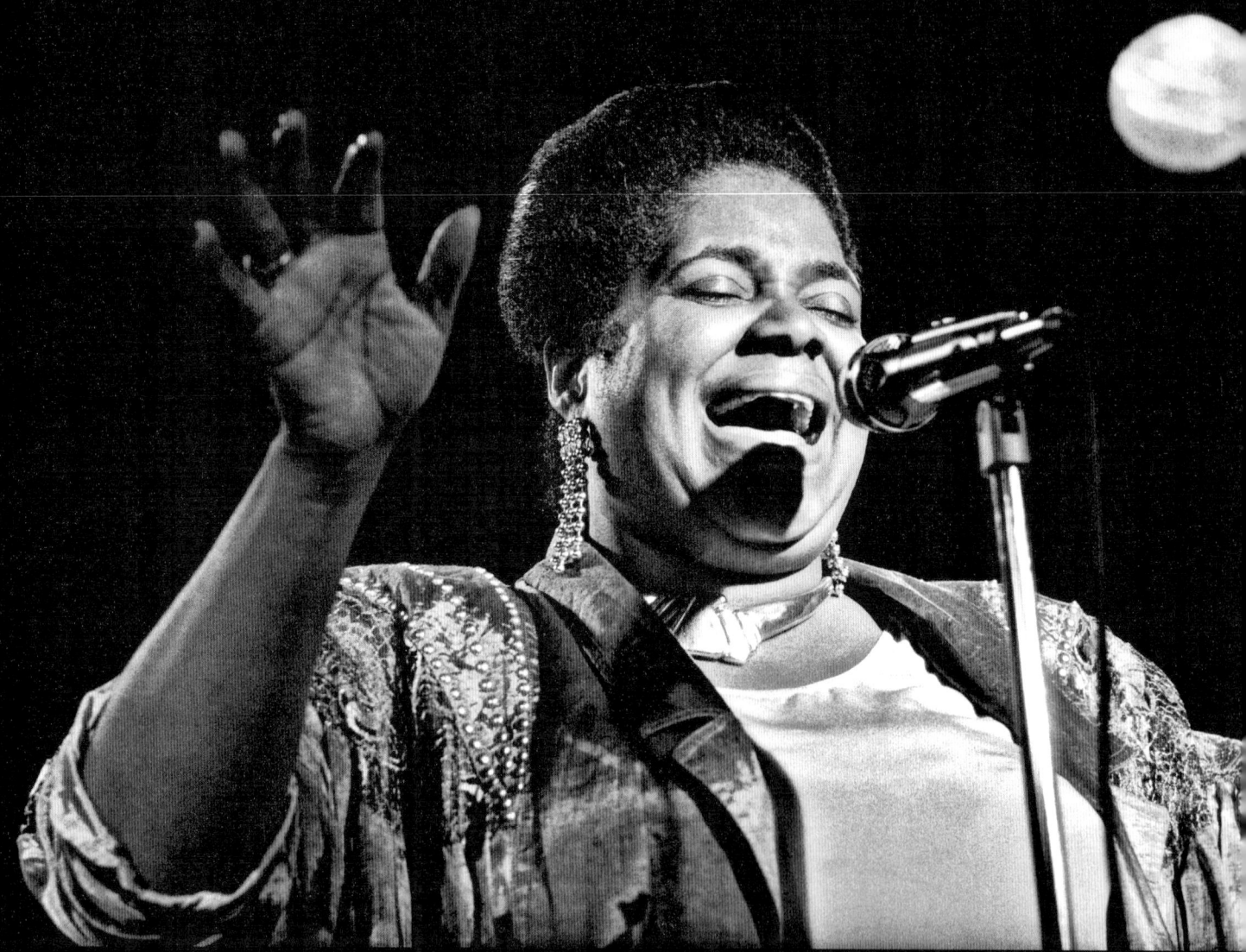

Carla Thomas

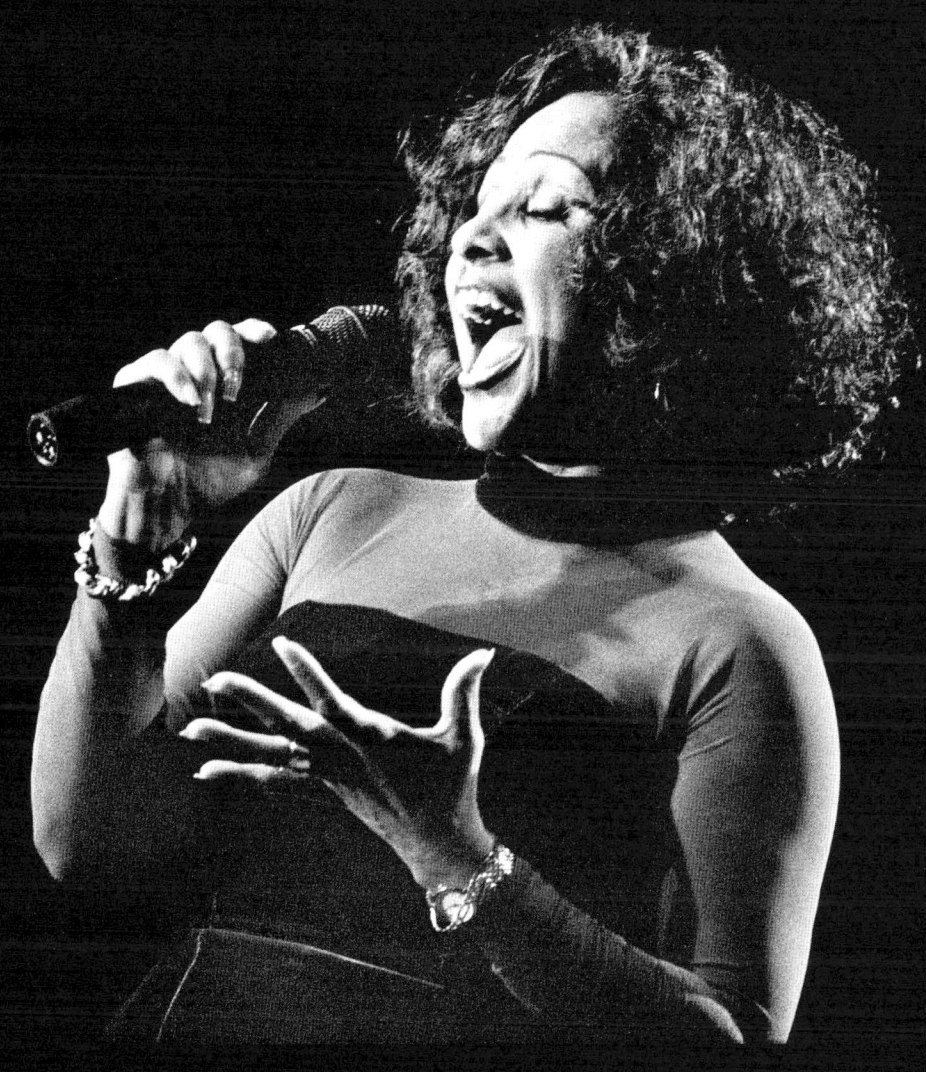

Darlene Love

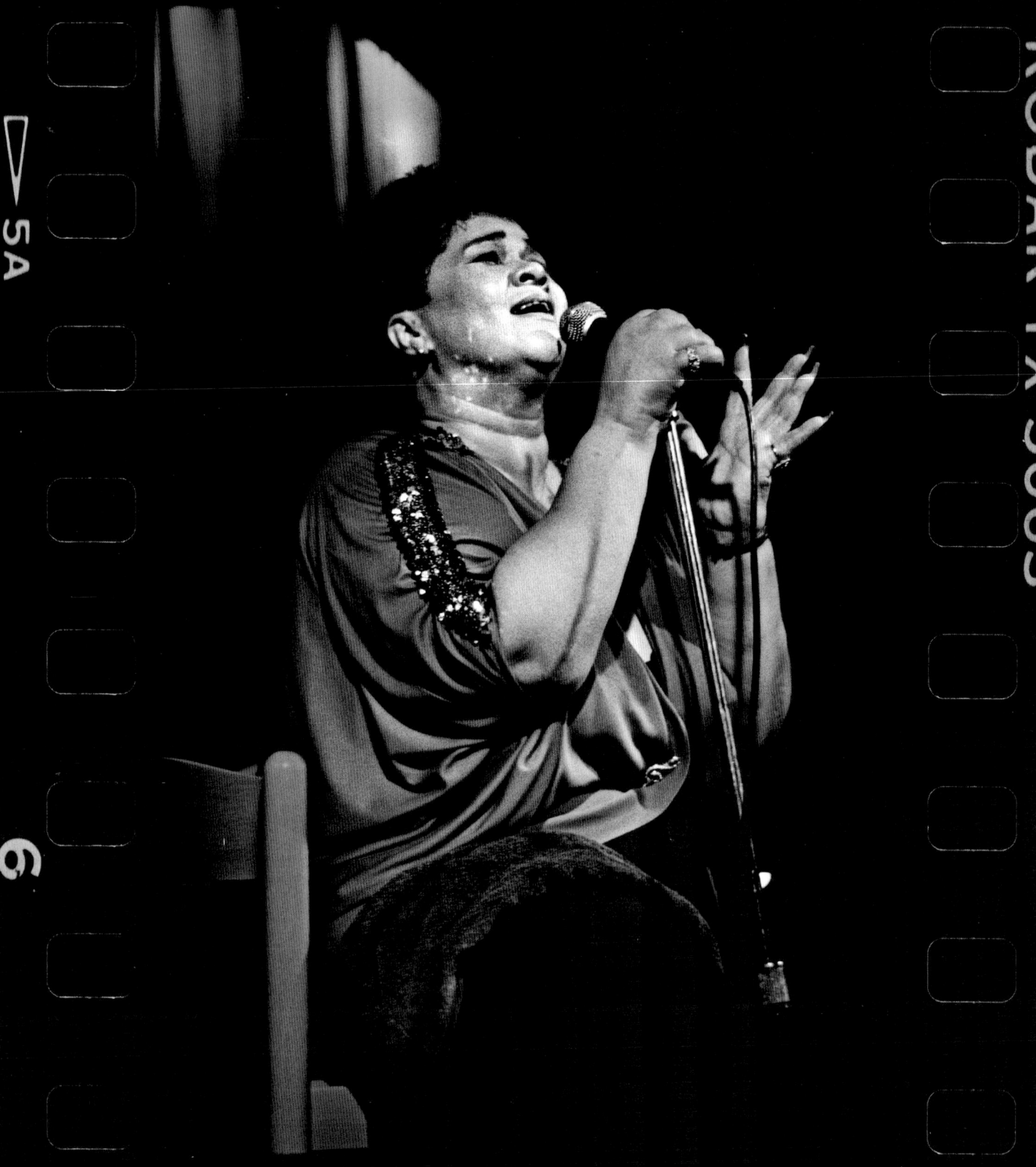

Etta James

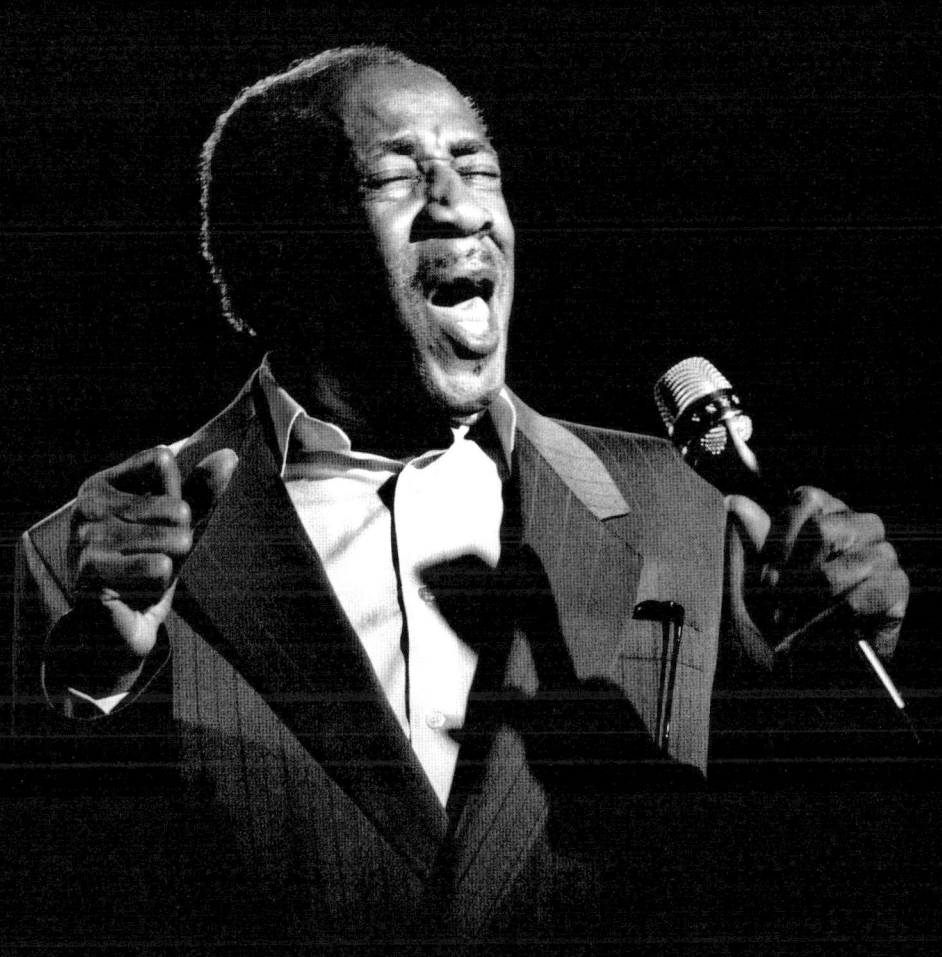

James Carr

William Bell

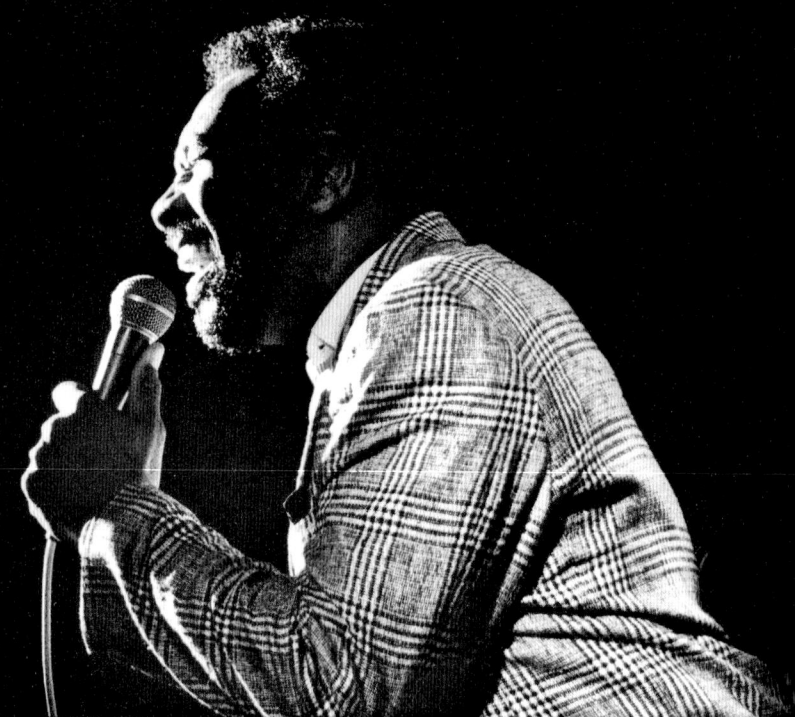

Wilson Pickett

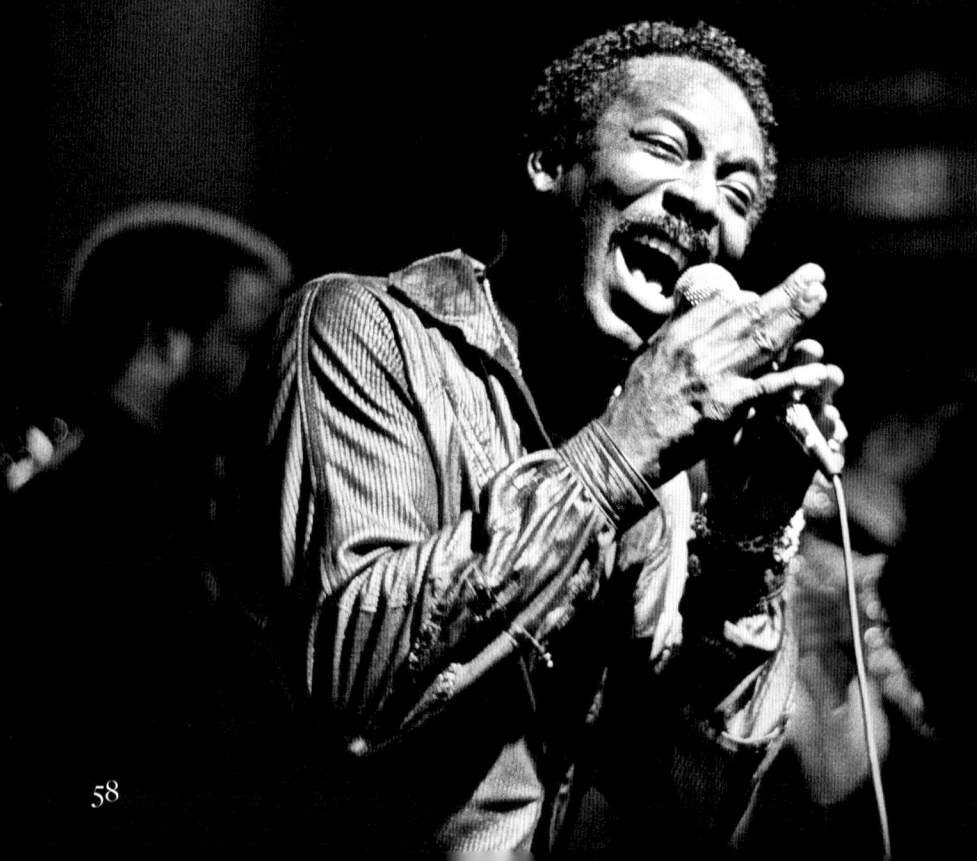

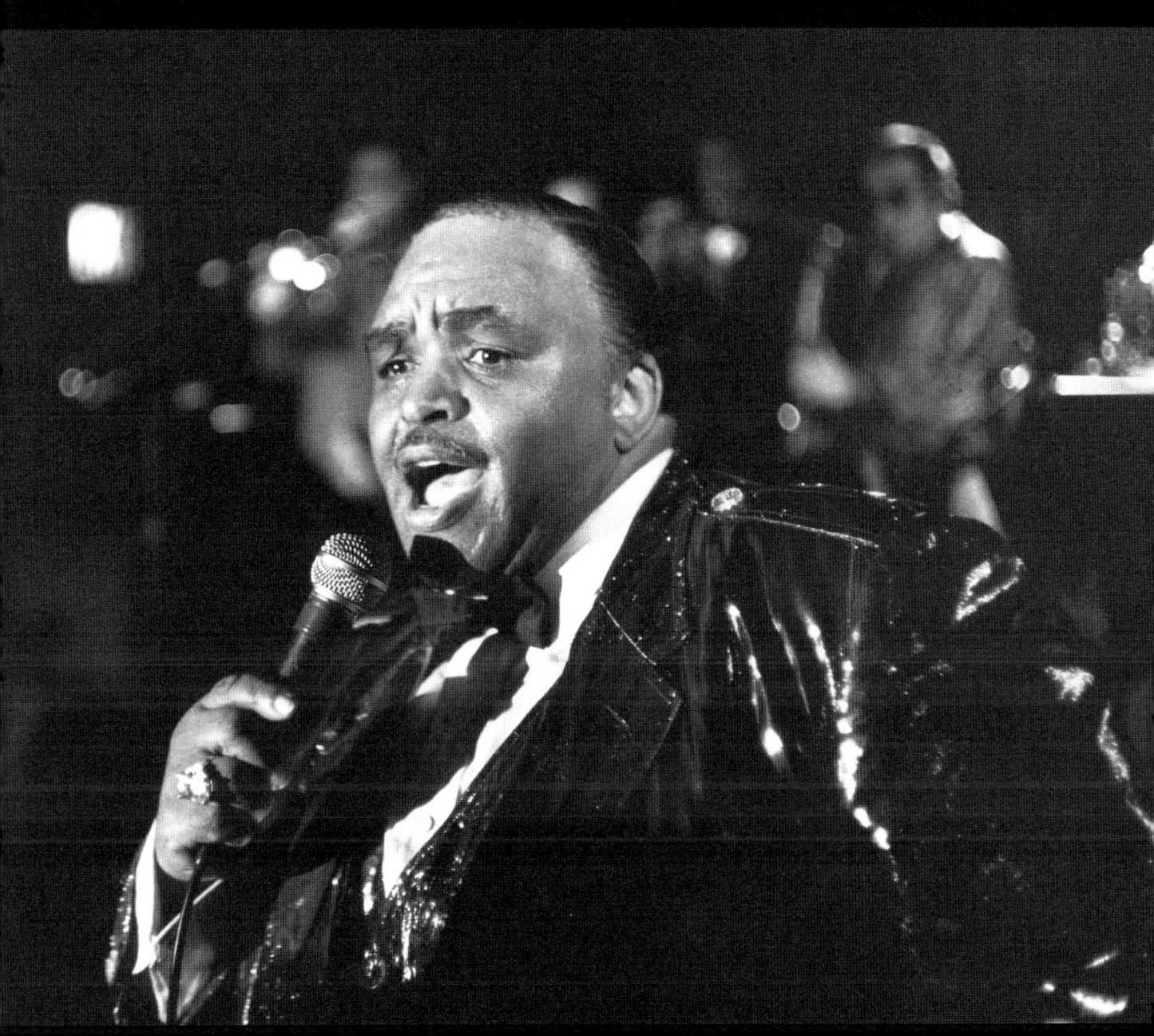

Wilson Pickett

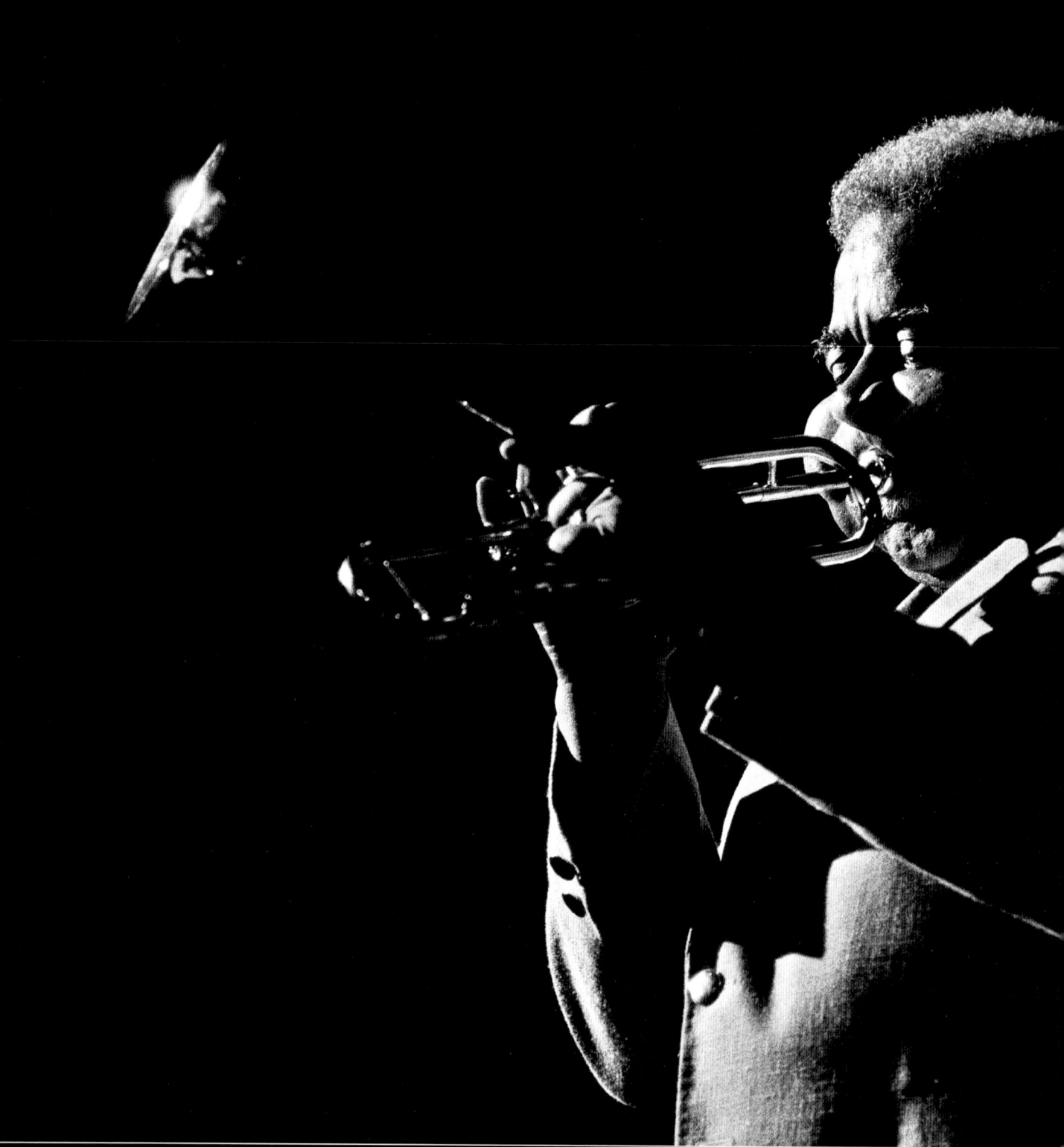

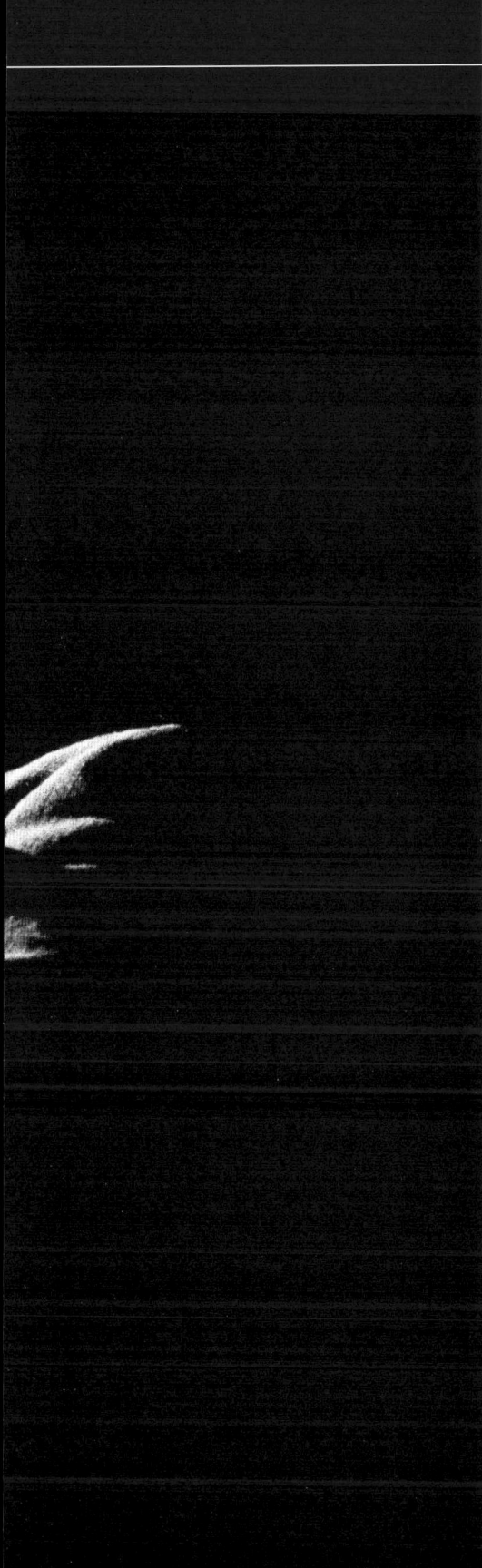

CHAPTER 3

JAZZ

Jazz is an American creation, and, from the earliest days, jazz musicians have played the blues. The repertory of jazz contains literally thousands of tunes with "Blues" in the title, and the twelve-bar blues structure is the most basic musical form in jazz.

The standard blues vocal consists of a line of lyric, which is then repeated and followed by a different line that rhymes with it. When the song ends, a story has been told—yet, a jazz-blues instrumental also tells a story, ideally beginning with a forceful and insinuating line that then develops through the thoughtful and inventive lines of improvisation that follow to a well-defined conclusion. The first notes of the solo draw the listener in, the building of the solo holds the listener, and the final phrases tie it all together.

Louis Armstrong's 1928 recording of "West End Blues," with its startling introductory cadenza, has long been seen as evidence demonstrating that jazz could be both equal in artistic expression to other musical genres and a legitimate musical genre itself.

Throughout its long history, jazz players—whether formally or informally known as "blues players" individually—have played the blues while improvising on popular standards along with blues tunes and other material. Swing-era trumpeters Roy Eldridge and Charlie Shavers, master improvisers, were brilliant blues soloists, as were their pianist contemporaries Fats Waller, Teddy Wilson, and the incomparable Art Tatum.

It was perhaps the saxophonists, many straddling the line between jazz and R&B, who most naturally made the blues their home. Coleman Hawkins, who almost single-handedly brought the tenor saxophone to prominence, played his first recorded solo on singer Mamie Smith's "Mean Daddy Blues" in 1922. Lester Young's many solos with Count Basie and backing Billie Holiday were notable for their smoother and more mellow sound. Both men, early giants on the tenor sax and the two greatest influences on those who followed, were formidable blues players.

During the early New York jam sessions at Minton's Playhouse in Harlem, where the style and basic lexicon of be-bop were developed after 1940, much of the early repertoire was blues or blues-tinged twelve-bar derivatives of such popular standards as "I Got Rhythm" and "Indiana," many of them jazz standards to this day. The great Charlie Parker, one of the handful of musicians who invented the be-bop style, was an exceptional blues player.

The pioneer honking tenor saxophonists of the late 1940s—Illinois Jacquet, Arnett Cobb, Hal Singer, and, a few years later, their R&B brethren Red Prysock, Sil Austin, and Willis "Gator Tail" Jackson, among many others—played the blues, but they were all jazz men who eventually returned to jazz. Buddy Tate and Dexter Gordon played R&B dates in the late 1940s, then returned to their roots as jazz men, but they always sounded bluesy. Sam "The Man" Taylor and "Big" Al Sears were blues-playing jazz men who worked for—and were given their nicknames by—rock-and-roll impresario Alan Freed; yet, Taylor had been featured in earlier years with the bandleader-showman Cab Calloway, and Sears was featured with Duke Ellington.

In 1956, Jimmy Smith suddenly appeared to show everyone that the cumbersome Hammond organ was much more than the "miscellaneous instrument" defined in jazz polls and that he himself was a master blues player, as influential and inspirational as Armstrong, Hawkins, Young, and Parker had been years earlier. And all the players who followed Smith were bluesy: "Brother" Jack McDuff, Shirley Scott, John Patton, Richard "Groove" Holmes, and numerous others worked in most American cities after the "organ circuit" established itself in the 1950s. Jimmy McGriff, one of the very best, said that "I'm a blues player, basically—what I play isn't really jazz, it's sort of in between. Just old-time swing with a jazz effect to it."

As they became prominent, Eddie "Lockjaw" Davis, Lou Donaldson, Stanley Turrentine, Willis Jackson, Gene Ammons, and other saxophonists established organ groups; the deep, mellow groove of the organ setting up a blues-chorded and heavily rhythmic background much beloved by Black audiences in the inner-city "organ rooms."

Jazz bassist Charles Mingus loved the blues and gospel material, often exhorting his groups to "play the blues, man, just play the blues," and he also incorporated a gospel feeling because "the blues was in the churches."

With the advent of the jazz avant garde and free jazz during the 1960s, unfortunately, the tradition and comfort of inspired blues improvisation became, to many modernists, old hat. Prominent jazz critic Ira Gitler once lamented the "blues is the enemy" attitude of many young musicians who no longer believed in the long-standing tradition so precious and natural to their predecessors and focused instead on their own original compositions, many generic, unmusical, and unswinging, with little blues feeling.

George Benson

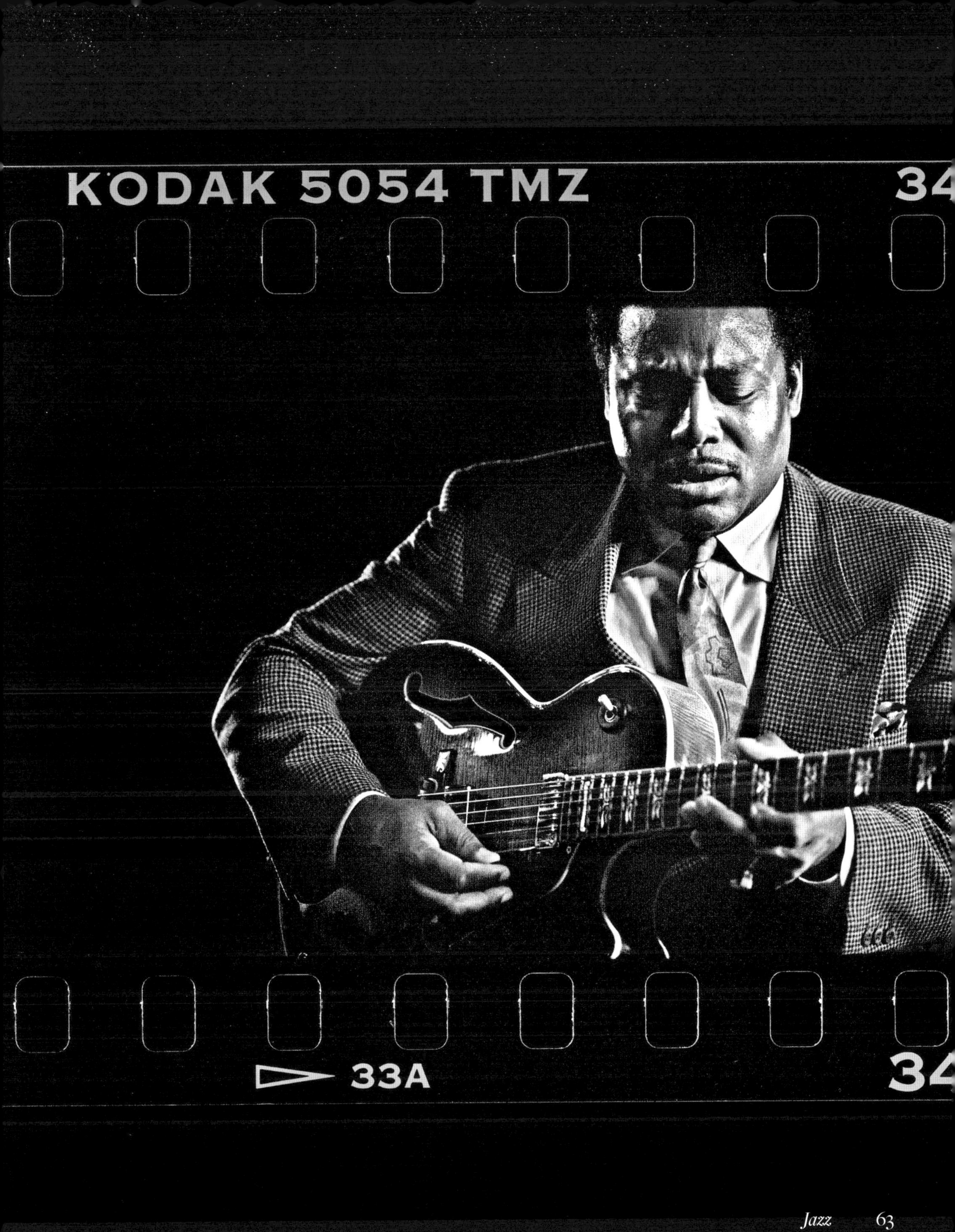
KODAK 5054 TMZ
34
33A
34

Jazz is a creative improvisational music, something of an eternal work in progress, and live performances have historically showed it at its best, from mainstream clubs to more-formal concert halls to the organ rooms, where, as a critic once observed, "You can feel the music in the air like heat," and where inspired bluesy improvisation startles and delights the listener.

As blues-oriented saxophonist Hank Crawford, who doubled as player and arranger in Ray Charles's band between 1958 and 1963 and later recorded often with his own groups and co-led a group with Jimmy McGriff for some fifteen years, said of club appearances that "as a jazz man, you make your money as a touring musician. And whatever kind of club it is, it's never too early to play a good blues."

TONY OUTHWAITE
Literary agent, writer, and jazz historian

Dexter Gordon

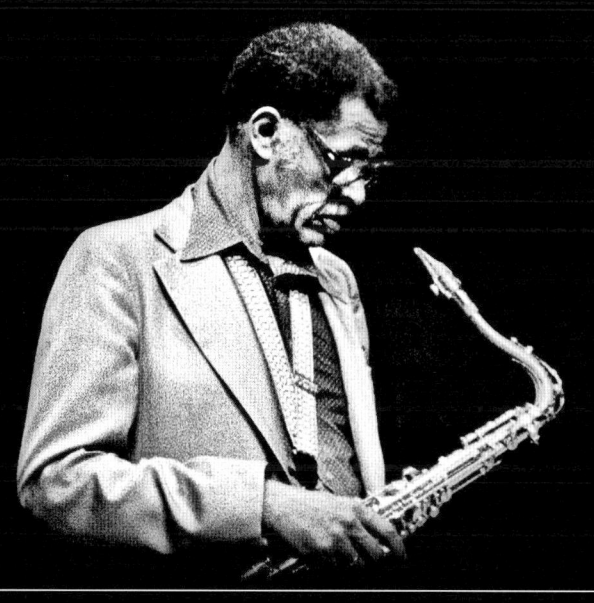

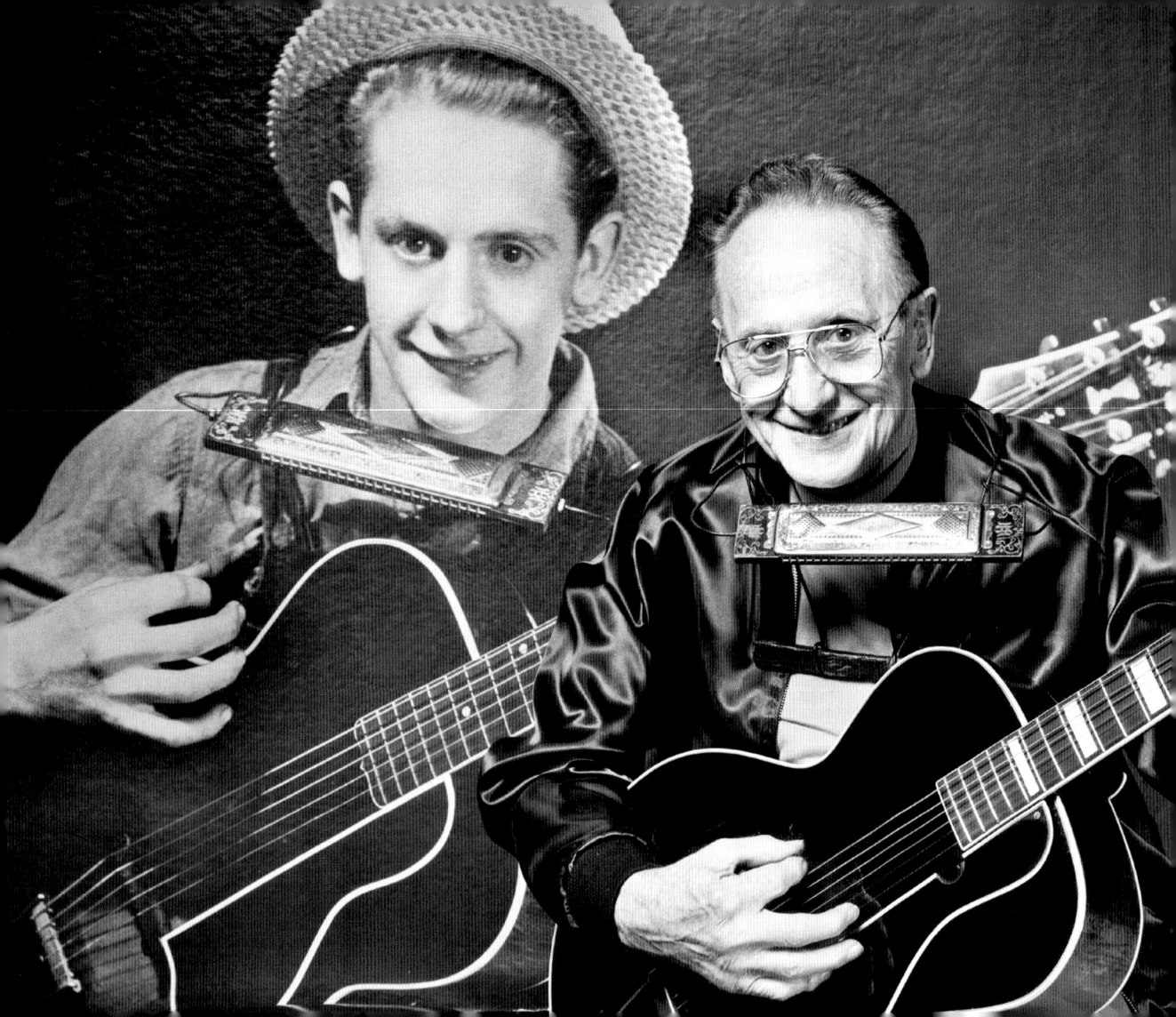

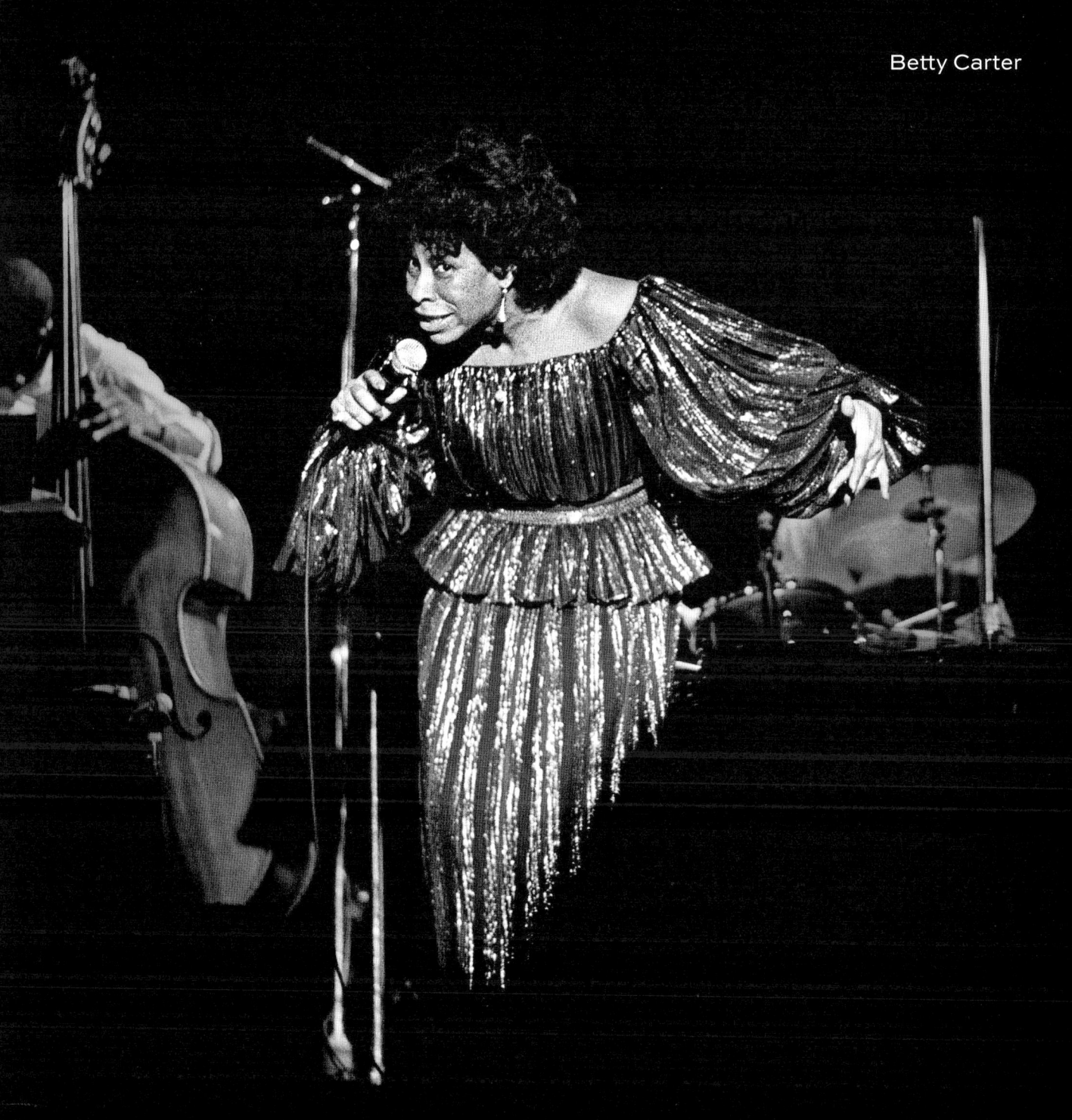

Betty Carter

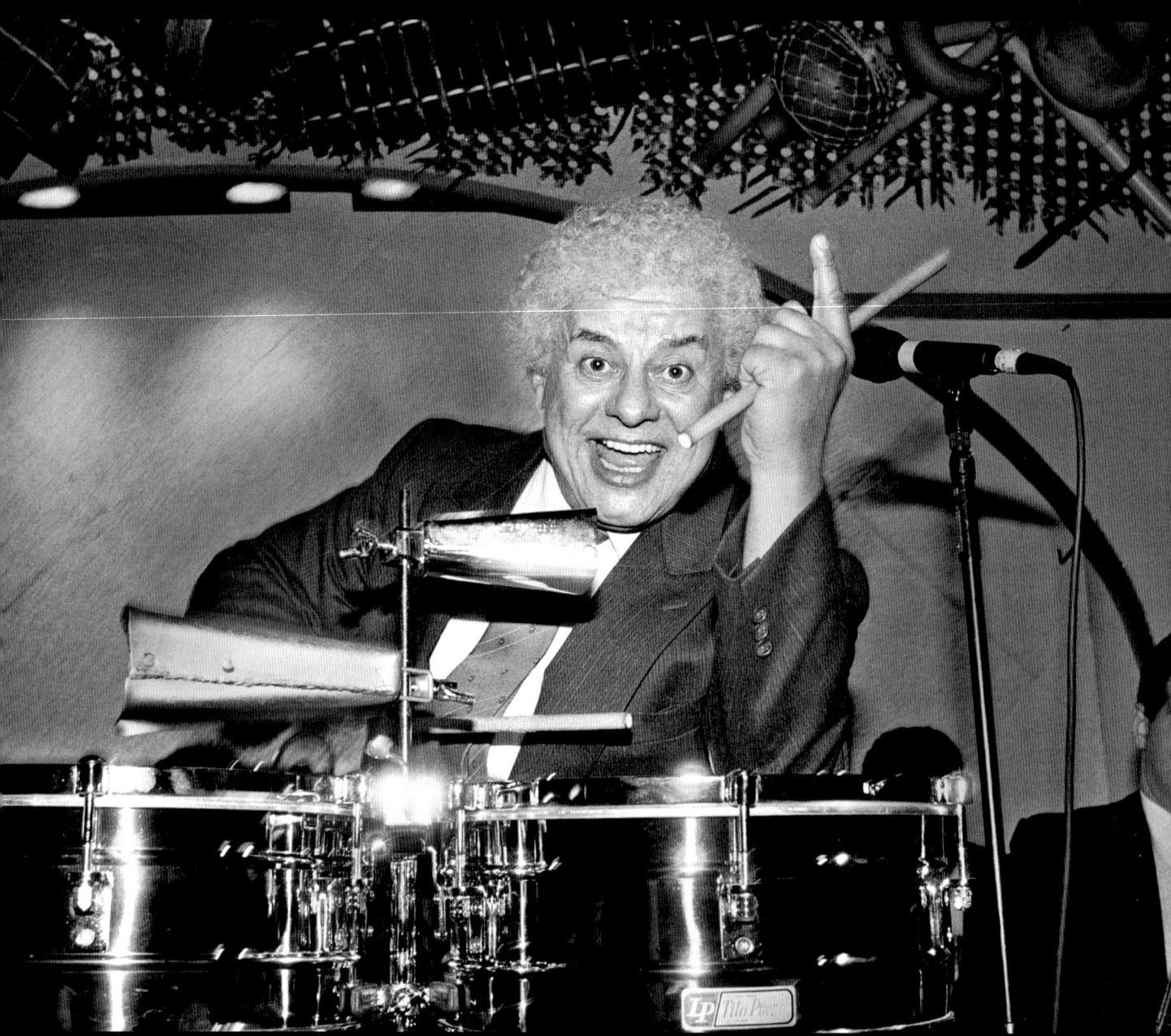

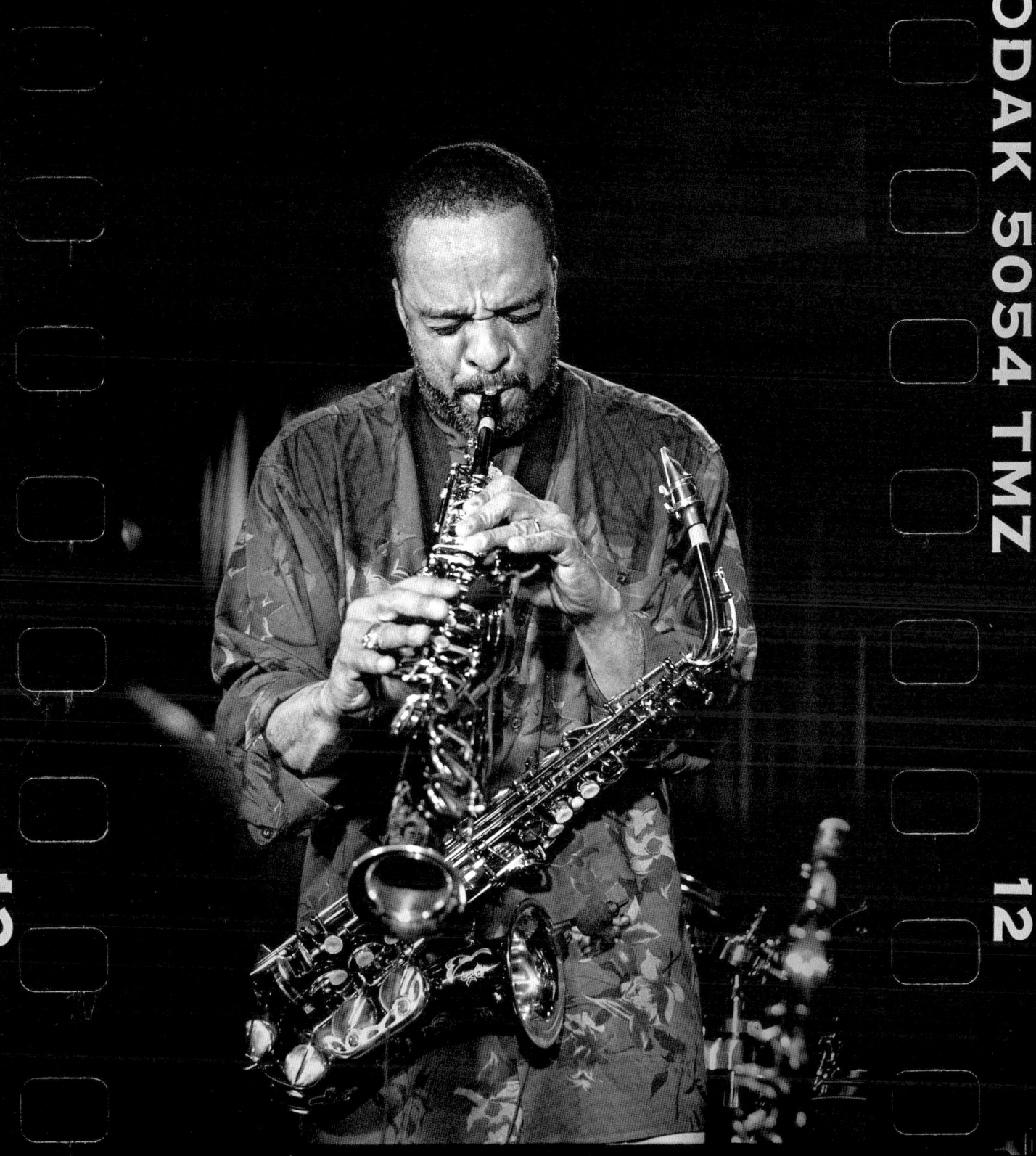

Grover Washington Jr.

KODAK 5054 TMZ

12

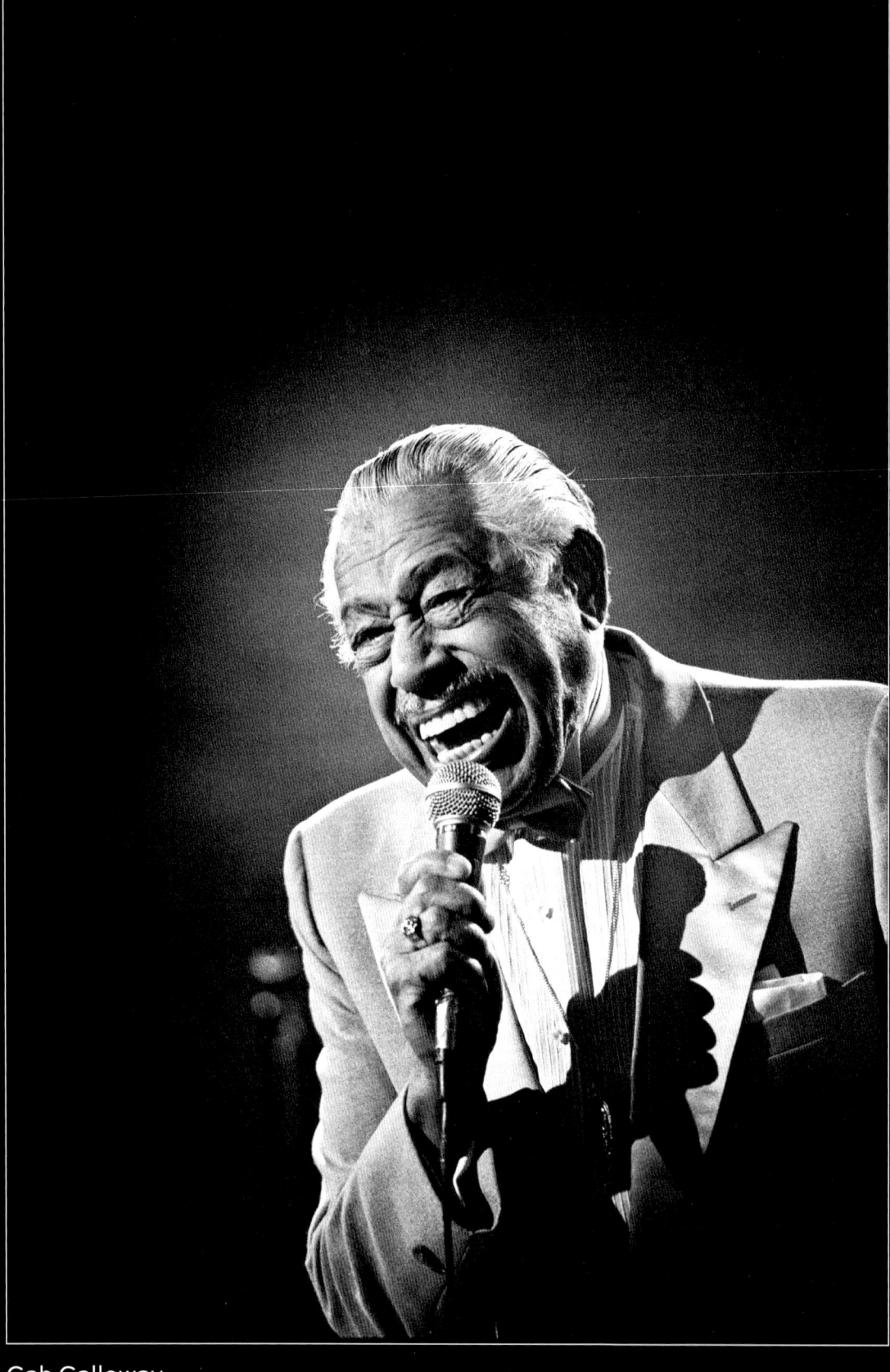

Cab Calloway

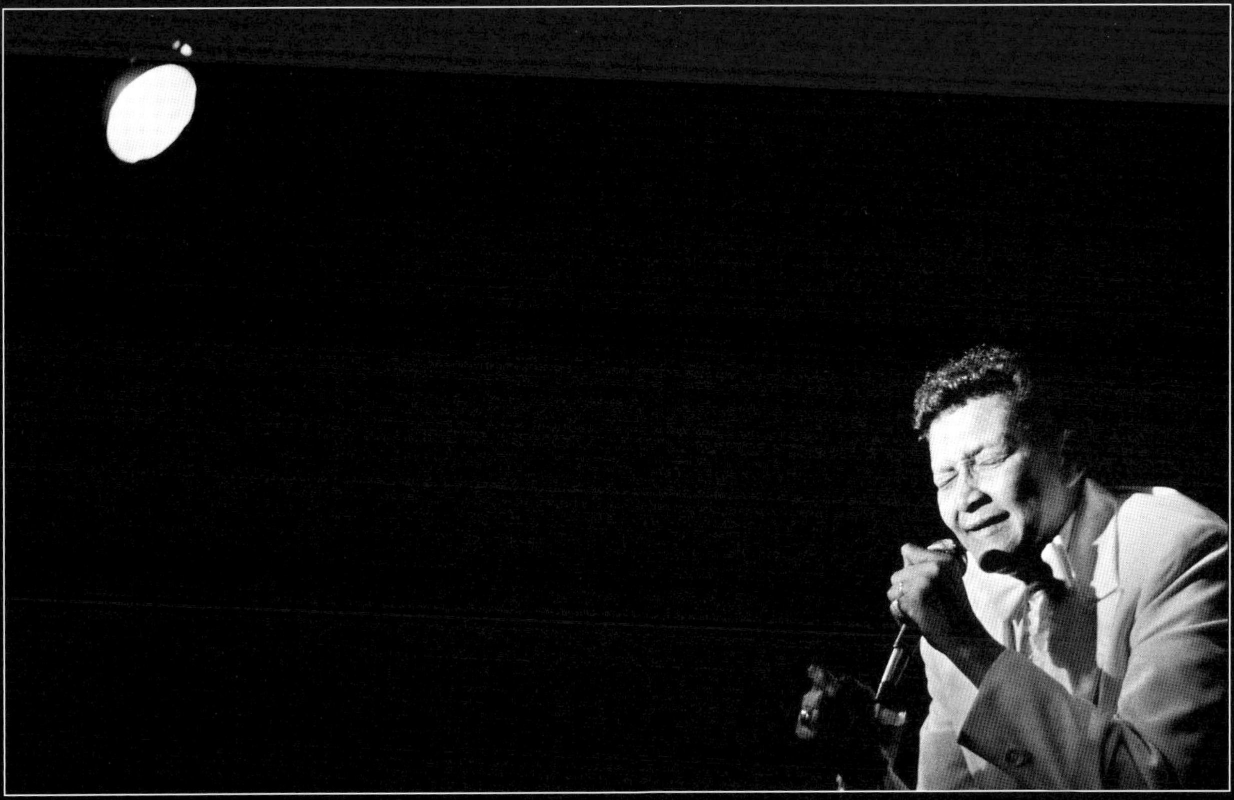

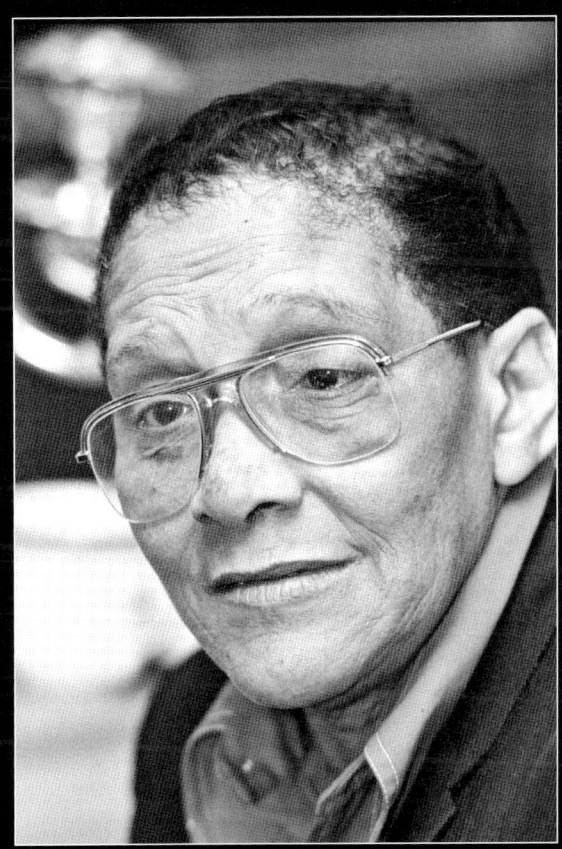

Little Jimmy Scott

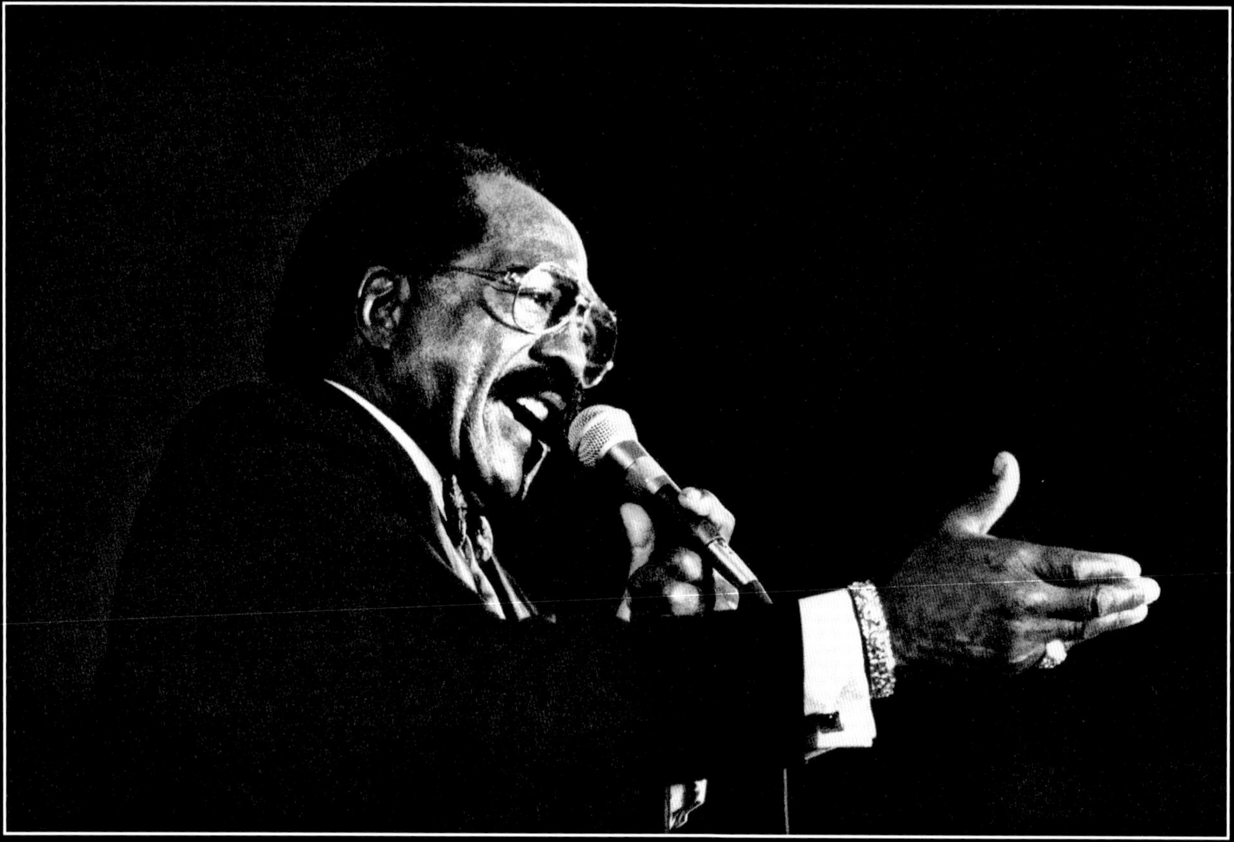

Jimmy Witherspoon

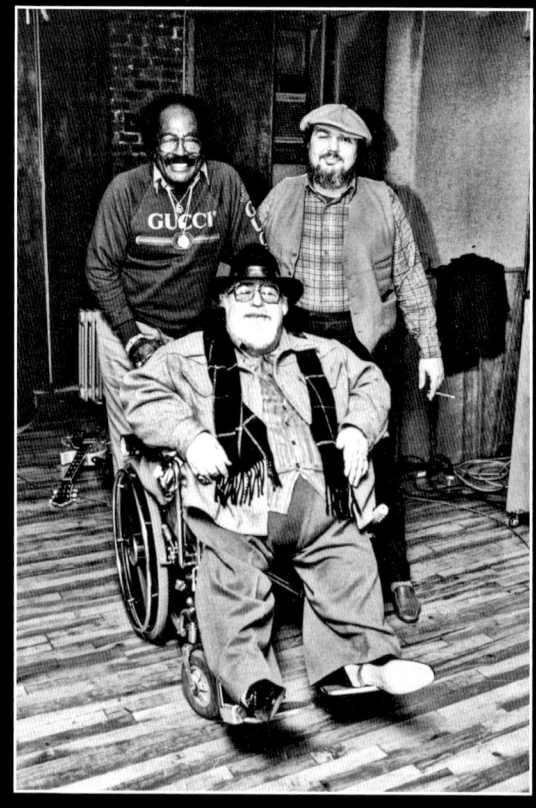

Jimmy Witherspoon, Mac "Dr. John" Rebennack, and Doc Pomus

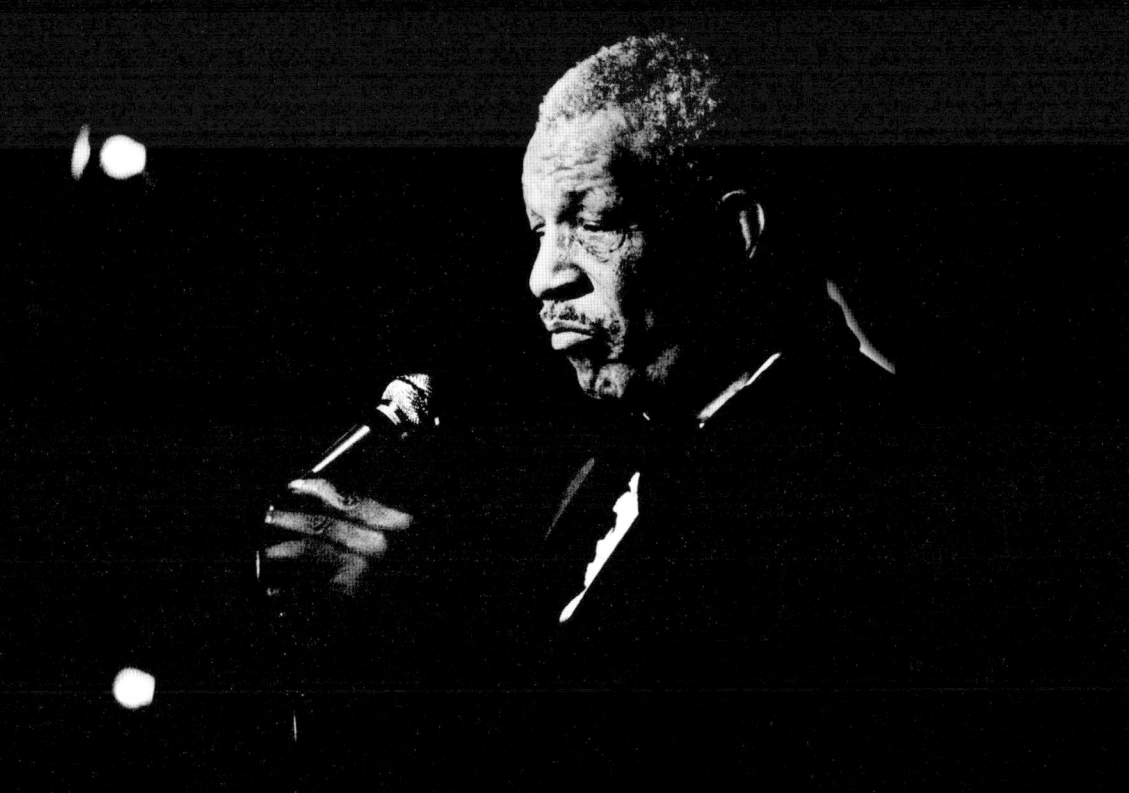

Al Hibbler

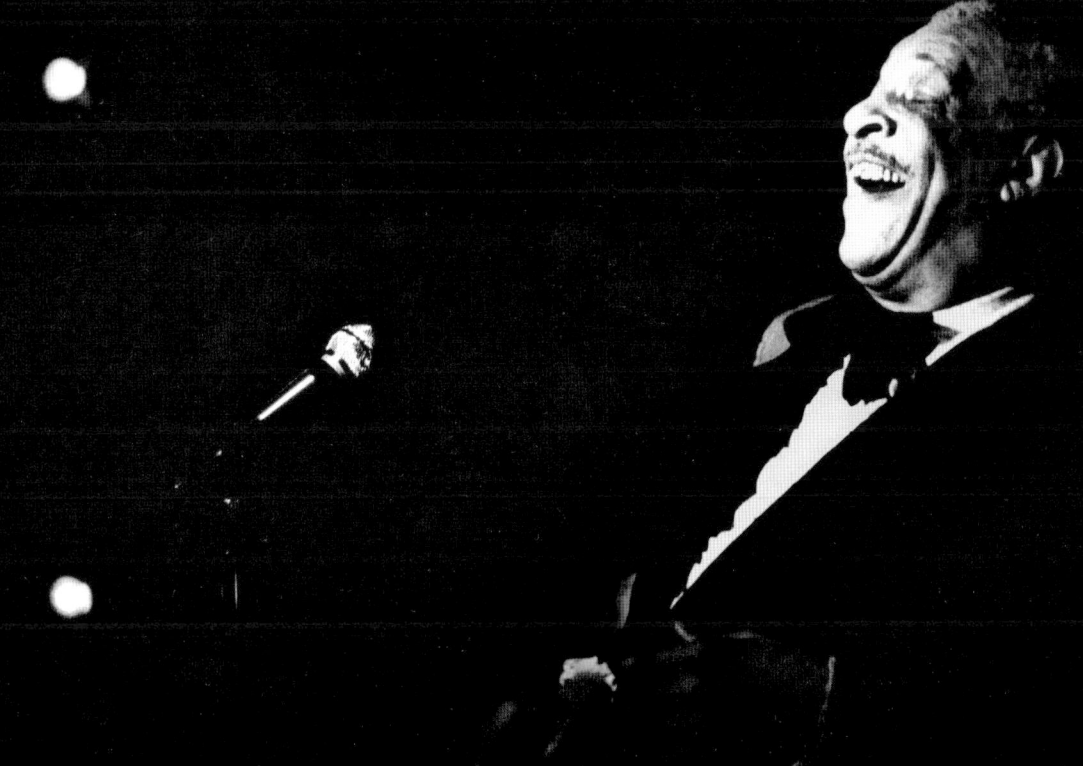

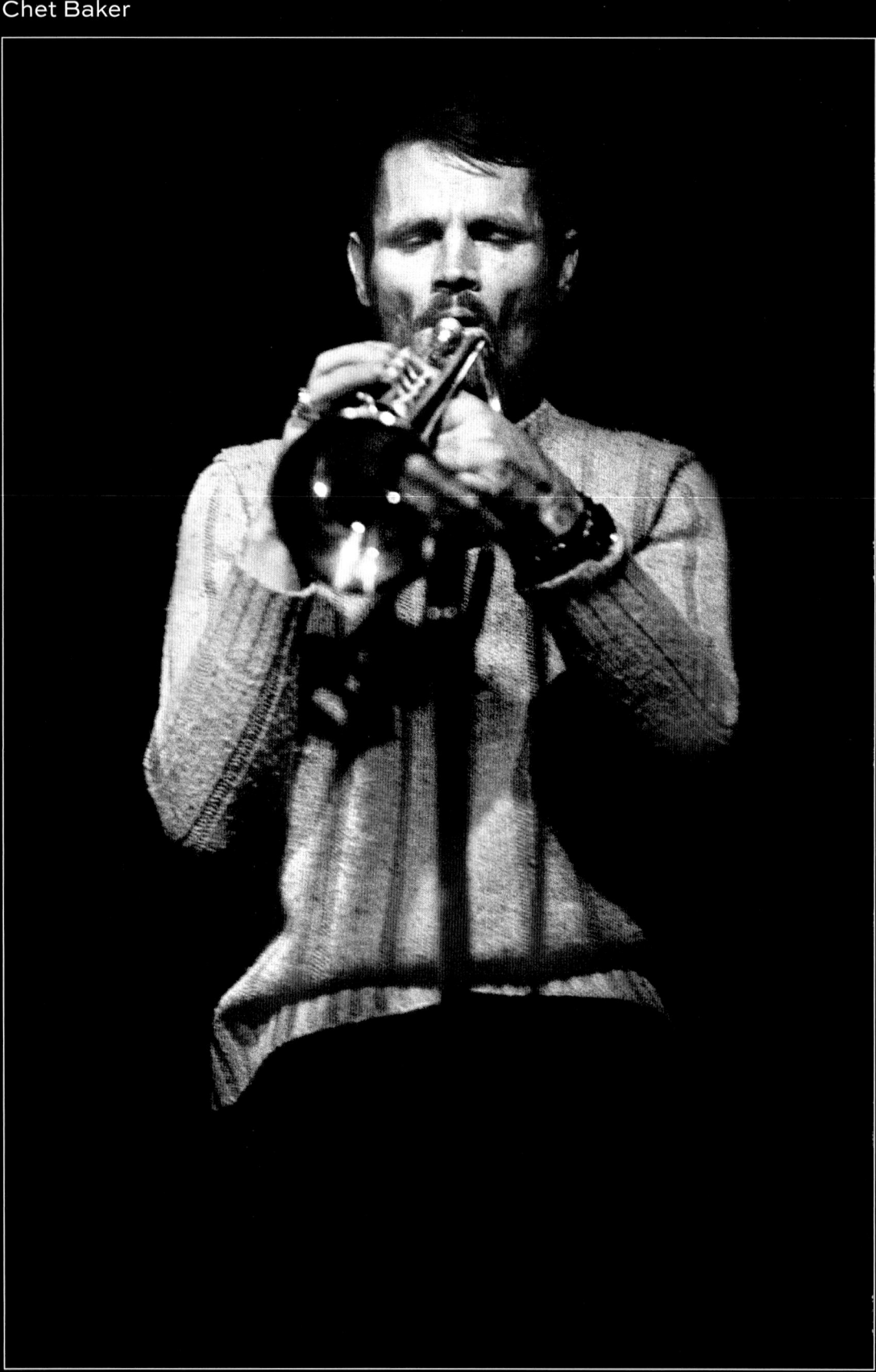

David "Fathead" Newman

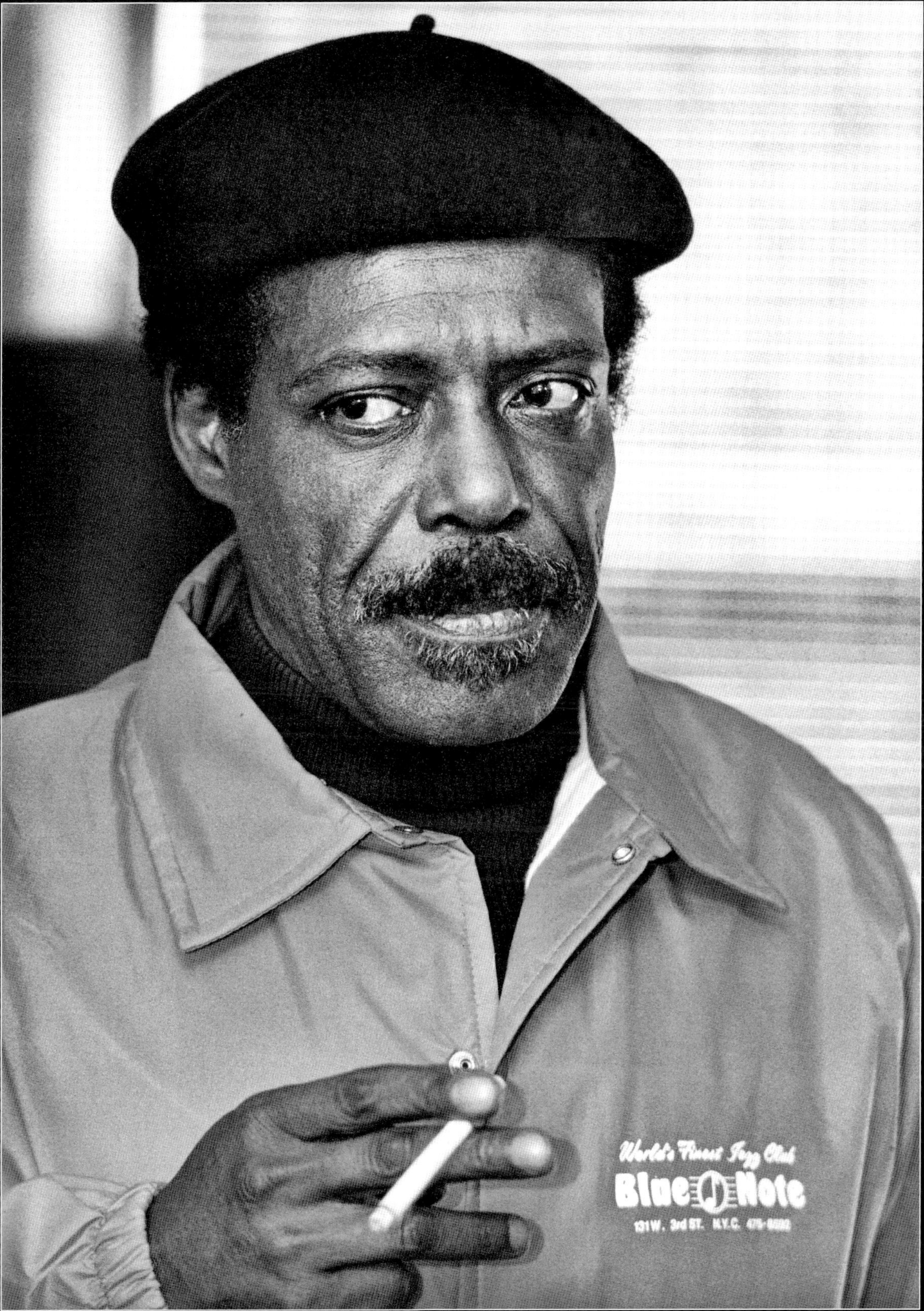

ORD FP4 PLUS

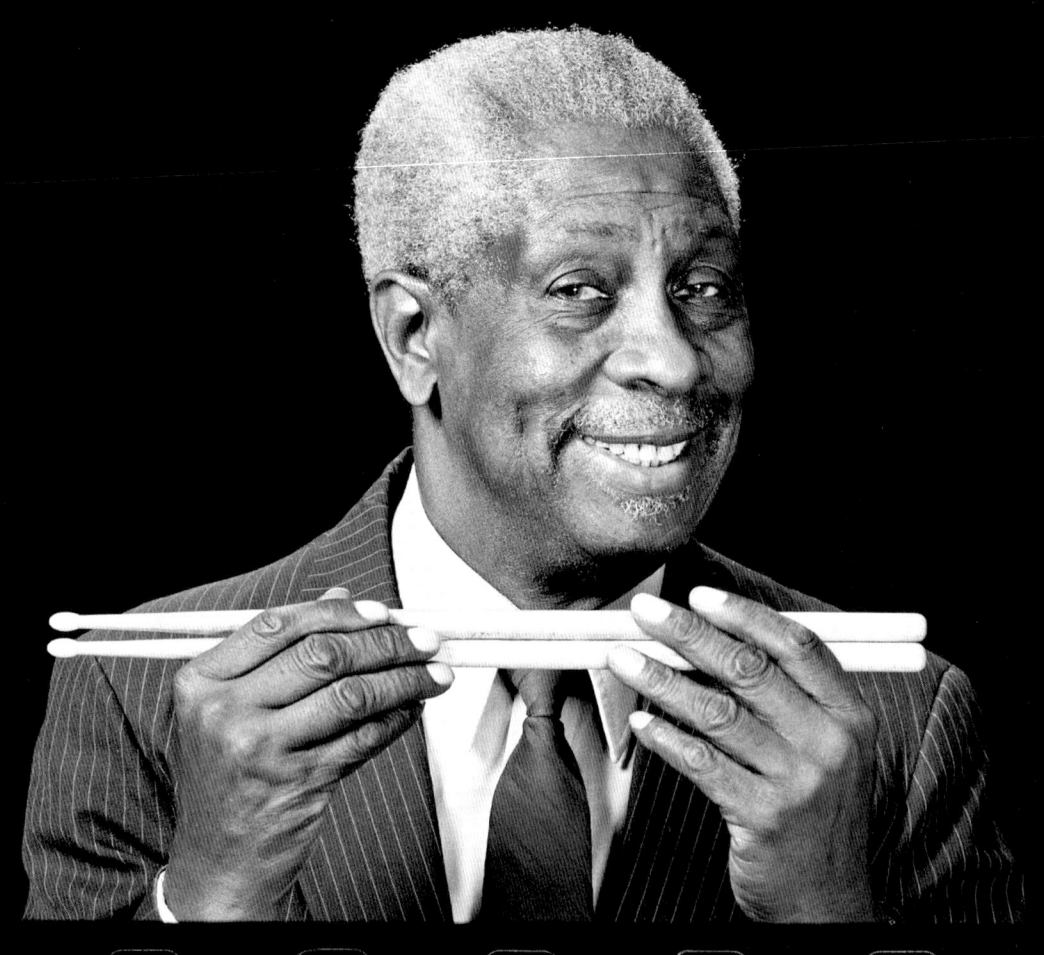

33A   34

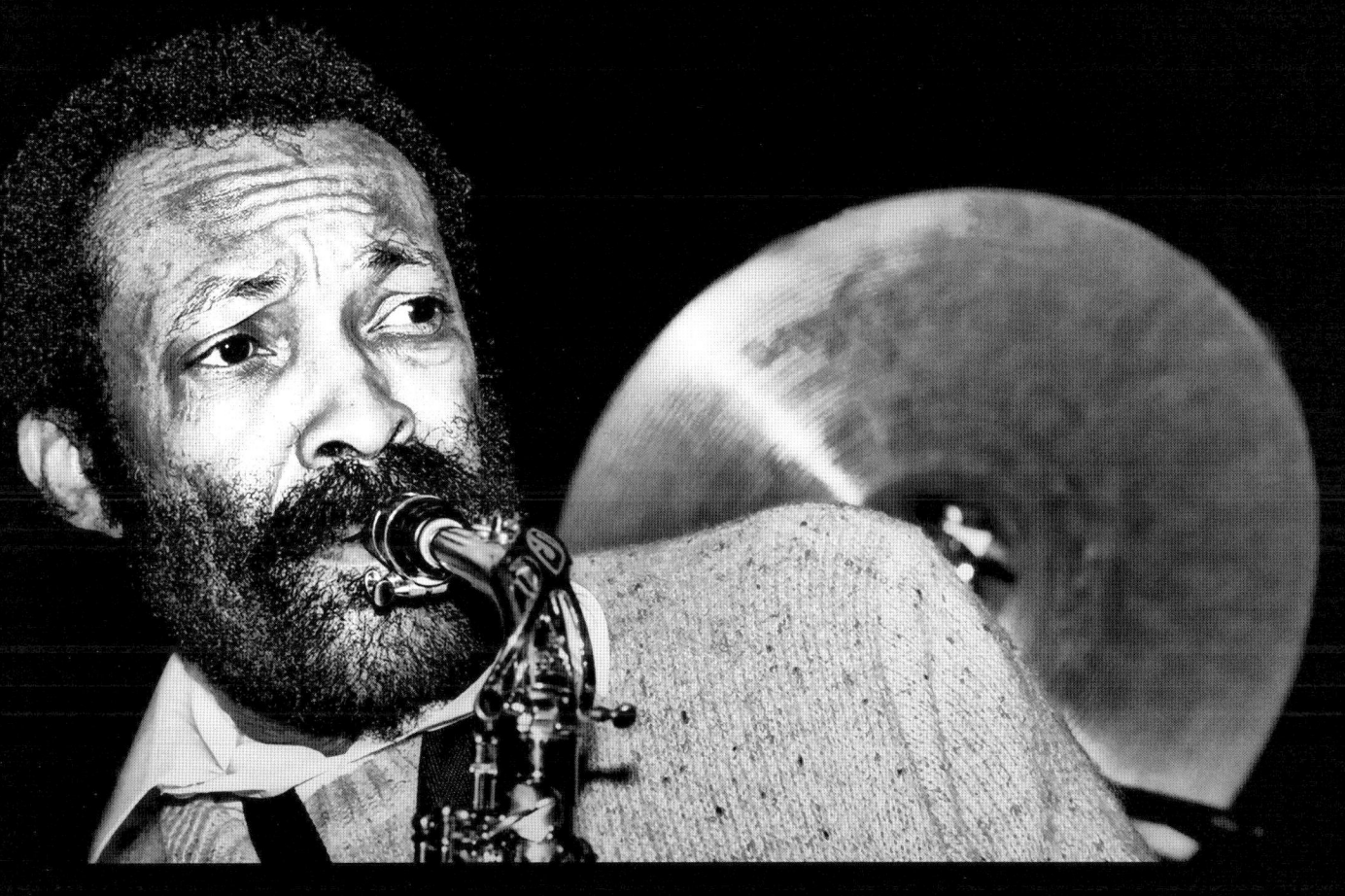

Illinois Jacquet

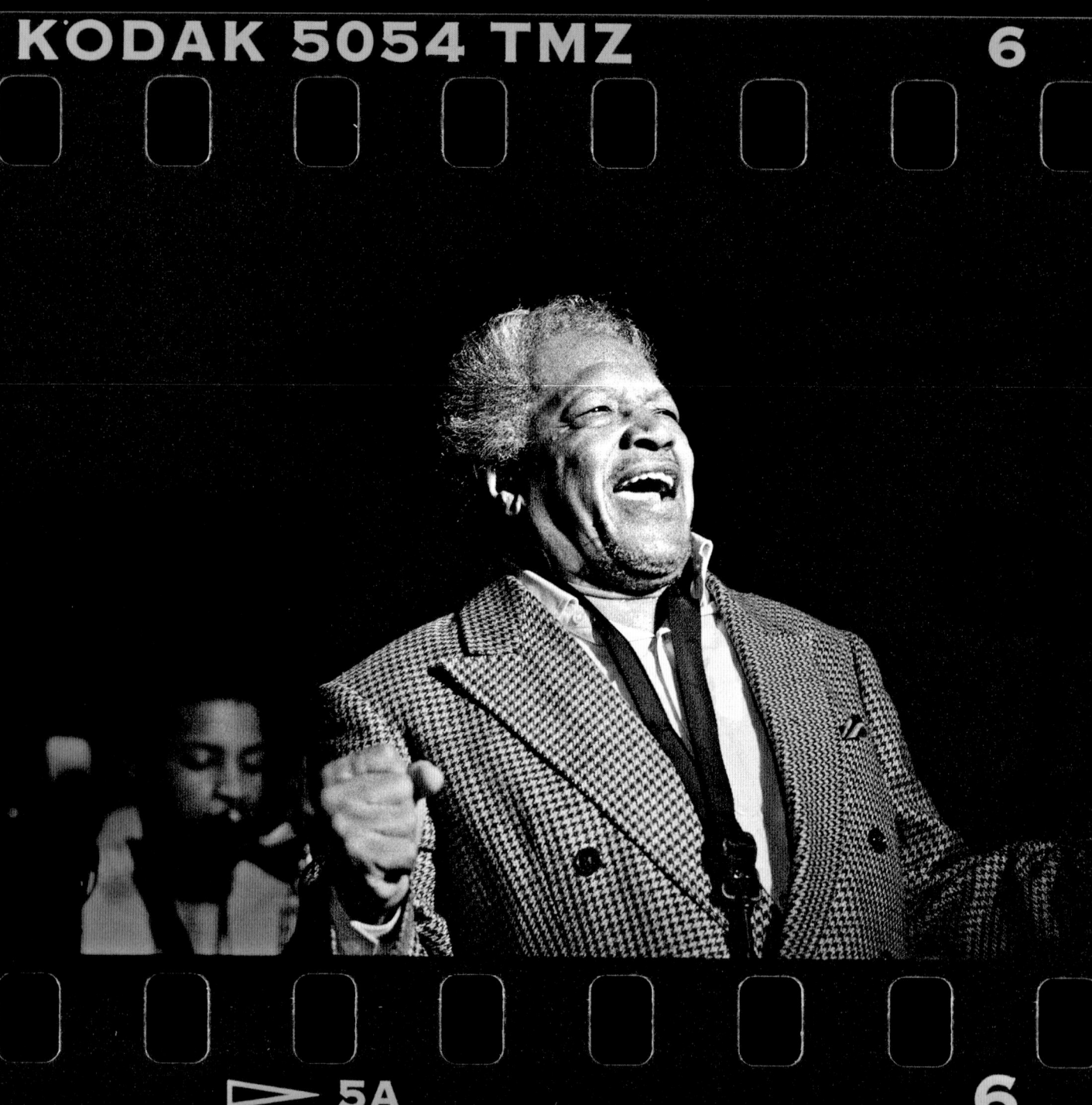

KODAK 5054 TMZ   6

▷━ 5A   6

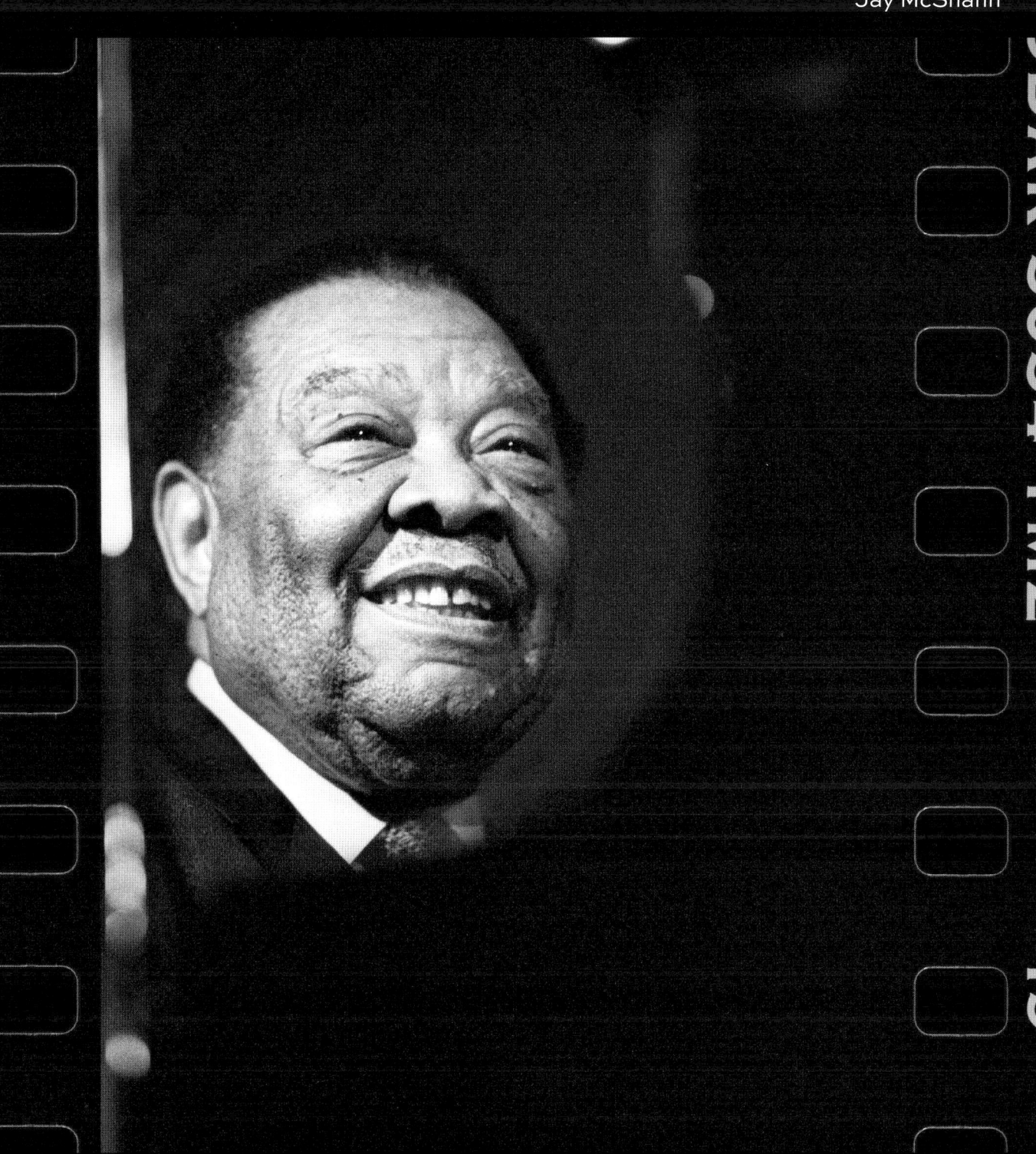

Jay McShann

KODAK 5054 TMZ

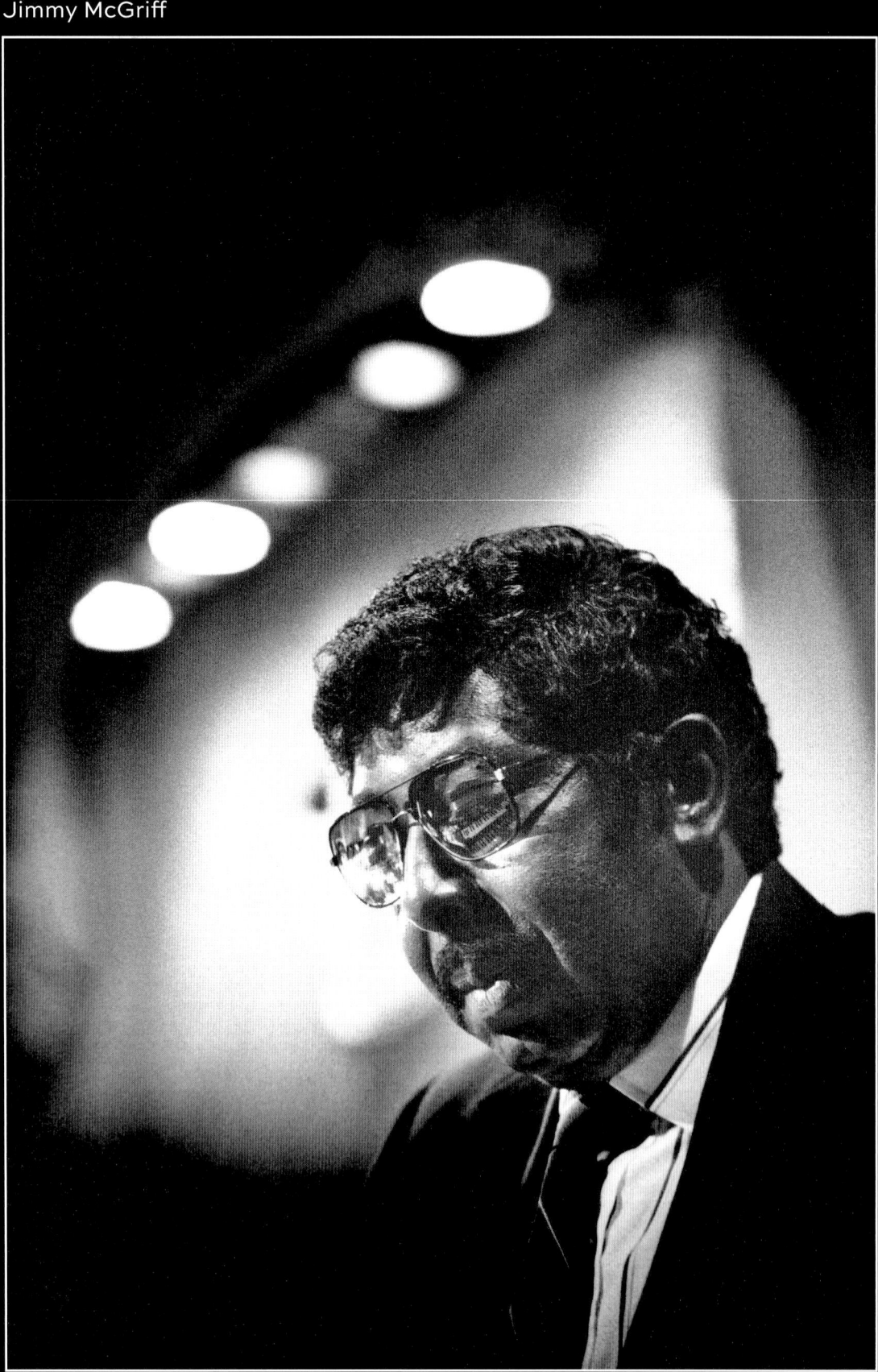

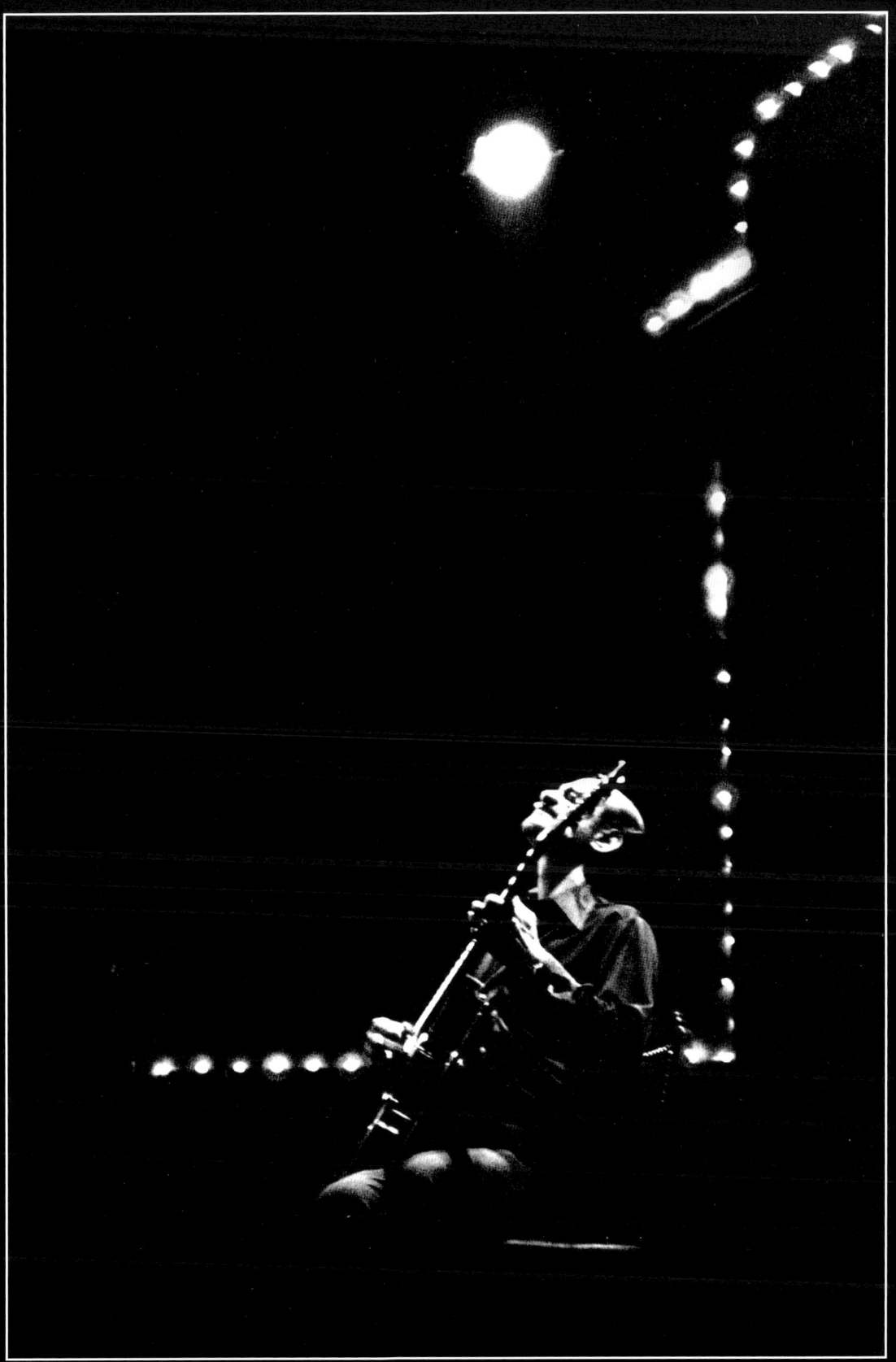

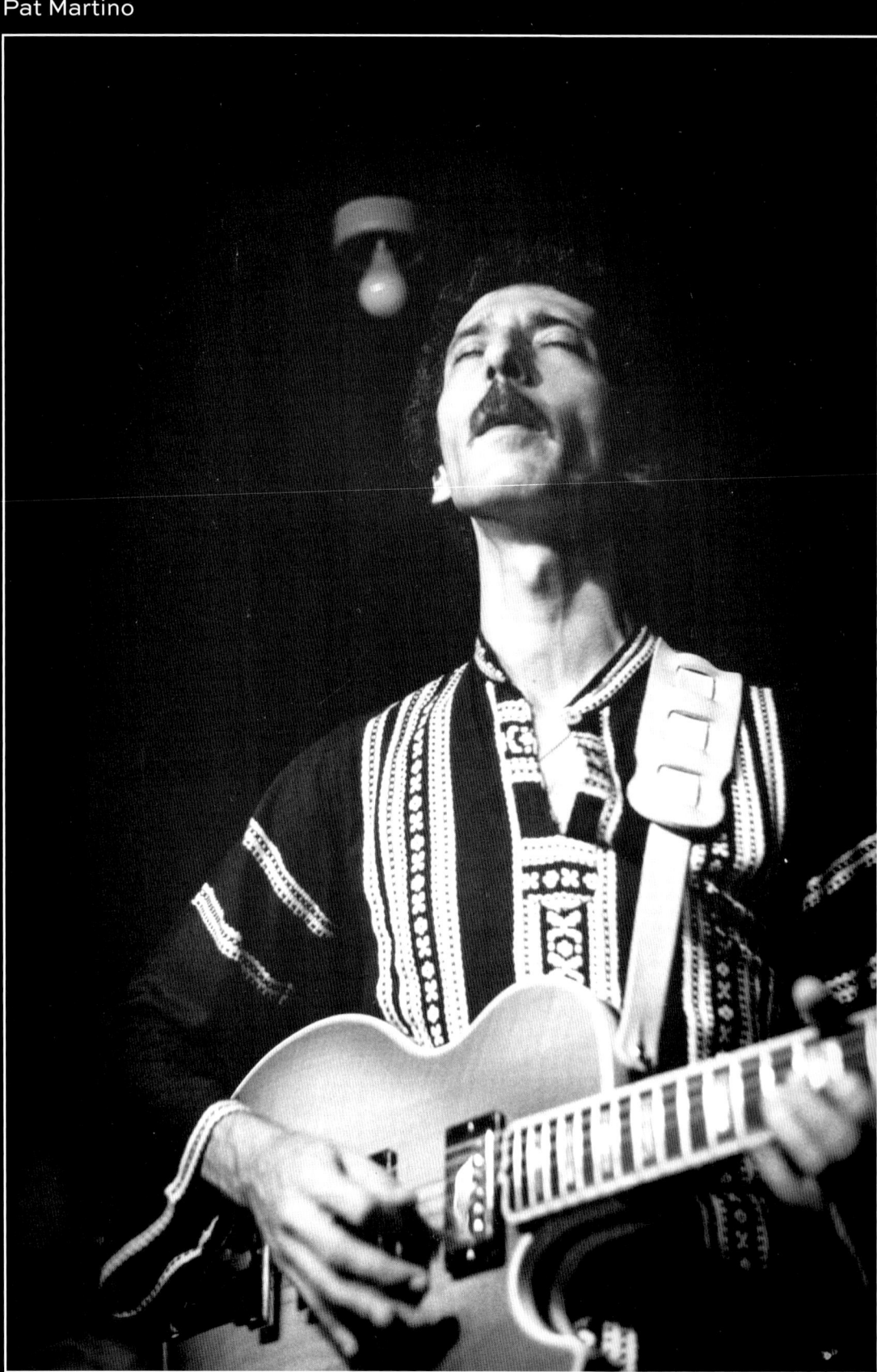

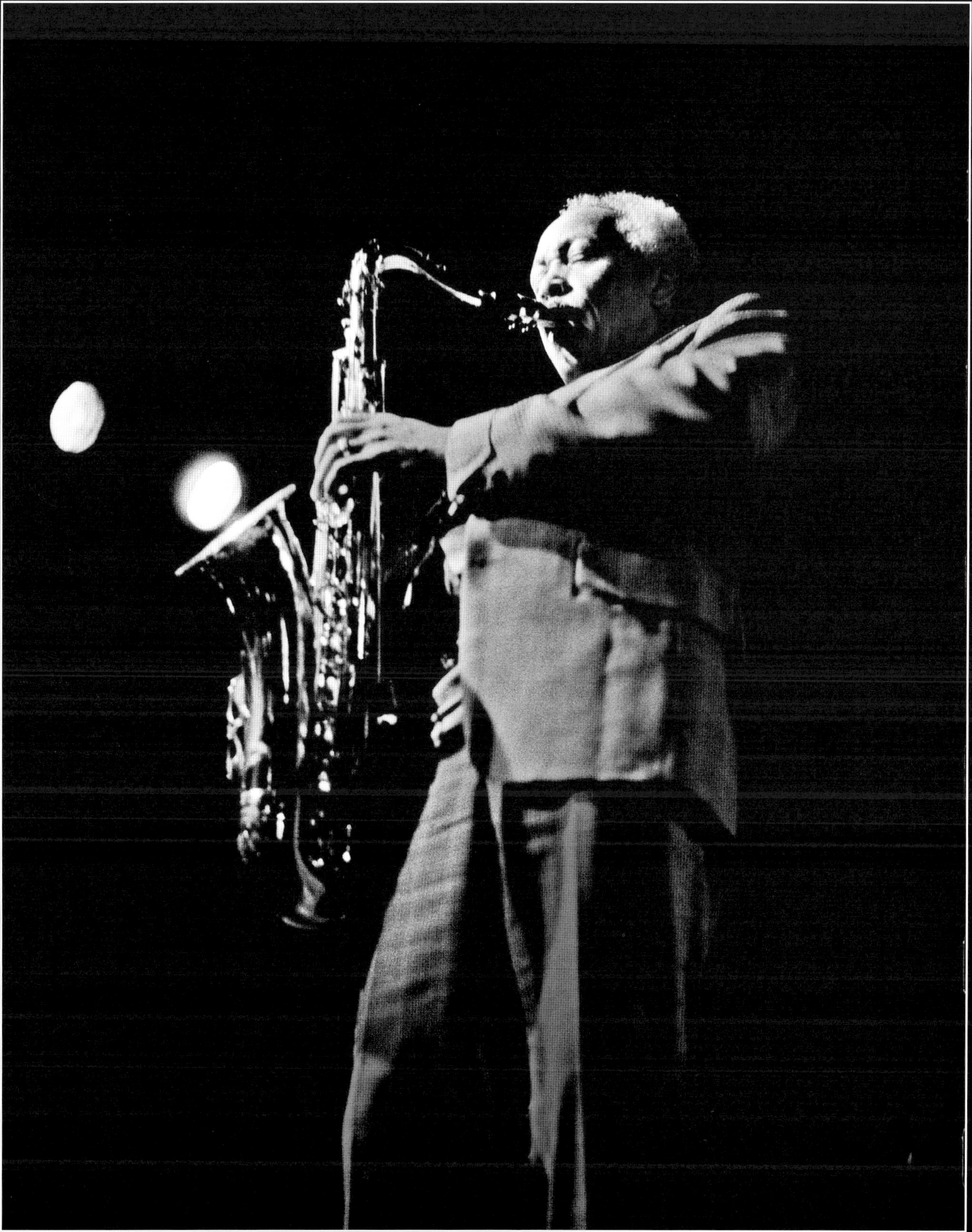

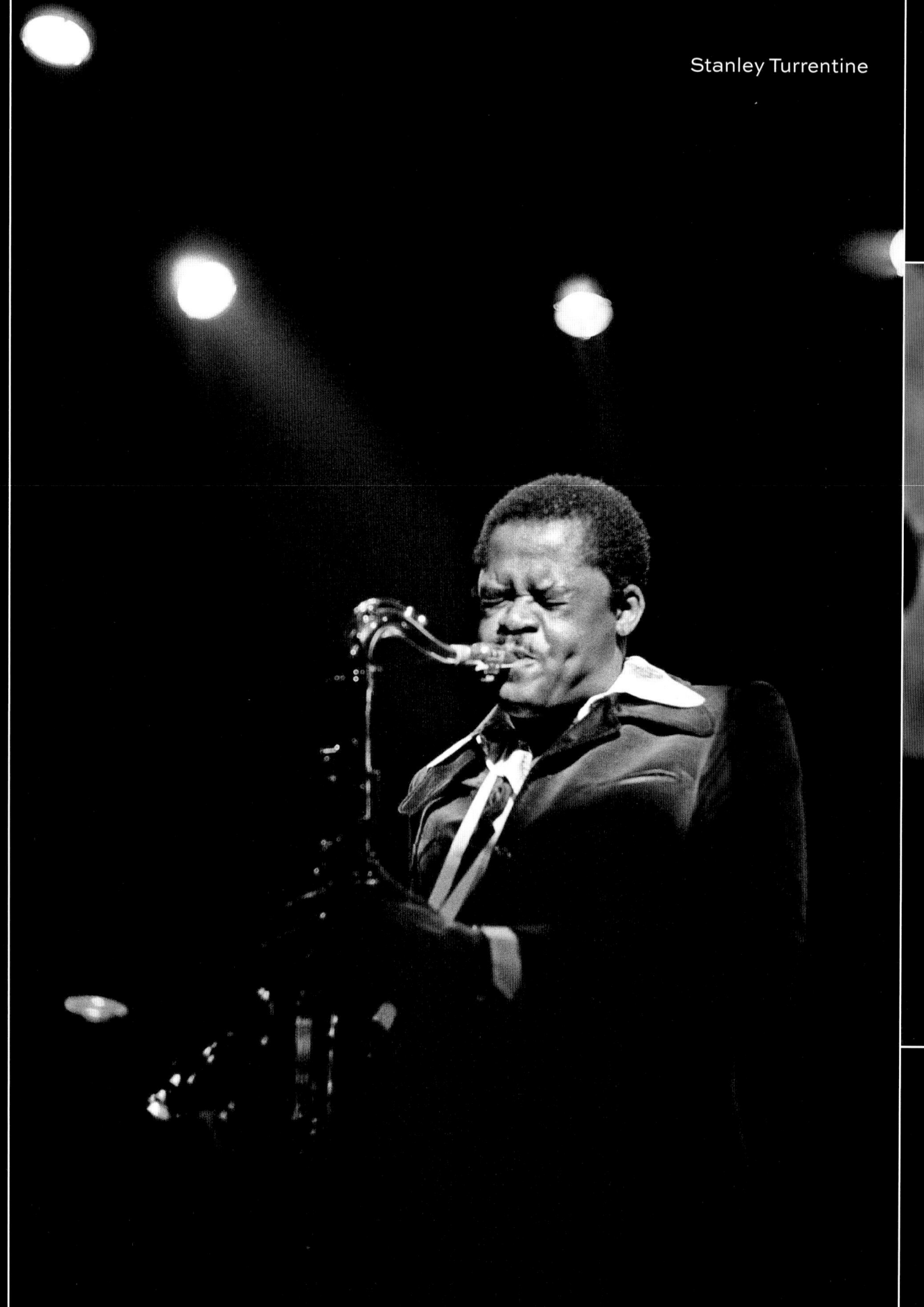

Stanley Turrentine

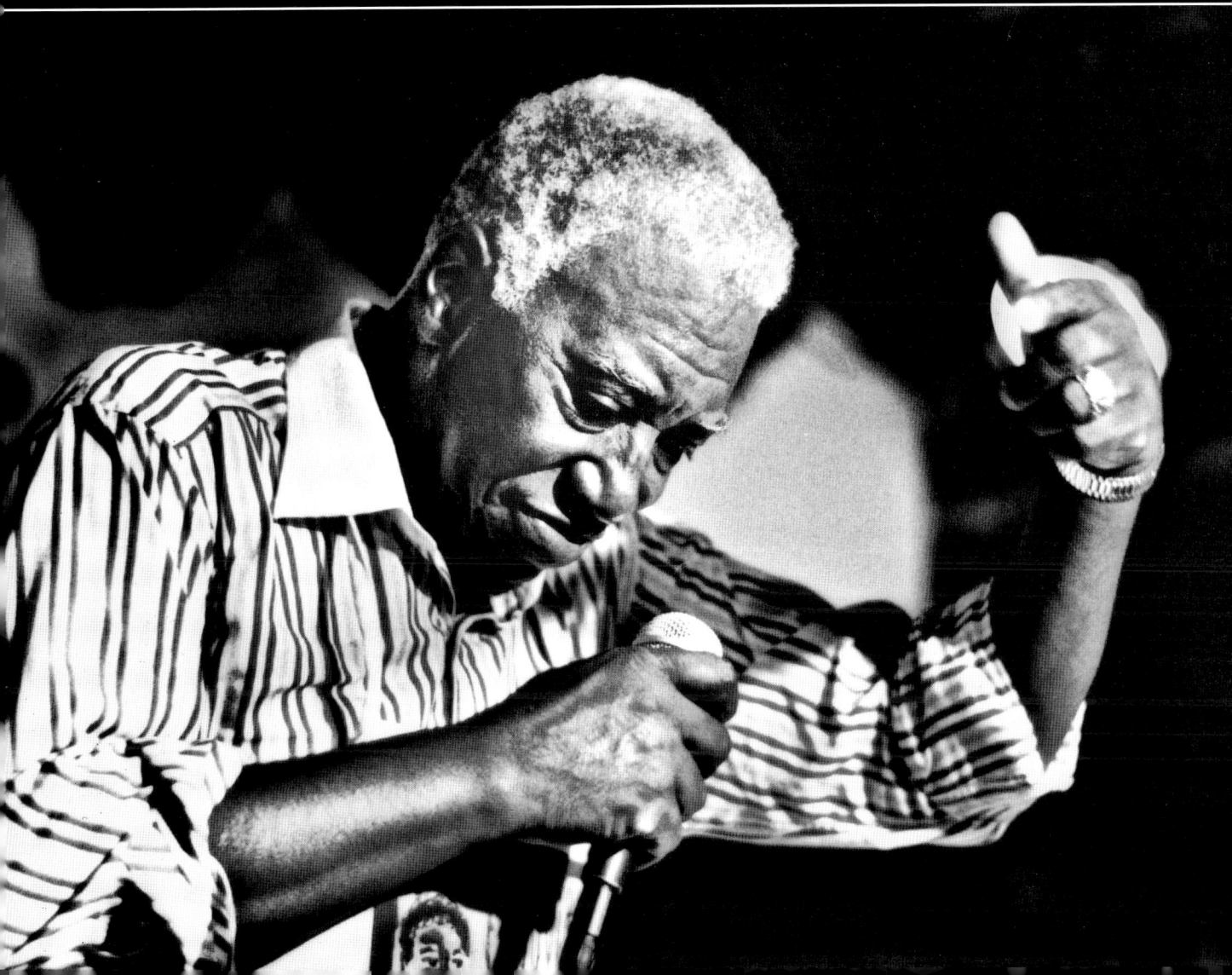

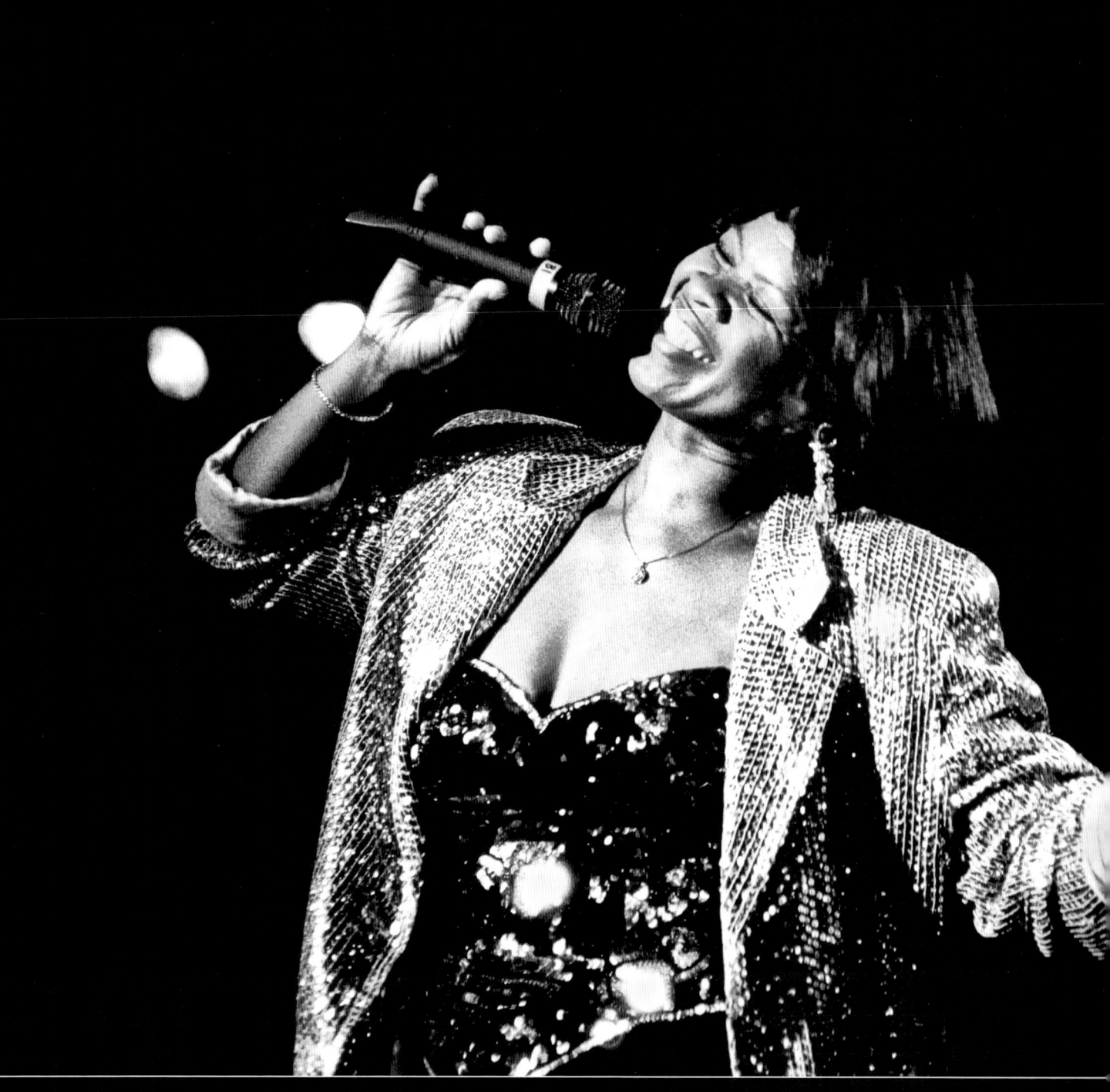

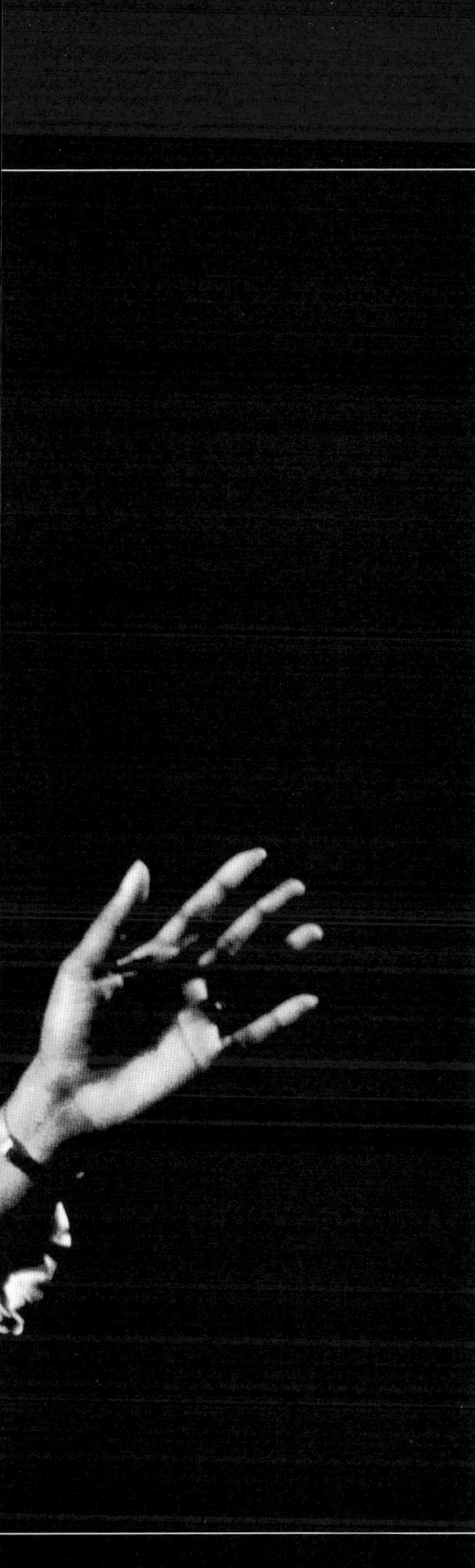

CHAPTER 4

The South Louisiana music scene, past and present, is often described as "an embarrassment of riches." This accurate assessment certainly applies to the abundant wealth of blues, rhythm and blues, and zydeco that all flourish in the state's southern parishes.

Blues is a bedrock common denominator in each of these great overlapping sounds, both in Louisiana and around the South. In New Orleans, the beloved guitarist Walter "Wolfman" Washington crafted a seamless blend of blues, 1960s soul, funk, and Crescent City R&B. And Snooks Eaglin's deft, dexterous guitar work—plus his eclectic, thousands-of-songs repertoire—included plenty of blues standards.

The blues figures prominently in New Orleans rhythm and blues too, but there's also an important difference. Many blues songs use traditional folk-rooted lyrics that are also heard in many other blues songs. These are known as "floating verses." But R&B songs combine a blues sensibility with professional songwriting skills and arrangements. The result is fresh new commercial material that's aimed at the major radio airplay, which leads to lucrative hit records.

Since the late 1940s onward, New Orleans has made incredibly rich contributions to R&B worldwide. The crooning pianist Fats Domino, working with the trumpeter/producer/songwriter/singer Dave Bartholomew, racked up eleven Top 10 hits, propelled by the master drummer Earl Palmer. Palmer later left New Orleans for Los Angeles, where he became a top session musician.

Irma Thomas

In the early 1950s, the prolific New Orleans songwriter and distinctive guitarist/singer Earl King first came on the scene. Some years later, so did the exquisite singers Irma Thomas and Aaron Neville and pianist Art Neville. And so did the gifted pianist, producer/arranger, singer, and songwriter Allen Toussaint, who significantly enhanced the careers of many local and national artists. Toussaint produced some epic albums by the singer, pianist, and songwriter Mac Rebennack, better known as Dr. John, whose deep knowledge of New Orleans R&B and voodoo forged a unique sound and persona. In his later years, Toussaint stepped out as a performer and recording artist in his own right.

Heading west from New Orleans to Lafayette, Lake Charles, Eunice, Opelousas, and environs, the accordion-and-rub-board sounds of zydeco draw on blues, R&B, Afro-Caribbean rhythms, and Cajun music to forge one of the world's great danceable genres. As the revered elder statesman, accordionist, and singer Clifton Chenier put it simply and directly: "If you can't dance to zydeco, you can't dance—period!"

Chenier's colleague Boozoo Chavis recorded zydeco's first hit record in 1954 but then left the music business in disgust and worked for decades training racehorses. Chavis roared back in the 1980s, though, as evidenced by the mile-long lines of cars parked at the rural dance halls where he packed in huge crowds.

Rockin' Dopsie, seven years Clifton Chenier's junior, maintained the zydeco tradition of accordionists who sported regal crowns. Two of his sons, Dopsie Jr. and Dwayne, carry their dad's torch by leading their own popular zydeco bands. So does Chenier's son, CJ.

After years of playing mainstream R&B and soul music, Stanley "Buckwheat Zydeco" Dural got schooled in zydeco as a keyboardist in Clifton Chenier's aptly named Red Hot Louisiana Band. Heading out on his own, Dural took up the accordion and took zydeco to unprecedented heights of exposure. He opened stadium concerts for major rock stars such as U2 and Eric Clapton. But whenever he was back home, Buckwheat still played dances for his loyal fans in the local community. Terrance Simien followed Buckwheat's footsteps into mainstream crossover circles, bringing zydeco to even-more-far-flung audiences and adventurous cross-cultural collaborations.

But zydeco prowess is not limited to accordionists. The lengthy résumé of versatile and highly respected guitarist Paul "Little Buck" Senegal (sometimes spelled Sinegal) included tenures with Chenier, Buckwheat Zydeco, the Lil' Band o' Gold, and Carol Fran. And the singing pianist Katie Webster played in Otis Redding's band in the 1960s before developing her own diverse, commanding blend of soul, blues, R&B, swamp pop, and zydeco. Such abundant talent made Webster one of South Louisiana's most in-demand and prolific studio musicians, and a popular performer on the European festival circuit.

Joe Rosen has walked many streets and beaten many bushes to document South Louisiana's musical riches. We are the grateful beneficiaries of his hard work and discerning dedication.

BEN SANDMEL

Author of *Ernie K-Doc: The R&B Emperor of New Orleans and Zydeco*, producer for the Music Heritage Stage, the oral-history and interview venue at the New Orleans Jazz & Heritage Festival, and holds an MA in musicology from Tulane University

Aaron Neville

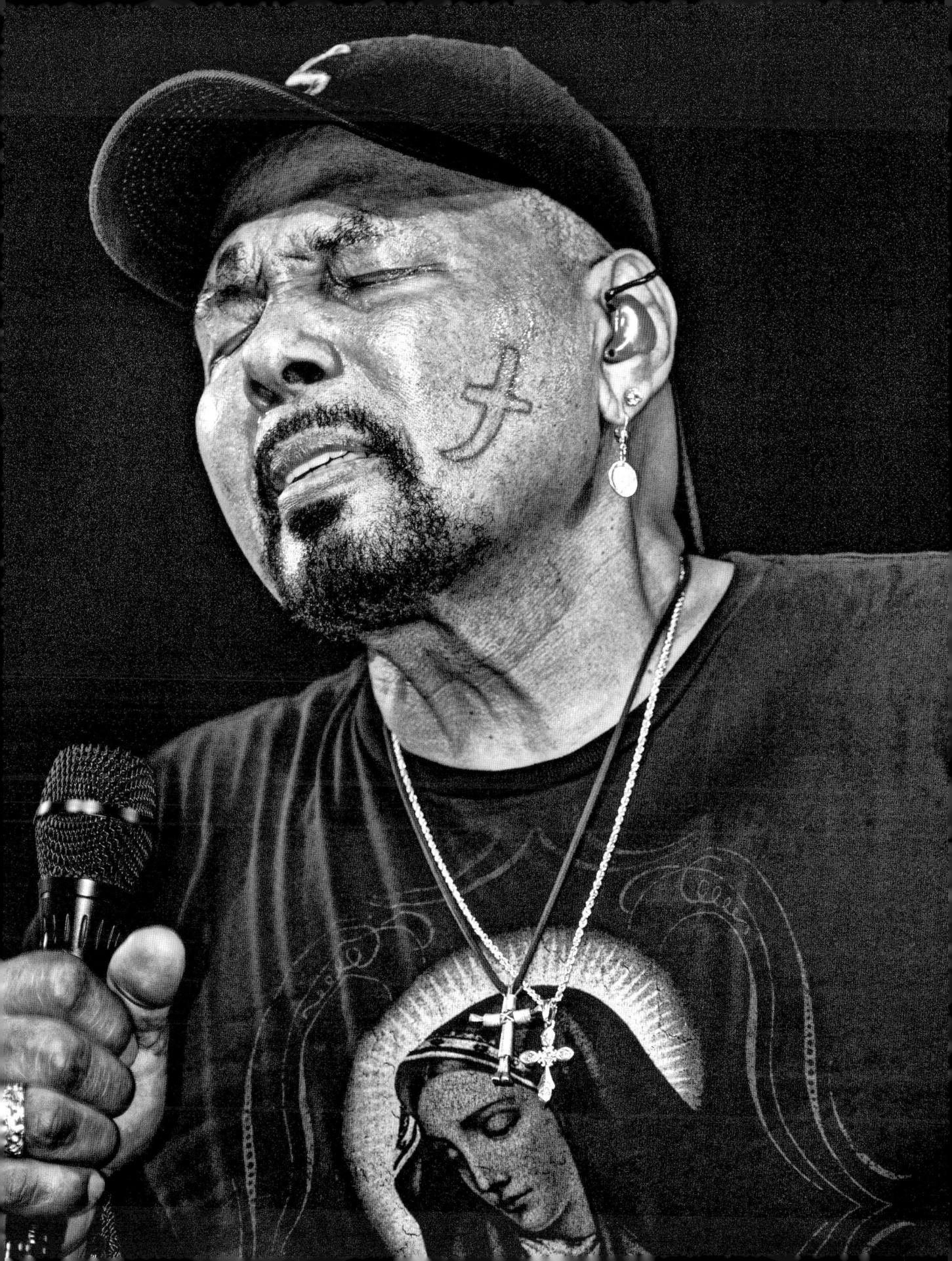

Henry Butler

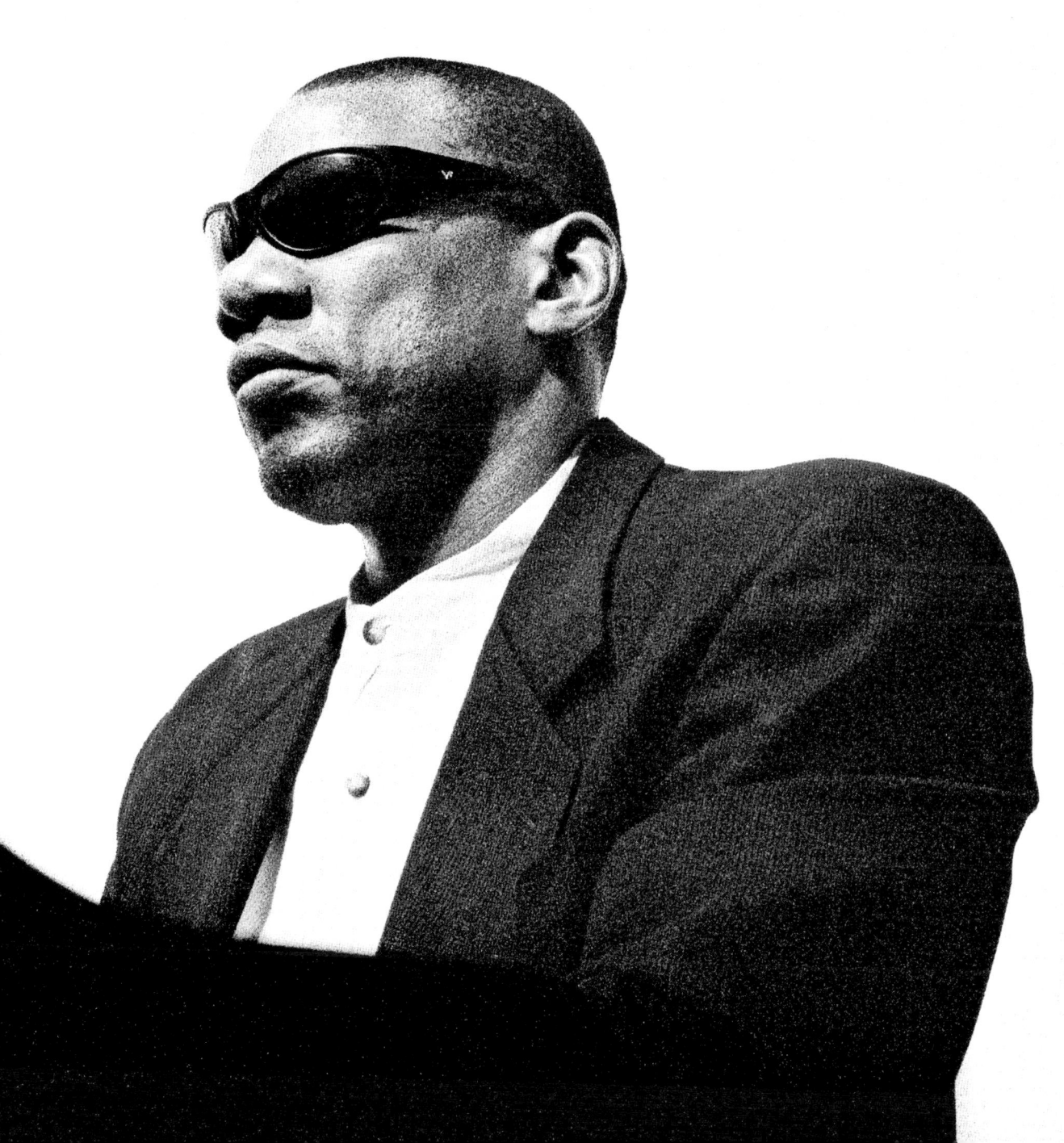

Mac "Dr. John" Rebennack

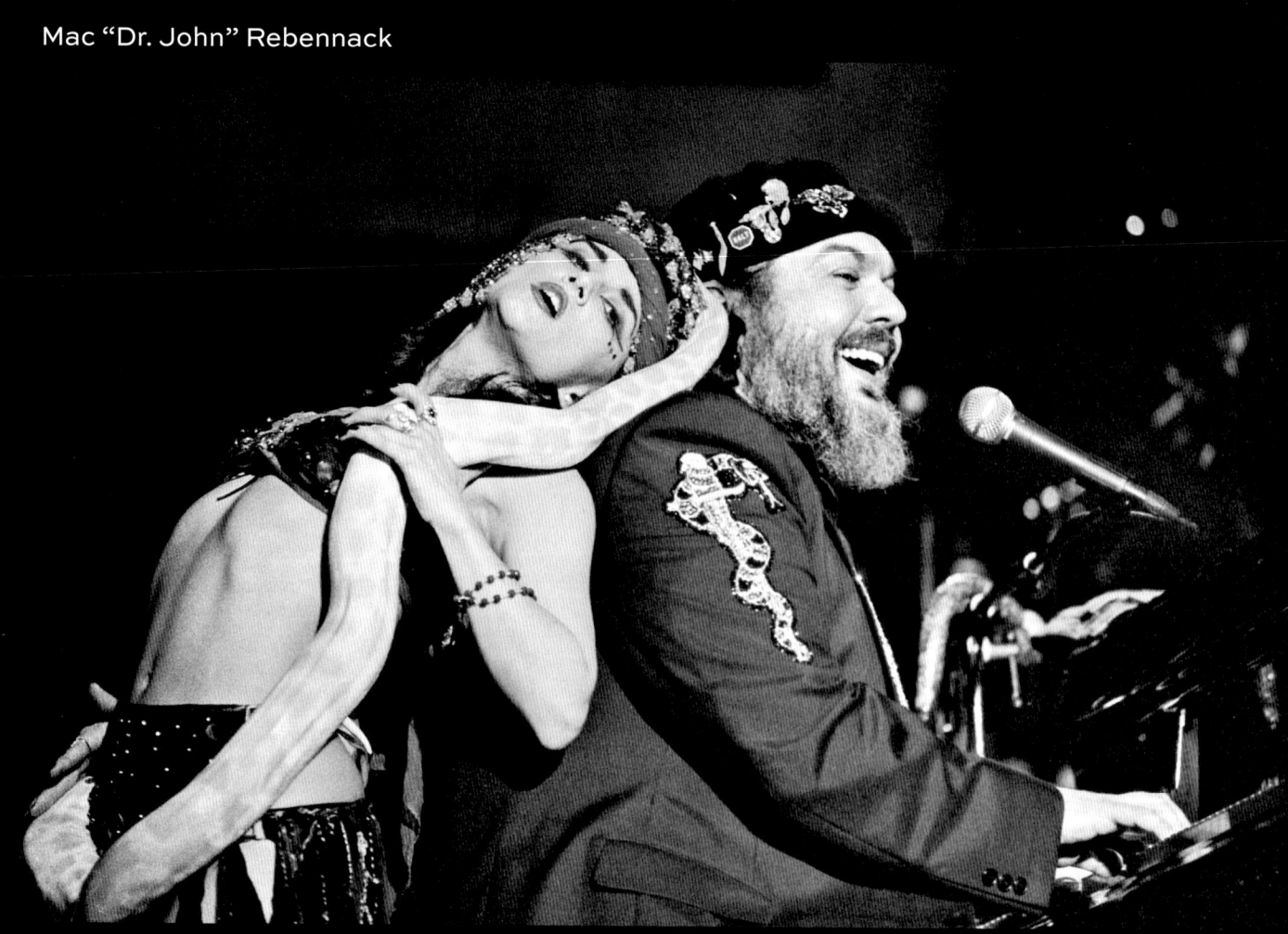

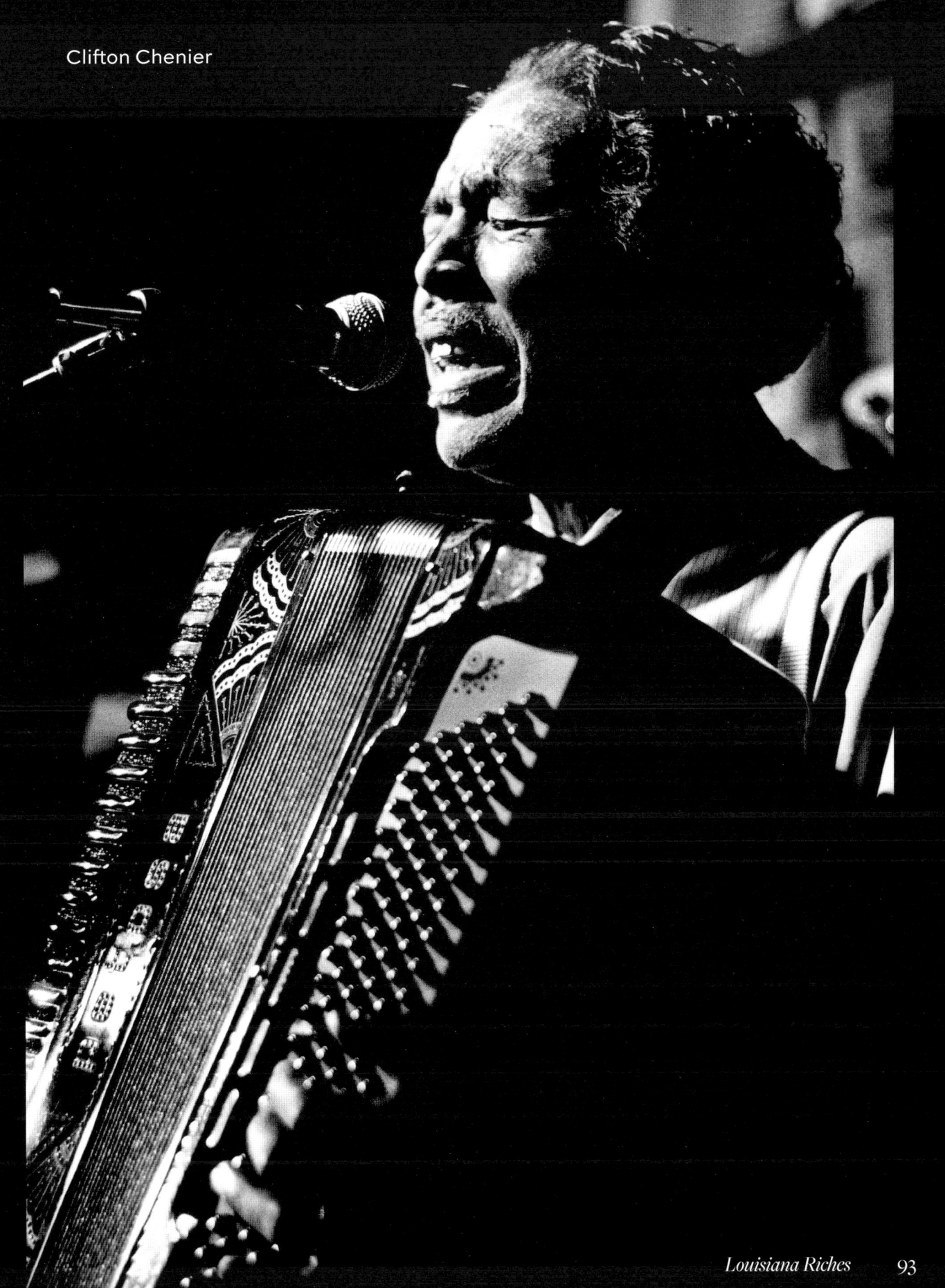

Clifton Chenier

Kermit Ruffins

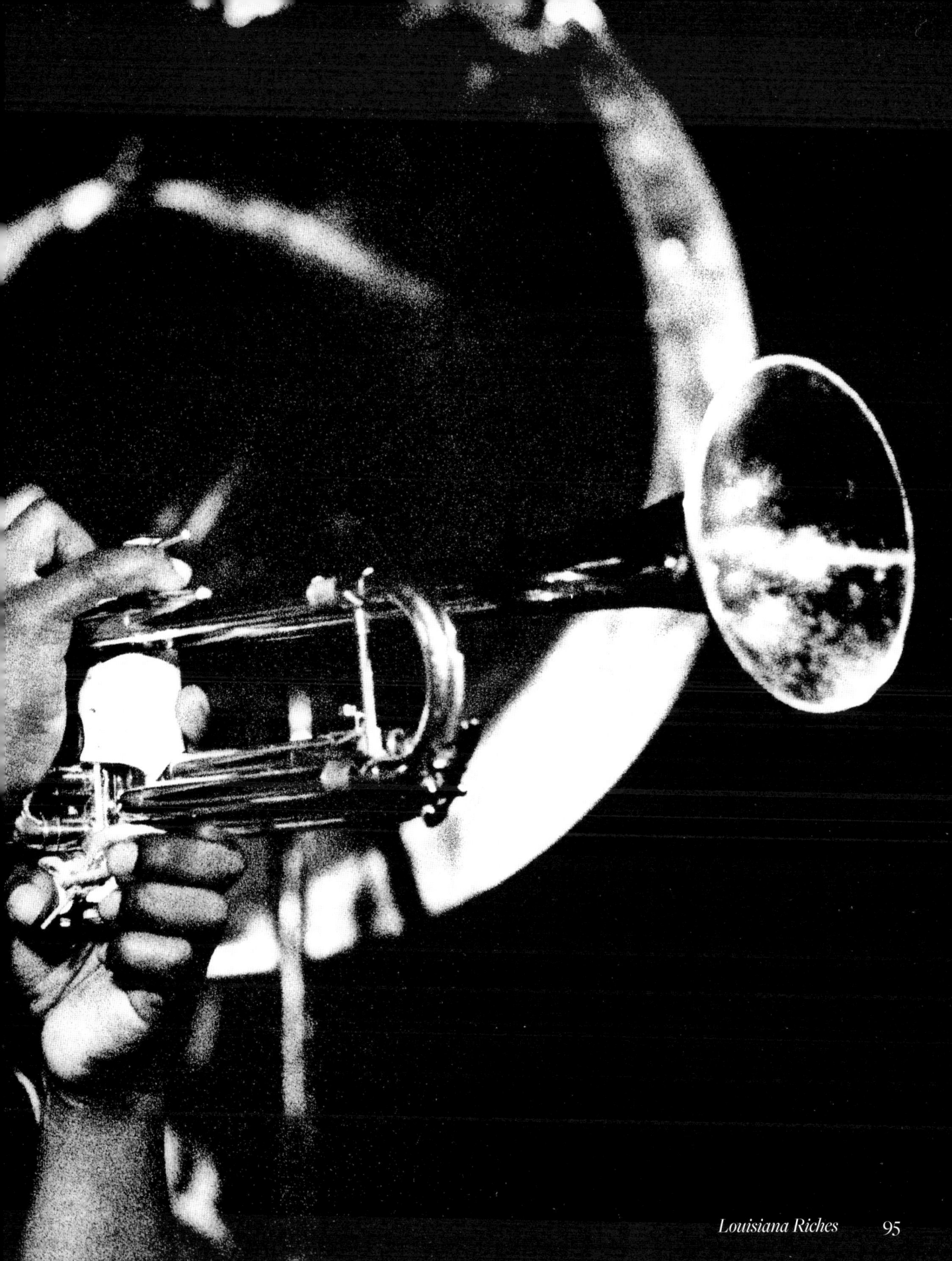

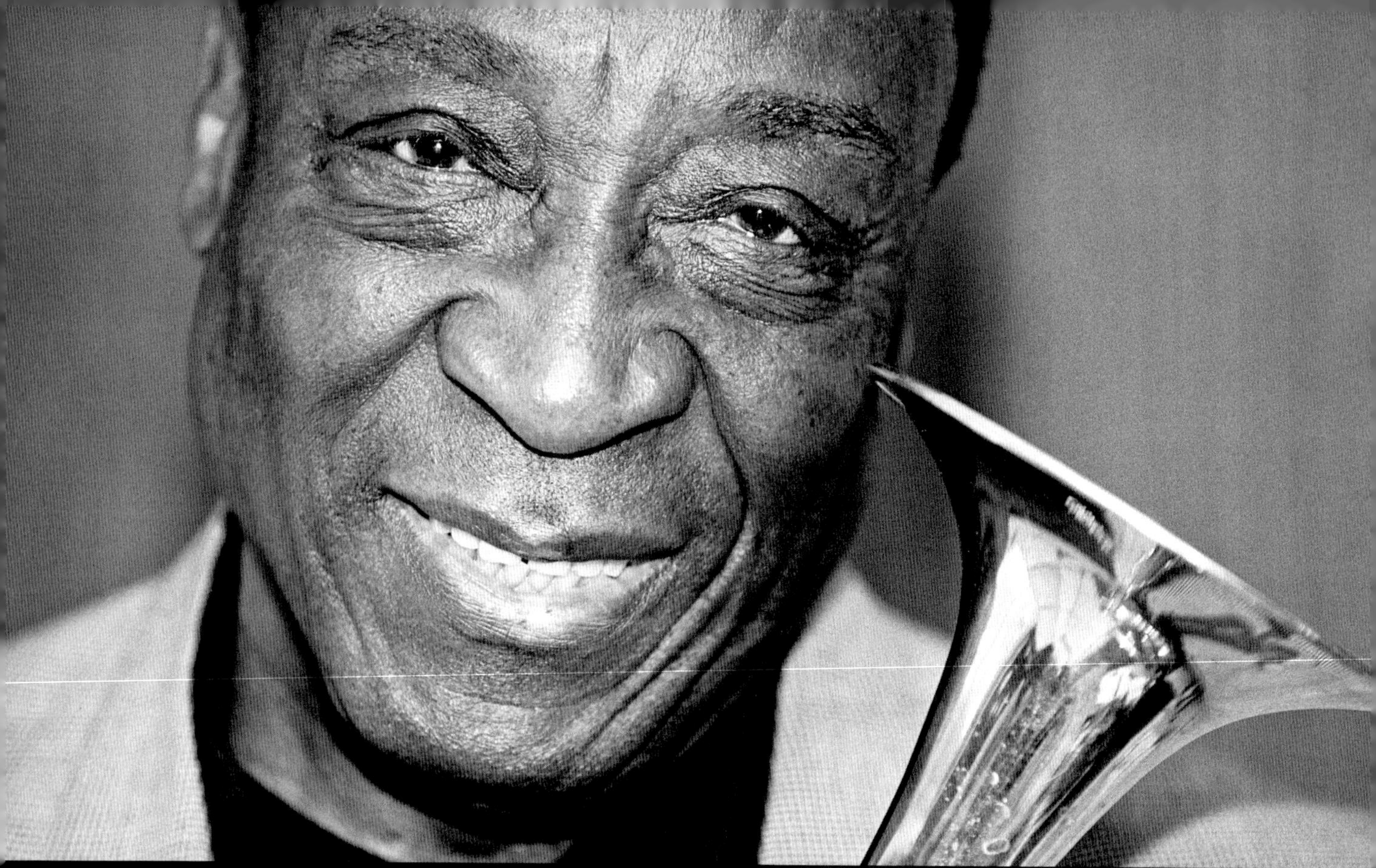

Dave Bartholomew

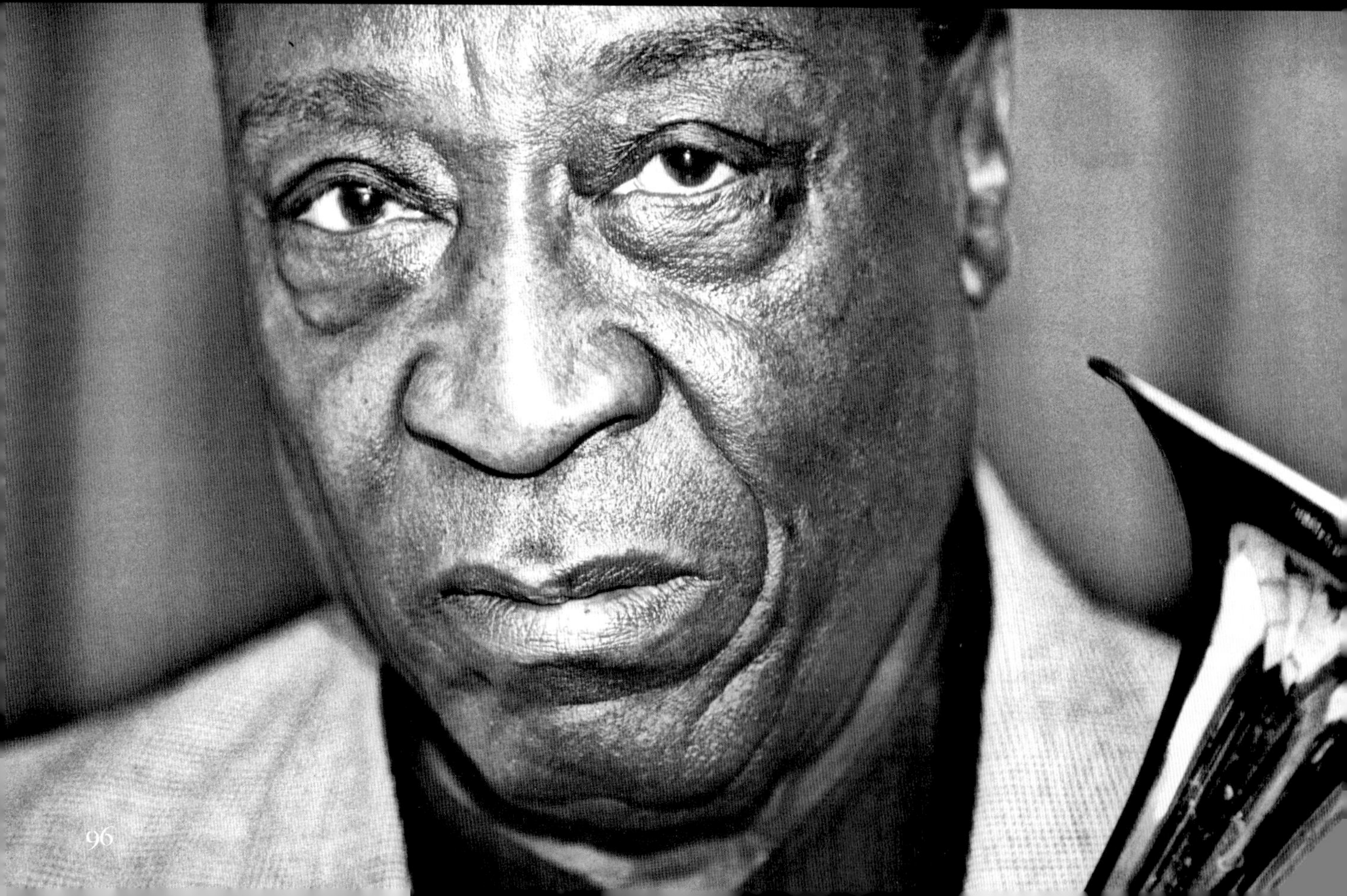

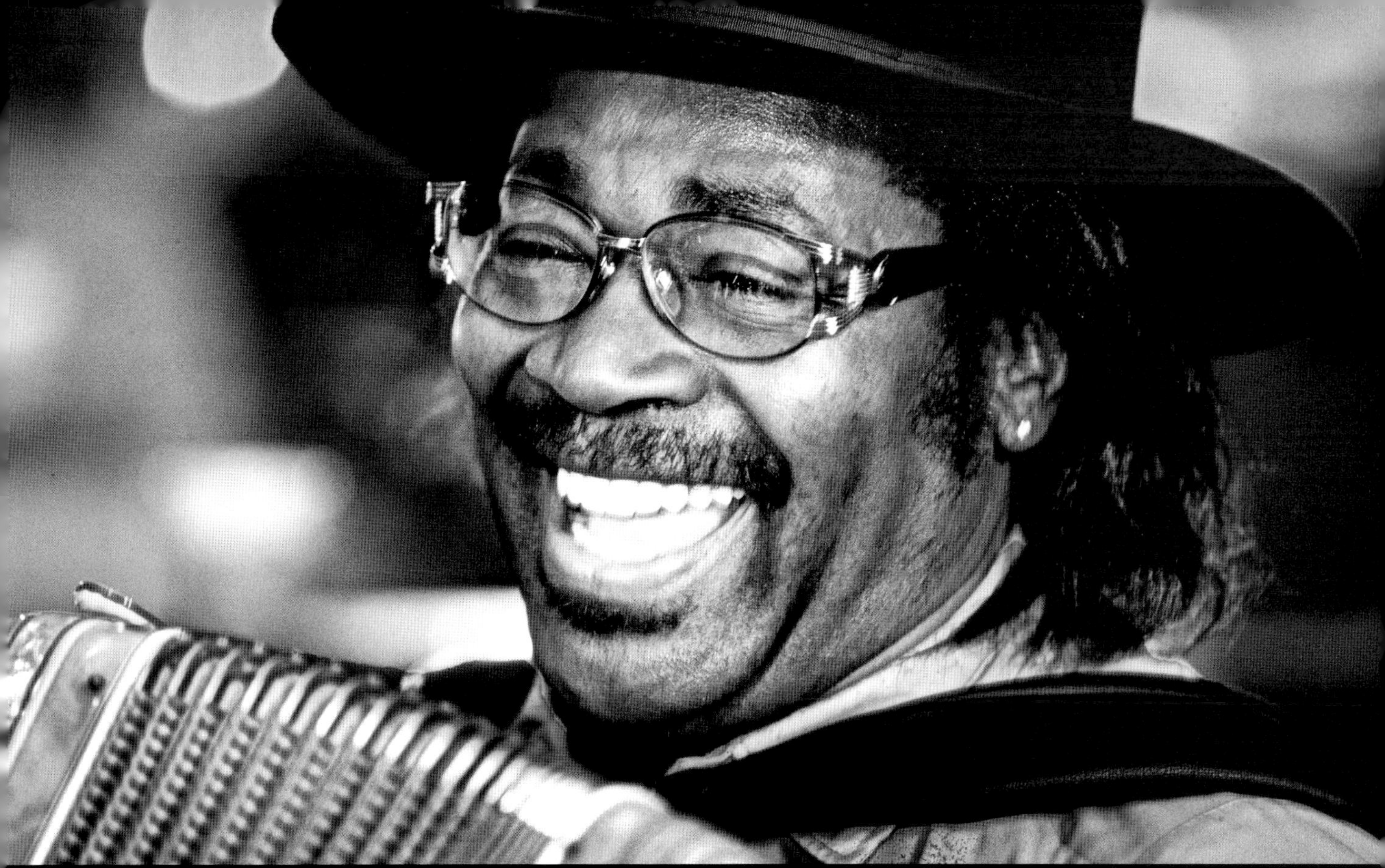

Buckwheat Zydeco & Lee Zeno

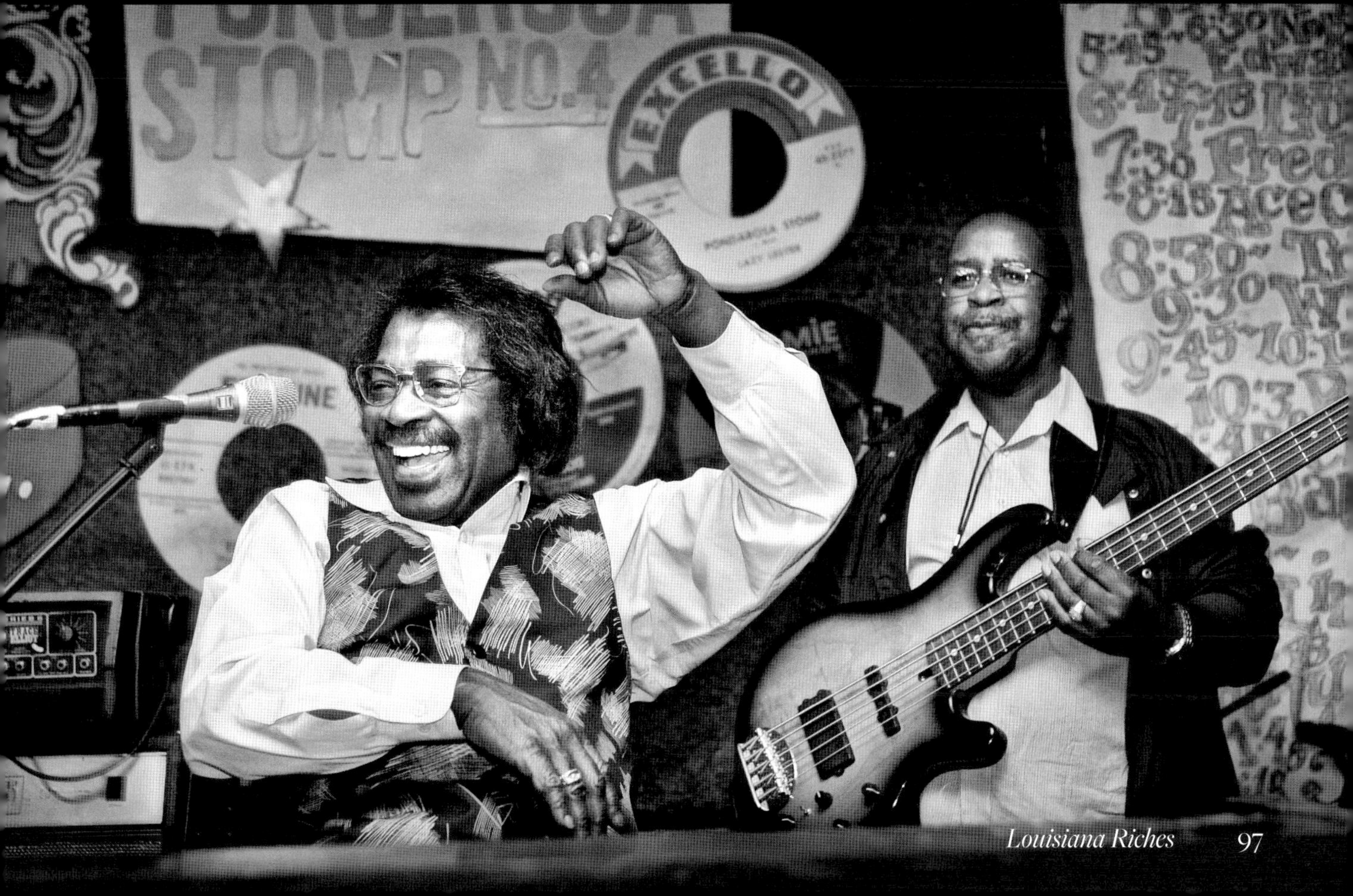

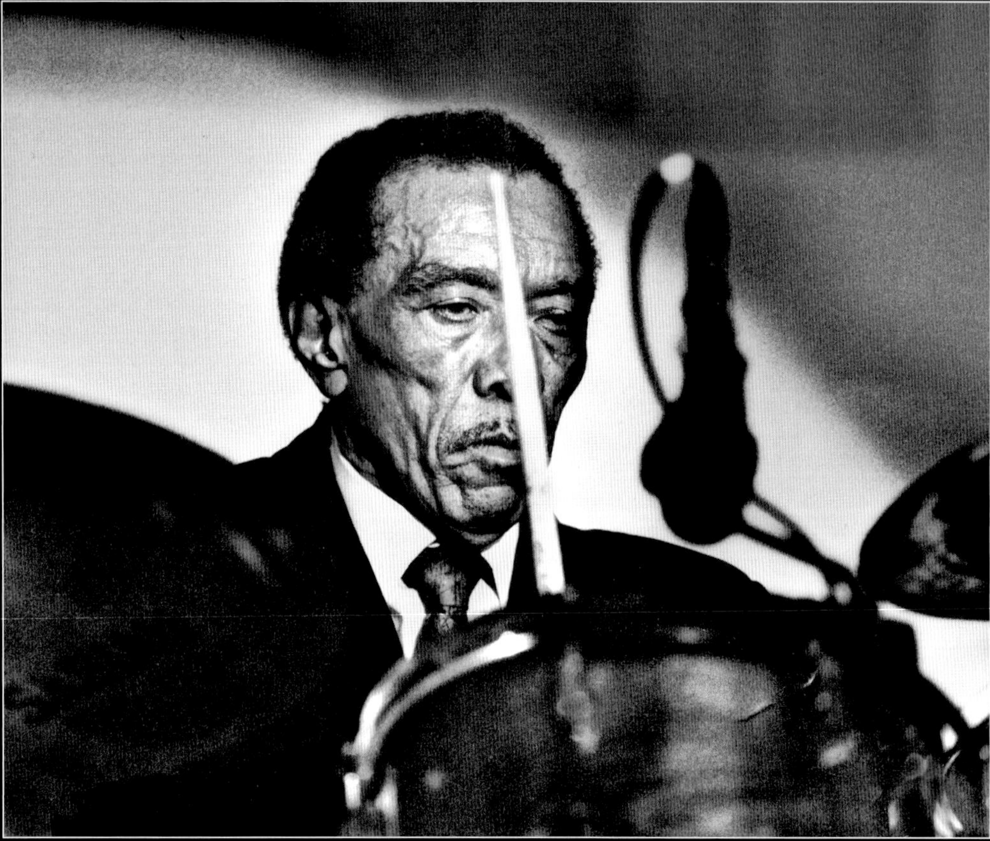

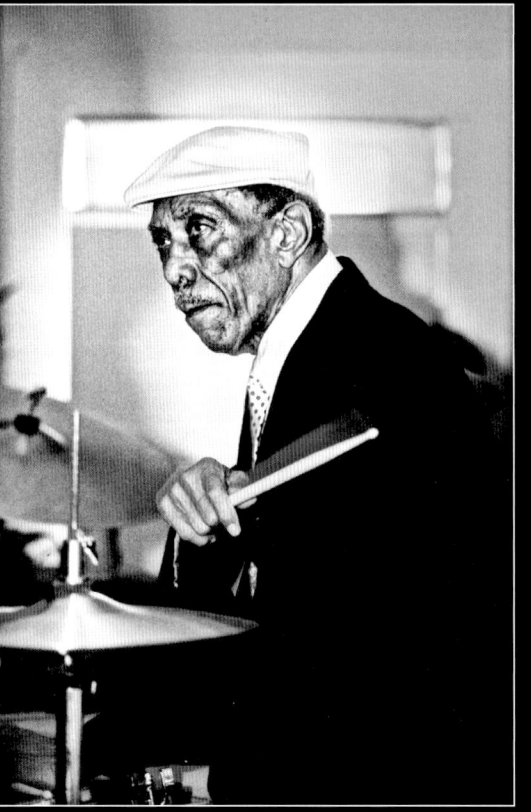

Earl Palmer

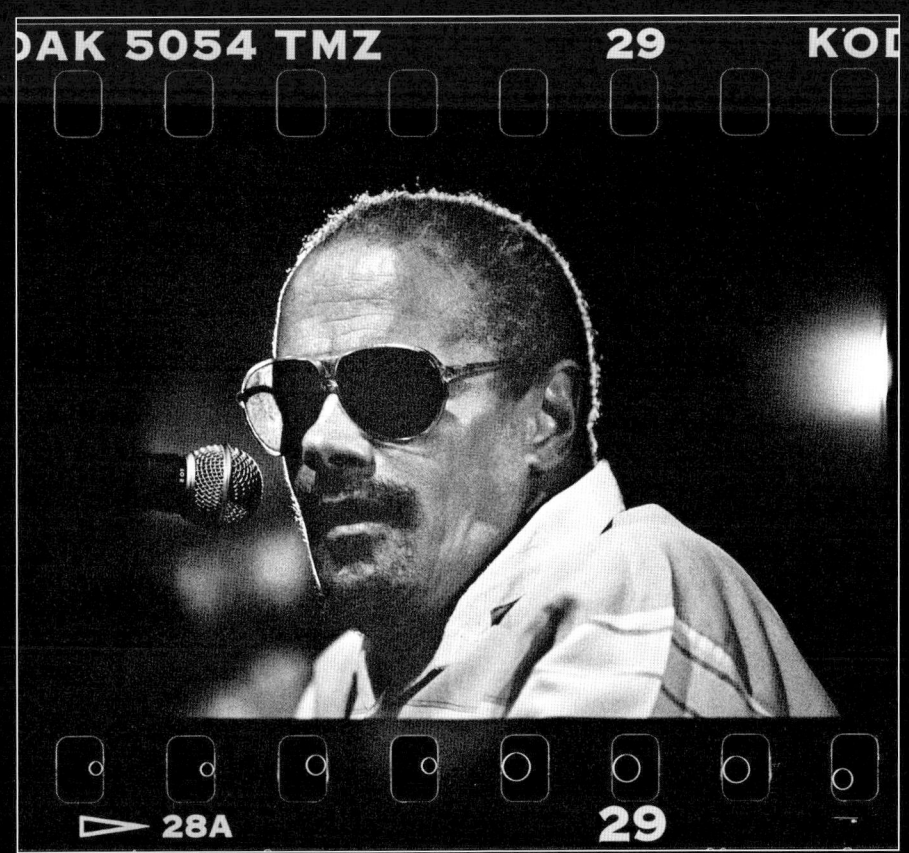

Fird "Snooks" Eaglin

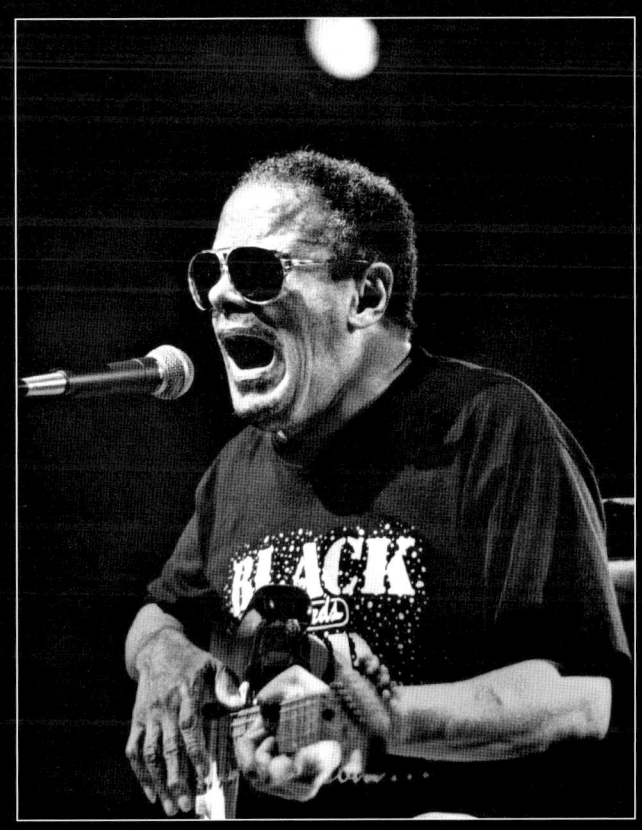

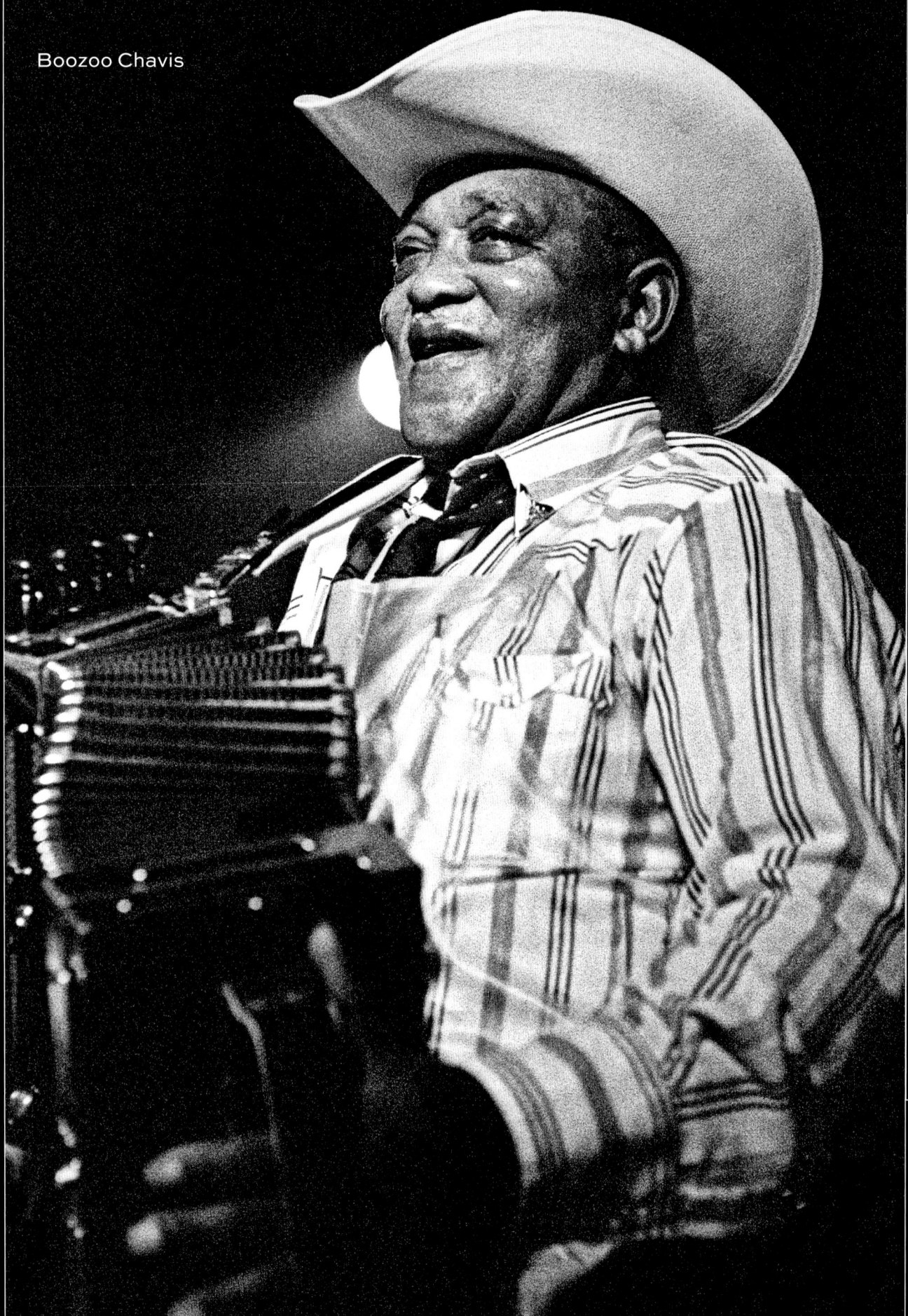
Boozoo Chavis

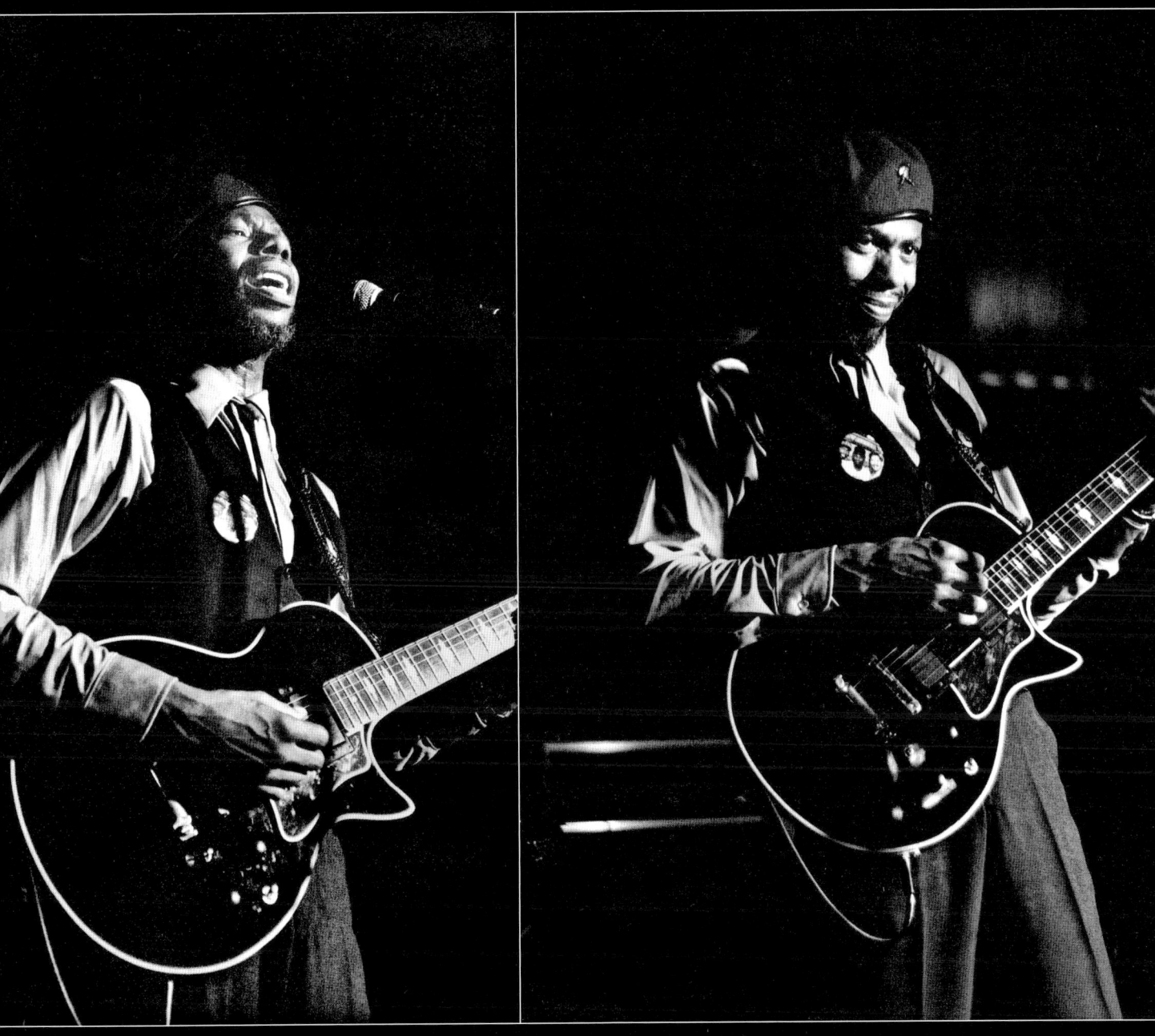

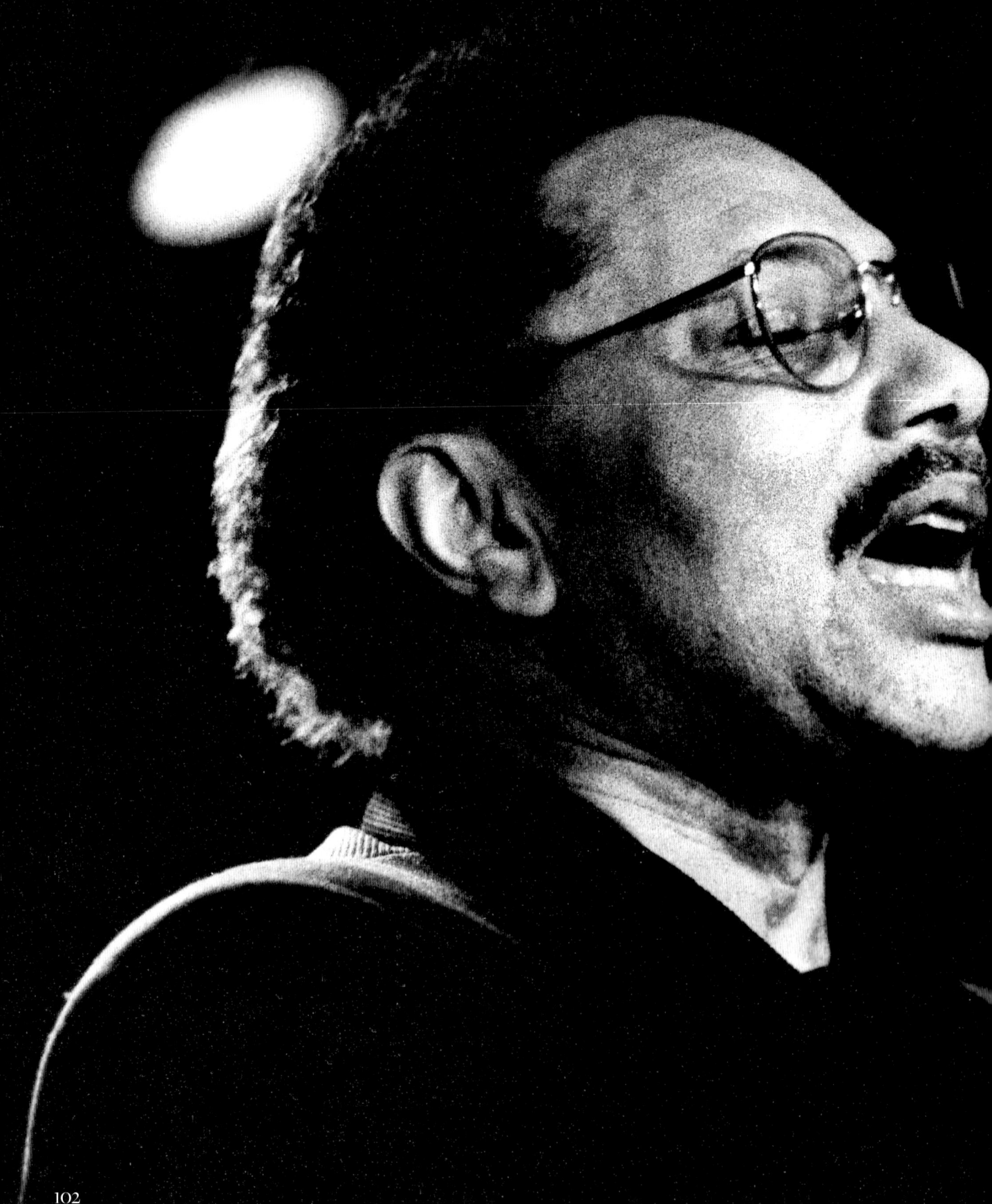

Carol Fran

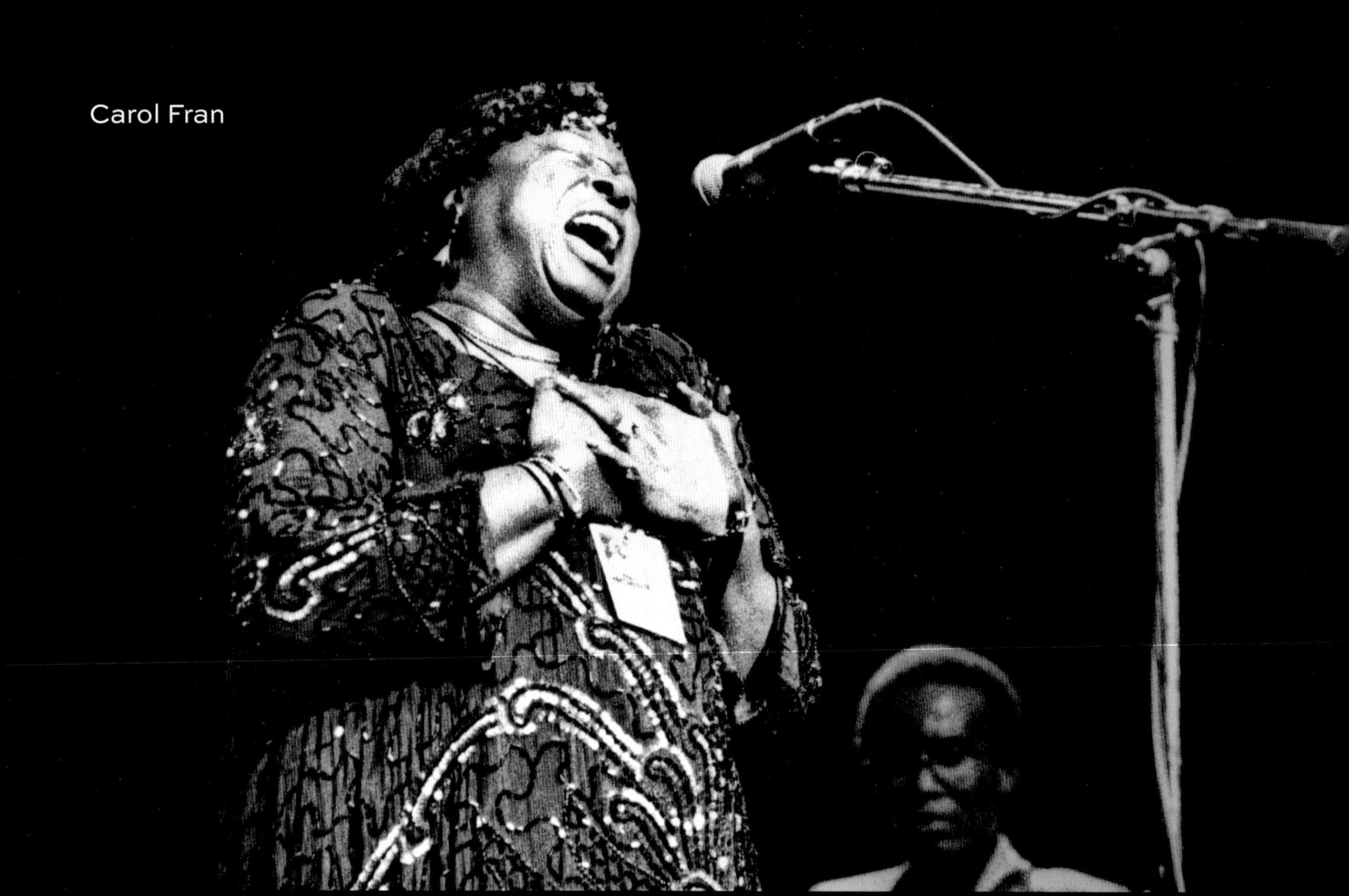

Ernie K-Doe

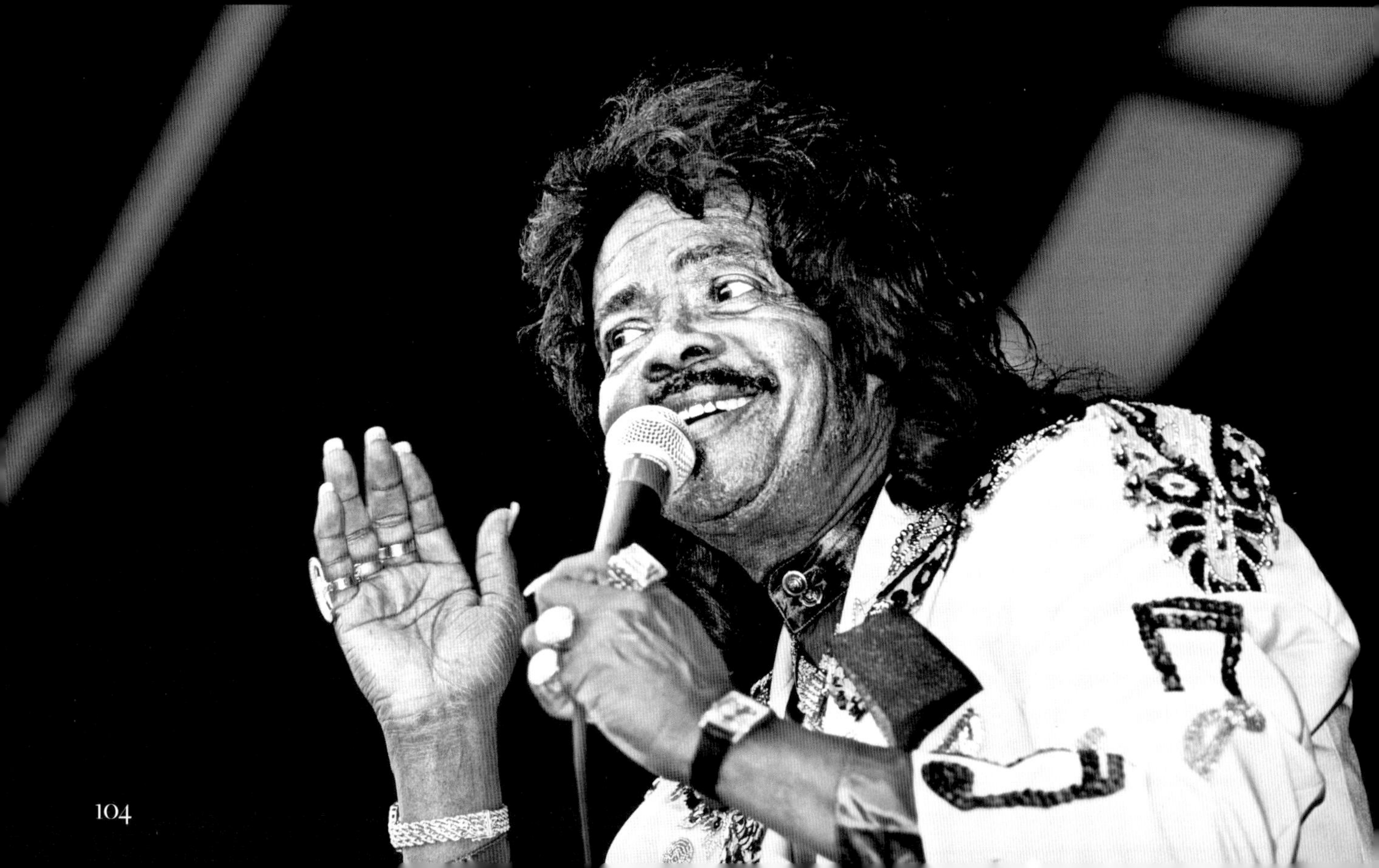

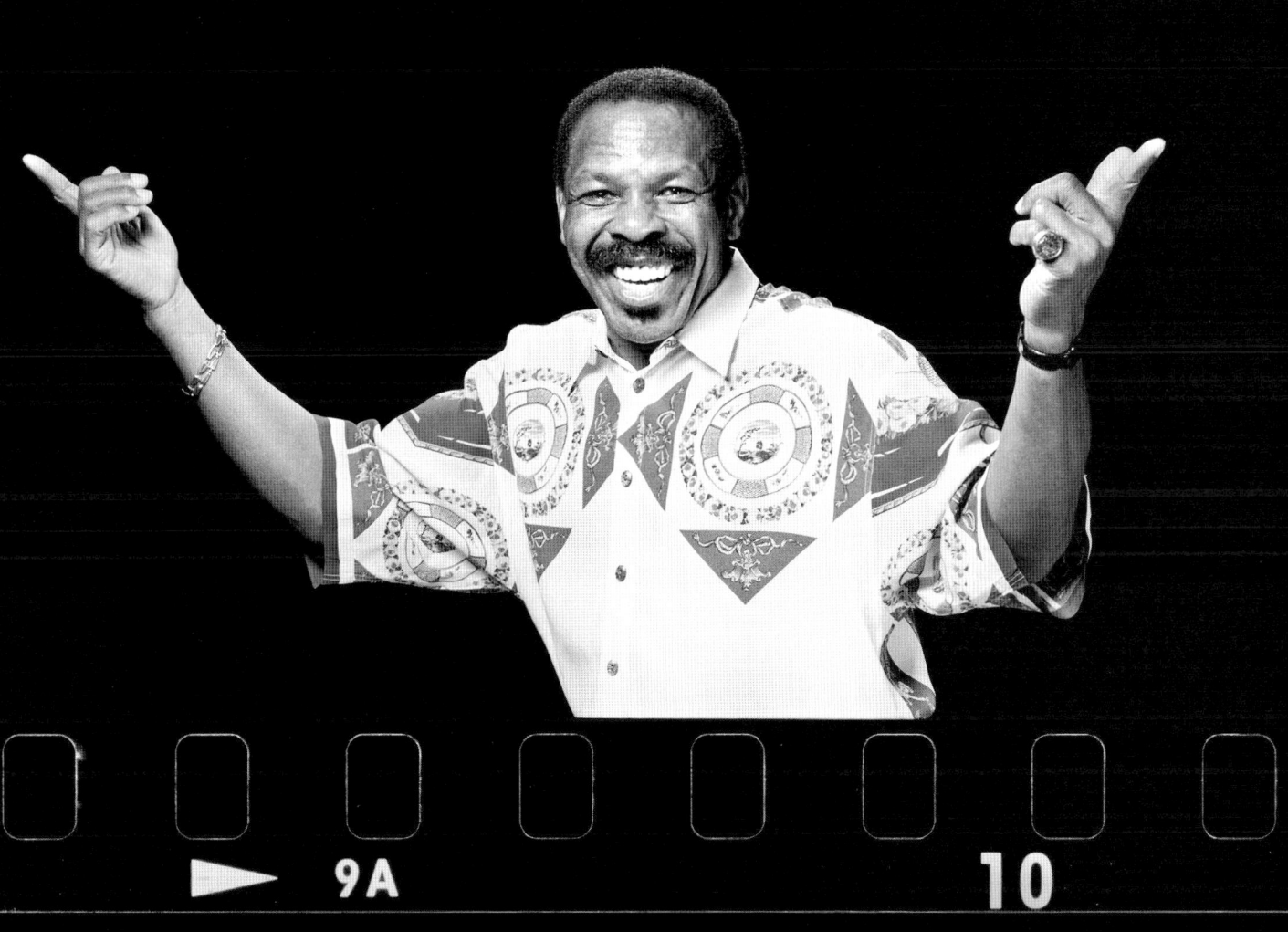

ILFORD FP4 PLUS

▶ 9A   10

Paul "Lil Buck" Sinegal

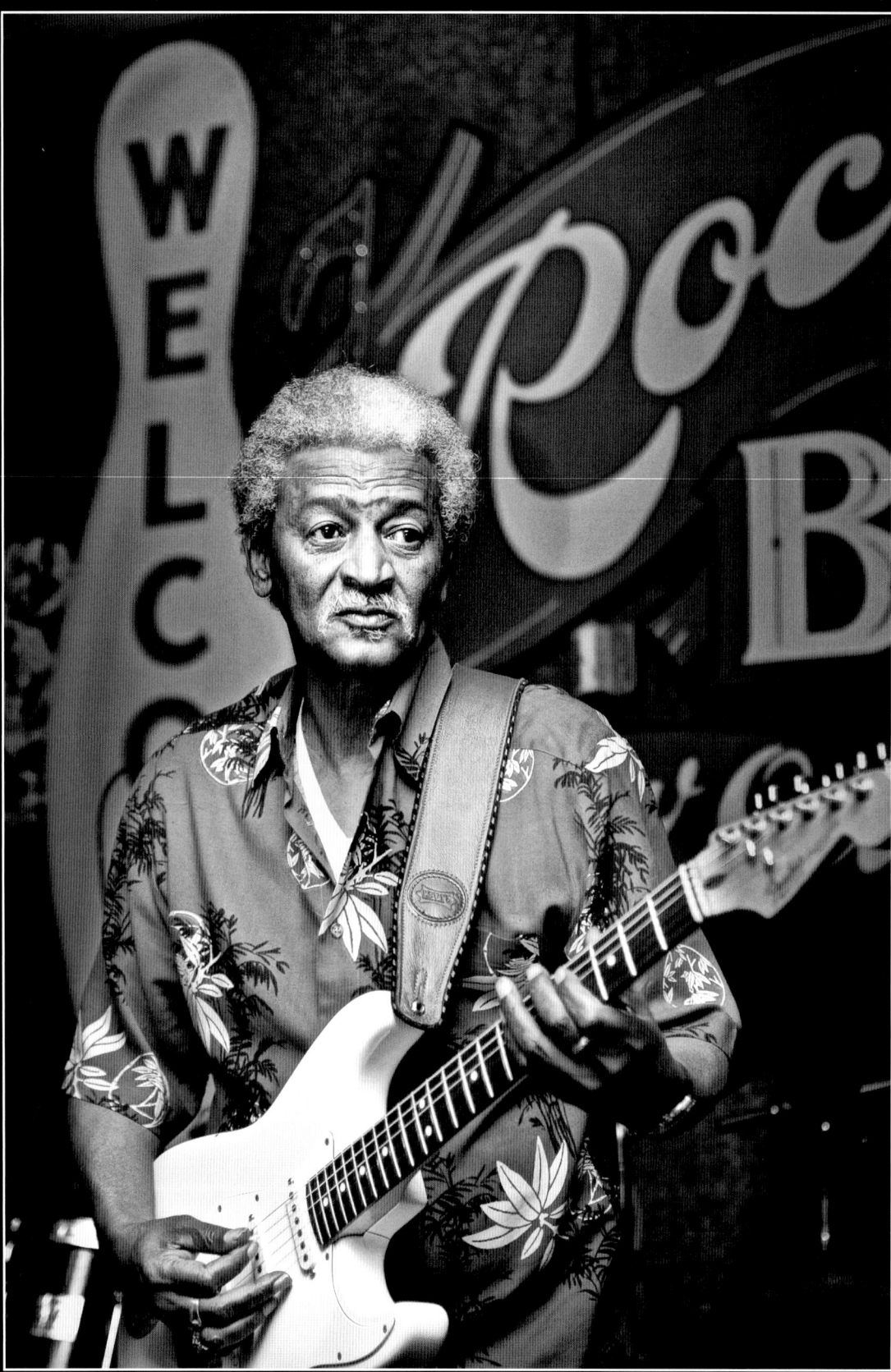

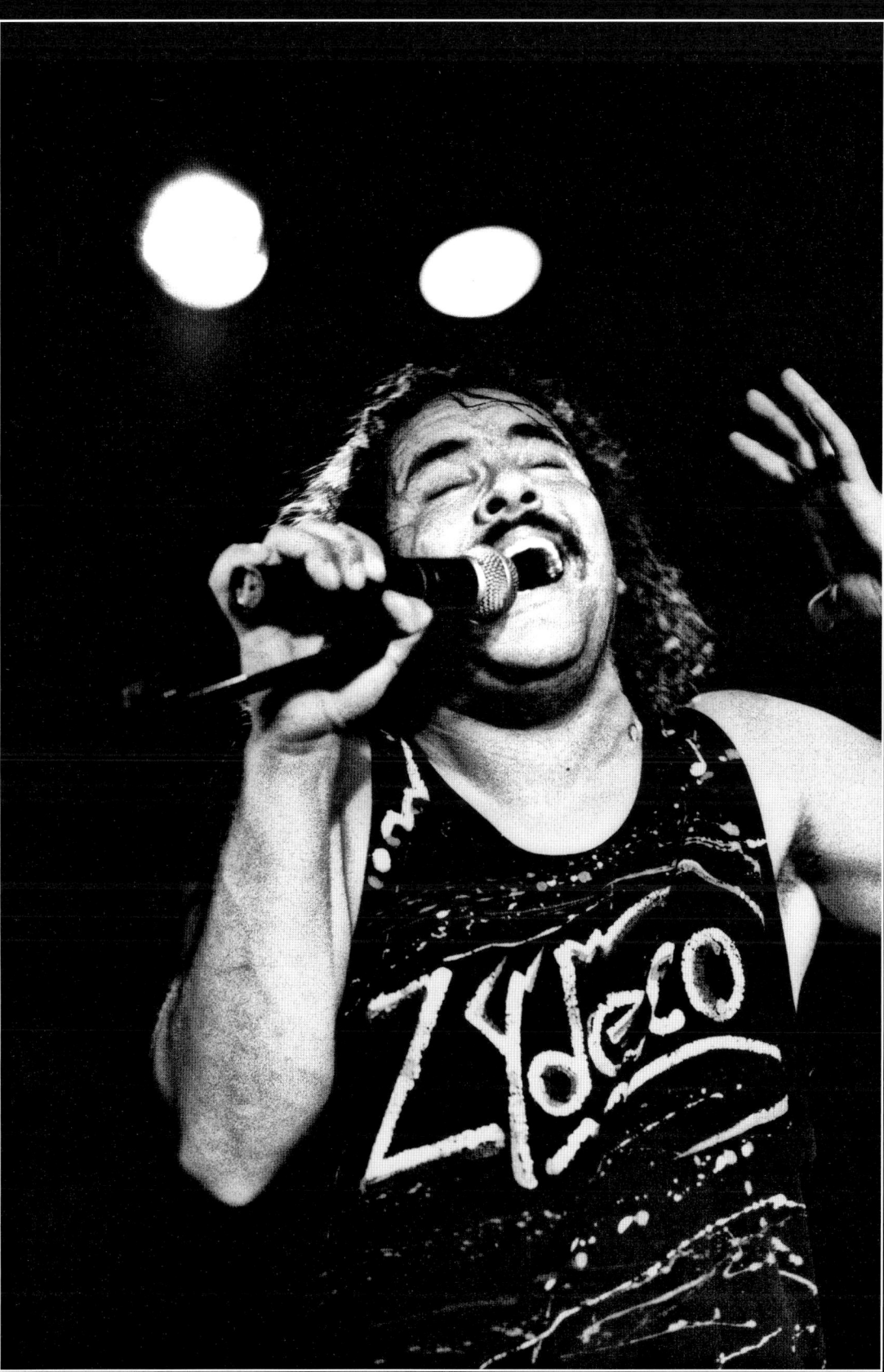

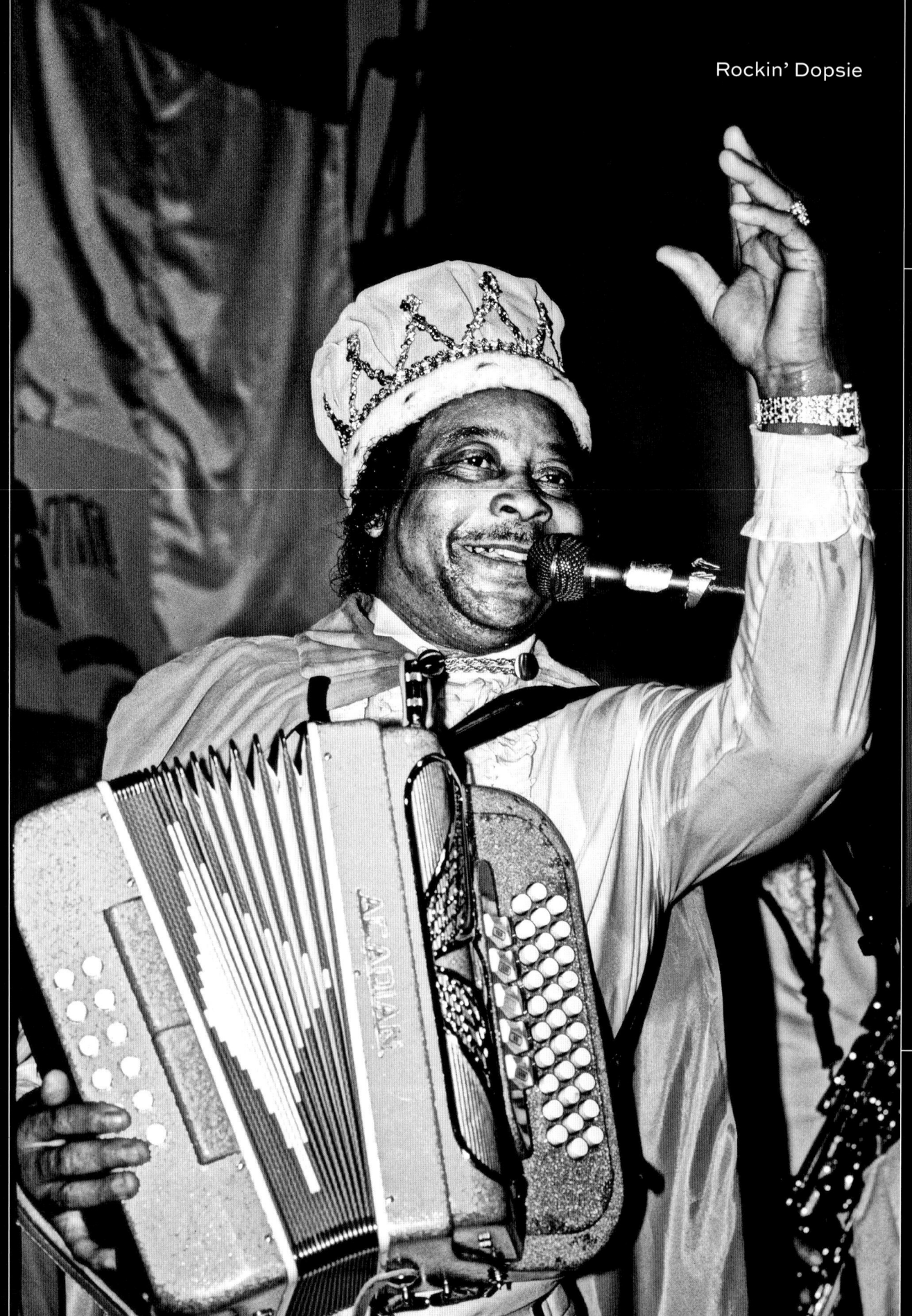

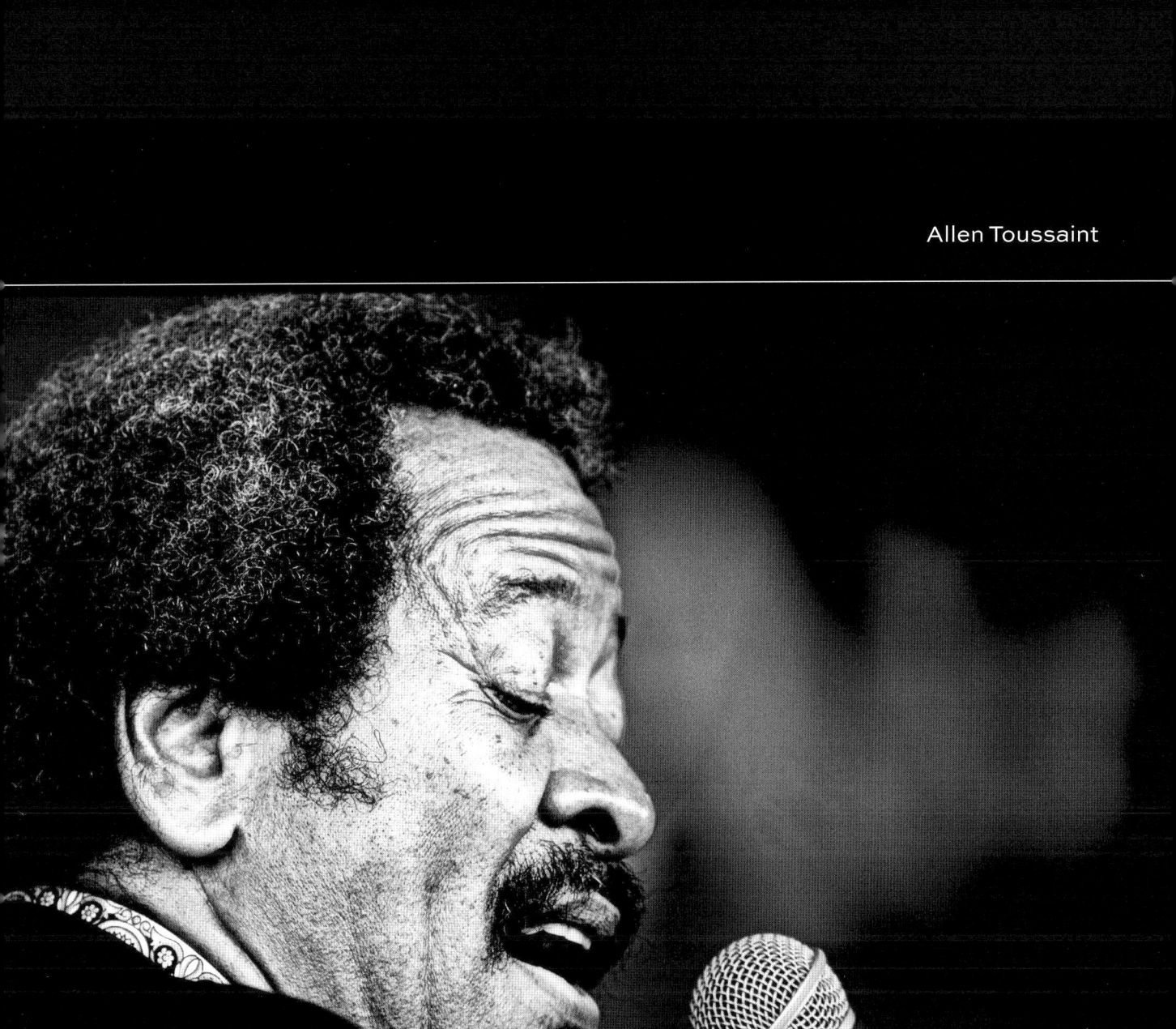

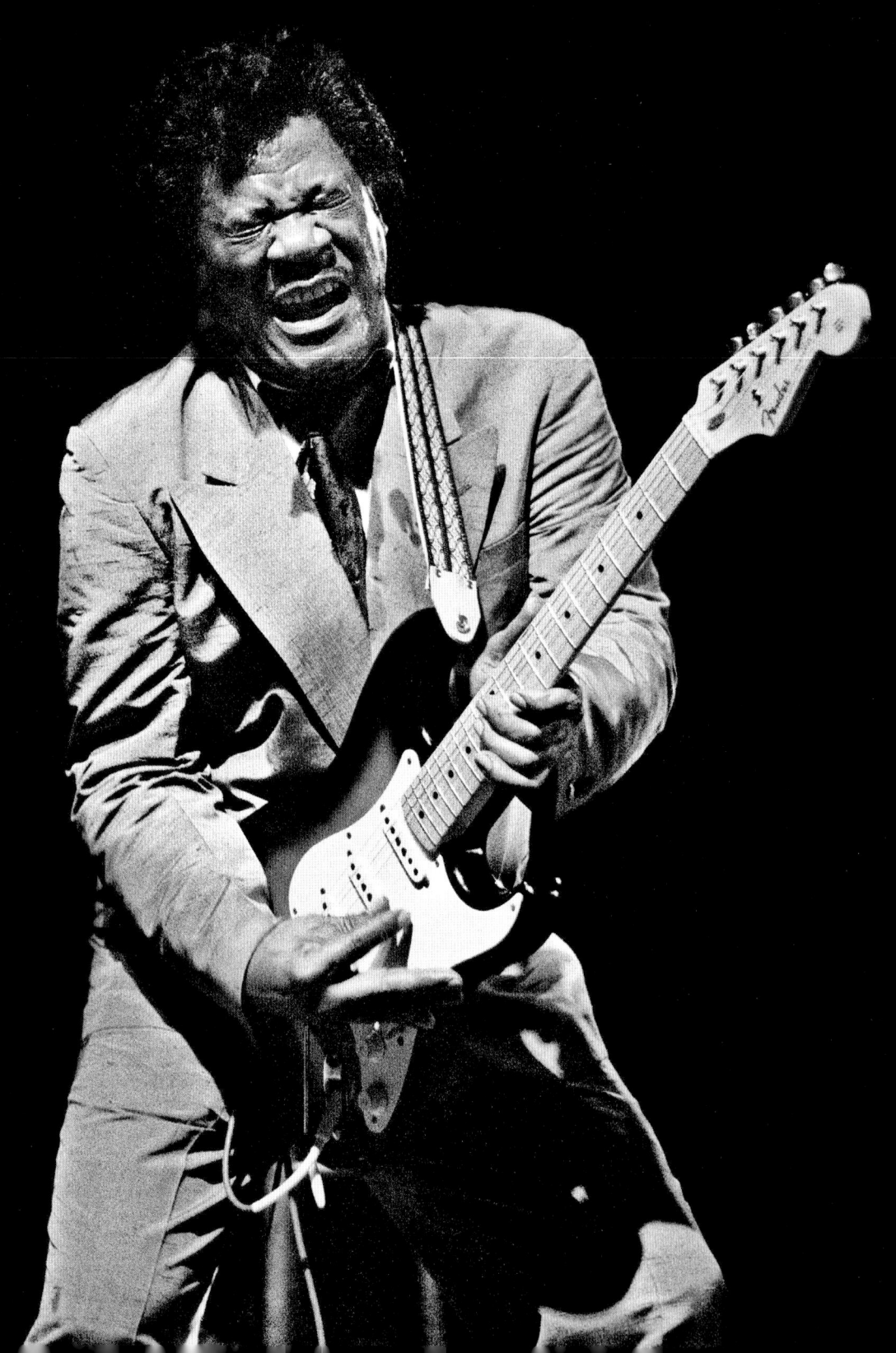

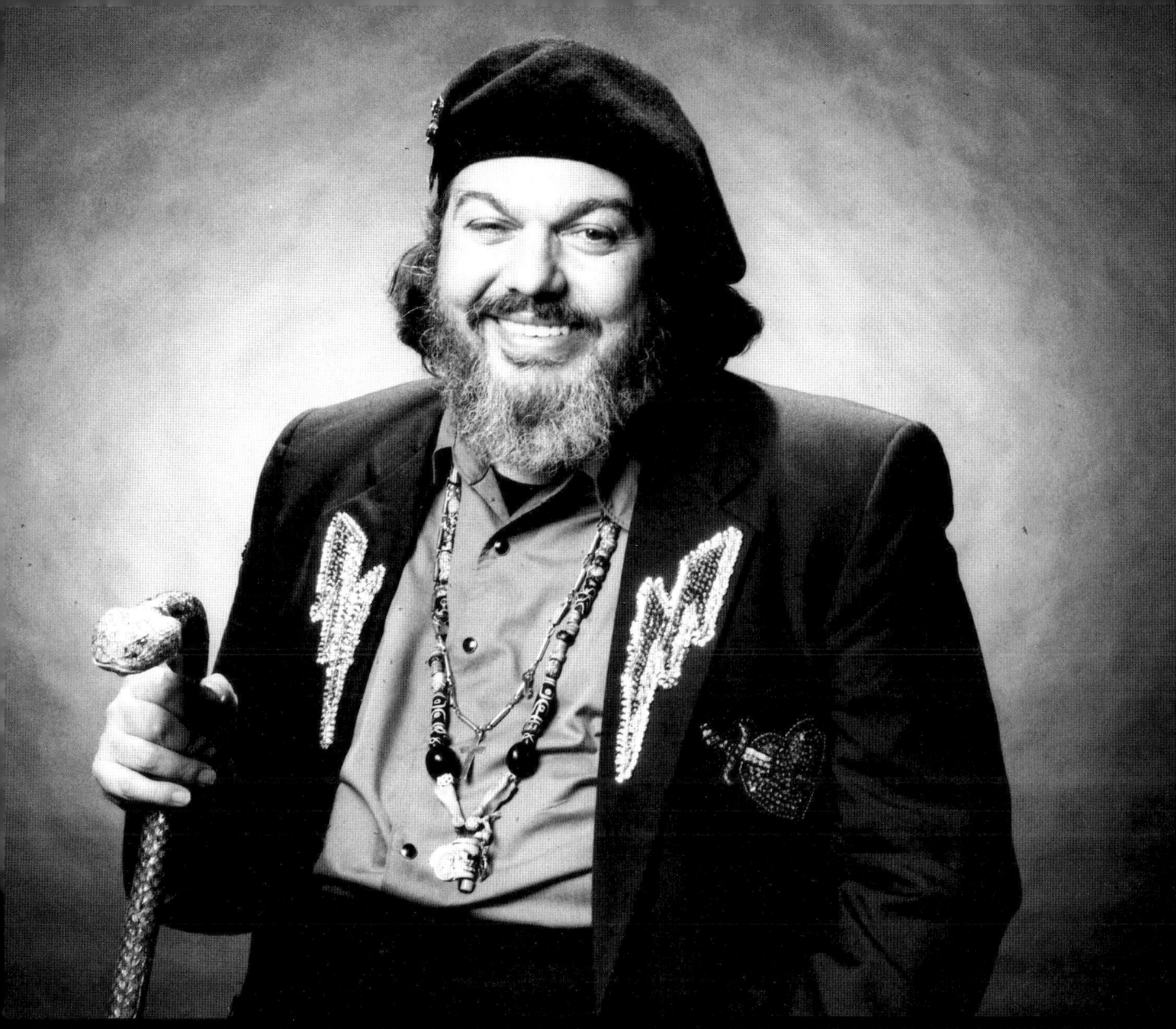

Mac "Dr. John" Rebennack

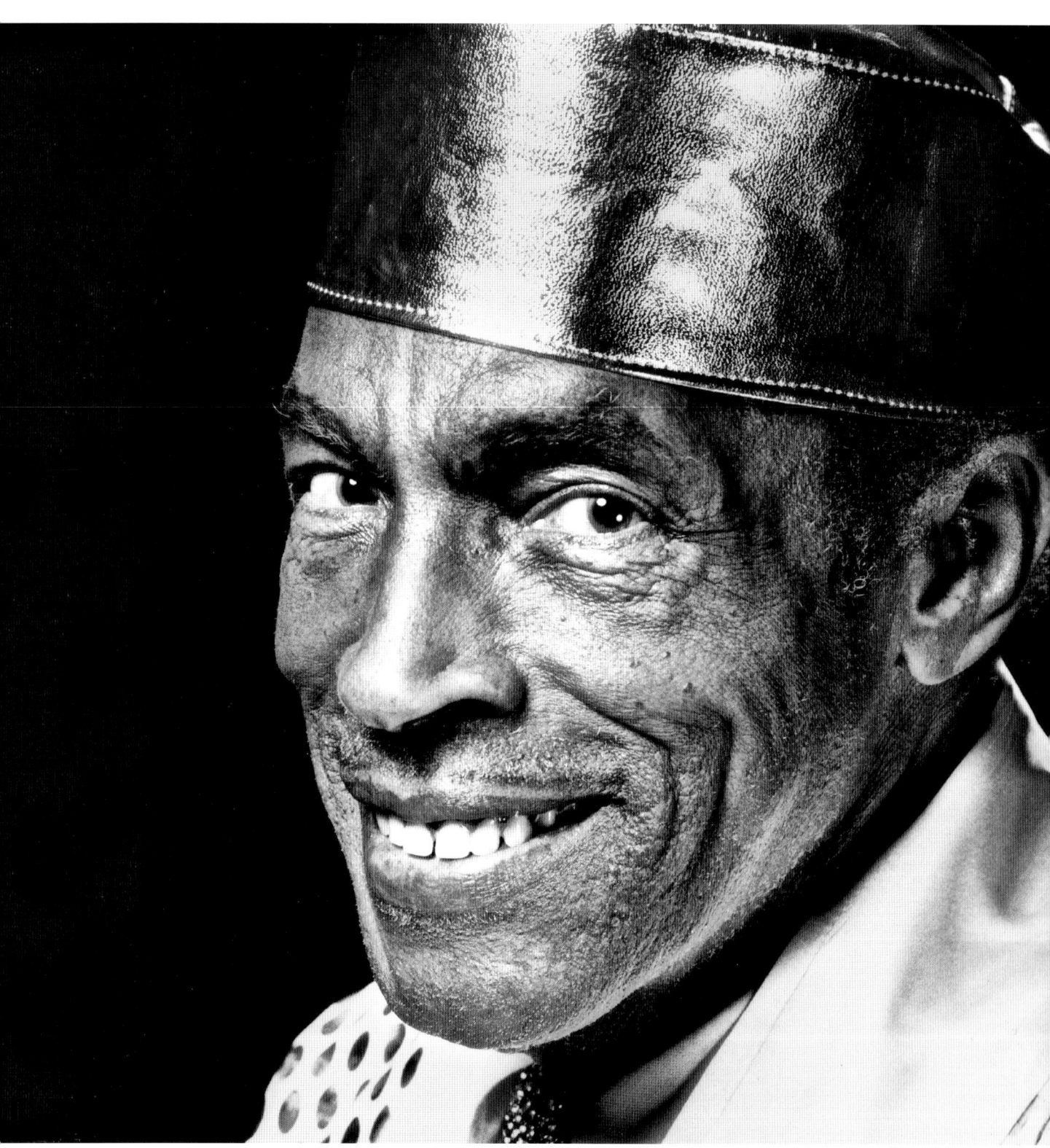

Charles Brown

CHAPTER 5

SOUL ON FIRE

Mr. Blues stepped out on stage,
in some wine-red alligator shoes,
hair slicked back, a diamond ring,
and he went to shouting the blues …

—Excerpt from the poem
"Thursday Night Blues,"
by Douglas Curry

Hailed as honkers and shouters, Sepia Sinatras, and vivacious vixens of va-va-voom, here they are, the kings and queens of royal-blue urbanity, the denizens of "Lonely Avenue." At once brassy and smooth, their blues were anything but down home. It was for them and their audiences an insistence to make it there, exalting life in the big city. These music makers joined the ordinary Black folk, shouldering their way into burgeoning population centers such as Memphis, Houston, Los Angeles, New York, Chicago—anyplace that didn't feel and smell "country."

It was after the war, before the Space Race; things were changing. Nothing would ever be the same again.

The lure of the main stem drew some of the best howlers and crooners from the pulpit and out of gospel quartets to create impassioned blues and R&B. From the teenaged temptress Little Esther, who never sounded like she'd been to church, to Bobby "Blue" Bland, whose stylings constantly returned there, suggesting, perhaps, the blues as a confession of sins, they preached to both sinners and saints and held court for the city slickers. Their music formed a bridge from the age of the bobby soxers, who bipped and bopped and Lindy-hopped, to the rebellious age of rock and roll. Roy Brown issued forth with smooth croon that paved the way for a young Jackie Wilson, while also creating "Good Rockin' Tonight," a jumper irresistible to Wynonie Harris and to Elvis.

Yet, amid the crackle of blare and glare, sonic boom, and shimmer, genuine artistry gave voice to changing times and technology. Charlie Parker's iconoclastic bebop was transformed by Eddie "Cleanhead" Vinson's honking, squeaking, and blue squalls, while 'Spoon turned swing into jump blues, calling on Hootie and declaring that Bessie Smith was right: "'Tain't Nobody's Biz'ness If I Do."

One of the era's finest blues shouters and balladeers was Nappy Brown. He doesn't always make everyone's list of top R&B stars, but maybe he should. Suffice it to say that he was equally a big-voiced shouter, crooner, and rocker—sporting a virtuosity seldom achieved. He should be better known for having sung the paint off the walls on the original "The Right Time," later covered and best remembered for Ray Charles's version. Nappy Brown hung on through many lean years, later to come back an acknowledged urban blues survivor.

Cascades of arpeggios rained, and torrents of ham-fisted boogie thundered, from the fingertips of men in silk suits and women adorned with gardenias and high-slit cocktail dresses. Bridging the gap from the old-time boogie and blues of a Walter Davis and a Memphis Slim to the fusion of secular and gospel music emerging in the mid-1950s stood singer/songwriter/bandleader Jimmy McCracklin. He recorded hits and enduring standards during the emergence of the blues/soul amalgam that still finds favor within the core blues audience. His hard-driving piano style often graced many recordings as well.

The more delicately fingered cocktail piano style of Charles Brown created a reflective mood, bluer than Nat King Cole's, yet never close to anything "country." He embodied the spirit of a man adrift, "like a ship out on the sea," but whose suffering would be vindicated. Champion Jack Dupree, who once sang of being a "junker"—a reefer smoker—was well ahead of any notion of legal cannabis or of the world becoming "420 friendly." He played around the precarious edges of the blues, from solo piano to full-band blues, from New Orleans to Harlem.

Like Champion Jack, right up to the time of his passing, Doc Pomus was no stranger to New York City's bars and blues joints. Perhaps that is where and why he became so informed of the language and mood of the city. Maybe that is where his telling observations of the human condition, which created the backdrop for his songs, were formed. Like Champion Jack, Doc wrote and sang about "My Good Pott," but in a way that was plausibly deniable. Doc was a master storyteller and a songwriter whose list of hit records reads as a definitive history of rhythm 'n' rock.

Starlets similar to Lavern Baker and Ruth Brown simply do not exist; there were only the two of them. Lavern, with a range that spanned foremother Bessie's moaning blues to the innocuously girlie "Tweedle Dee," and Ruth, who exclaimed, "Mama, He Treats Your Daughter Mean," blazed a path for femme rockers and girl groups who followed. These sultry, seductive, brown beauties aged like fine wine, as living proof of blessings that money just can't buy.

The sly and ribald singing and raucous, rhythm-rocking instrumentation have been preserved for posterity on record. But it was the look—the glad rags, the below-the-belt moves, the attitudes—that set their audience's souls on fire, that made these performers unforgettable.

Here's to not forgetting.

DOUG CURRY
Historian, disc jockey, actor, author

Bill Doggett

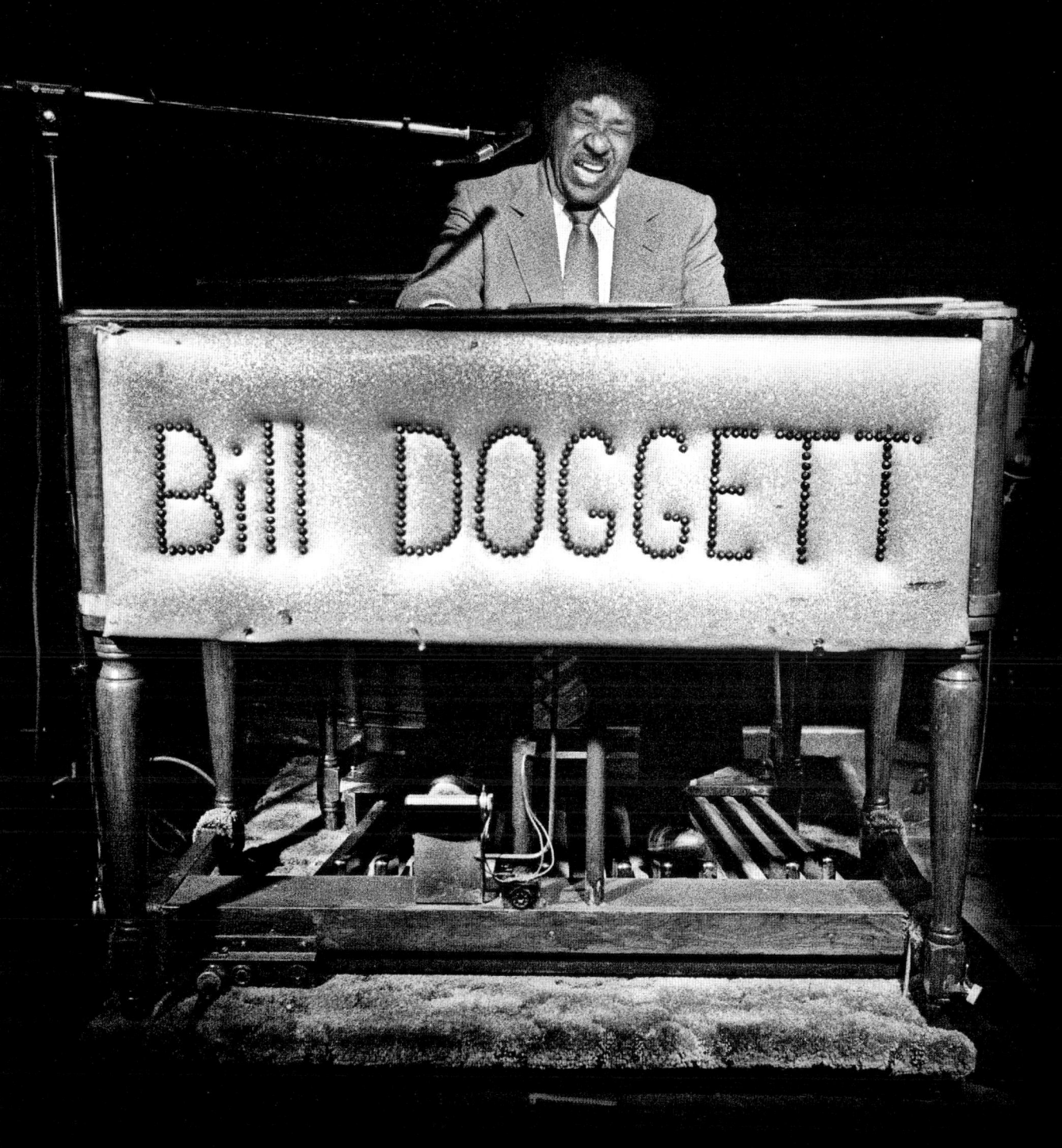

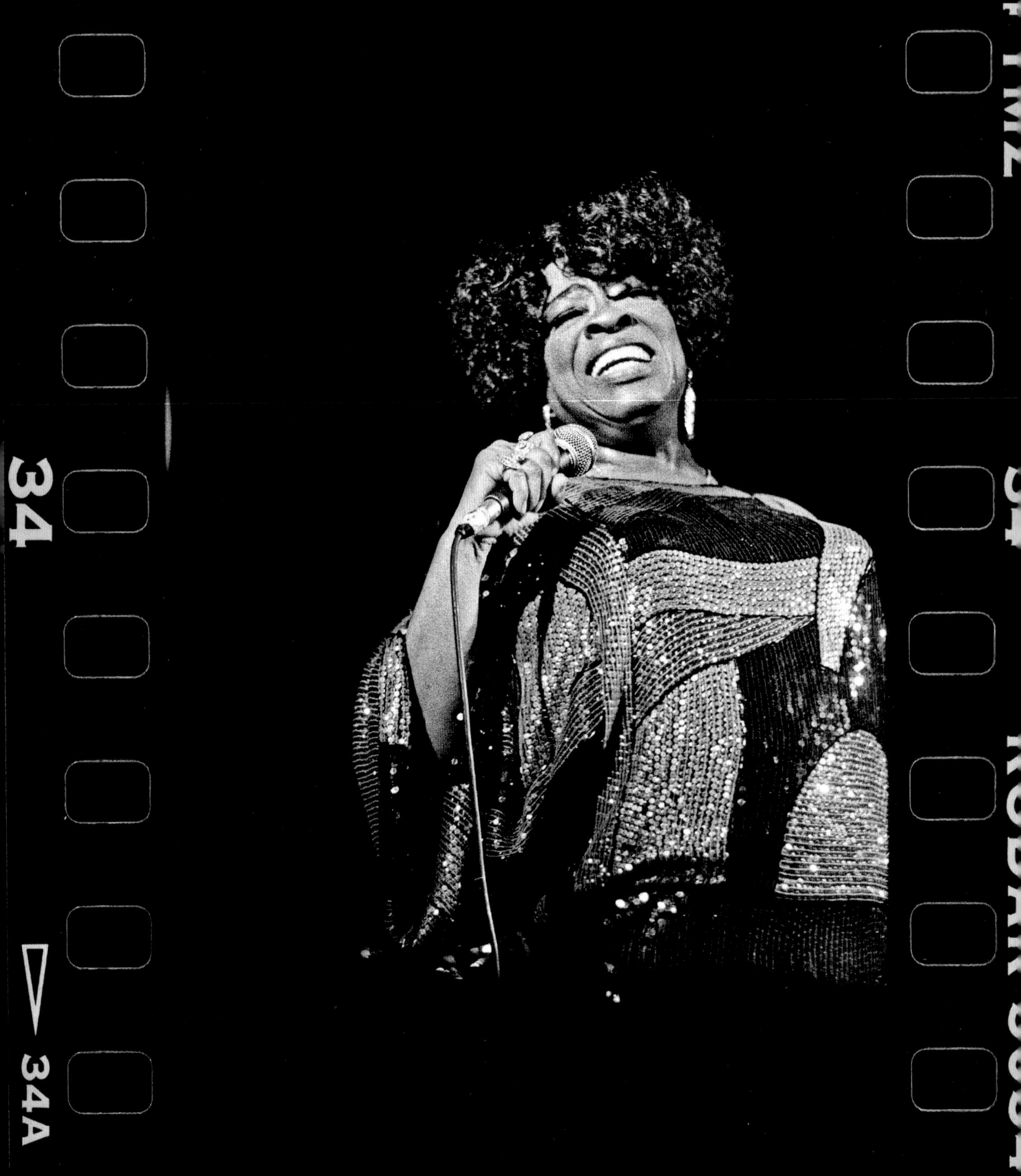

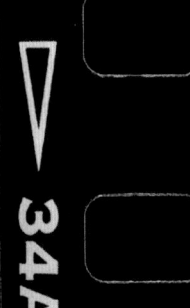

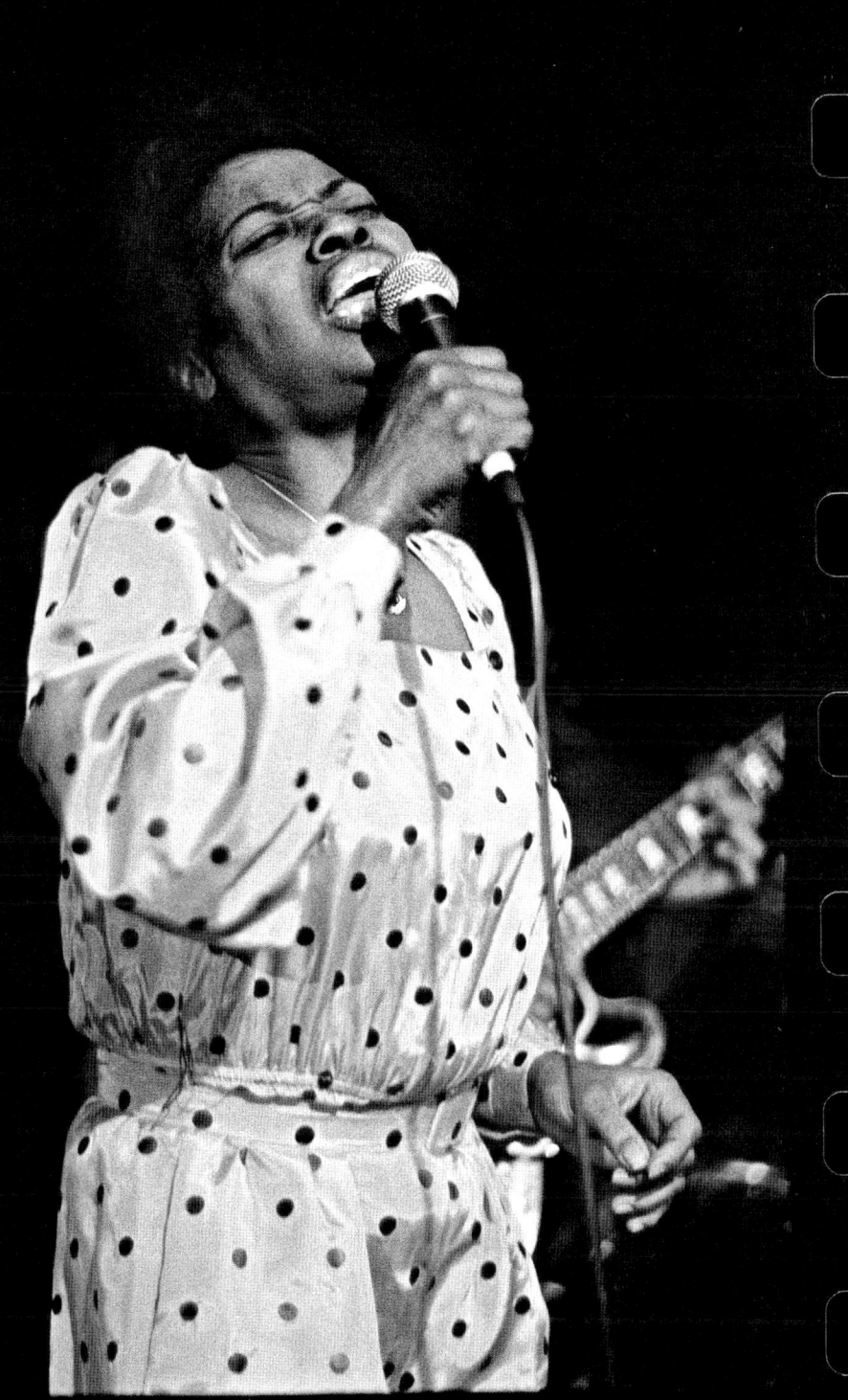

Roy "Good Rockin" Brown

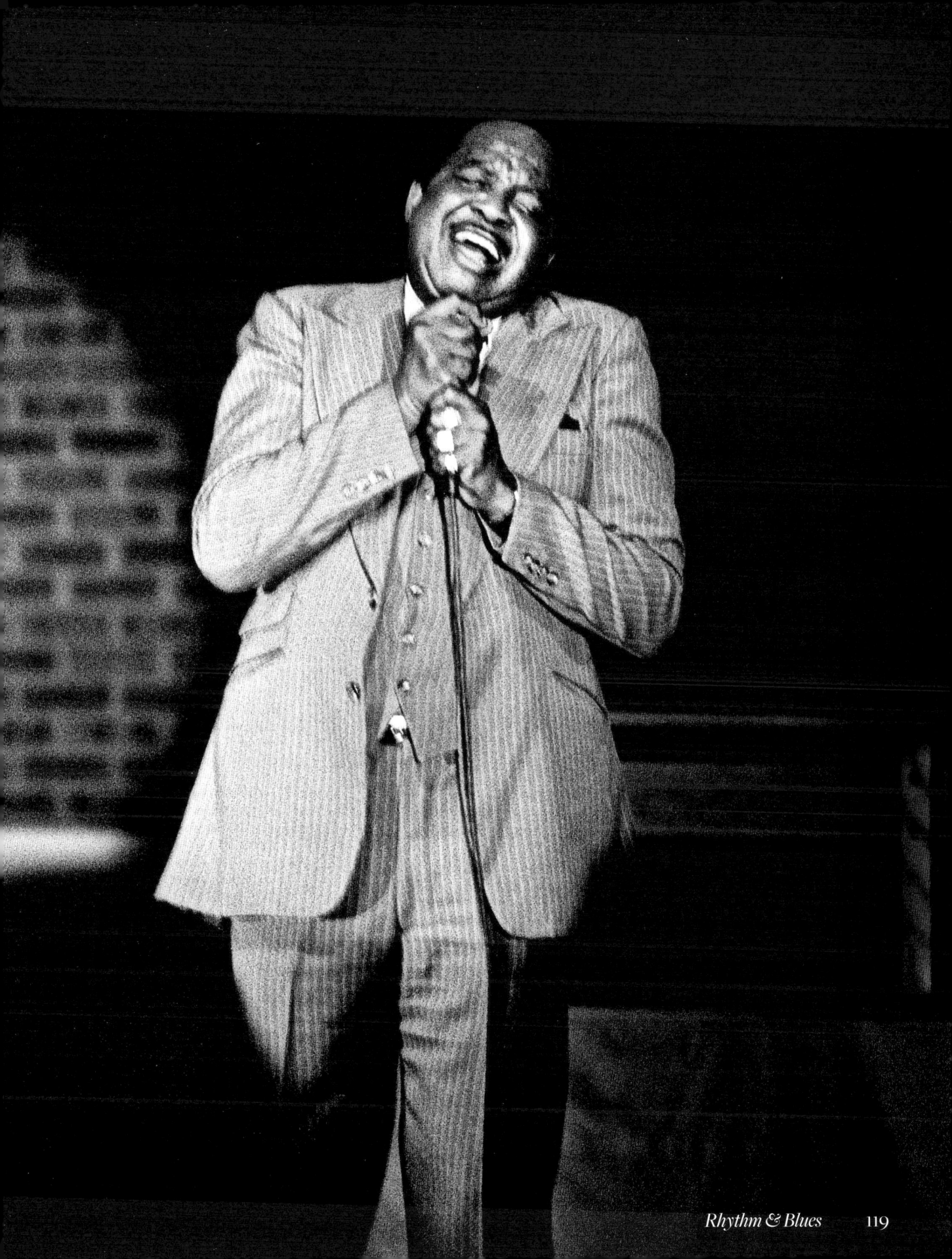

Andre Williams

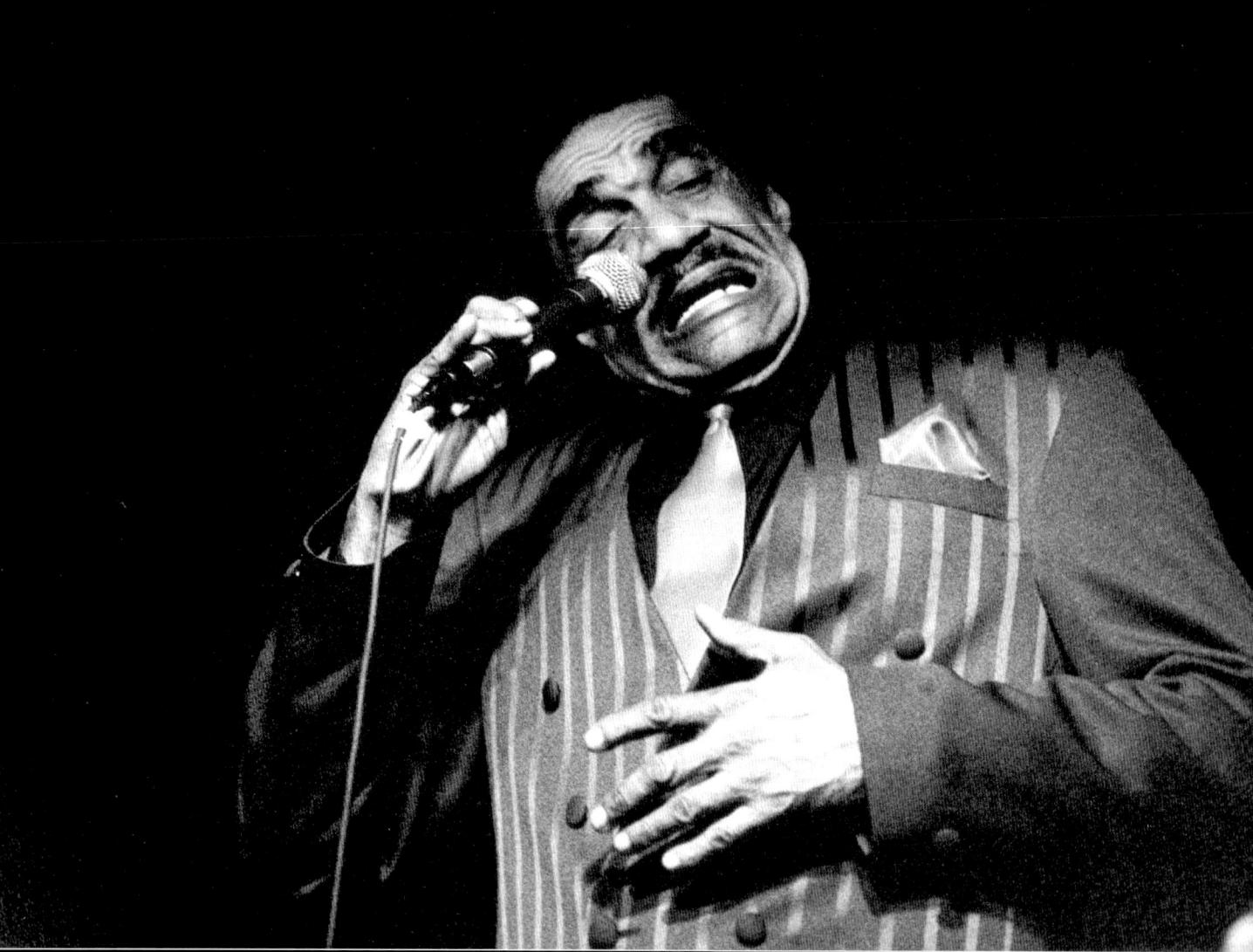

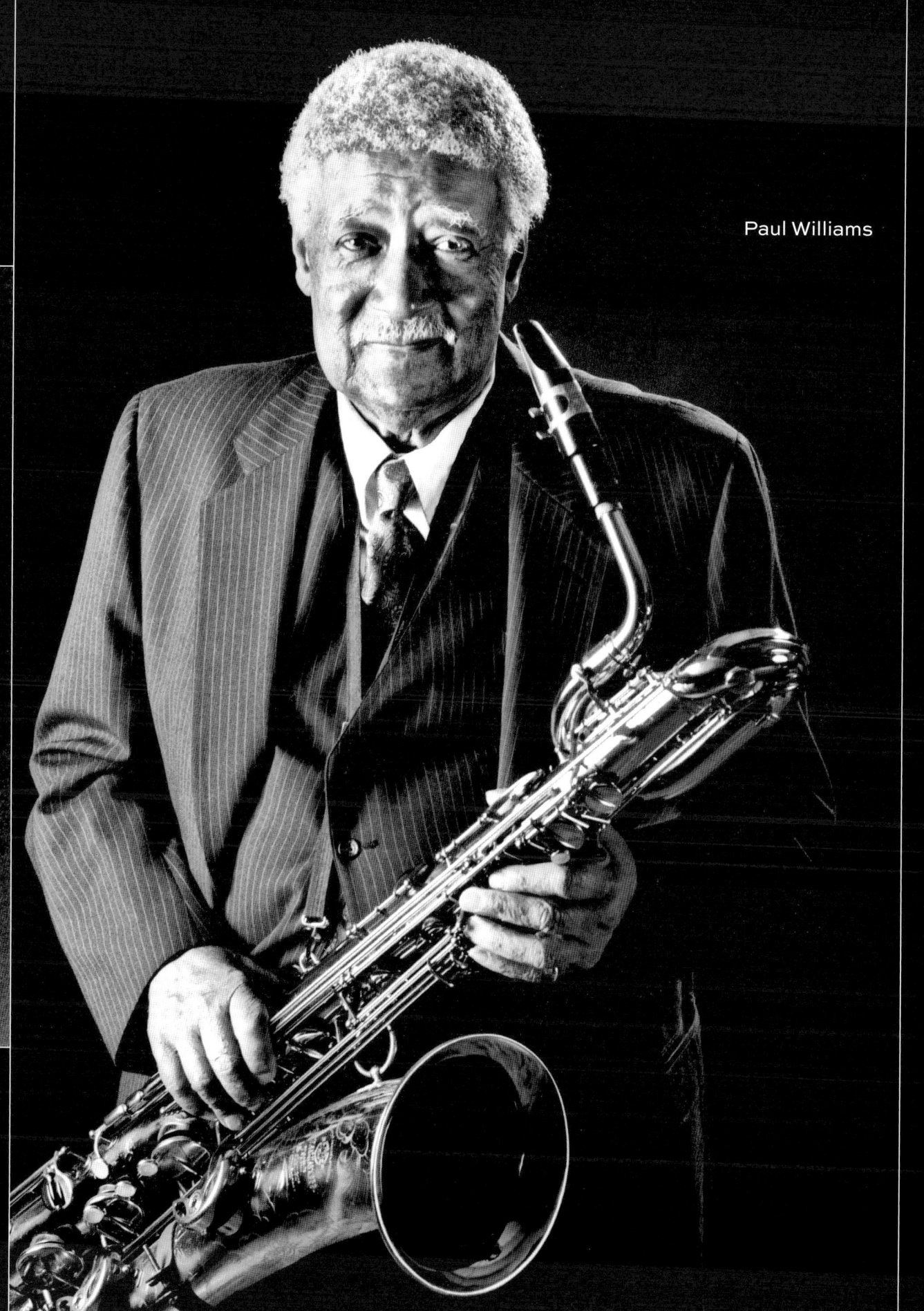

Paul Williams

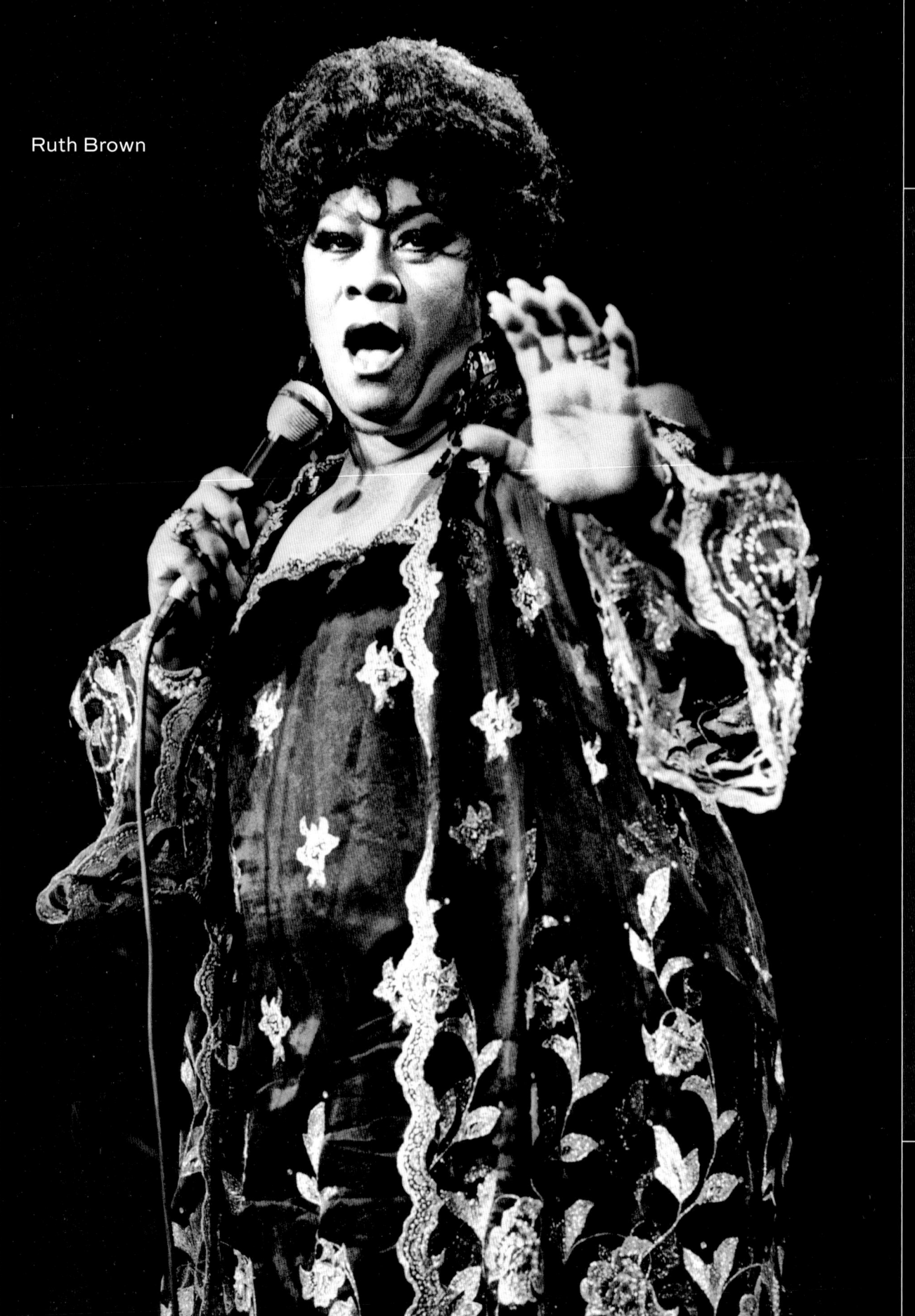

Ruth Brown

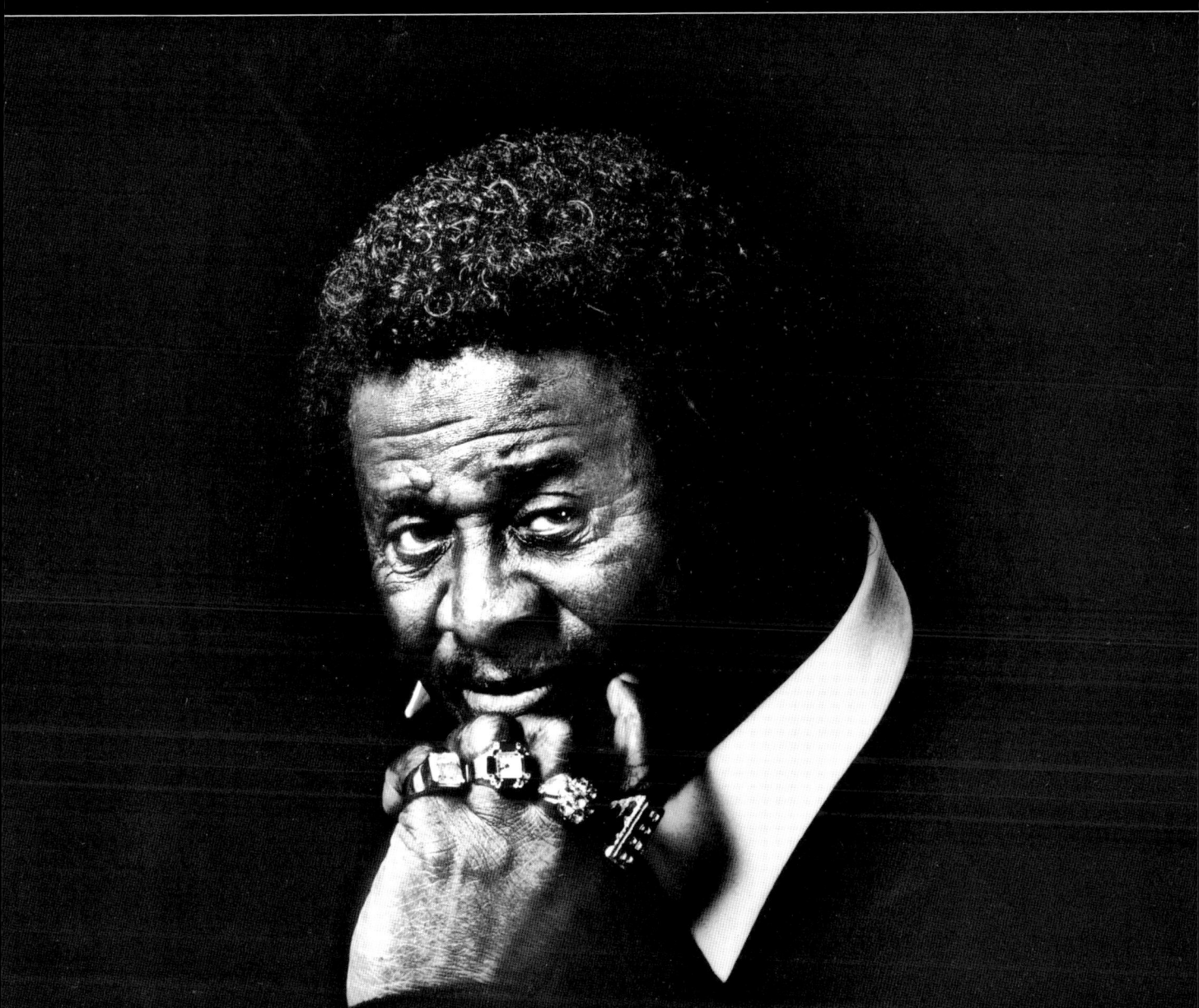

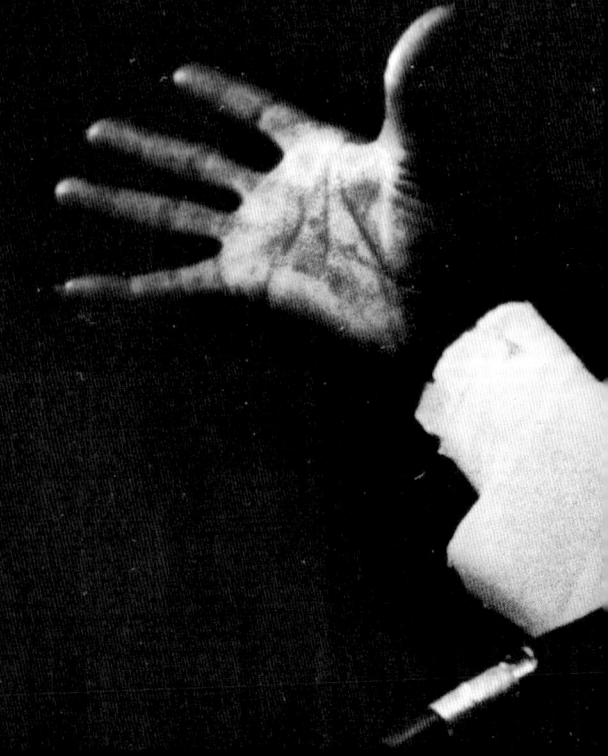

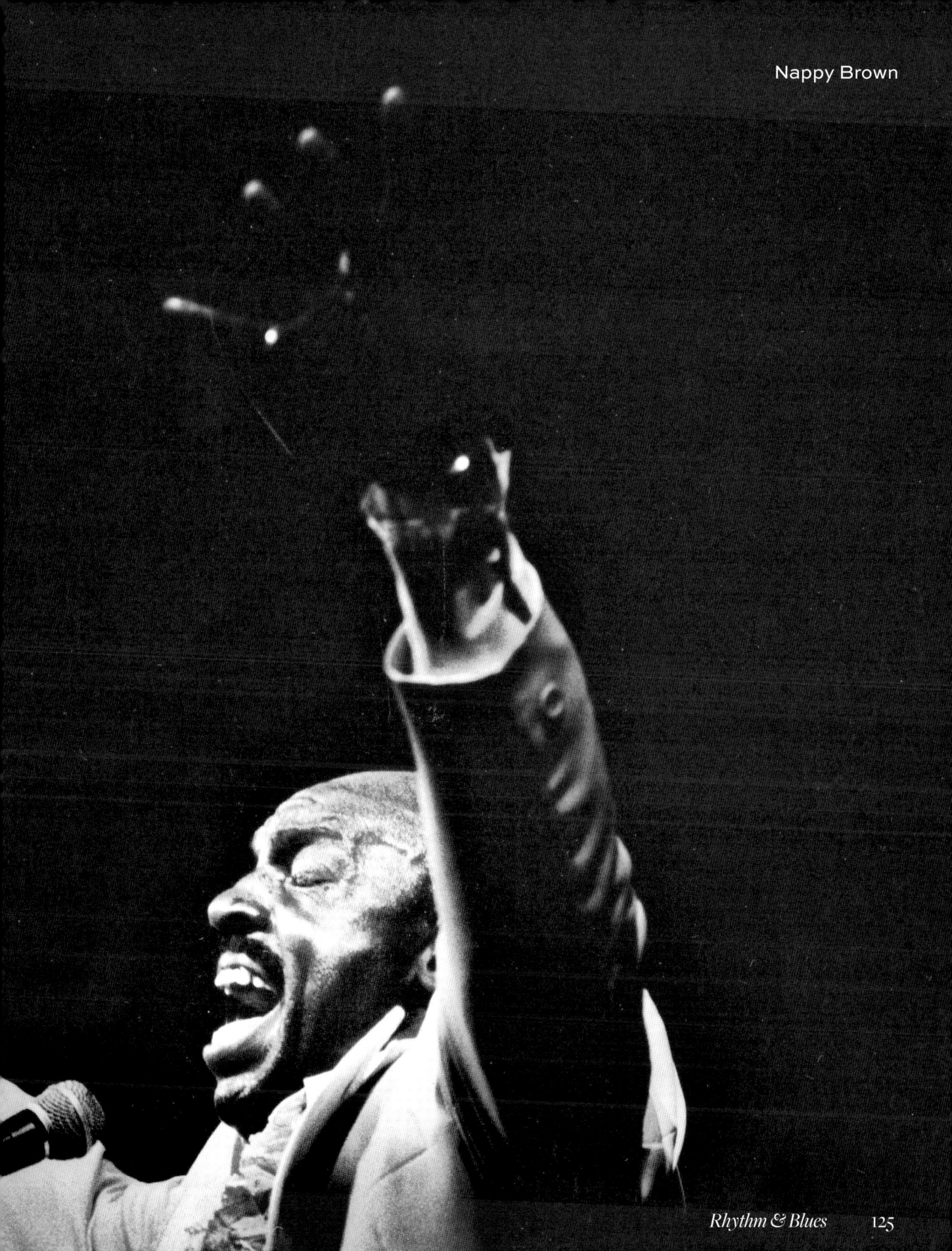

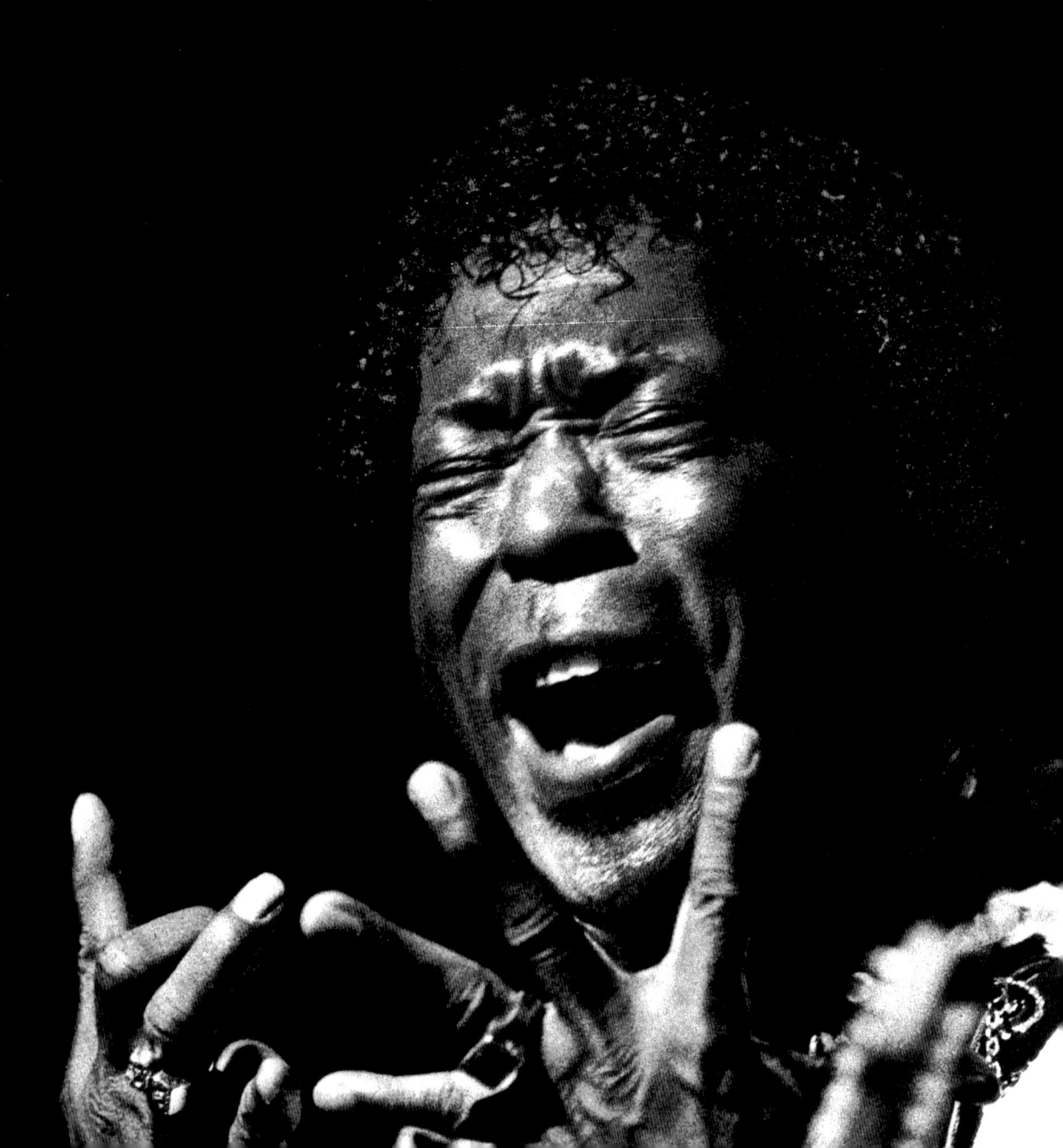

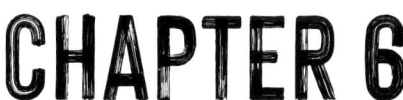

CHAPTER 6

BLUES MOVING FORWARD

In search of greater opportunities, especially with the World War II jobs boom, and an escape from racism, many African Americans from the Deep South headed north to Memphis, and on to St. Louis, Chicago, and Detroit. Others from Texas and Louisiana headed west to Los Angeles, the San Francisco Bay Area, and other urban centers. Those metropolitan areas were a gold mine of blues musicians, each region with a strong network of blues clubs as well as employment opportunities. The hours were long, the pay was short, and bands quickly adapted to playing amplified to be heard over the din of big-city life.

A new generation of blues artists, schooled in the South, began to stake their claims in the big towns, each a giant musical melting pot of blues, jazz, R&B, gospel, and swing. Numerous independent record labels provided recording opportunities to the artists and these sounds to consumers. Songs about cotton and Mr. Charlie gave way to odes about stockyards and steel mills, automobiles, and a more modern approach to the joys and heartaches of love. With the postwar rise of amplification, these artists relished the freedom to create music that rang out **in bold tones, colored with vibrant electrified** instrumental accompaniment.

In addition, the growing folk boom of the 1960s gave traditional artists newfound exposure and spurred on the careers of many blues-based artists. The increase in interest in the 1960s led a number of small, independent record labels to

Buddy Guy

record artists who had been limited to playing local clubs. In Chicago the legendary Bob Koester at Delmark Records led the way, recording the classic *Hoodoo Man Blues* album with Junior Wells and Buddy Guy, a pioneering record for a real working electric Chicago blues band. Guitarist/vocalist Magic Sam blended elements of soul music into his tough Chicago West Side sound, a sensational mixture that had him marked for stardom before his untimely passing in 1969. Others such as Luther Allison and Otis Rush kept the West Side sound vital. Blues got an additional boost with the British Invasion of the 1960s. Bands such as the Rolling Stones, the Yardbirds, and the Beatles sparked interest in the music for a host of mostly white rock-oriented listeners. Once artists deeply steeped in the blues tradition such as Dave Van Ronk, Paul Butterfield, Charlie Musselwhite, John Hammond, and others started recording, the music began its steady climb to international acclaim.

The demand for the music in its real, unfiltered form continued to grow on college campuses across the country. Eventually, legendary artists such as B.B., Albert, and Freddie King were booked at larger venues, such as Bill Graham's Fillmores East and West, often getting standing ovations from an entirely new audience of young whites. Another boost occurred when such songs as B.B. King's classic "The Thrill Is Gone" or Albert King's "Born Under a Bad Sign" placed on the record charts and play lists along with soul, Motown, and pop.

The Alligator Records label, started in 1971 because owner Bruce Iglauer wanted to cut a record documenting the raw sound of Hound Dog Taylor and the House Rockers, and later guitarist Son Seals, harp player Carey Bell, and more, saw their profiles expand from regional to international audiences. Albert Collins played the blues with a cool, modern sound rooted in his Texas heritage. Lee Baker Jr., known as "Guitar Junior" in Louisiana, had a regional hit there, "The Crawl," then moved to Chicago, where he updated his sound, becoming known the world over as Lonnie Brooks. Other labels such as Rounder and Black Top recorded artists such as Texan Johnny Copeland, Louisiana's Gatemouth Brown, Snooks Eaglin, and many more and expanded the horizons of the music.

As the 1980s dawned, a new generation appeared, serving up their own vibrant interpretations on the traditions. The Fabulous Thunderbirds, led by singer/harmonica ace Kim Wilson and guitarist Jimmie Vaughan, took the Texas blues sound to a whole new level. On the East Coast, guitarist Duke Robillard started Roomful of Blues, a band with a jumping, swaggering sound with a killer horn section. Other regions had similar, equally great bands bringing the music forward.

Blues was taken further forward by artists based in blues yet blended with soul, such as Little Milton, Latimore, Z.Z. Hill, and Johnny Rawls. Soul blues maintained and expanded its popularity, especially in the South.

The music's popularity and exposure reached a peak in the early 1980s with the arrival of two seminal artists who, along with the Fabulous Thunderbirds, brought blues to the masses on MTV. The soulful vocal and guitar stylings of Robert Cray garnered five Grammy awards for his album *Strong Persuader*. And Stevie Ray Vaughan, Jimmie's younger brother, gave listeners a taste of his guitar prowess, which still reverberates and influences today. His first release under his own name, *Texas Flood*, and his subsequent career marked him as a guitarist for the ages. His life was cut short by a tragic accident; one can only wonder where he might have taken the music if given more time.

Artists such as Taj Mahal, Keb Mo, Ronnie Earl, and many, many more have had long careers and sustained popularity, and devoted fan bases keep the blues alive and moving forward, while staying deeply connected to the music's origins and traditions.

MARK THOMPSON
Senior writer for *Blues Blast* and *Blues Music* magazines and a past member of the board of directors of the Blues Foundation

Buddy Guy

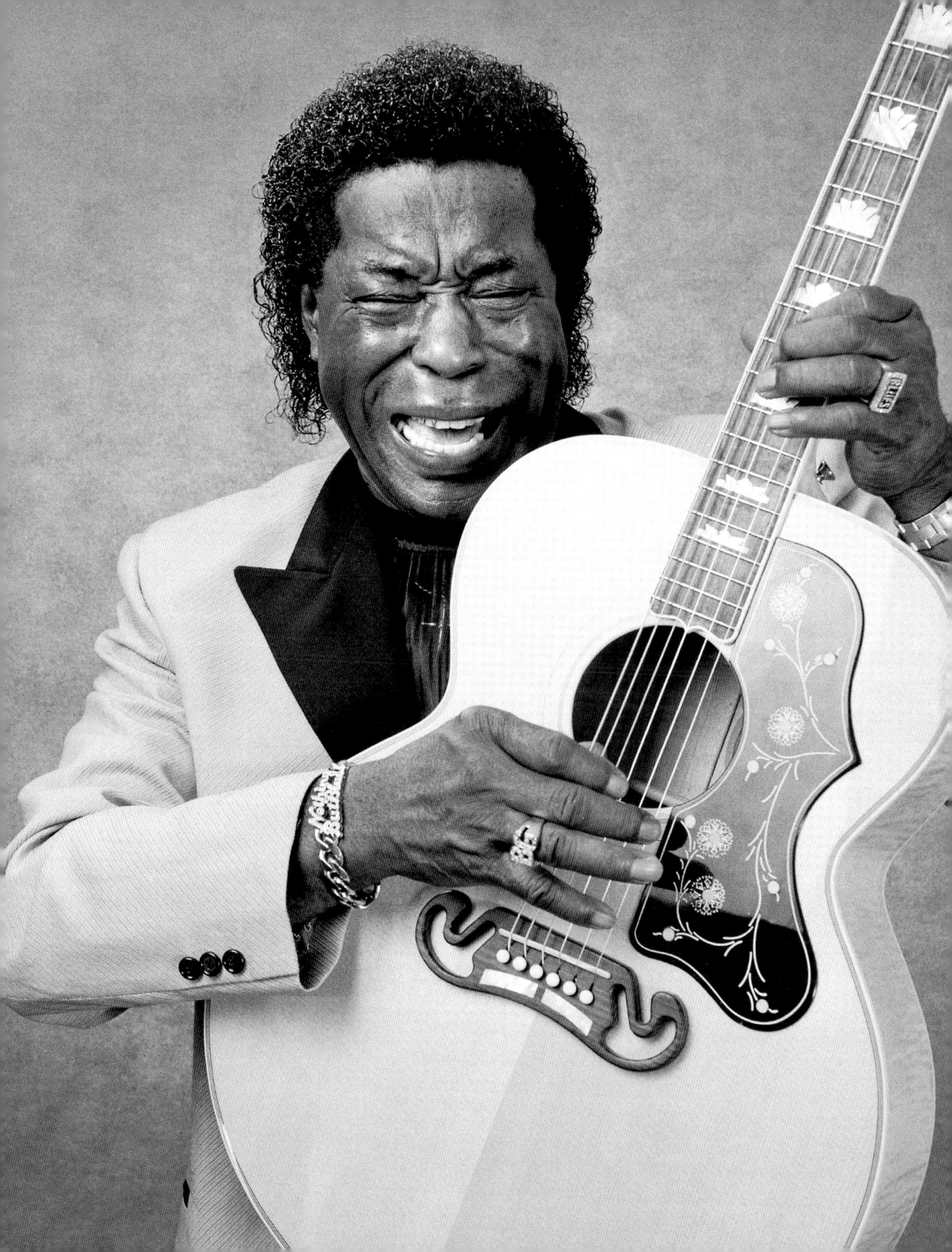

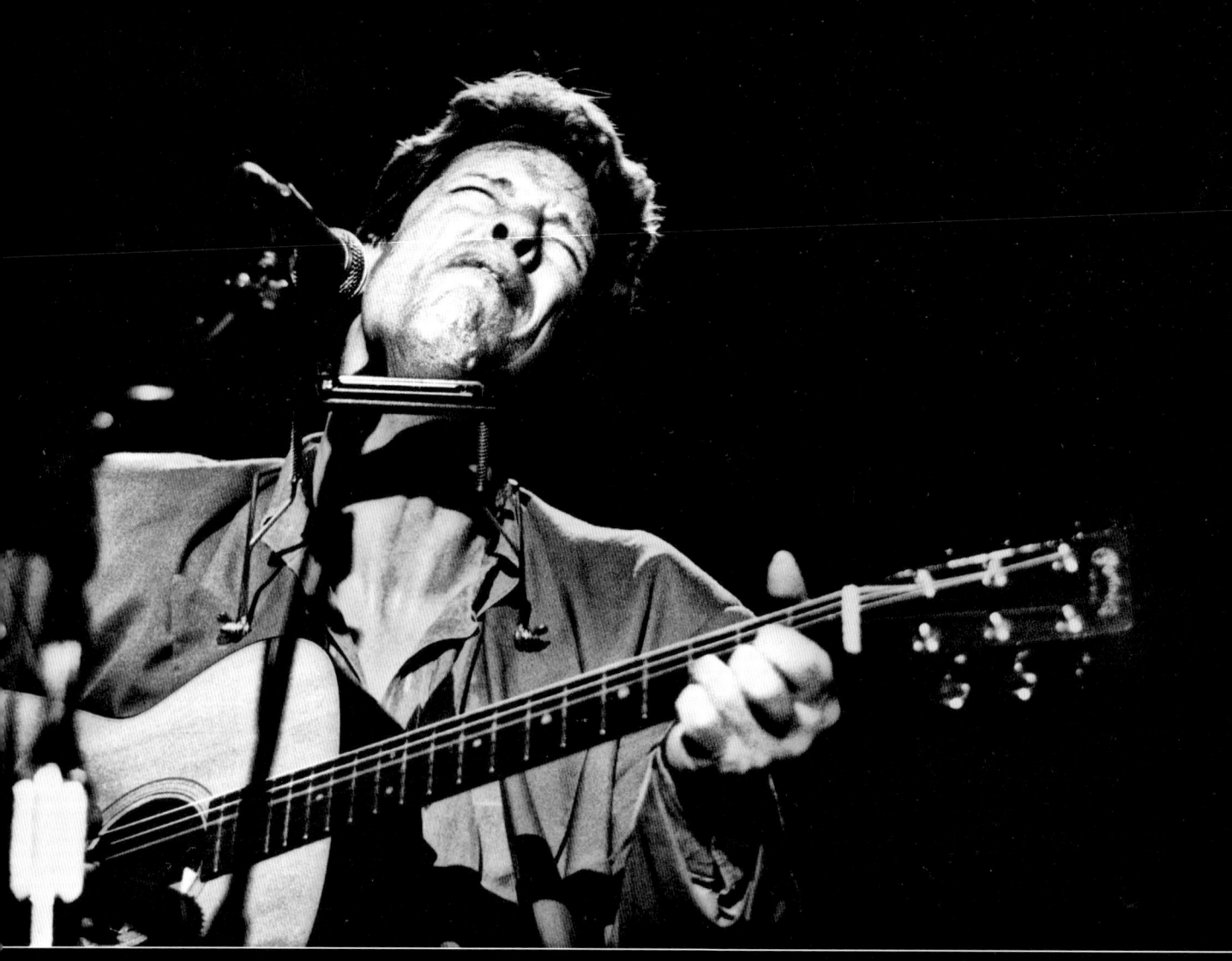

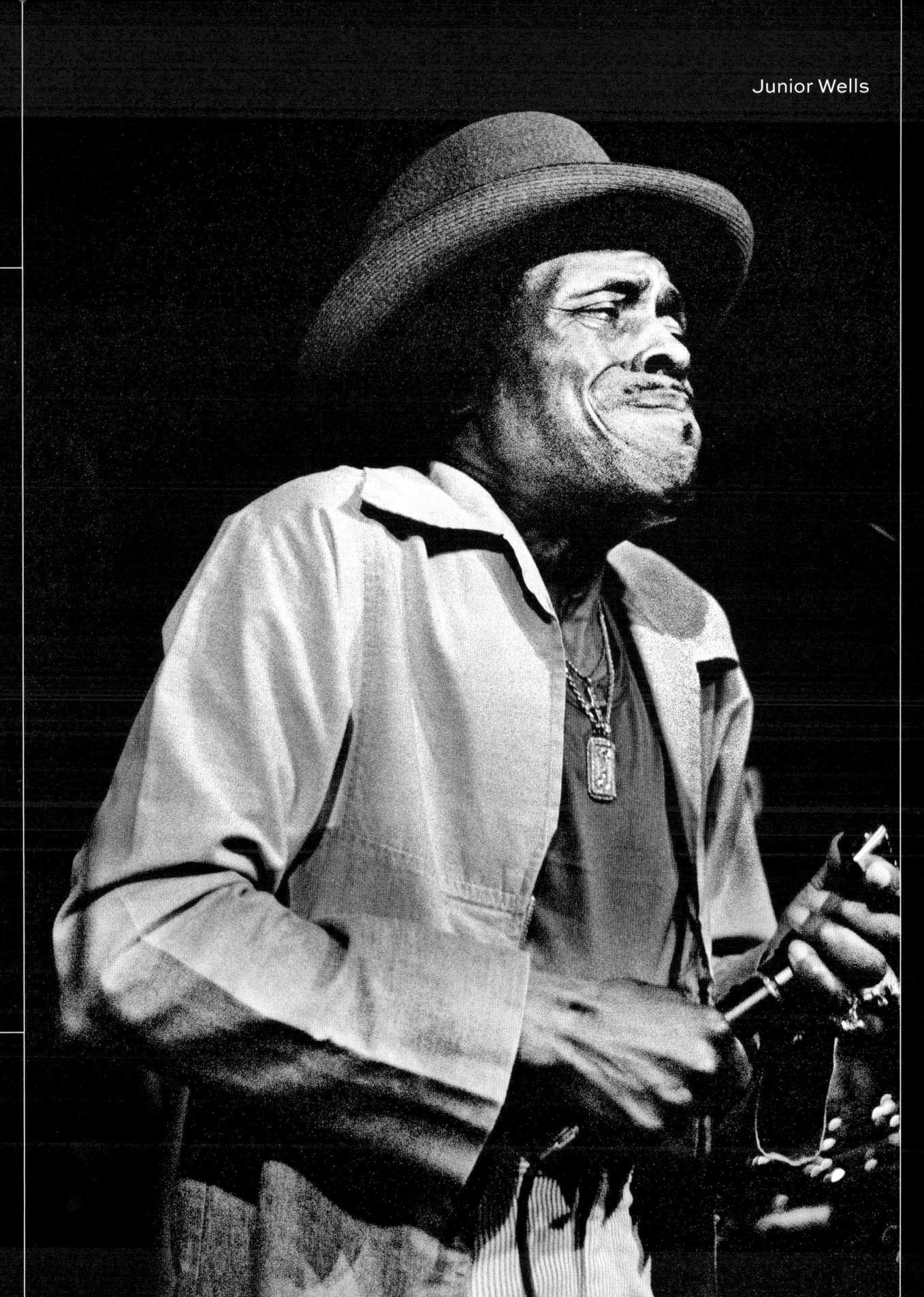

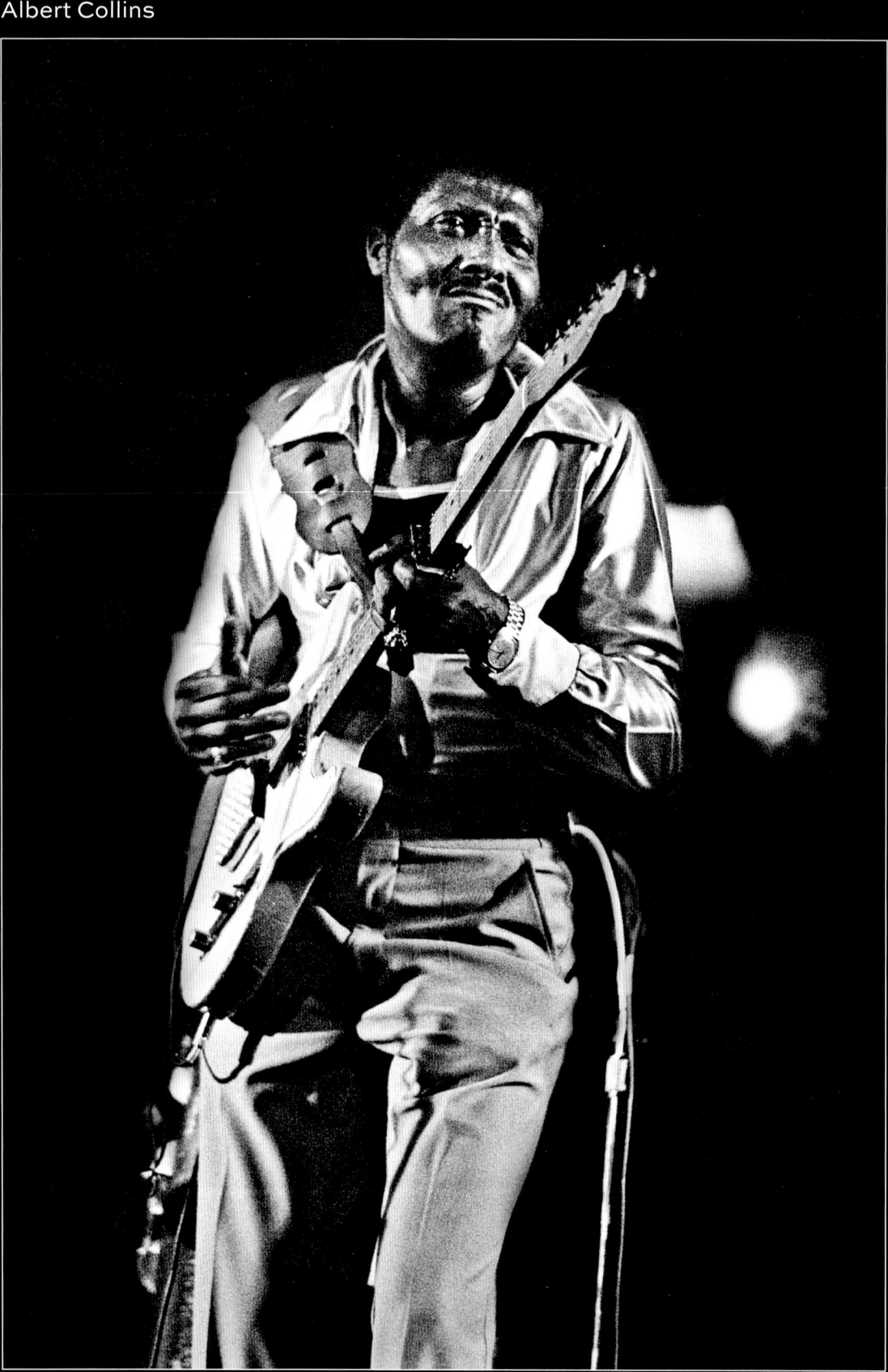

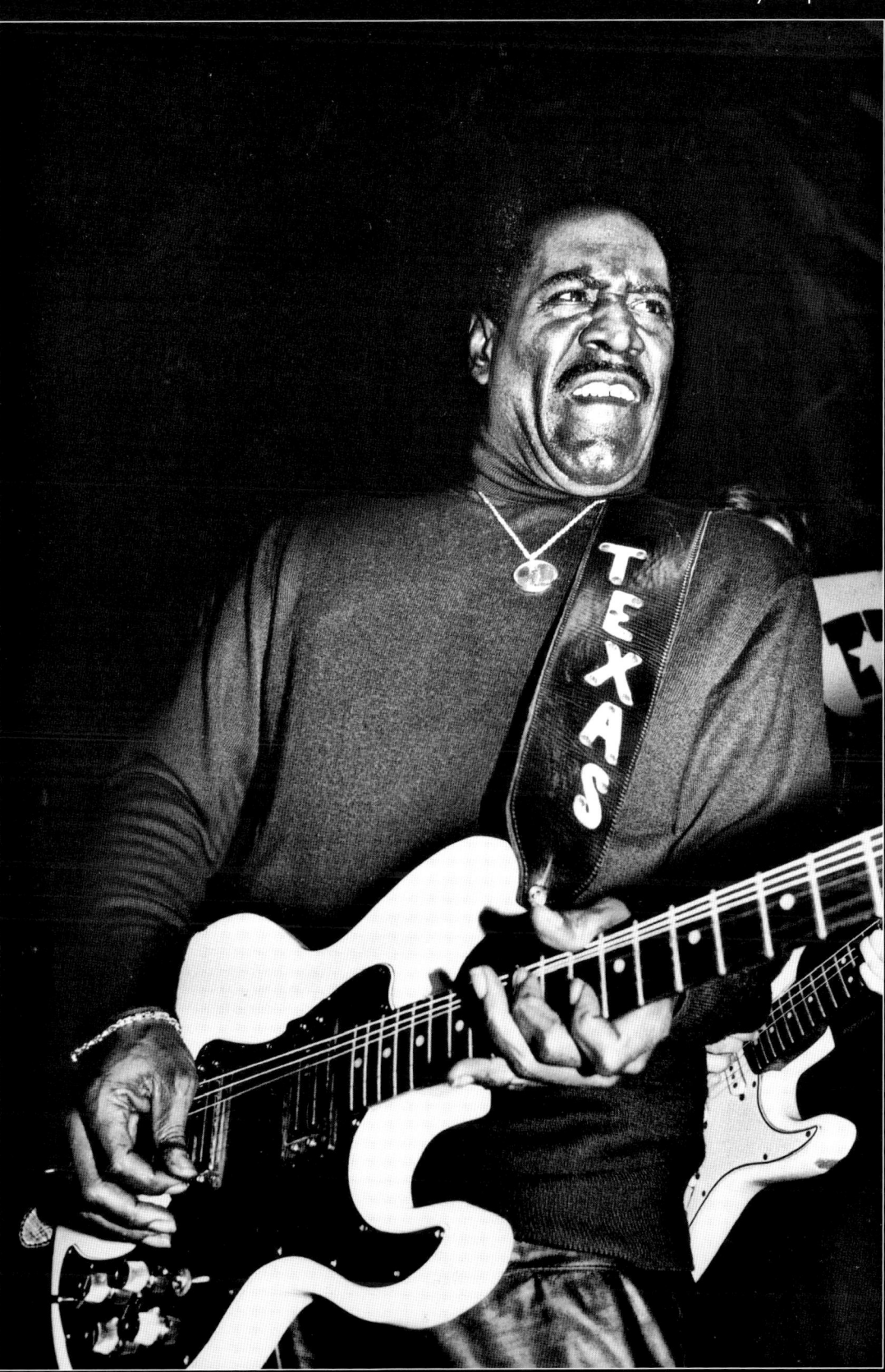

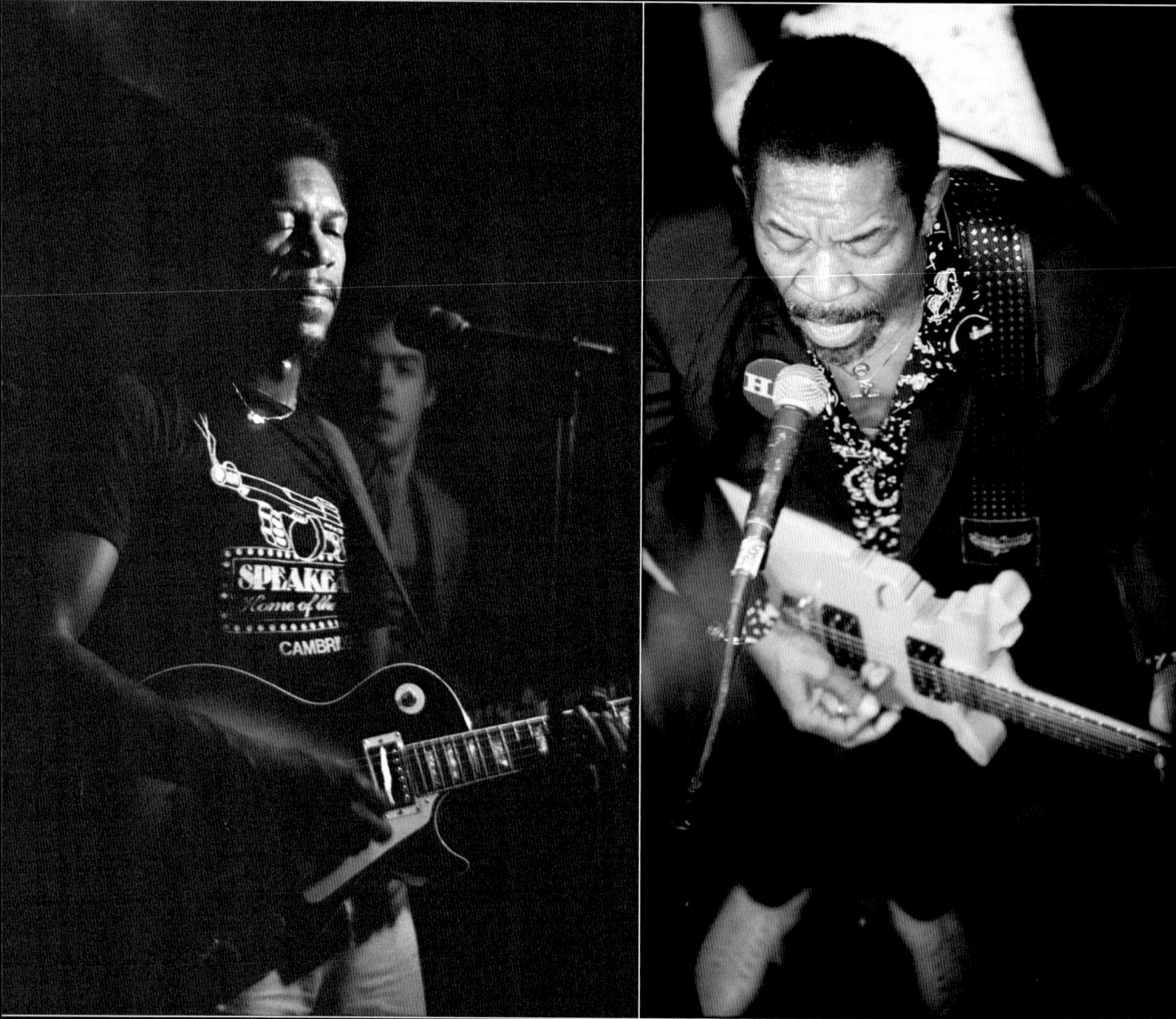

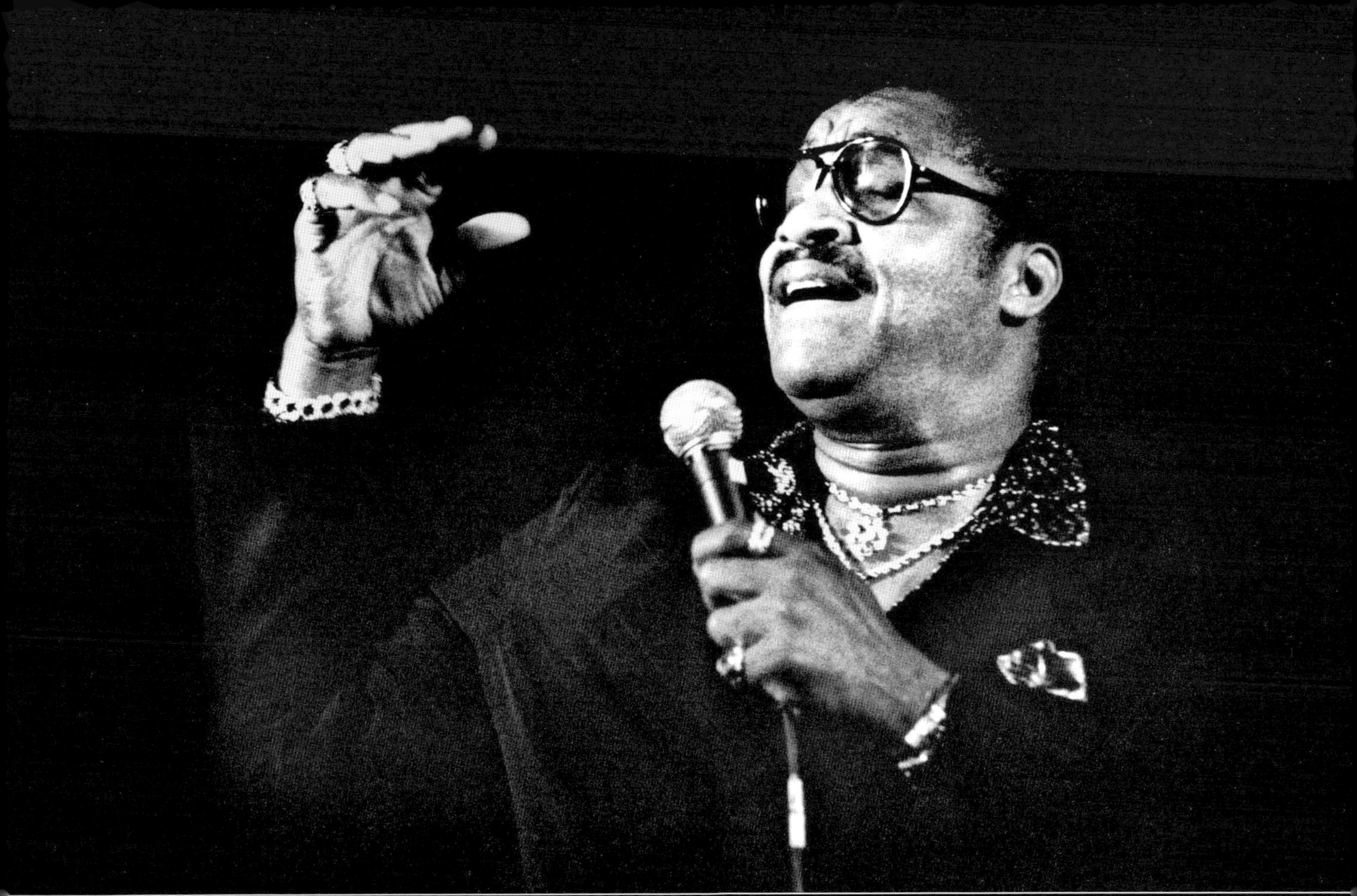

Little Milton Campbell

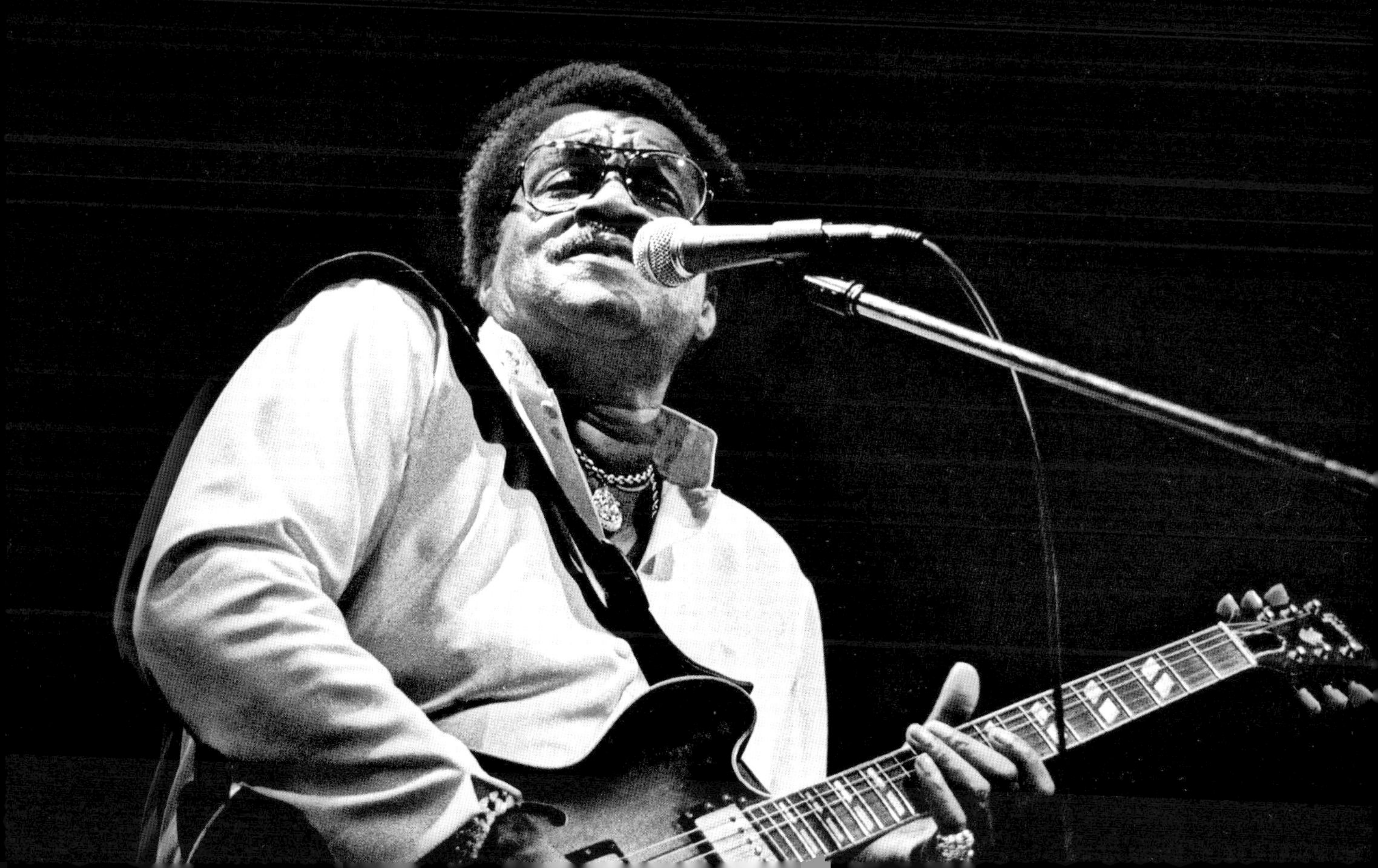

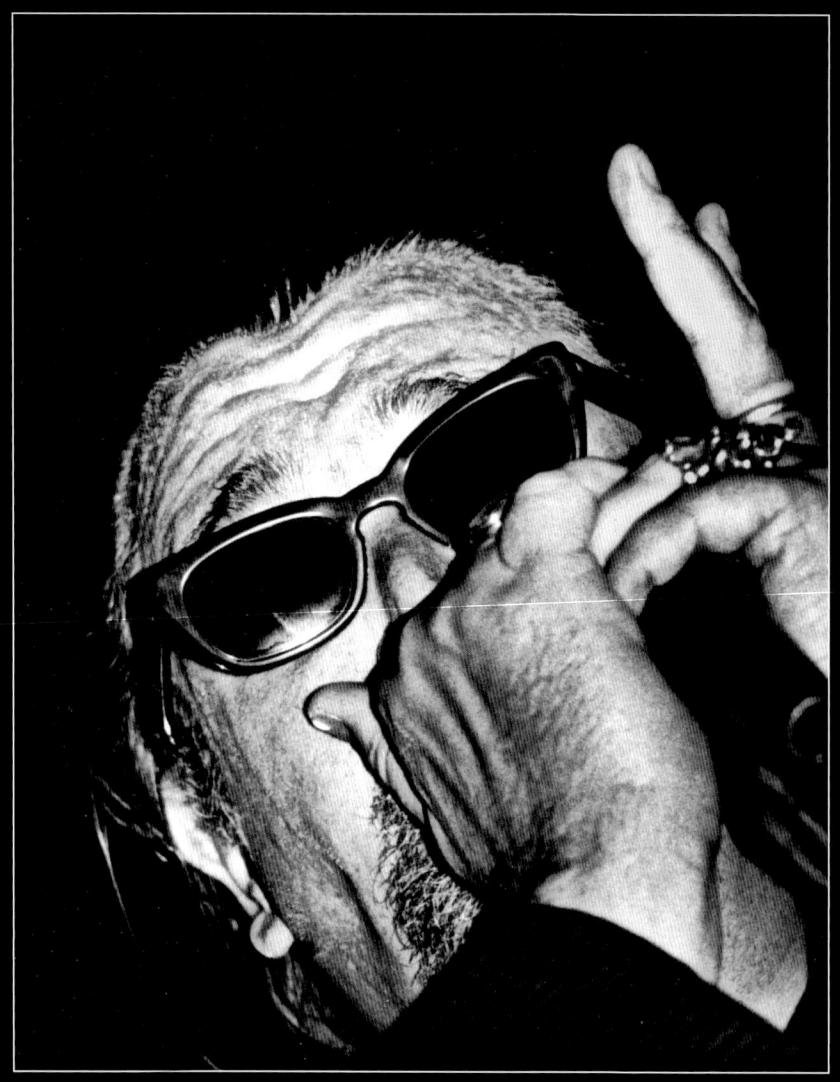

Charlie Musselwhite

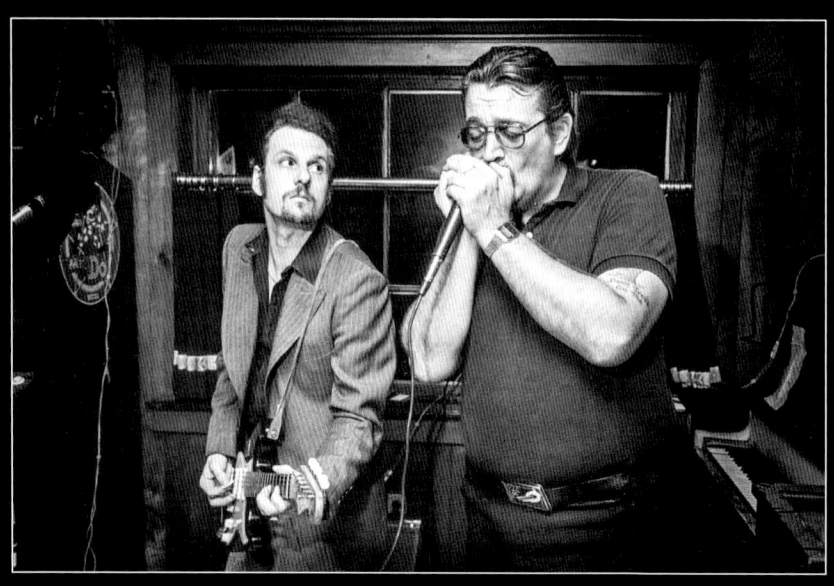

Charlie Musselwhite
and Ronnie Earl

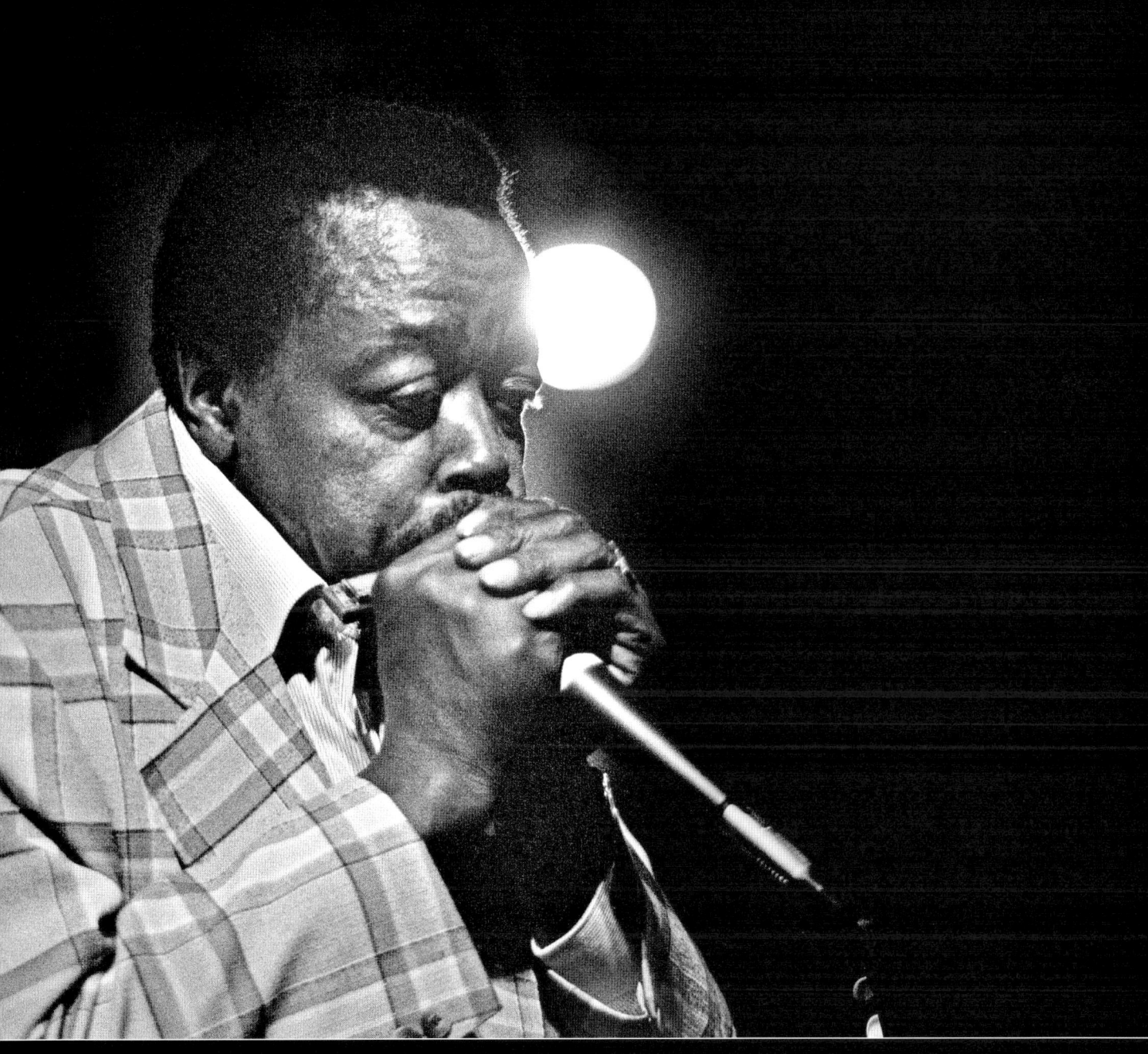

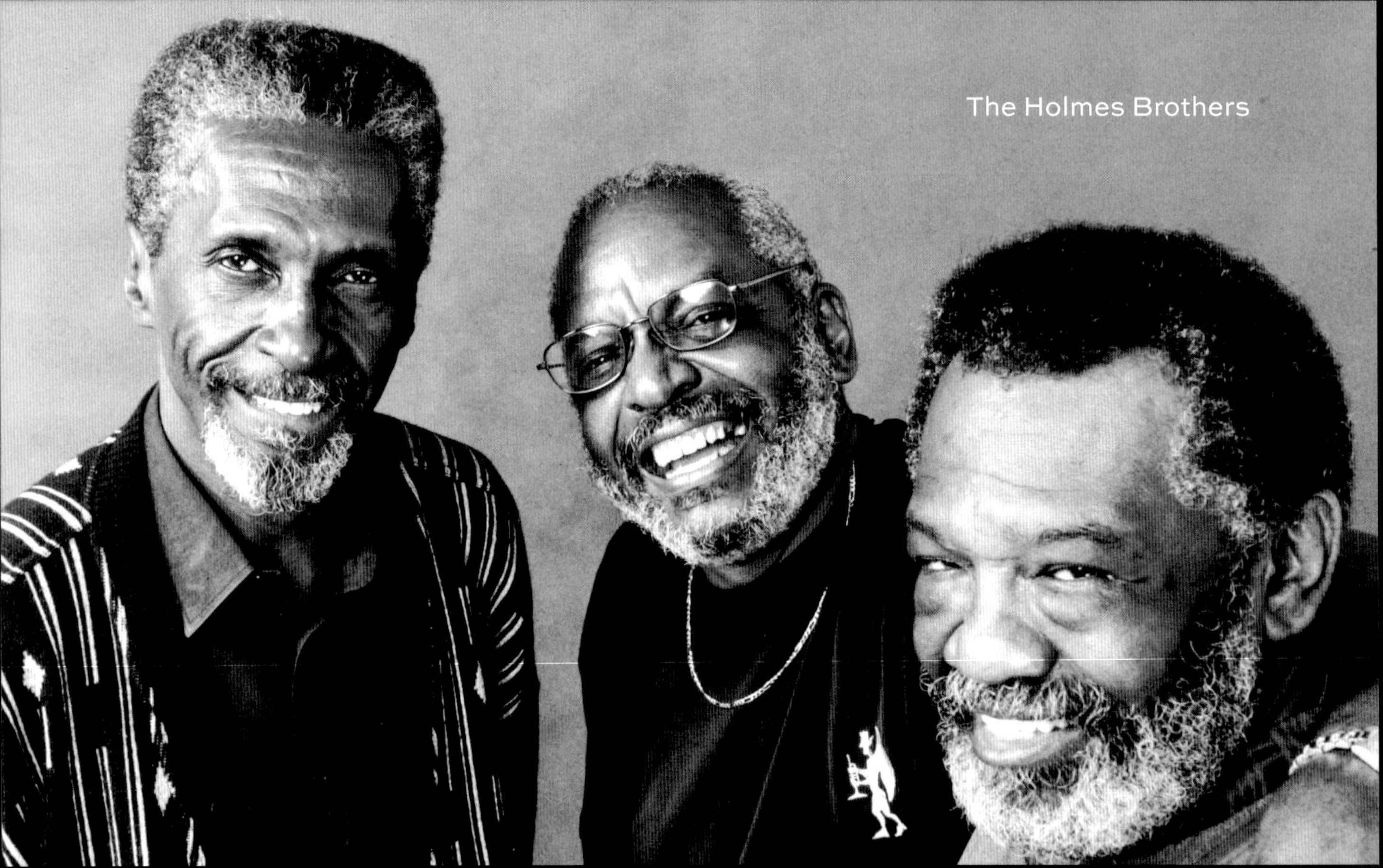

The Holmes Brothers

Hubert Sumlin

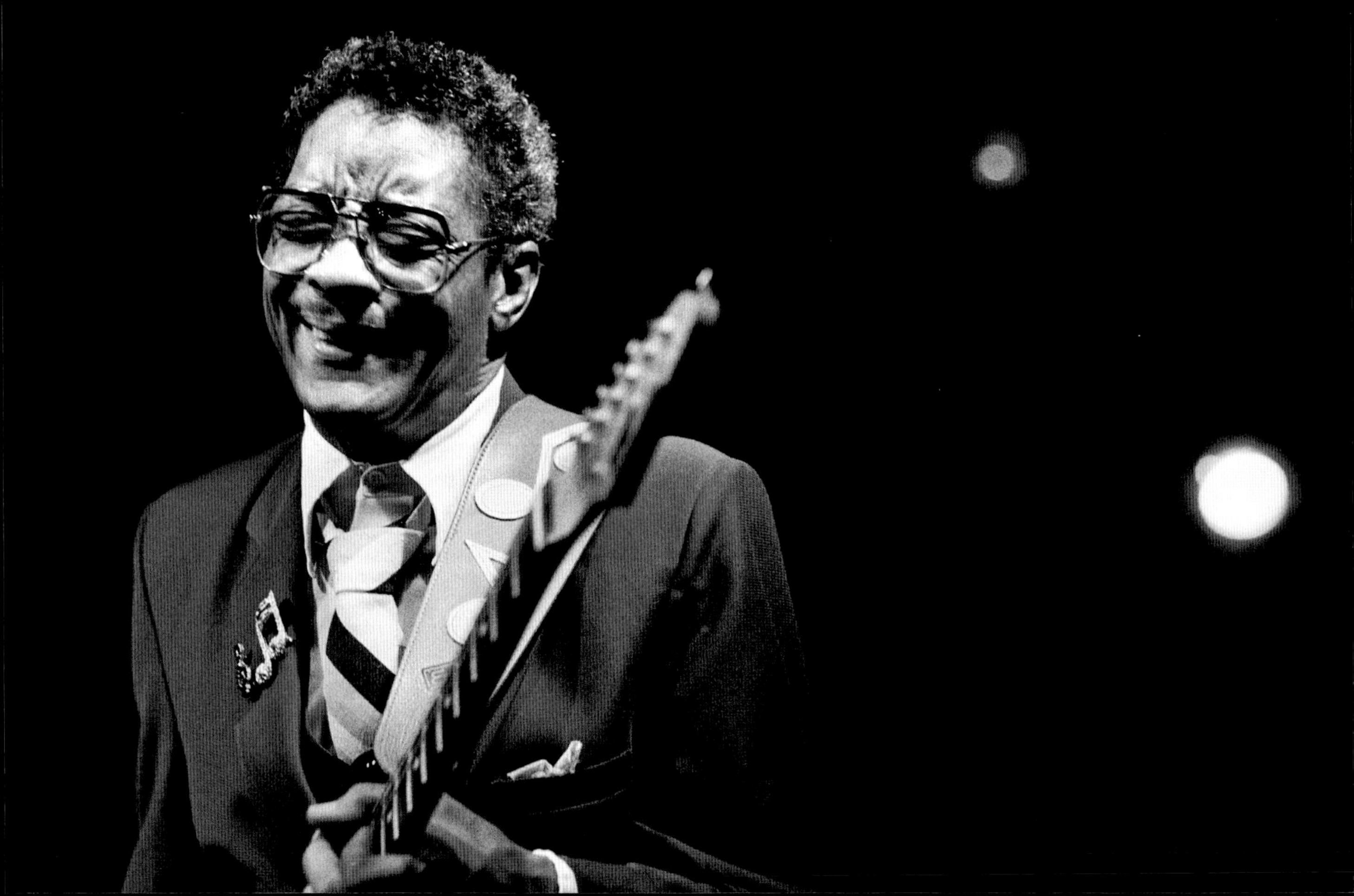

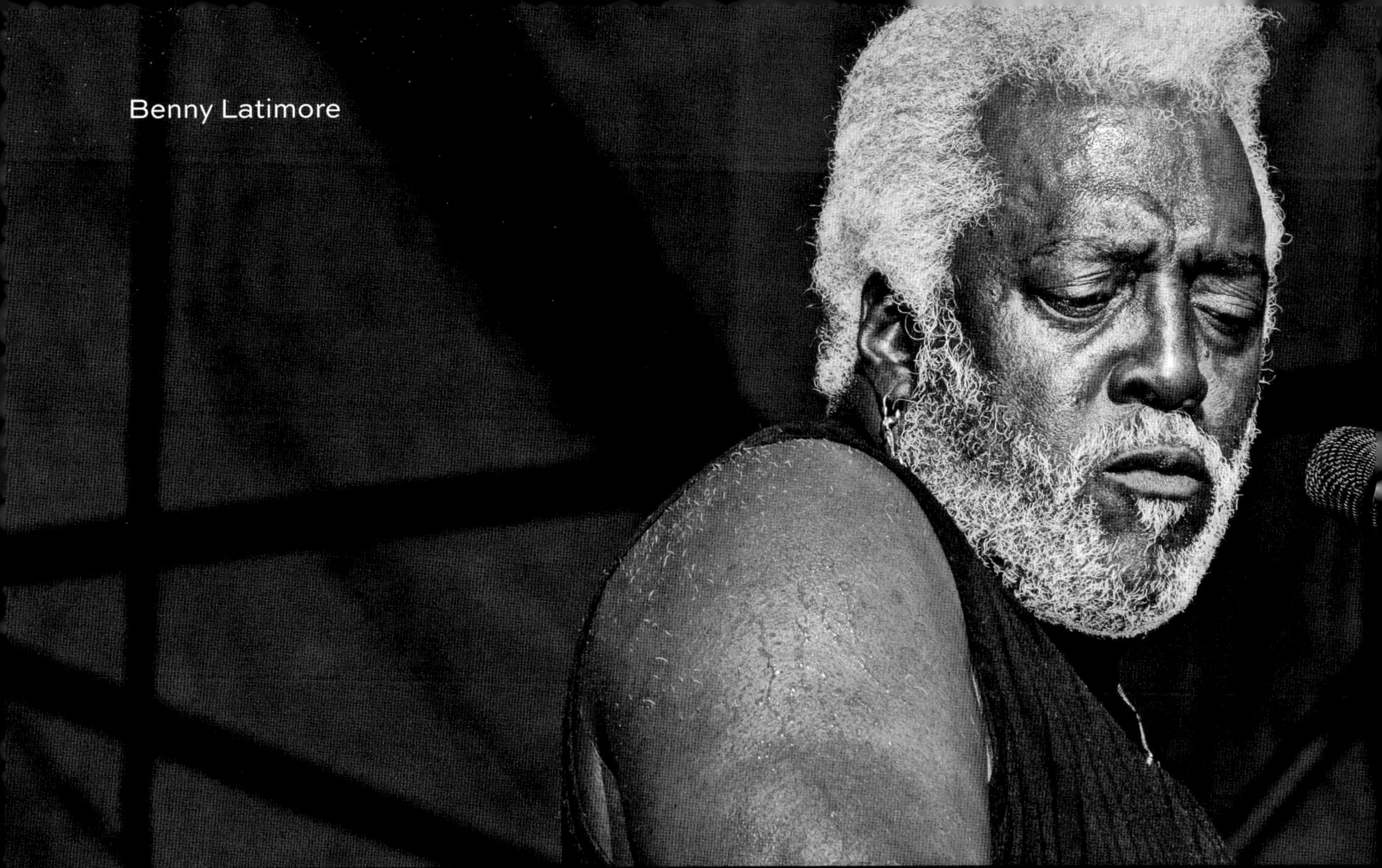

Benny Latimore

Lonnie Brooks

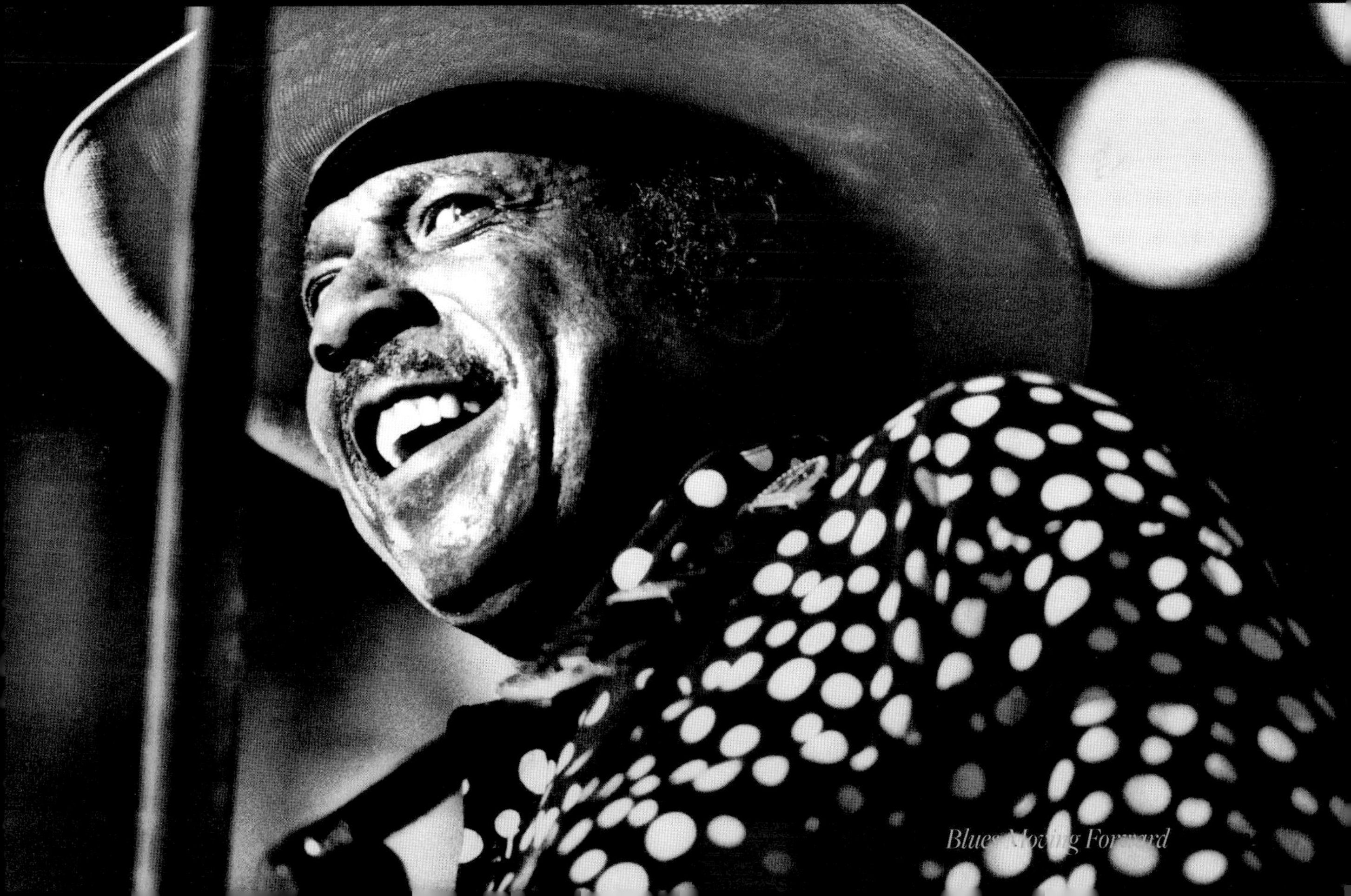

Blues Moving Forward

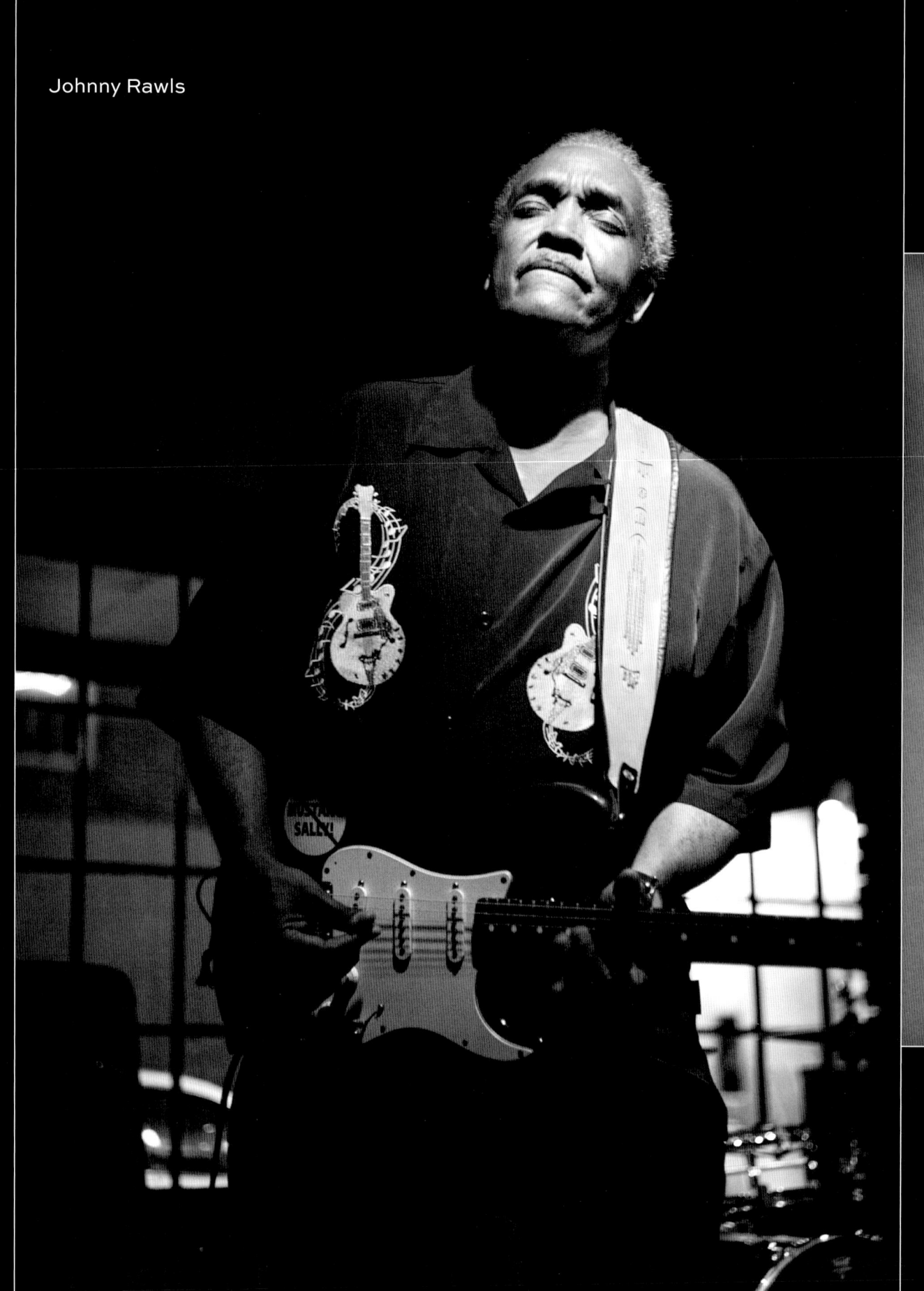

Johnny Rawls

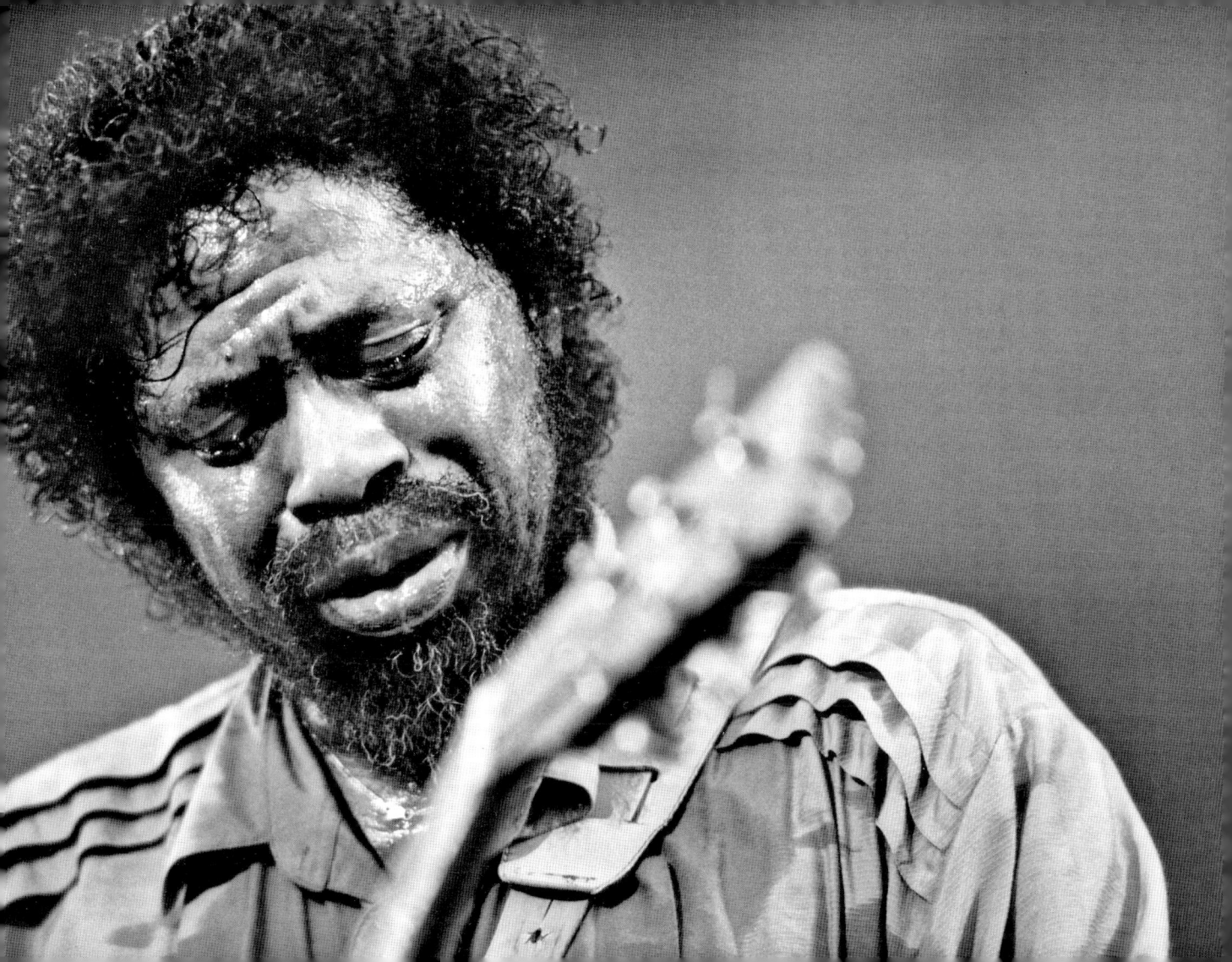

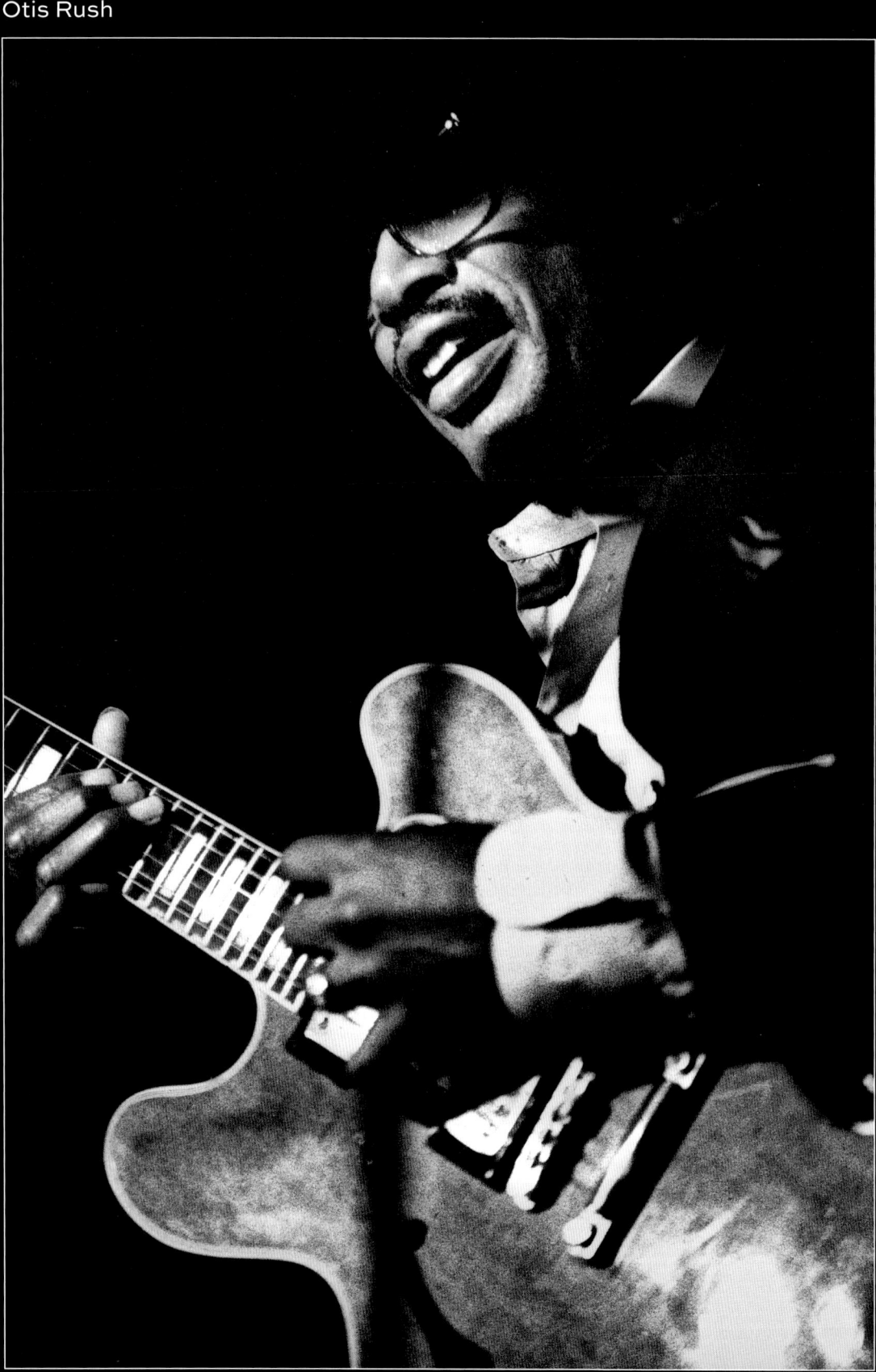

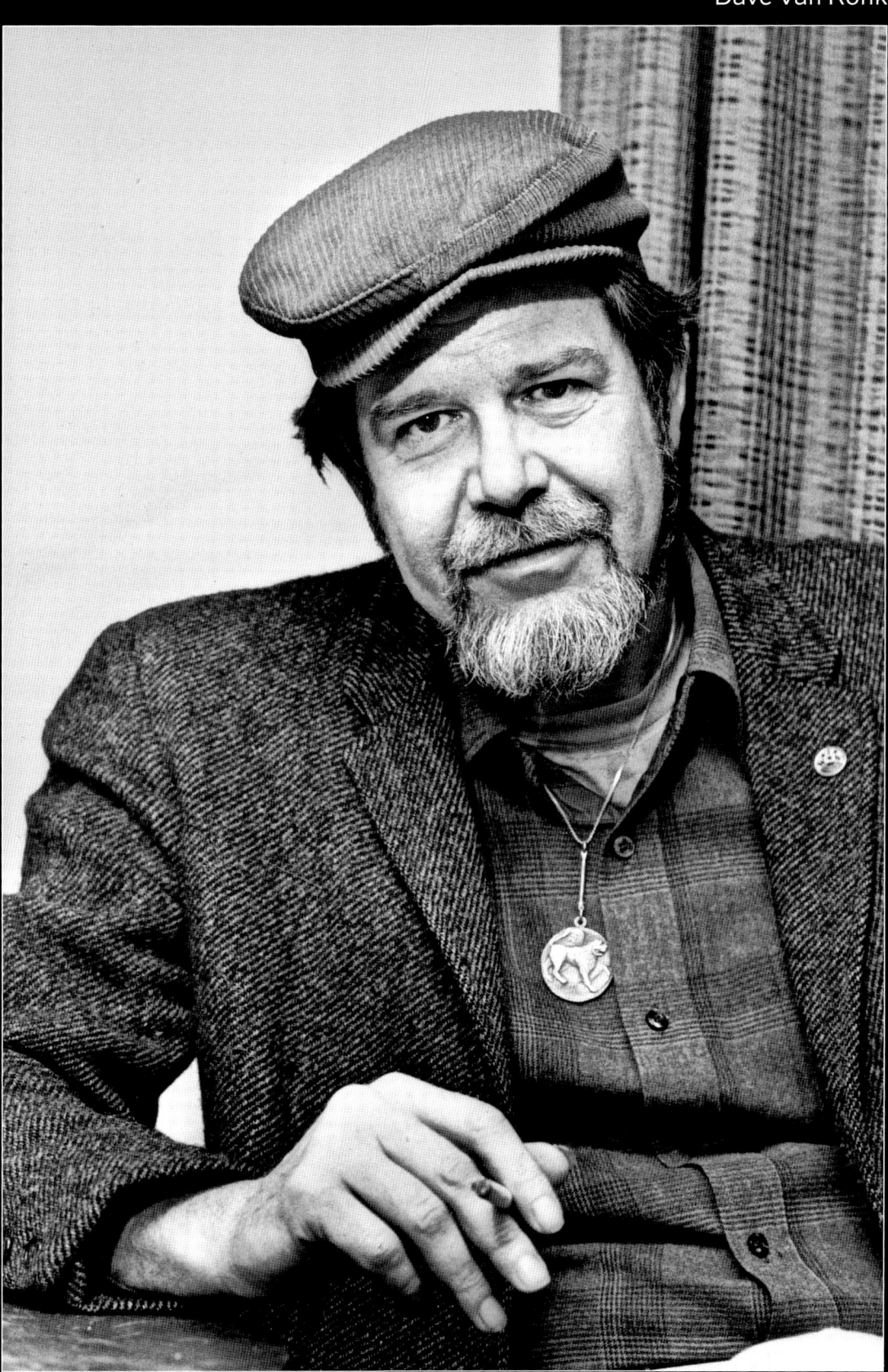

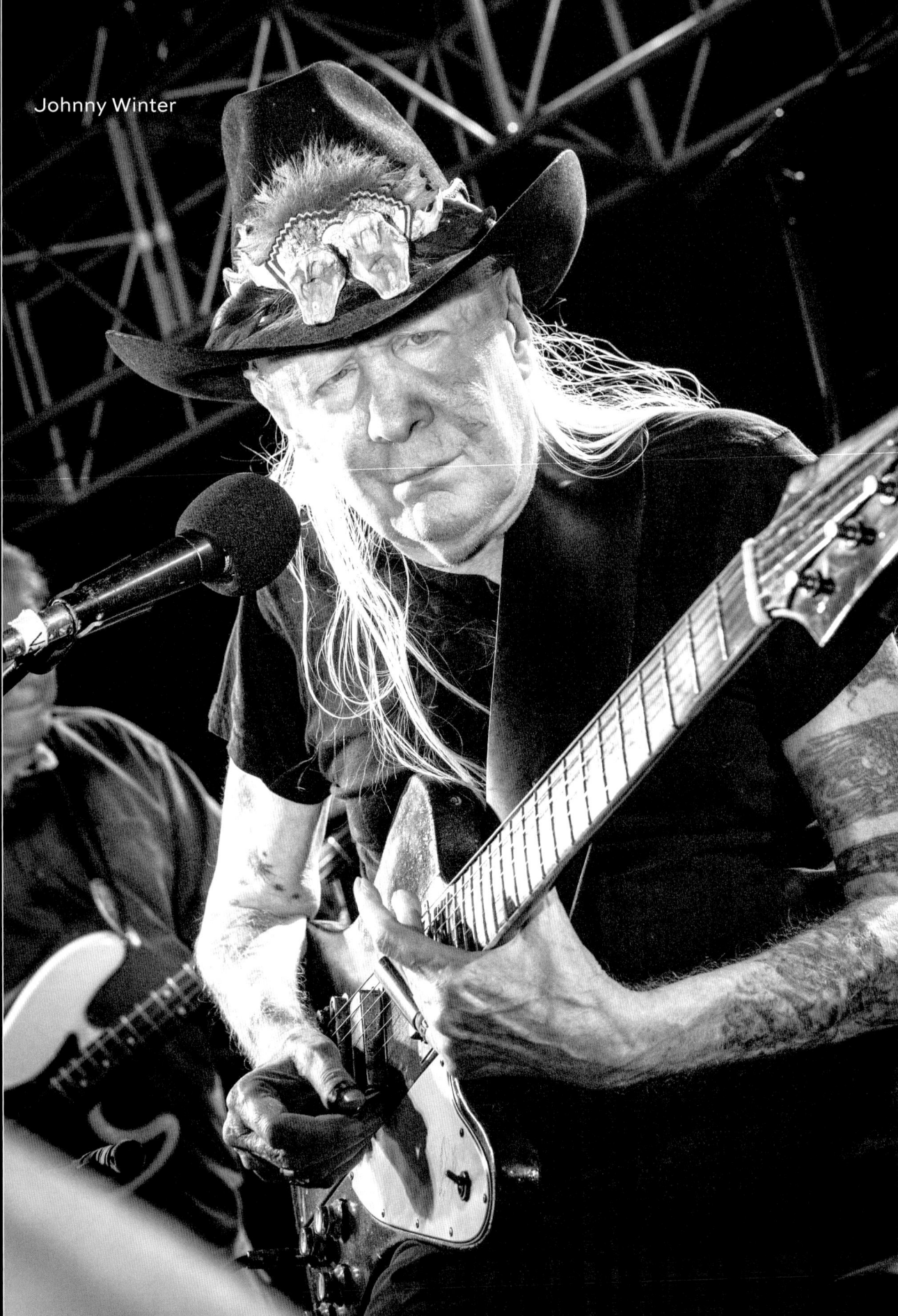

Johnny Winter

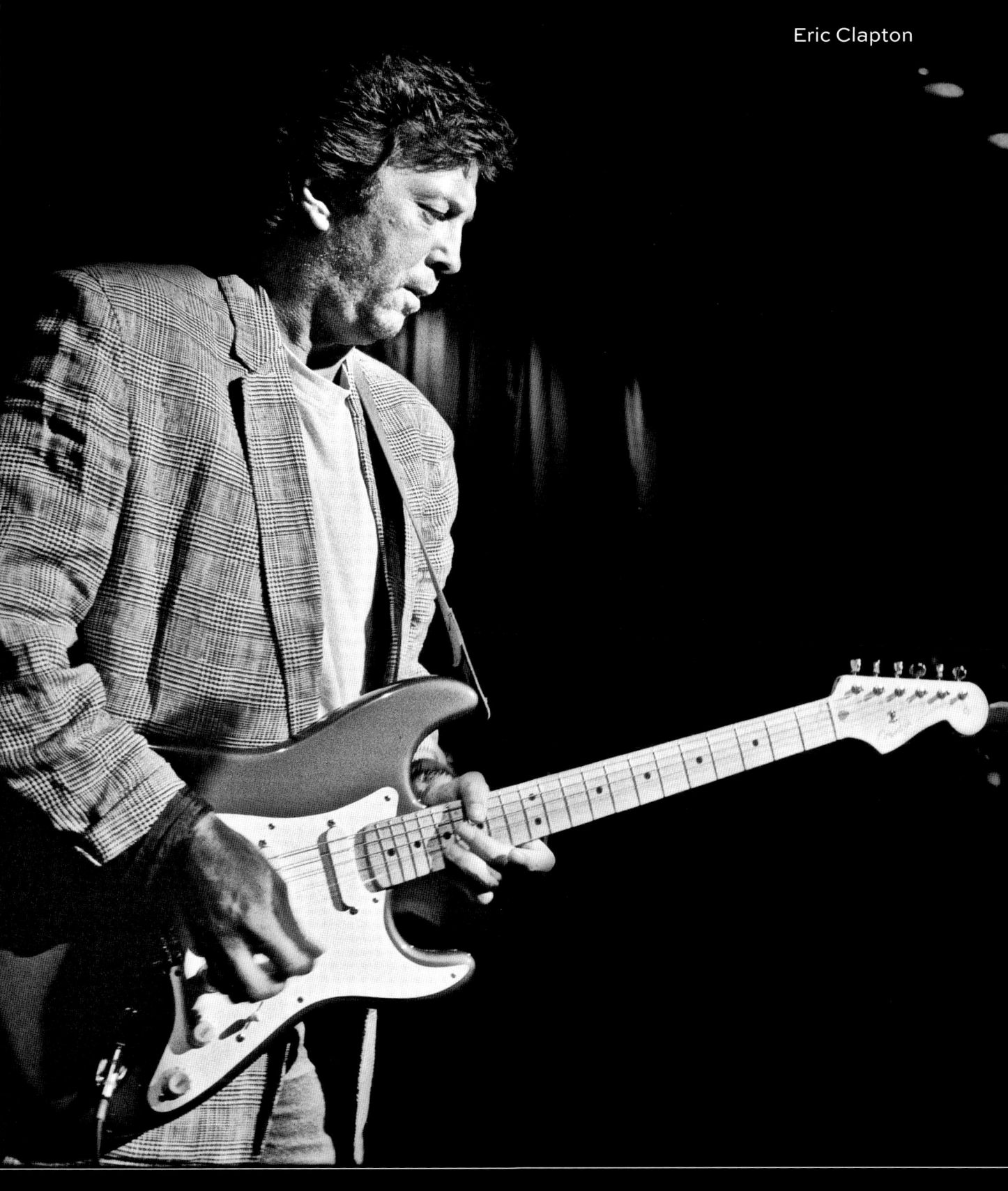

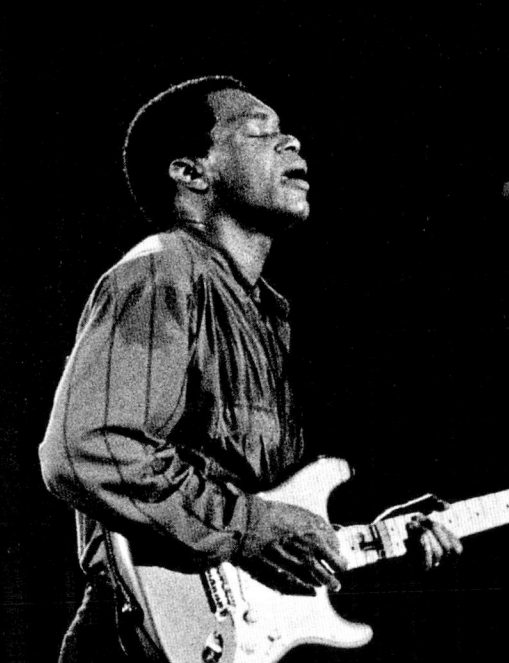

Robert Cray

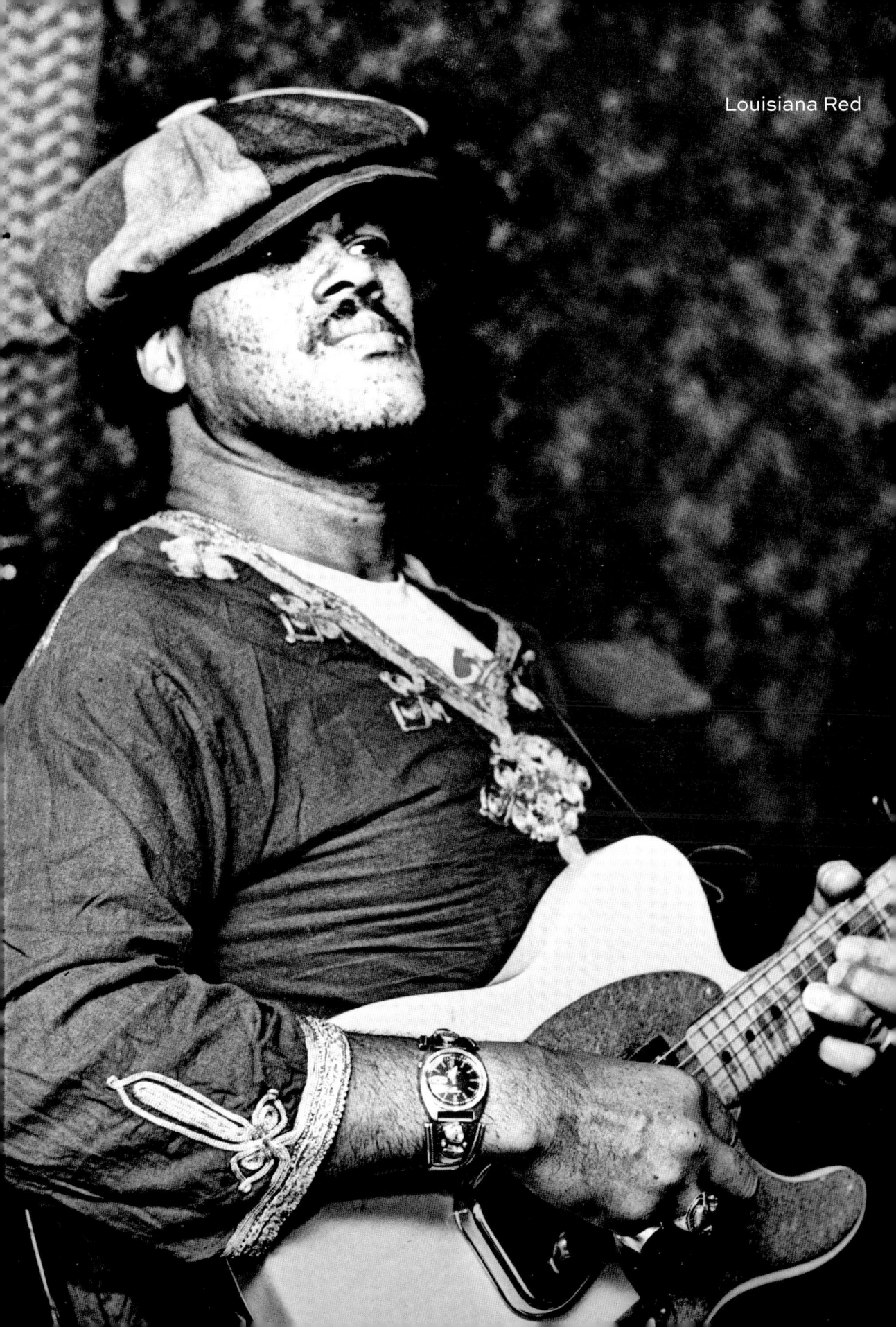

Louisiana Red

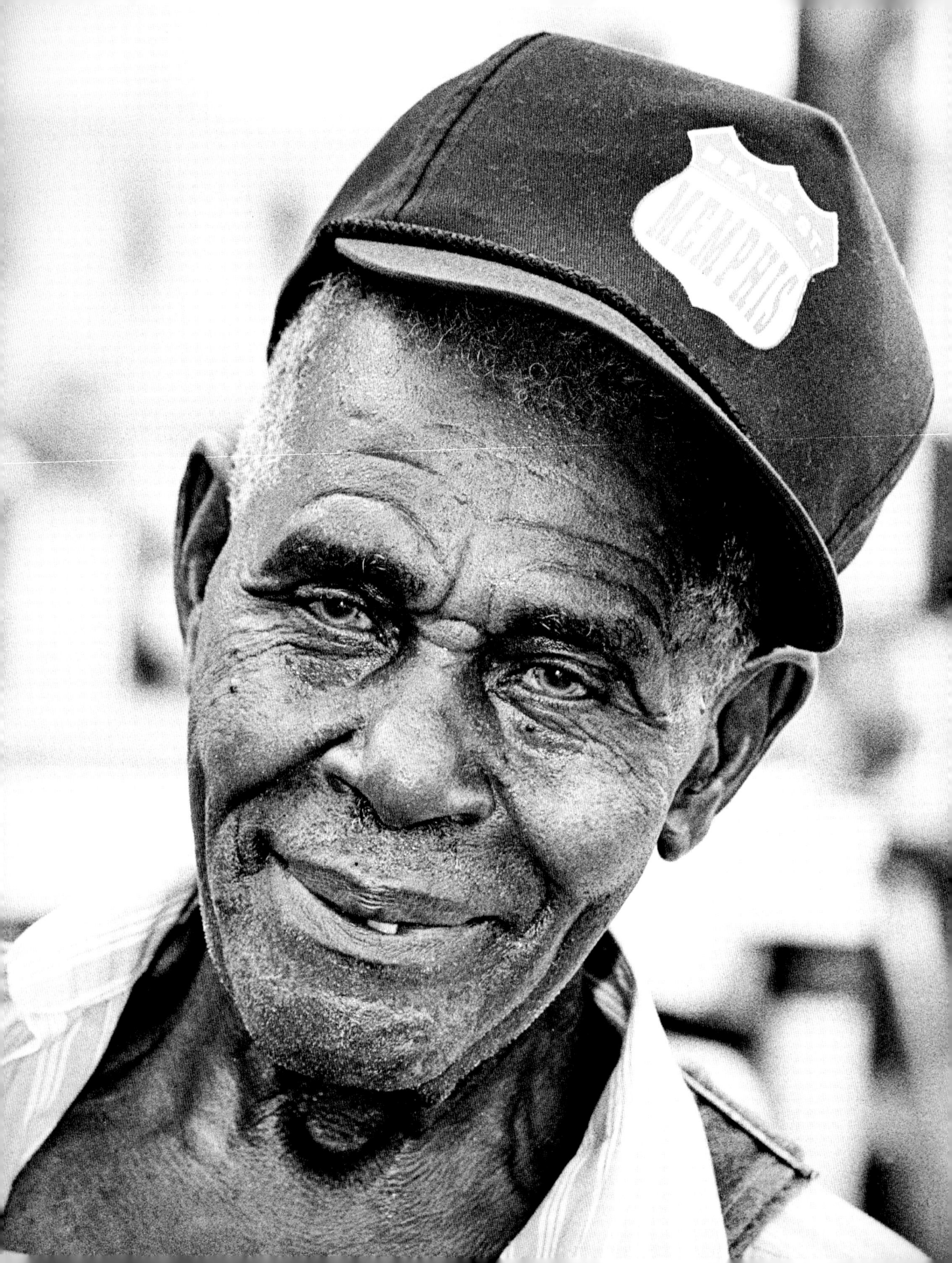

CHAPTER 7

MISSISSIPPI BLUES

There is a vibe, a frequency that you feel, when you are in Mississippi. Even if you are interacting with someone from there, you feel the spirit of the Mississippian. It resembles other spaces in the Delta, but it is unique to the soul of Mississippi alone. Like most Black culture, Mississippi is believed to be a one-trick pony or a monolithic Southern Black experience. However, contrary to that narrative, Mississippi is one of the few ground zeros of the root of many authentic Black cultures and traditions that migrated throughout the Americas. It's a culmination of the Delta and the Hill Country, flatlands lived on by agrarian-lifeway progenitors and sharecroppers to the owners of farms and bars on the Hill Country, the First Nation location mixed with African, Caribbean, Haitian, Cuban, Orisha, Black Magic, and Pentecostal worship that mirrors voodoo, hoodoo, and Sunday Baptist church, and one might say that the most-potent musicians and songwriters ever to walk the planet come from Mississippi. David Ruffin's roots began in Mississippi, Sam Cooke comes out of Mississippi, and Pops Staples, founder of the Staple Singers, not only comes out of Mississippi but comes from the camp of Rube Lacy like so many of our blues ancestors. As the food and music reflect the people, Mississippi is also ground zero to the civil rights movement, with folks such as Medgar Evers and his brother Charles. According to the Mississippi Blues Trail Marker, in 1954, Charles Evers was one of the first African American deejays in Mississippi. He became a conduit for social change via voting and introduced many blues musicians, who later became legendary household names, to the masses.

When thinking of the song "Mississippi Goddam" by Nina Simone, I am reminded of the blatant racialized bigotry and segregation inflicted on Black Americans. However, those experiences birthed a resilience that is found in the blues. Ownership and straightforward lyrics are the essence of the Bentonia blues legend Jimmy "Duck" Holmes. Holmes, the owner of the Blue Front Café (a business started by his parents), runs what is known to be the last official juke joint in America, and he is a practitioner of the family tree of traditional Bentonia blues created by Henry "Son" Stuckey. Another Mississippi blues man who has deeply rooted lineage in the culture, tradition, and practice is L. C. (Lester Chester) Ulmer, who was a Mississippi blues man from a generation of traditional Black musicians and the life of a large family working the plantation. Is that the only narrative that makes Black blues authentic? Absolutely not! However, it is a piece of African American blues history that keeps the story of the blues honest rather than perpetuating the nostalgia of traditional practice and the space in which it was experienced. If you ask any old-timer or member of the younger generation still connected to the tradition of blues, they will tell you that hard work is a major fact and component of the Mississippi Delta culture, and that component is evident in the expression and performance of the blues. The great Lil Joe Ayers shared with me about the years he plowed the mule. Terry "Harmonica" Bean shared the history of hard work in his family. Vencie Varnado also told me stories of his work, all solidifying the notion that the blues, Mississippi, and hard work are inextricably linked.

Othar Turner

Cedell Davis, from Arkansas, who used a knife for a guitar slide, established another aspect to the story of Mississippi blues, since his mother was known to be a faith healer and, according to legend, considered blues to be devil music. Spirituality, God, the devil, and folk beliefs play huge roles in the blues and Southern Black culture. Listeners of the music can hear many singers wail about mojo hands and different dusts that would put spells on either unsuspecting love interests or harsh overseers. The story of Tommy Johnson, Robert Johnson, and many others going to the crossroads and making a deal with the devil is a reconstructed story that originated with entities such as Poppa Legba, Esu, Anansi, Aunt Nancy, and other Orisha, Ifa, and Voodun spirits venerated through praise and worship. From the Pentecostal church to the praise dance of Bush Harbor (also known as Hush Harbor or Brush Harbor), the supernatural has been a large part of the blues people and their musical practice. Blues are sacred, and the traditions that accompany blues are as well. We honor our legends, such as Big George Brock, Frank Frost, and R. L. Boyce. We remember Willie Foster, R. L. Burnside, and the legacy of the Burnside and Kimbrough families, who keep the music and culture alive. The tough T-Model Ford, who was described as playing North Mississippi Hill Country blues, is the representation of everything Mississippi. And as we remember and celebrate the people, space, and region of the blues, let us also appreciate those who take time to capture blues moments, the images that carry the story of the blues forward, and the photographs that solidify what we call the "Blues Face." The Blues Face is the performer's expression when either hitting a note vocally or instrumentally that resonates in and through their soul. The blues, baby! Mississippi blues . . . it is live and real!

LAMONT JACK PEARLY
Folklorist, author, disc jockey, ethnographer,
African American traditional music
historian and practitioner

George Brock

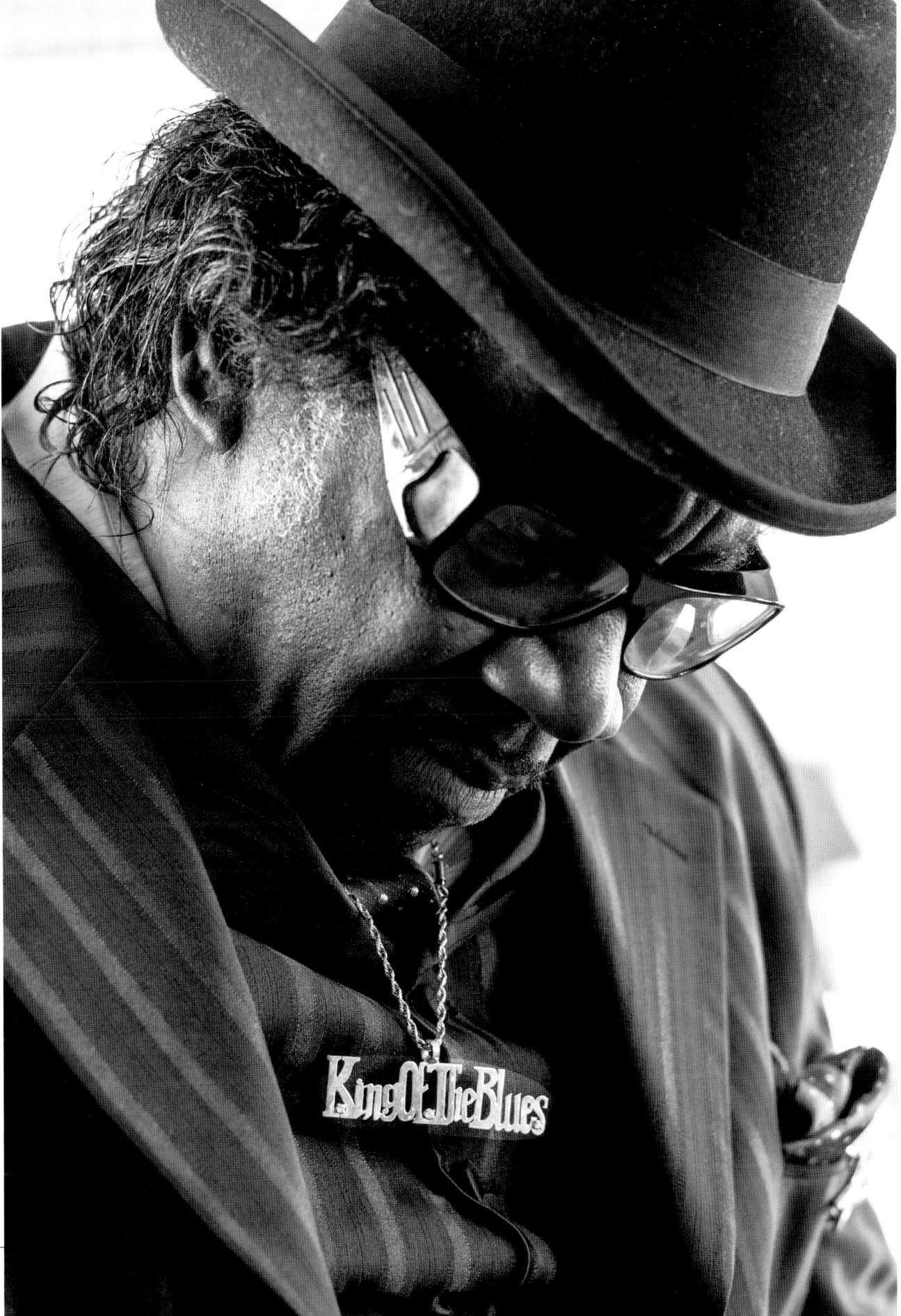

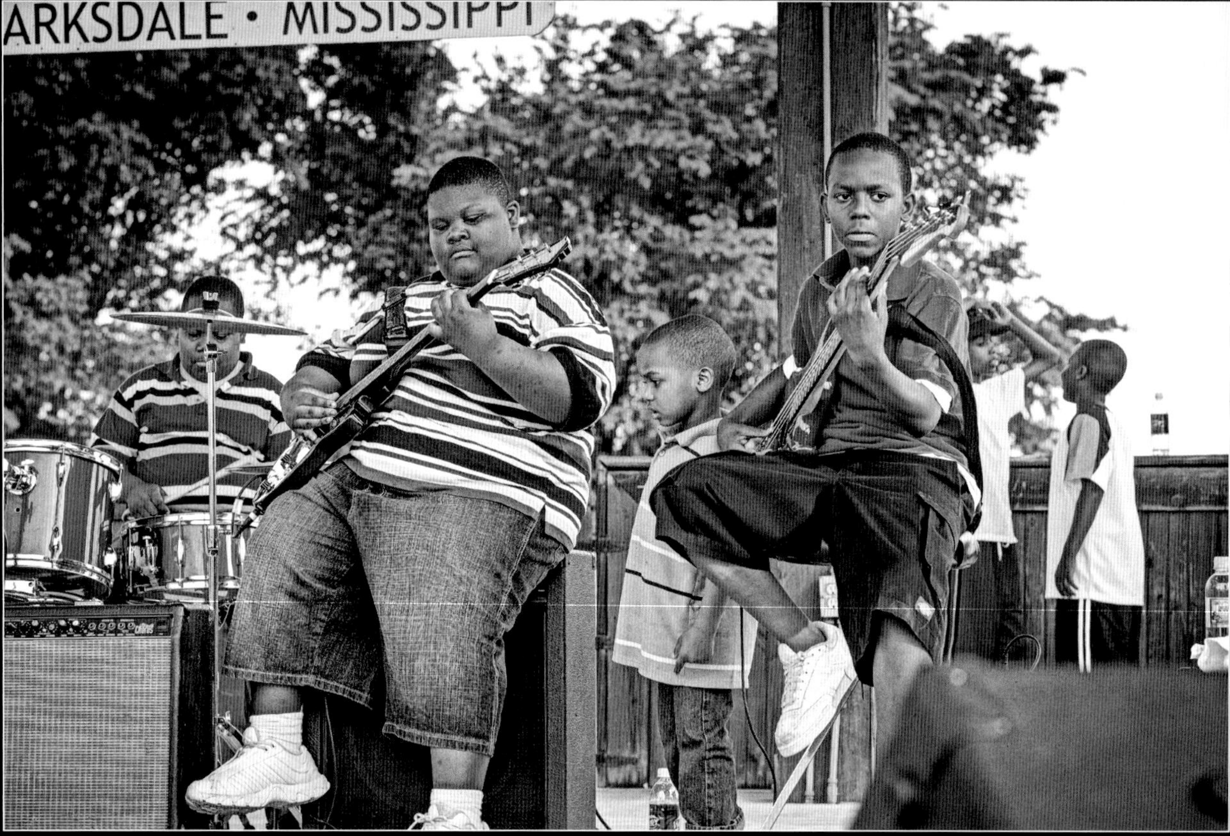

Christone "Kingfish" Ingram

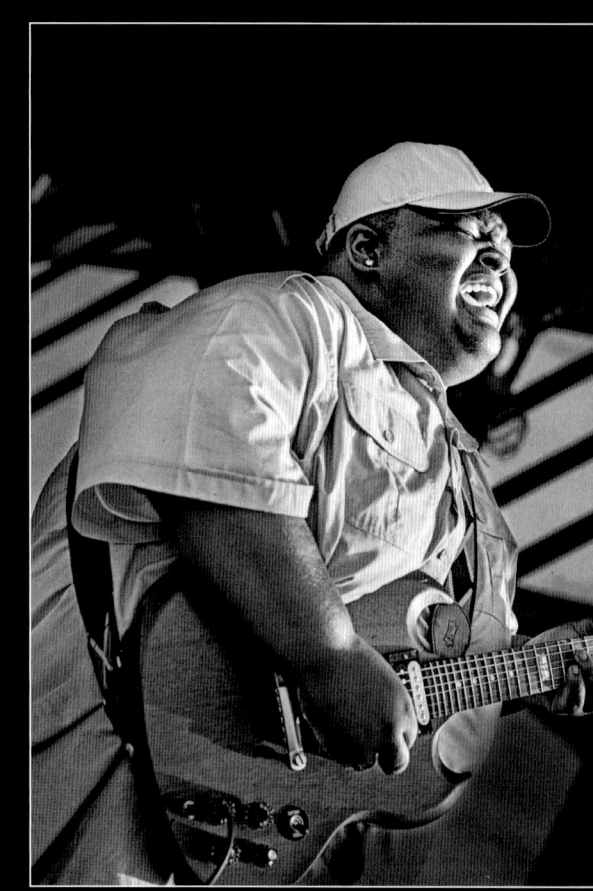

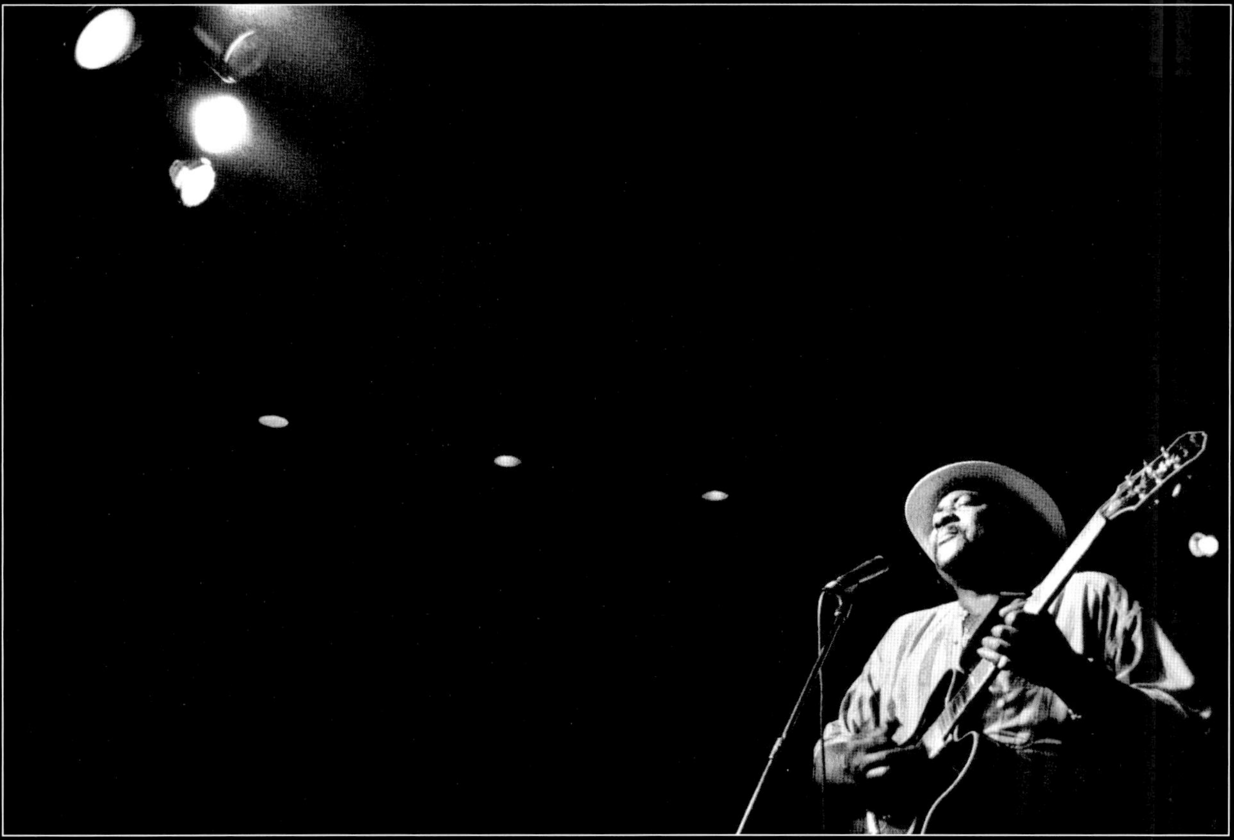

Big Jack Johnson

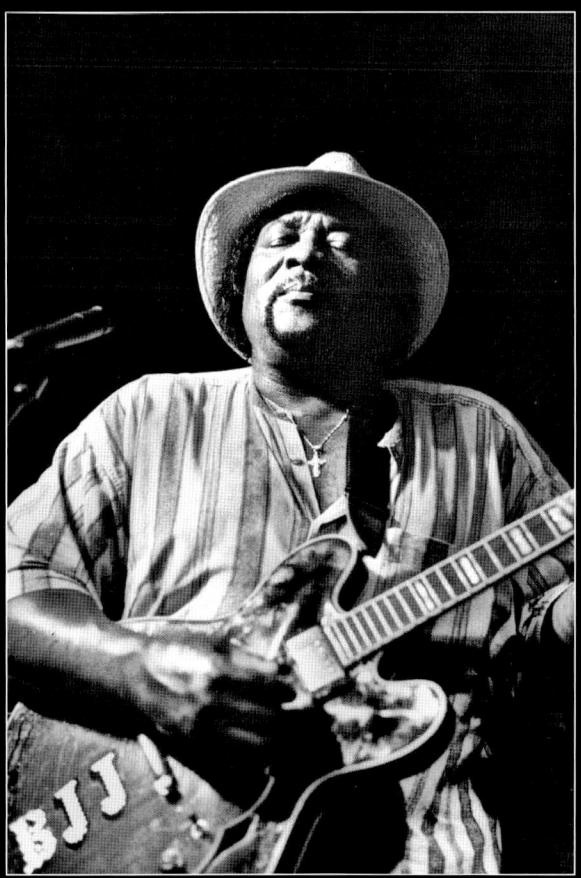

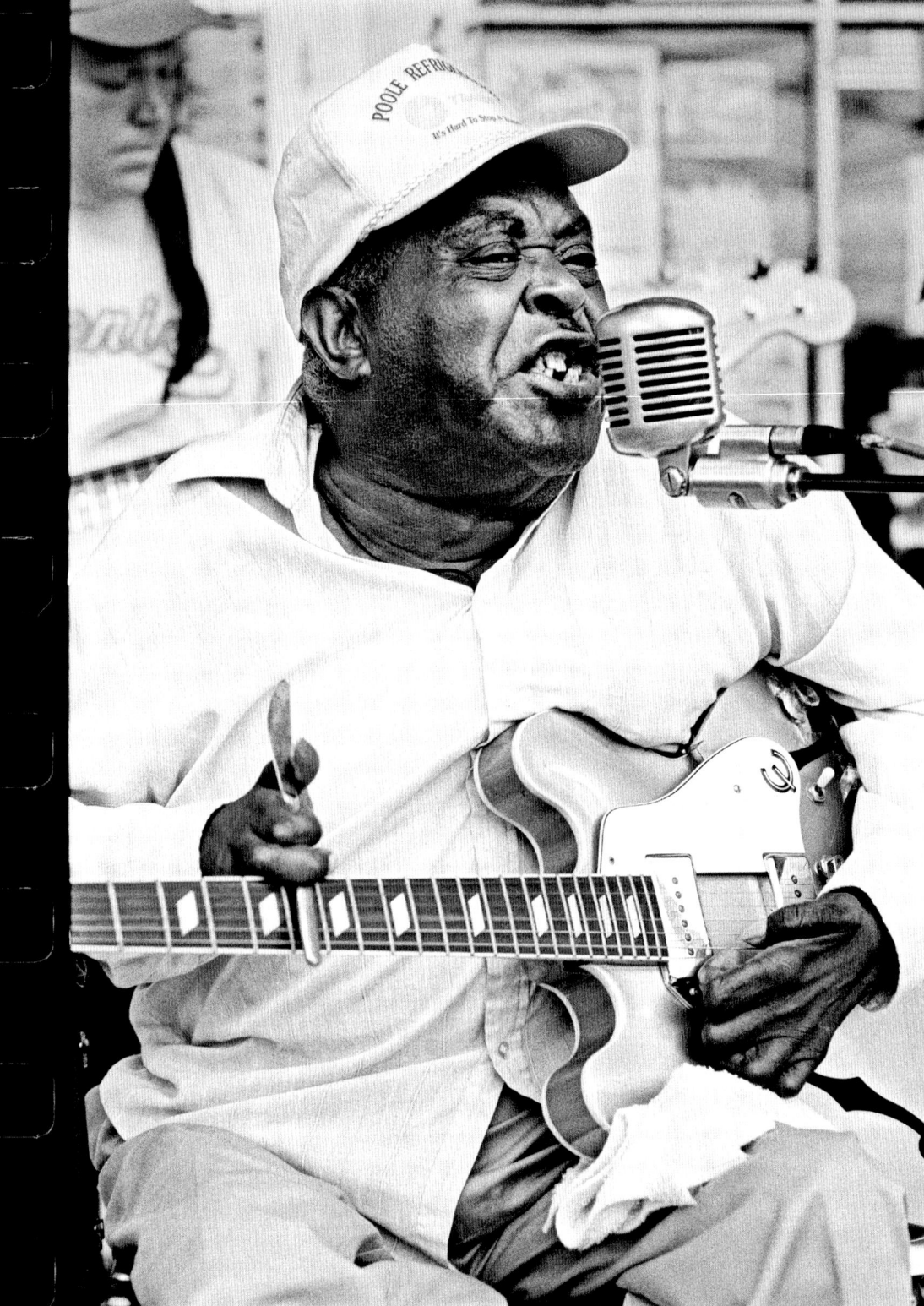

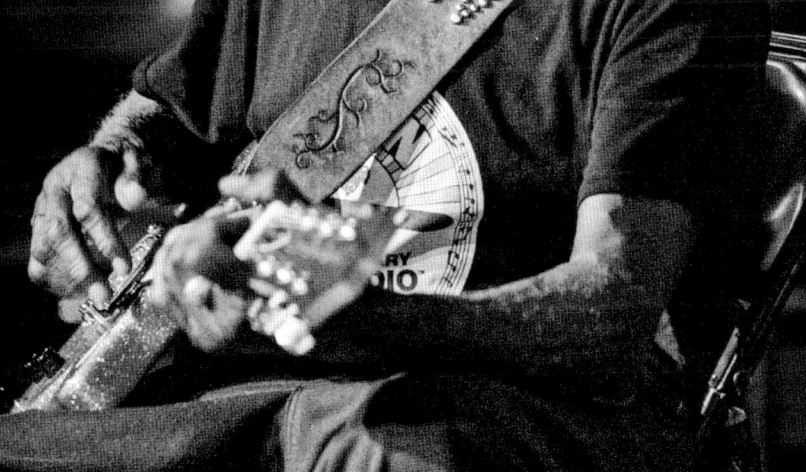

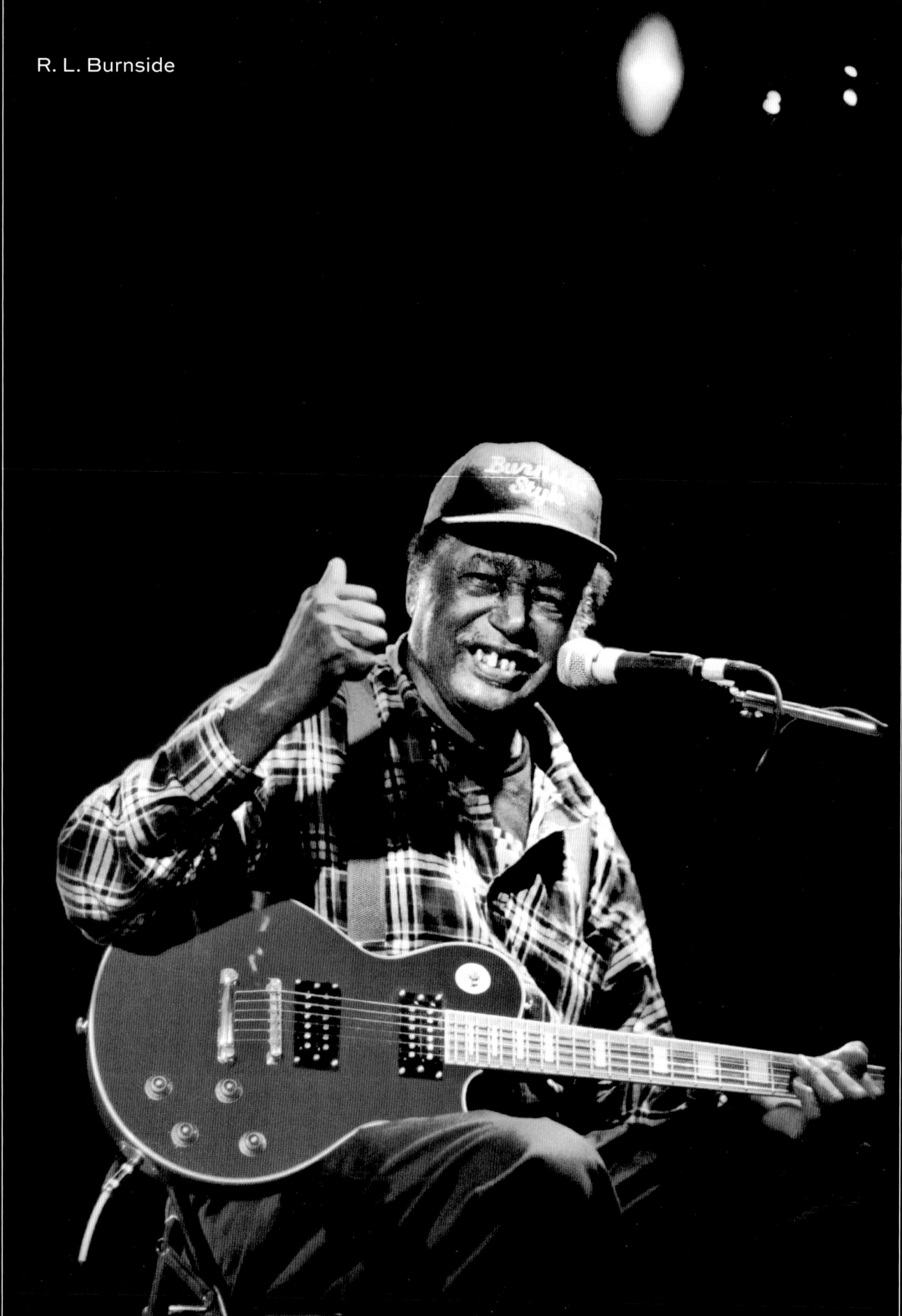

R. L. Burnside

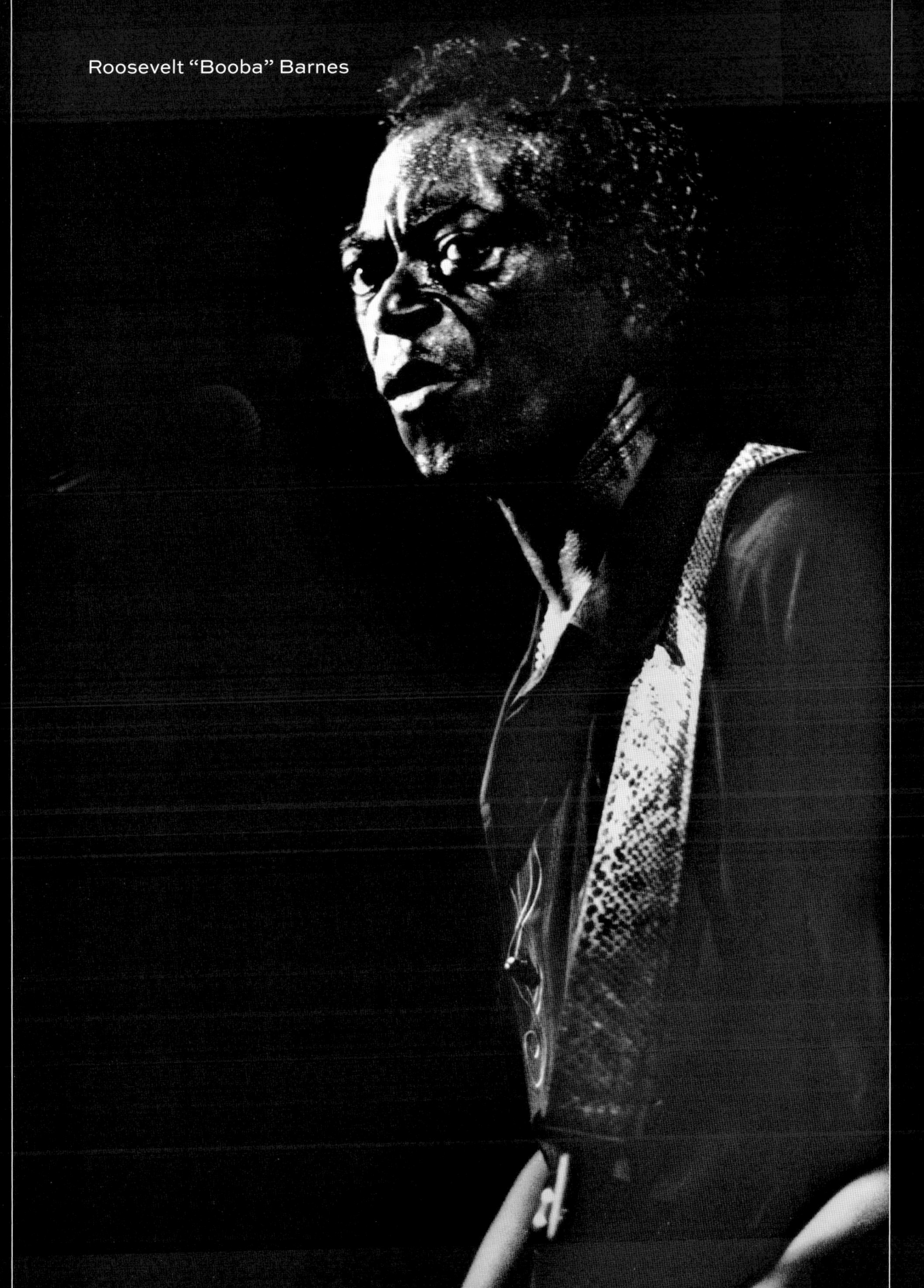

Roosevelt "Booba" Barnes

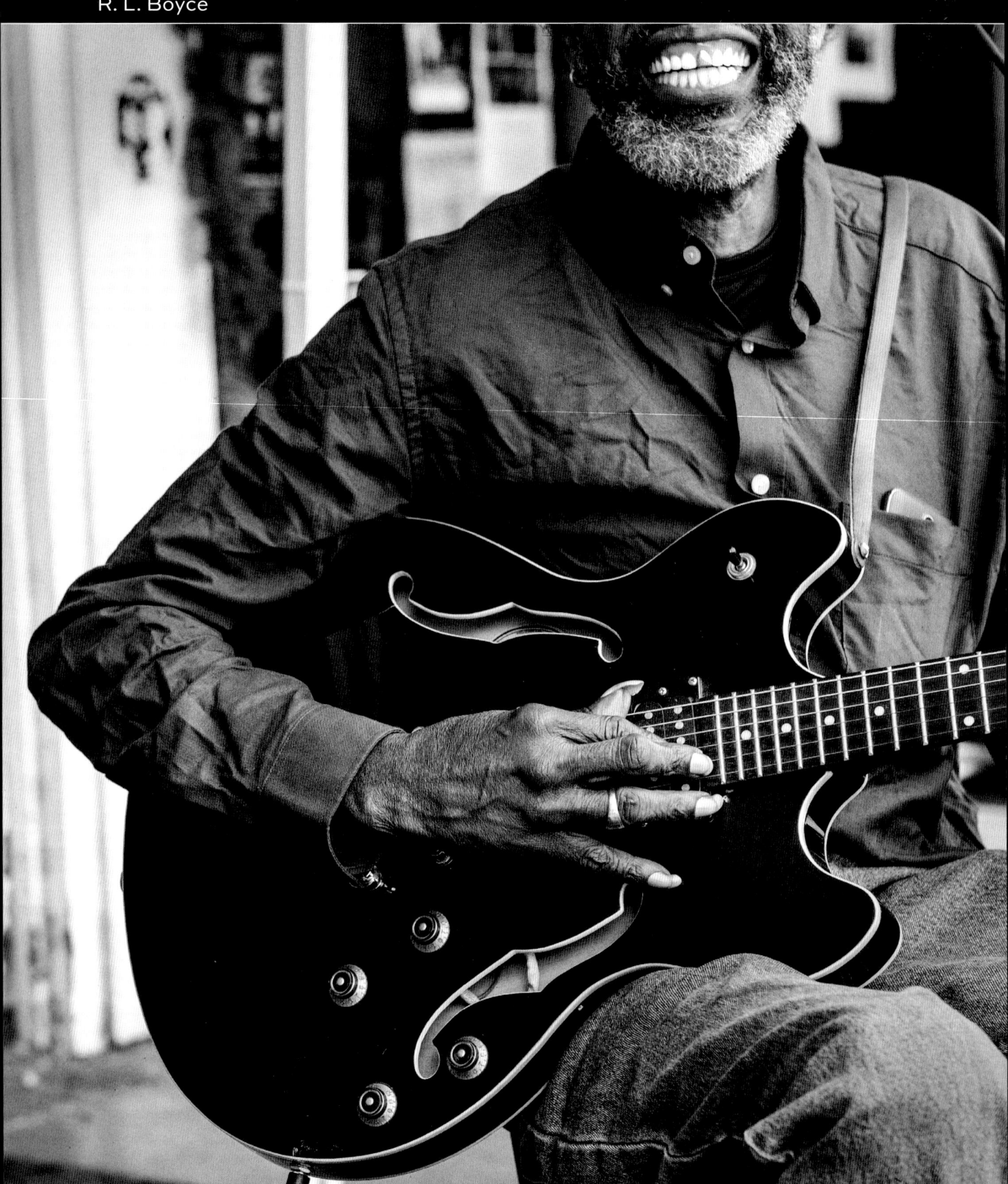

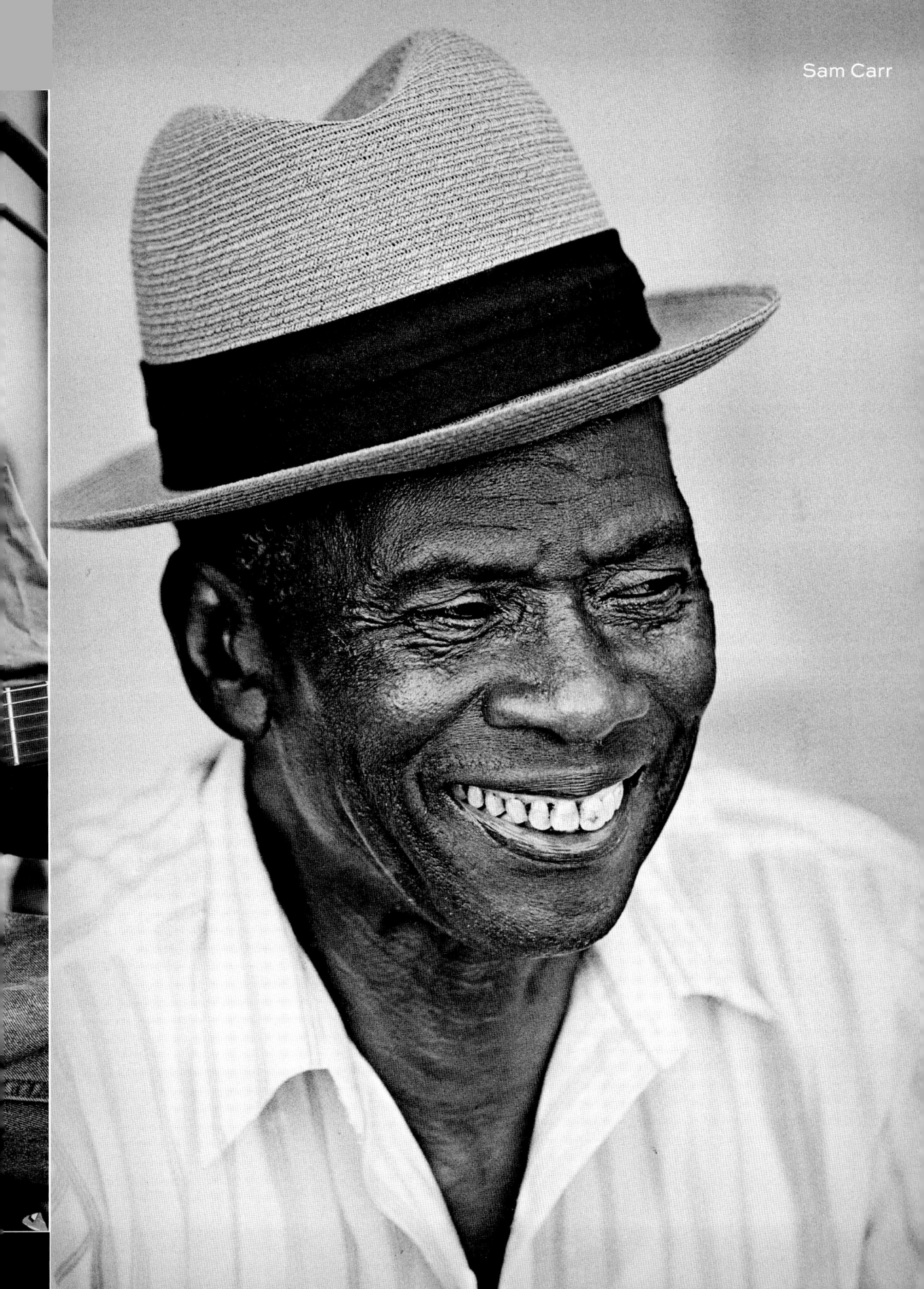

Sam Carr

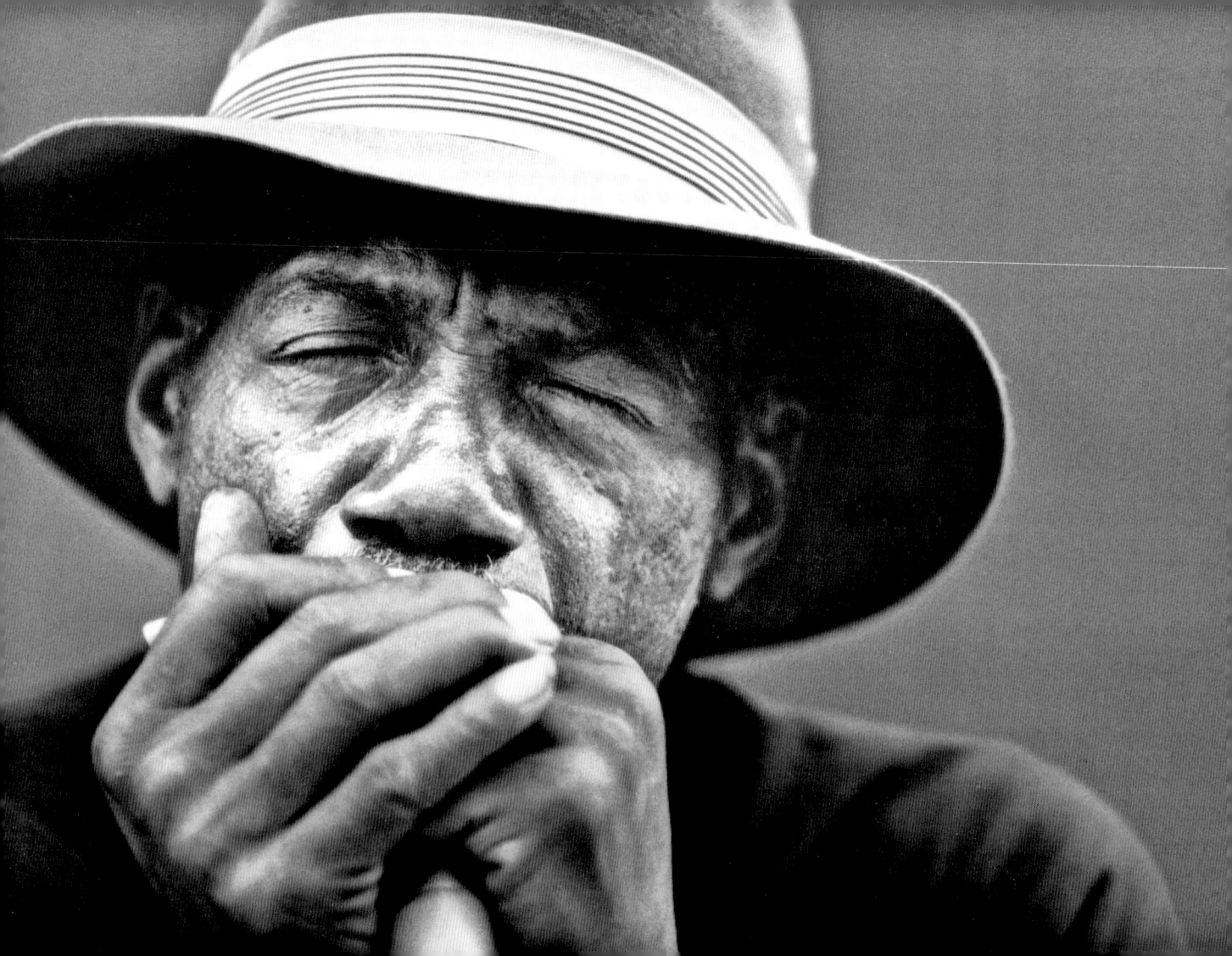

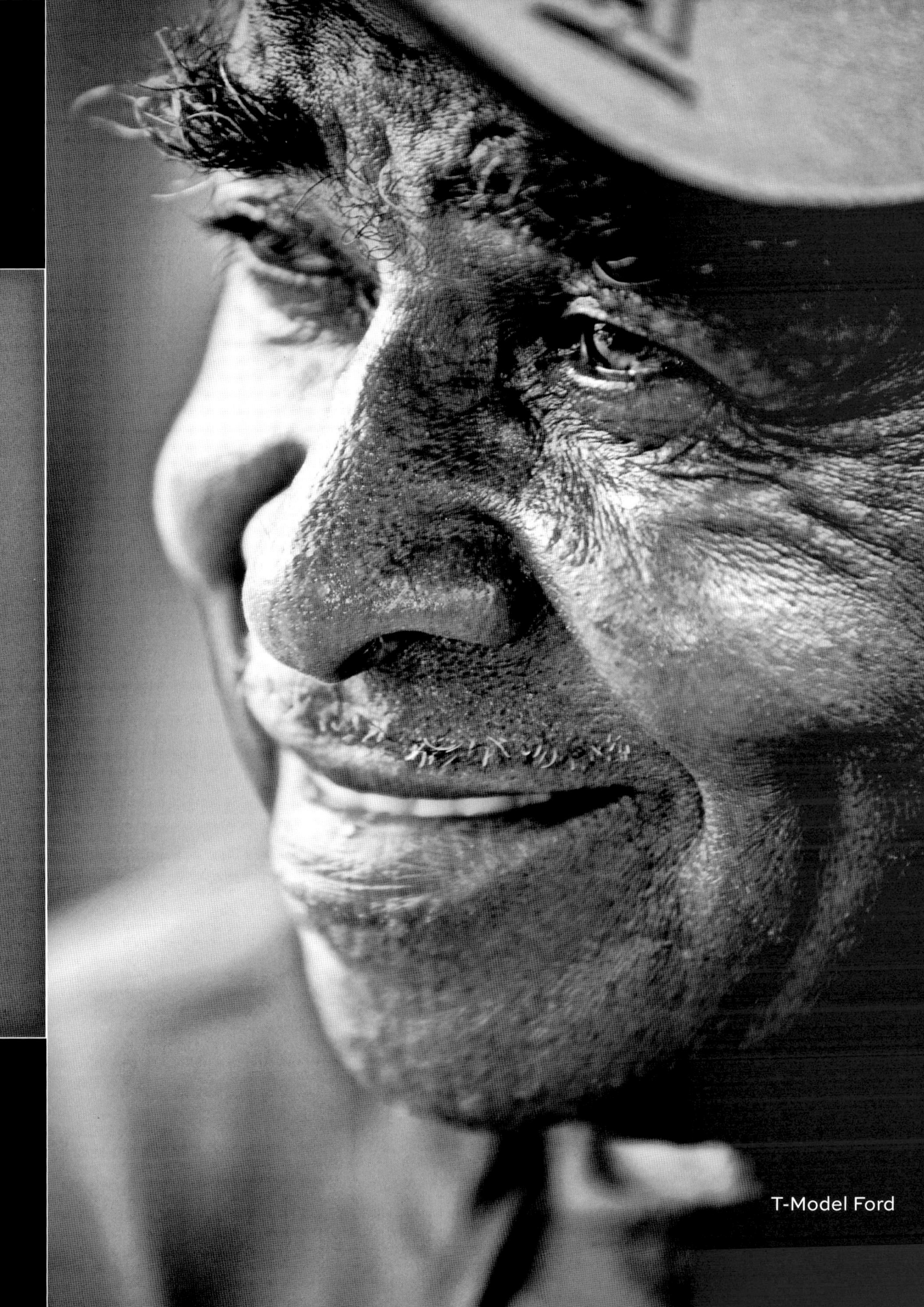

T-Model Ford

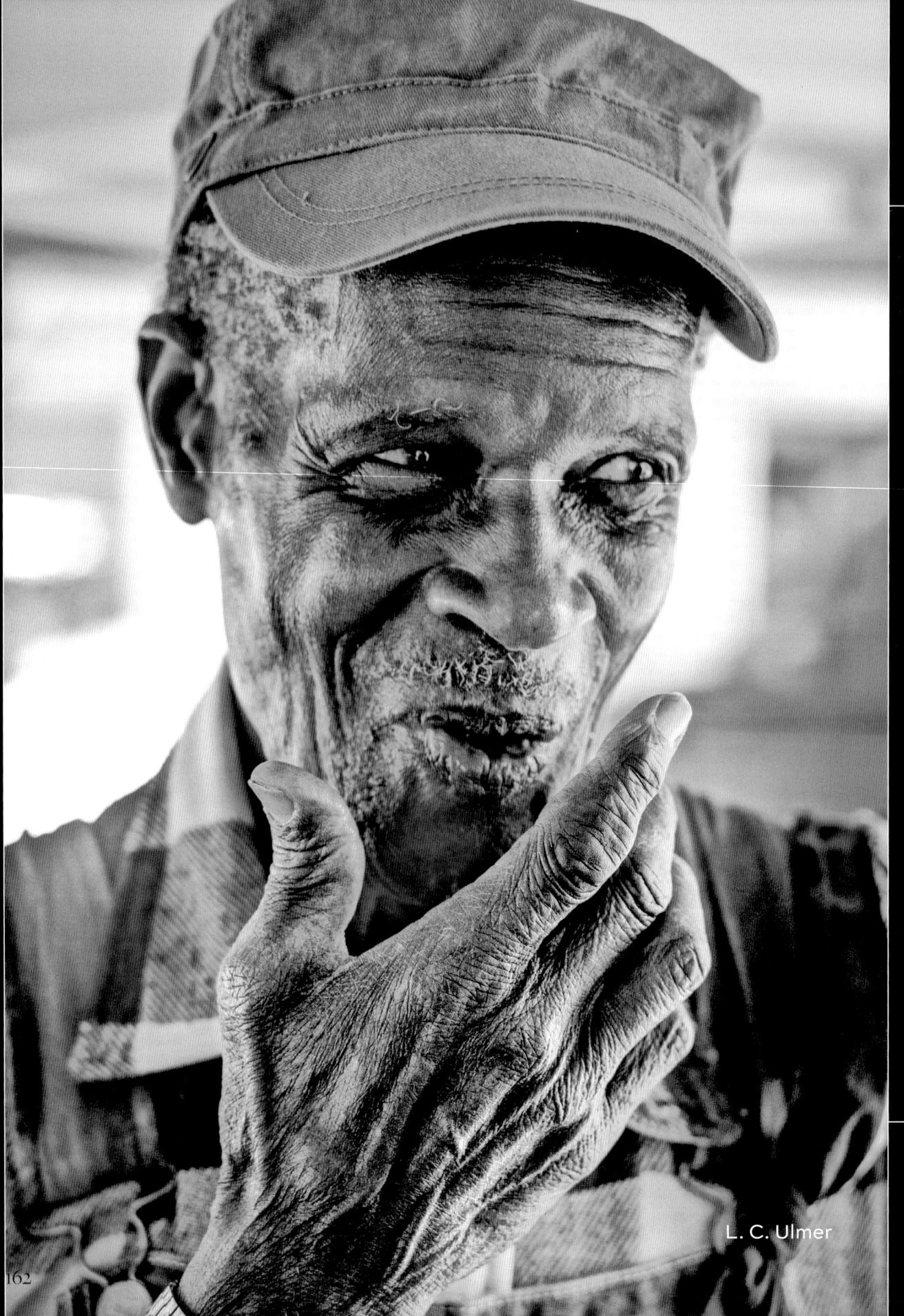

L. C. Ulmer

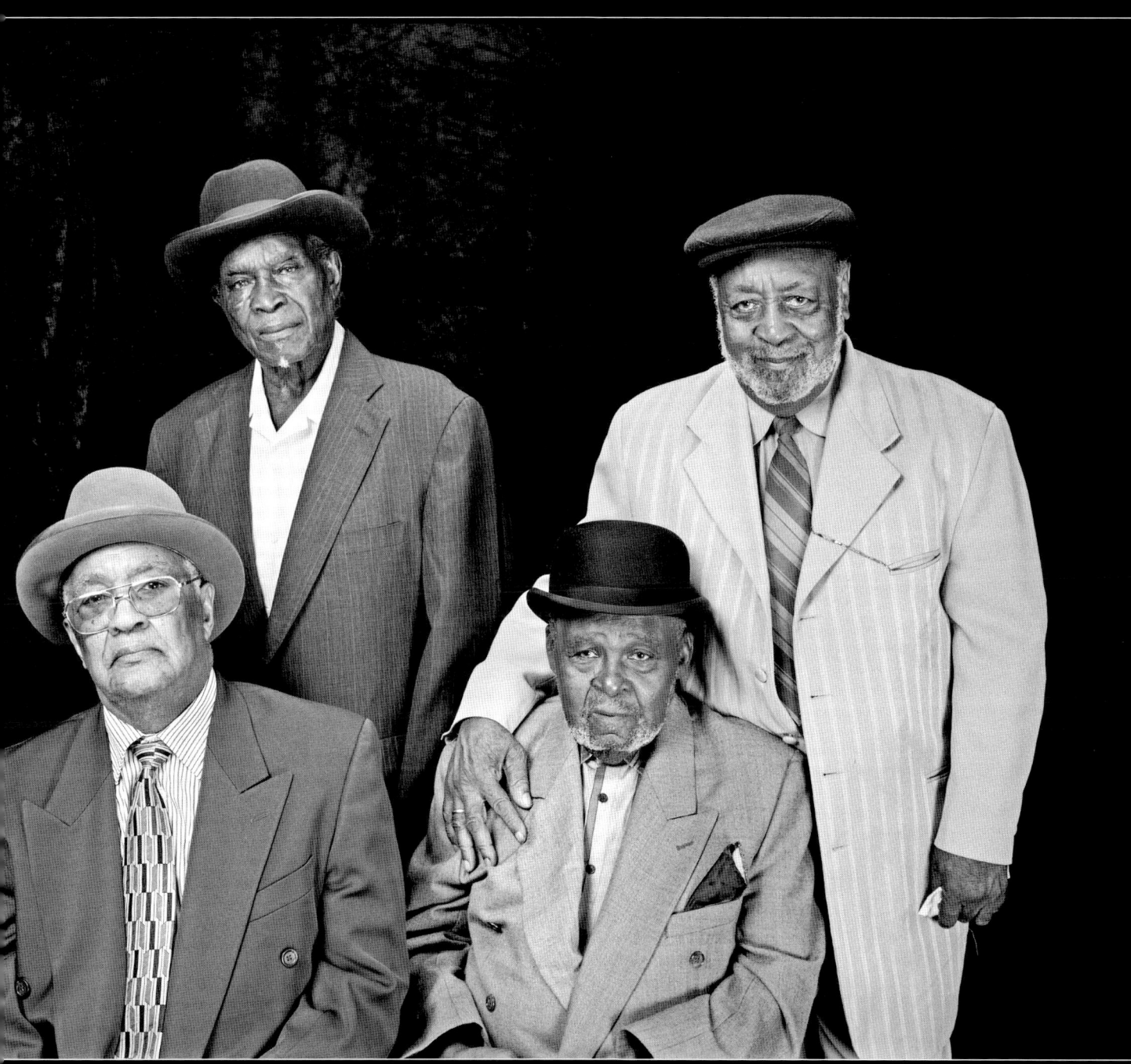

Delta Blues Cartel

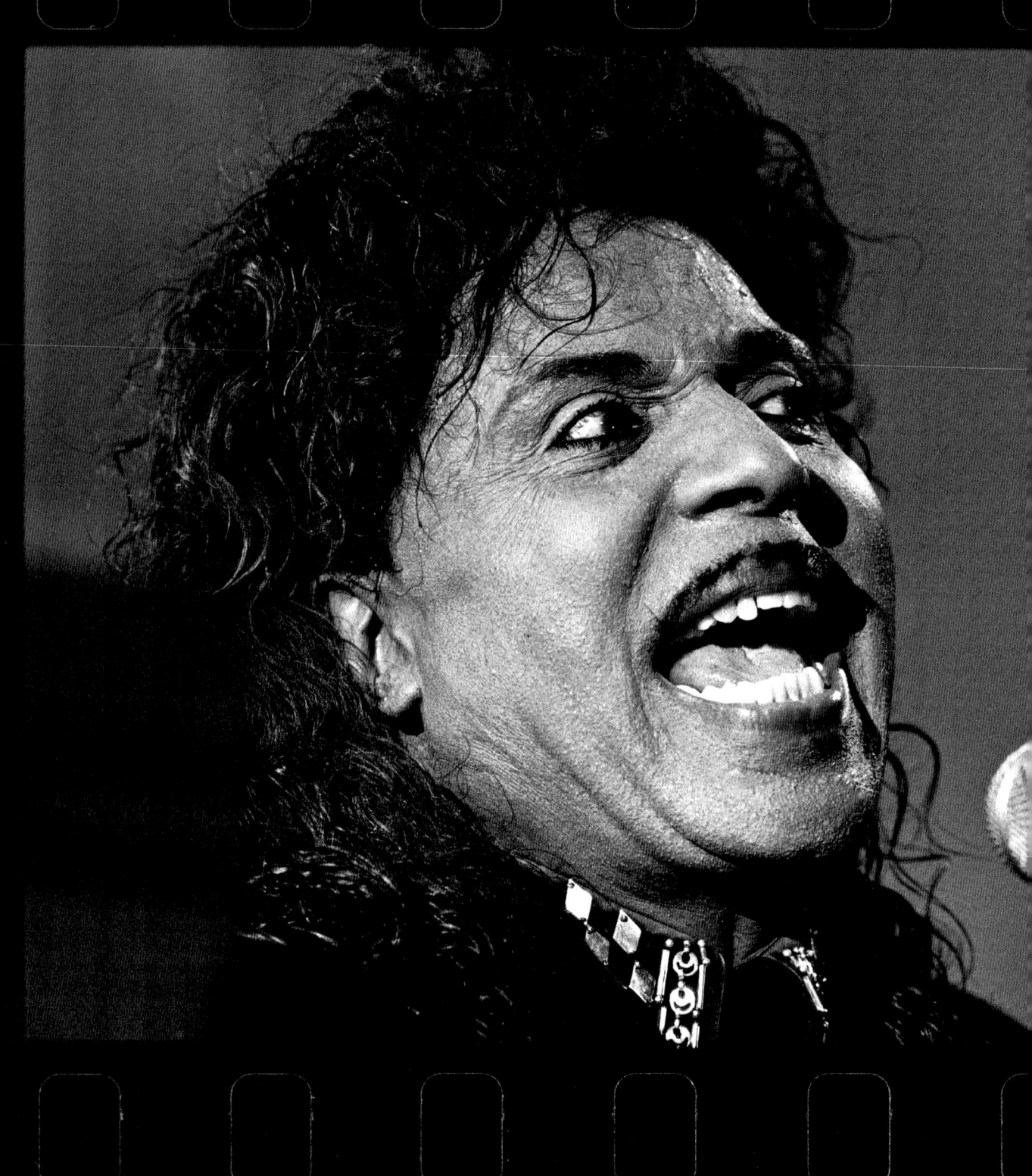

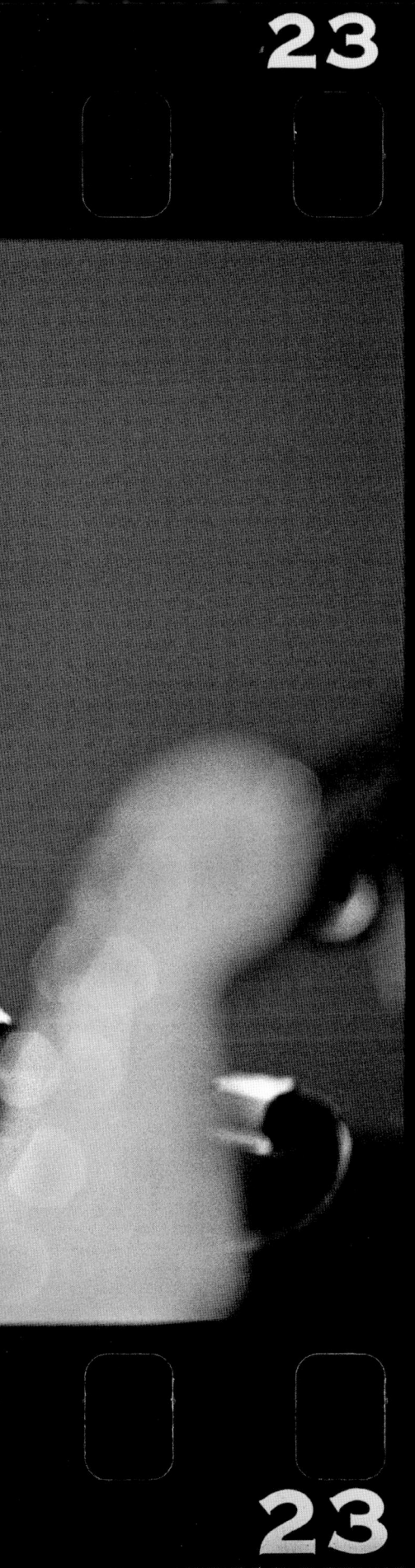

CHAPTER 8

ROCK & ROLL

It was all about that beat. Rev. Jimmy Snow would rave on about "The beat, the beat, the beat," and jazz-loving music critics laughed at this new groove, calling it "vulgar," "a soon-to-be-forgotten fad," and other, much less polite terms.

Some of the older Black musicians had already been making *the* music for years, flying under the radar of white, mainstream radio, scuffling along on the Chitlin' Circuit and airplay found on 50,000-watt clear-channel station WLAC out of Nashville.

In 1954, World War II was less than ten years in the rearview, and teenagers of all races and colors were ready for relief from Senator Joe McCarthy and *Brown vs. the Board of Education.*

The exciting new sound came from former gospel singers such as Hank Ballard, blues belters such as "Big Joe," a former hairdresser from St. Louis named Berry, an Assembly of God student from Louisiana named Jerry Lee, a Greek passing for Black named Otis, and a truck driver from Tupelo named Elvis.

This beat began as dance music for Black audiences, but somewhere along the way, as the gospel singers put it, "It jumped the fence."

The result?

An auditory grenade whose impact is still felt around the world today, known as "rock and roll."

WILLIAM WIRTHS
(REVEREND BILLY C. WIRTZ)
Historian, researcher, writer, humorist

Little Richard

Antoine "Fats" Domino

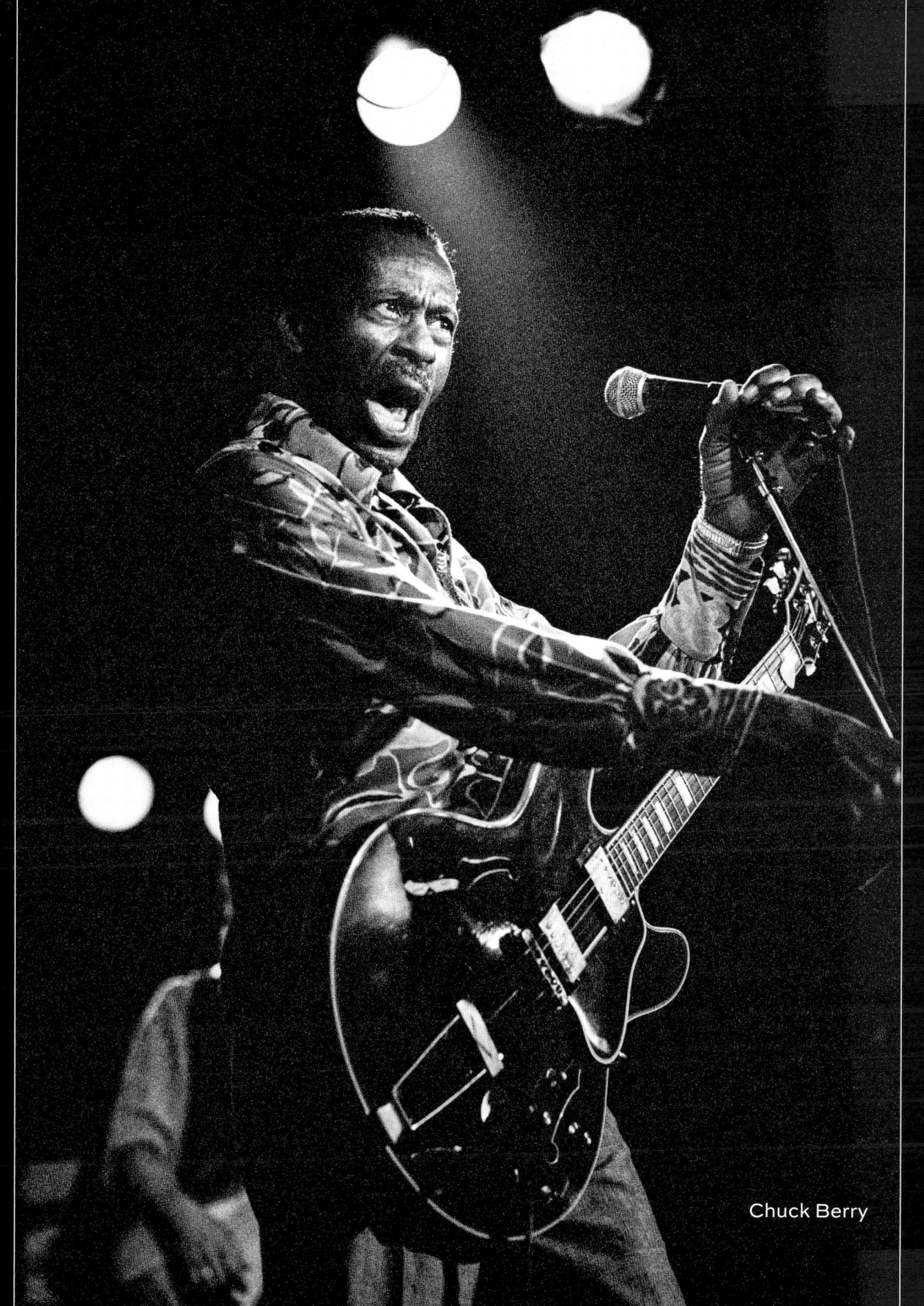

Chuck Berry

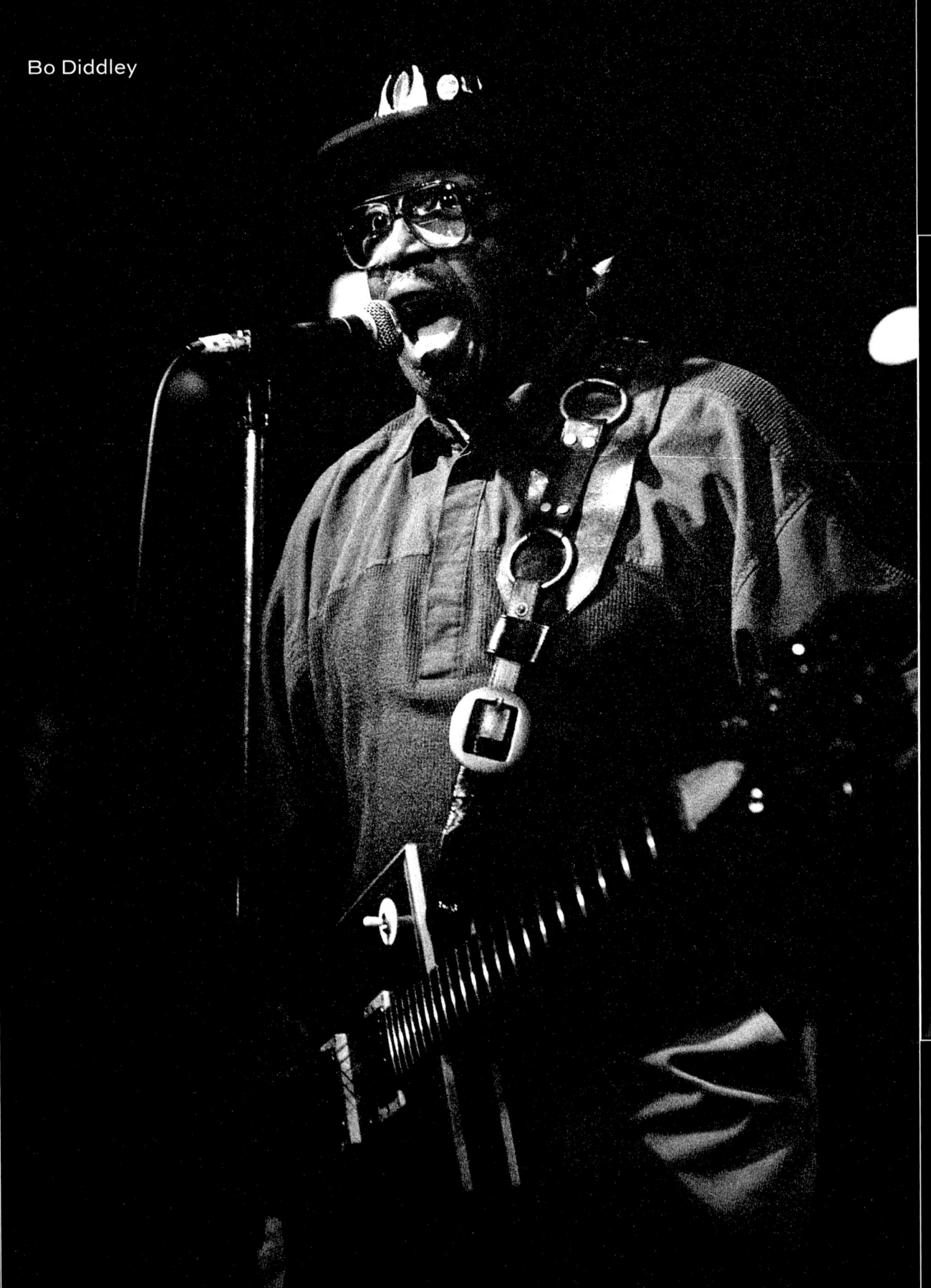

Bo Diddley

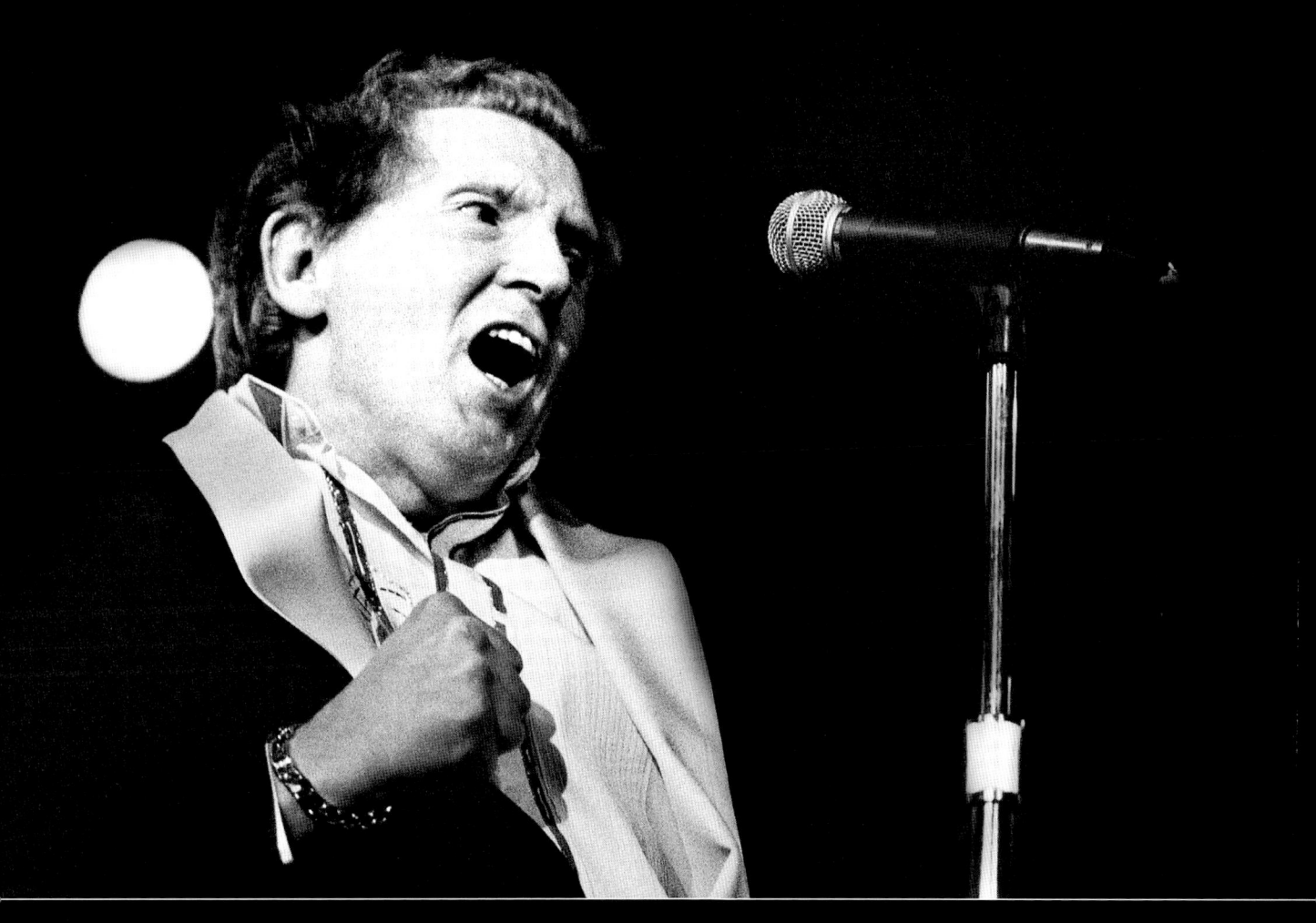

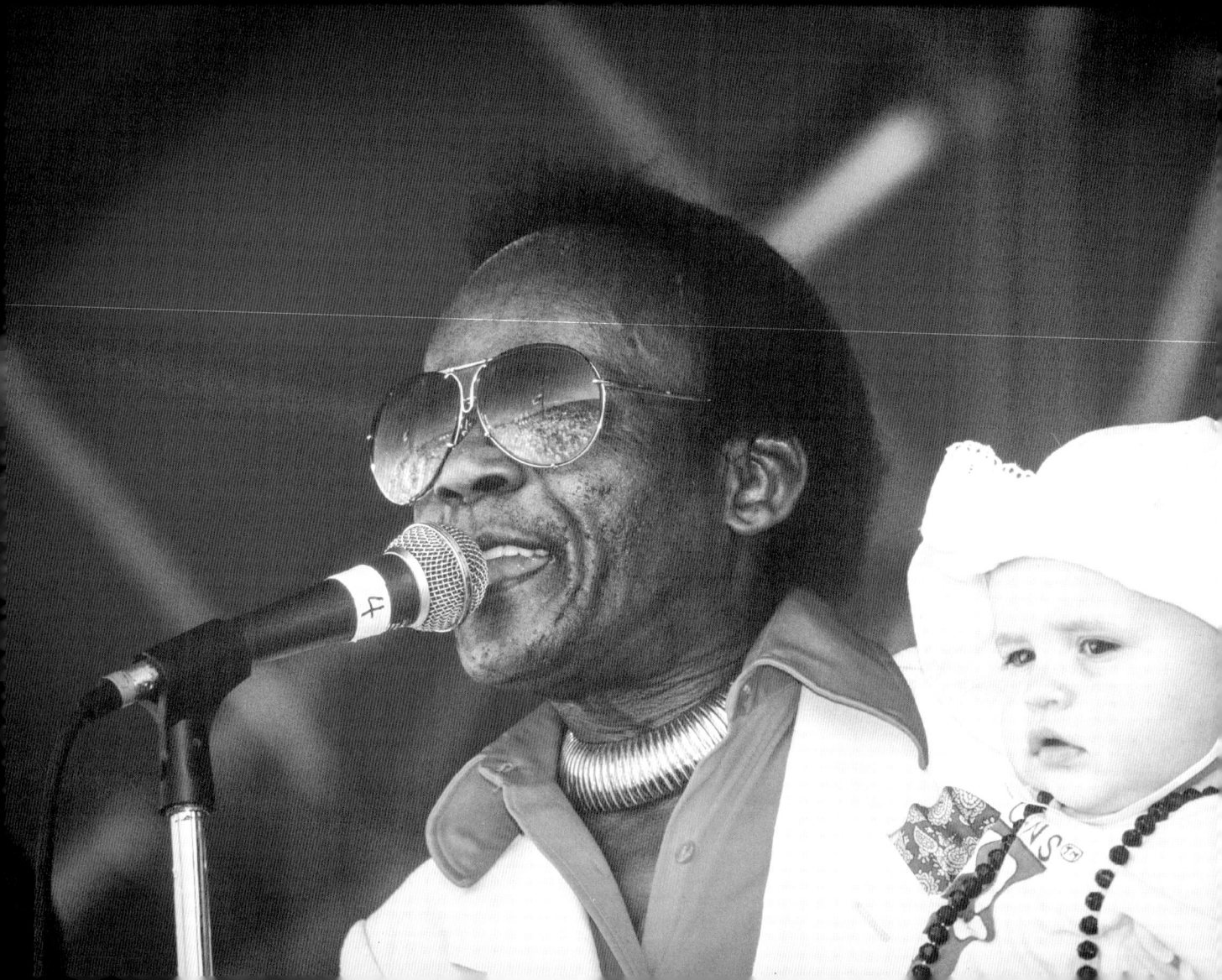

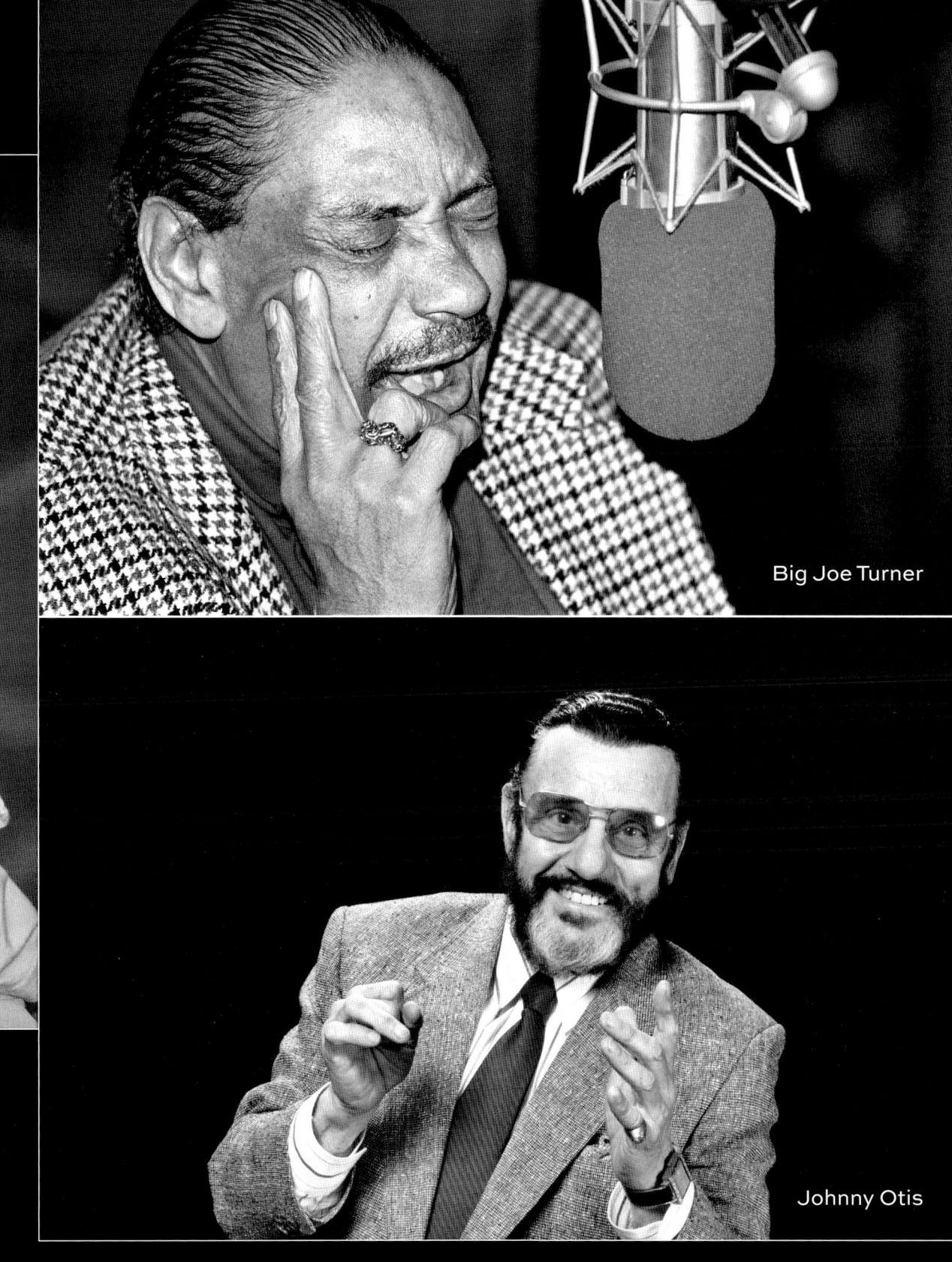

Big Joe Turner

Johnny Otis

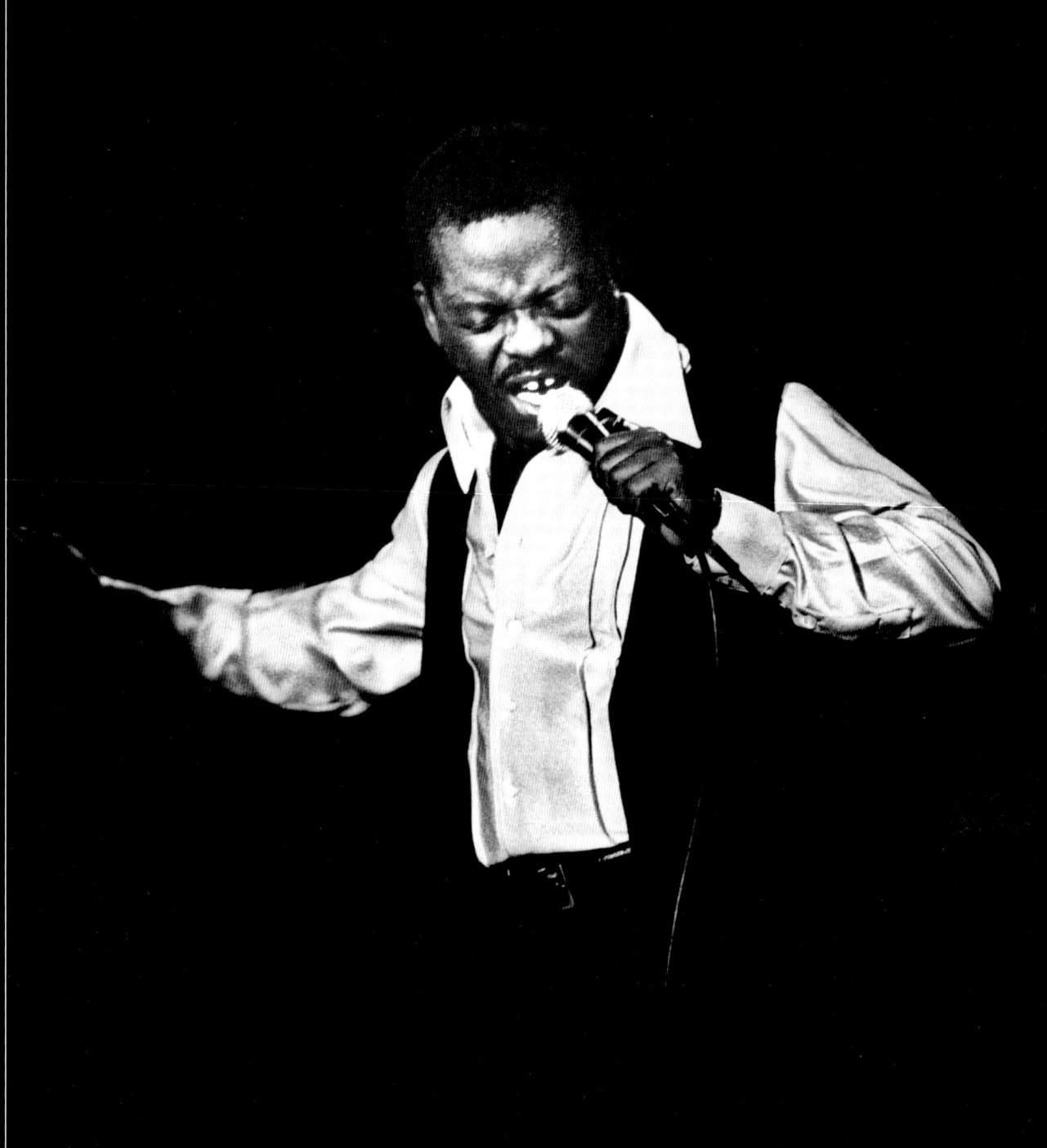

Otis Blackwell

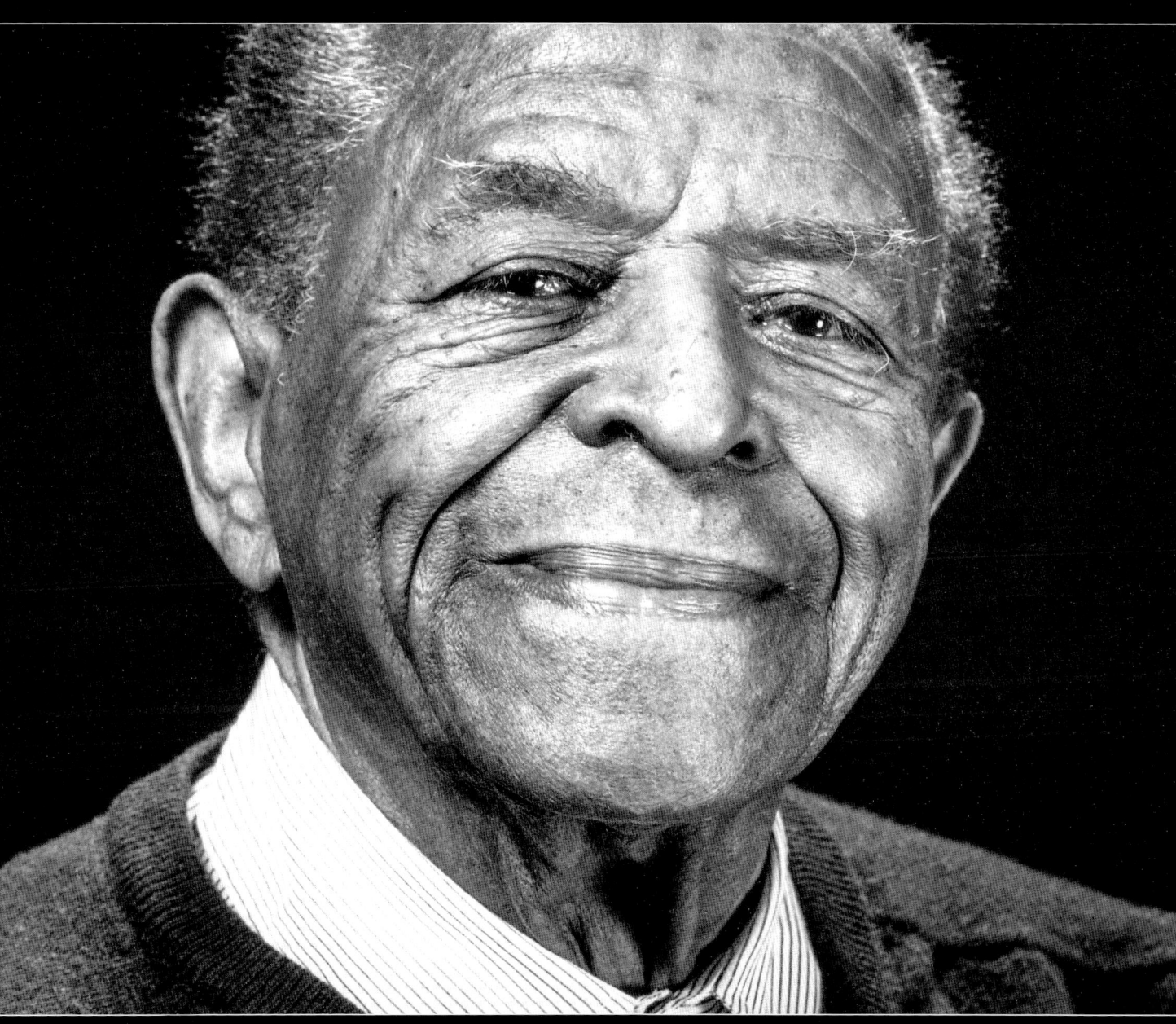

Jesse Stone

NOTES ABOUT THE PHOTOGRAPHS

JOSEPH A. ROSEN AND GARY HILL

John Lee Hooker

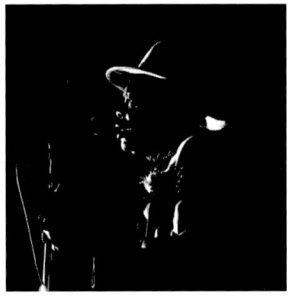

Mississippi-born bluesman John Lee Hooker personified deep blues and danceable boogie, which he delivered for over five decades.

Hooker made his earliest rhythm-and-blues chart hits—"Boogie Chillen'" and "Crawling King Snake" and others—in the late 1940s and had international hits such as "Boom, Boom" and "One Scotch, One Bourbon, and One Beer" in the 1960s. His album *The Healer* (1989) with Bonnie Raitt, Carlos Santana, Los Lobos, Charlie Musselwhite, and others led to revered elder-statesman status and revived his career.

John Lee Hooker was inducted into the Blues Hall of Fame in 1980 and the Rock & Roll Hall of Fame in 1991 and received a National Heritage Fellowship.

He possessed a growling, raspy voice and a driving, one-chord guitar style like no others. I saw him twice before his late 1980s career revival playing with just a trio at a small, rough club where I made this photo. It was very special to see him in this intimate environment.

After one of those shows, a happy accident in the darkroom resulting from some wildly overdeveloped film gave me the ultra-high-contrast photo, which has become a signature photo of mine and appears as the front cover of this book.

Albert King

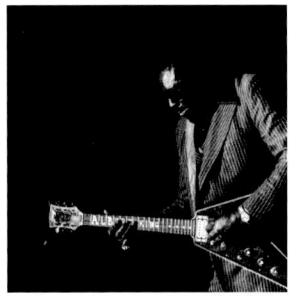

Born Albert Nelson in 1923, bluesman Albert King had a sound all his own: instantly identifiable and FIERCE. Self-taught, he played left-handed with the guitar upside down, and the unusual setup helped give his string bending a different tone from all others.

I remember watching him as he smoked a pipe while fiddling with the cover of his amplifier case, adjusting it as a sound baffle until he was satisfied. He'd turn up the amp, face the crowd, blow a puff of smoke, and

hit a note that sliced through the room like a knife: the show was ON. He was also a master of dynamics, going soft and making the strings cry and sing and then hitting notes that could peel paint.

A big, imposing man, he possessed a powerful, moving voice, and he brought an element of menace, in his person, and in his music.

He was a huge influence on rock players, most notably Stevie Ray Vaughan, who played with him frequently, and Eric Clapton, who covered his songs. His guitar style is often copied but never equaled. He along with Freddie and B.B. are the "Three Kings" of blues guitar.

Muddy Waters

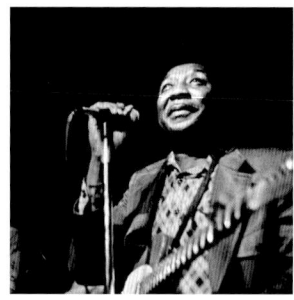

McKinley Morganfield (1913–83), born and raised in sharecropping poverty in the heart of the Mississippi Delta, rose to worldwide fame as Muddy Waters, establishing and defining the electric Chicago blues genre and changing music forever.

He was first recorded in Mississippi by Alan Lomax for the Library of Congress in 1941; he has said that hearing his voice played back gave him the confidence to move to Chicago to become a professional musician.

He eventually came to the attention of the brothers Chess, Leonard and Phil, and recorded for their Aristocrat label, which soon became the legendary Chess Records.

Among his many classics in a long career were "Hoochie Coochie Man," "I Just Want to Make Love to You," "Got My Mojo Working," and "Mannish Boy (I'm a Man)."

His records marked the transition of country blues to tough, urban, electric blues. The basic format was established for much of what was to follow in rock and roll, soul, pop, and more. The Rolling Stones and the most prominent US rock-and-roll magazine took their names from one of his songs.

I was so enamored of Muddy Waters and his music that I made a pilgrimage to Washington, DC, in 1976 to hear, see, and photograph the man himself—the beginning of my blues photography adventure, which continues to this day. I am so grateful that I got to see and photograph him and so thankful for all that he gave the world.

Lightnin' Hopkins

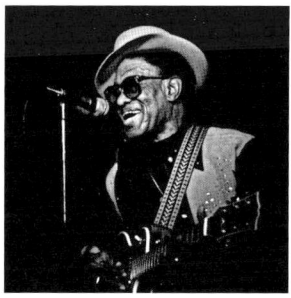

Sam John Hopkins—Lightnin'—personified Texas blues: guiding and accompanying the legendary Blind Lemon Jefferson as a boy, getting guitar lessons from his cousin Alger "Texas" Alexander, and on to cotton picking and a prison-farm chain gang.

He was a finger-style guitar virtuoso; a blues singer who could whisper, shout, or cast a spell with his naked voice; and a songwriter of unparalleled inventiveness and truth telling, sometimes making up his poetic lyrics on the spot.

He acquired his professional name when he made duo recordings with pianist Wilson Smith. A recording executive wanted a more impactful and memorable name, and they became "Lightnin' and Thunder."

He played rough Houston dives, major festivals, and Carnegie Hall. He made a lot of records—some for mainly white folky audiences interested in the real country blues, and others—my favorites—for a Black urban audience.

While he never made a bad record, those tough, gritty recordings for the local and regional audience in Houston from the late 1940s to the mid- to late 1950s (on Aladdin, Herald, and other labels, widely reissued) are pure, pharmaceutical blues. It does not get any better.

I got to see him only once in person, at the original Tramps in New York City just months before he passed.

I'm grateful for all he gave us.

Koko Taylor

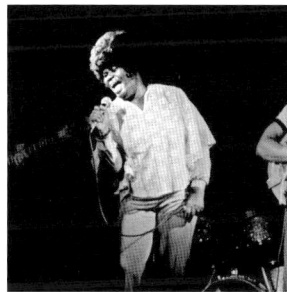

Cora Walton (1928–2009), better known as Koko Taylor and also called by some "the Queen of the Blues," was born to a sharecropping family in Tennessee in 1928 and migrated in the early 1950s to Chicago, where she began singing in clubs. It was there that she was discovered by songwriter / producer / bass player and Chess Records talent scout Willie Dixon, a central figure in the creation of the Chicago blues. Koko had made some small-label records, but it wasn't until Dixon called her to a late-night session to record "Wang Dang Doodle" that things clicked for her. Dixon's composition was based on a bawdy toast known as "The

Bulldagger's Ball" and featured such colorful characters as Automatic Slim and Razor Totin' Jim; Howlin' Wolf had recorded it five years earlier, and it didn't do well, but the Koko Taylor version took off, selling a million copies and reaching number 4 on the R&B chart in 1966. While she never again had a hit as big, she established herself as a club, festival, and touring favorite both domestically and internationally.

Koko Taylor's recordings for Chess and Alligator Records set the bar for tough Chicago-style blues from a women's point of view.

In her eighty years, she gave us great blues with strength, warmth, and dignity—a class act all the way.

Shown here are photos from the first time I saw her in 1978, and again in 1993.

Clarence "Gatemouth" Brown

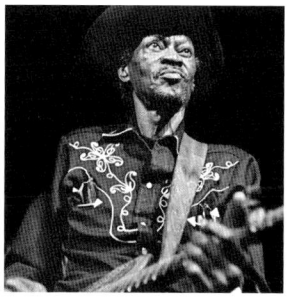

Clarence "Gatemouth" Brown was a singer and multi-instrumentalist with a career from the 1940s to the 2000s. While he is probably best known for his work as a blues musician, he melded country, jazz, Cajun, and R&B into his own style of American music (for which he became an official ambassador).

He was an admirer of the Texas guitarist T-Bone Walker, and his style evolved from there. His early recordings for (the notorious) Don Robey's Peacock and Duke labels are masterpieces of swing and jump blues, with "Okie Dokie Stomp" in particular setting the bar very high for instrumental blues guitar. He also set the standard for blues fiddle and went on to a long career as a performer and recording artist regionally, nationally, and all around the world. His tours of Europe and Africa were sponsored by the US State Department.

Gatemouth was also the bandleader on *The !!!! Beat*, a 1966 television show filmed in Dallas with a Nashville house band, where he backed up dozens of blues, R&B, and soul performers. This footage is beyond great! If you are not familiar, do yourself a favor and seek it out.

Sadly, his health was failing when Hurricane Katrina destroyed his home in Slidell, Louisiana, and he passed just days later. There will never be another like him.

Ike Turner

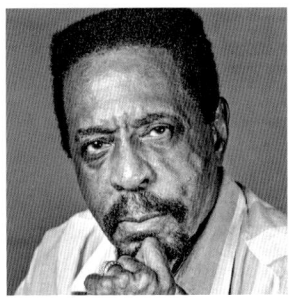

Bandleader, record producer, talent scout, guitarist, pianist, and songwriter, Izear Luster "Ike" Turner (1931–2007) was a musical giant. Setting aside judgment of a personal life marred by drug addiction and scarred by sexual abuse and violence he both received and delivered, one cannot overestimate his contribution to American music; in his lifetime, he traced the evolution of blues, rhythm and blues, rock and roll, soul, funk, and rock.

Born in Clarksdale, Mississippi, cradle of the Delta blues, Ike Turner was a Delta stalwart in his teens and twenties, playing juke joints and Chitlin Circuit clubs in the Deep South with his band the Kings of Rhythm. It was with this band that Annie Mae Bullock, who became known as Tina Turner, first performed. While still in the Delta, he learned piano from Pinetop Perkins. Early in his career he was the ultimate blues talent scout, bringing Bobby Bland and Howlin' Wolf and others to Sam Phillips at Sun Records as well as backing artists on records. His recording of "Rocket 88" (1951) with Jackie Brenston on vocals is considered by many to have been the first rock-and-roll song.

Ike is best known for his partnership with Tina, for their melding of soul and rock and roll and the showstopping megahit "Proud Mary," but he had a second blues career after they were inducted in absentia (he was in prison; she was taking the year off) into the Rock & Roll Hall of Fame.

During Ike's final run, I did a portrait of him on the Legendary R&B Cruise for the cover of *Blues Revue Magazine*. I don't remember what prompted it, but at breakfast preparing for the photo session, as simply as you might say, "I'd like my eggs over easy," he said, "Prison saved my life. I got clean and I made peace with my God." I was kind of stunned, but in that moment, at least, I believed him. He was direct, complex, fascinating to talk with, and generous to me.

B.B. King

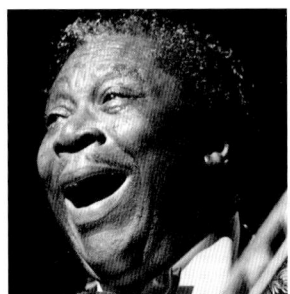

Riley B. King, better known as B.B. King, was the true King of the Blues. He had a deep history, stretching from the Mississippi Delta to a brief gospel career, to Memphis as a DJ and performer, to relentless touring for decades, to winning the hearts of younger white fans at the Fillmore West, to international acclaim and awards too numerous to mention. No one was better as a singer, guitar player, or human being. His music and humanity defined and shaped blues and all music forever. He was a true ambassador who brought blues to the world, always with taste, class, and dignity.

I have a fond memory from around the time his big hit "The Thrill Is Gone" was on the charts. I was so taken by his music that I sneaked into the Village Gate as an underage teen to see him in this intimate venue.

Another memorable show was when I went to the Fillmore East to see Super Session, who featured Al Kooper and one of the first guitar heroes, Mike Bloomfield. The show was running very late, and finally someone came out and said Bloomfield was delayed, but we have B.B. King in his place. The crowd went wild, they started playing, and then suddenly Bloomfield appeared. He and B.B. jammed for the whole set to an ecstatic audience, and it blew my teenaged mind. I cannot count the times I saw Mr. King after that, but I am grateful for every one.

Willie Mae "Big Mama" Thornton

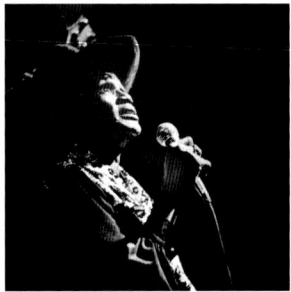

Willie Mae "Big Mama" Thornton was the large woman with the big voice who had the original hit with the Leiber and Stoller tune "Hound Dog," recorded on Duke Records in 1952 with Johnny Otis backing. Later covered by Elvis Presley on RCA in 1956, it became his first number one hit, but the song always made more sense to me sung from a woman's point of view.

Big Mama Thornton also made the original version of "Ball and Chain," with which Janis Joplin scored a big hit.

This photo was taken at the original Lone Star in New York City, early 1980s. She was cantankerous that night, chewing out band members onstage, but once things settled in and she threw back her head and sang, all was well again. I remember that during "Little Red Rooster," she sang all the barnyard sounds—clucking chickens, barking dogs, etc.

Big Mama Thornton passed in 1984 of liver disease caused by years of alcoholism. While she did receive some royalties from "Ball and Chain," she died penniless. She was just fifty-seven.

Bobby "Blue" Bland

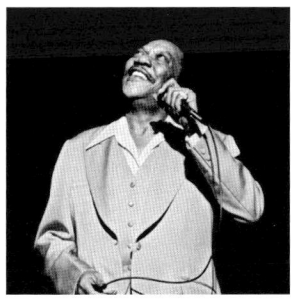

No one was more important to the blues as we know it today than singer Robert Calvin Brooks—Bobby "Blue" Bland (1930–2013).

Mixing gospel with blues and R&B, he had a long string of influential hits on the Duke Records label out of Houston and for decades reigned over the soul blues and Chitlin' Circuit world. He was perhaps the only blues artist to maintain that consistent popularity with his core African American audience.

Yes, he crossed over to broader audiences, playing clubs, festivals and cruises, but his original fan base never left him, nor did he ever abandon them. No one else could deliver a song and tell a story like he did.

He made driving blues with such songs as the Texas shuffle "Farther up the Road" (1957, also called "Further on up the Road") and the slower, grinding "I Smell Trouble" (1957). He sang danceable rockers such as "Turn On Your Lovelight" (1961) and "Good Time Charlie" (1965). And then he could turn around with softer, moody songs such as the tender "I'll Take Care of You" (1959) or his classic version of "Stormy Monday" (1962), based on T-Bone Walker's "Call It Stormy Monday (But Tuesday Is Just as Bad)." The list goes on and on: "I Pity the Fool" (1961), "That's the Way Love Is" (1963), Cry, Cry, Cry (1960), "Ain't Nothing You Can Do (1964). His later material told of real-life adult situations, as in "Ain't No Love in the Heart of the City" (1974) or "Take Your Shoes Off" (1990).

There never was, never will be anyone better. From the 1950s to his passing at age eighty-three he gave us classy and classic music for the ages.

Bobby Parker

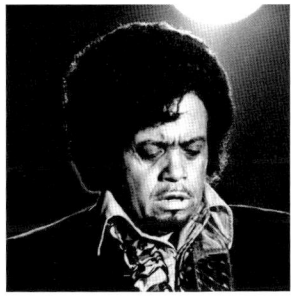

Guitarist and singer Robert Lee Parker was born in 1937 in Lafayette, Louisiana, and was raised in Los Angeles. By the 1950s, Bobby Parker (not to be confused with New Orleans artist Robert Parker of "Barefootin'" fame) was working with blues and R&B bands including Otis Williams and the Charms; Bo Diddley, including an appearance on *The Ed Sullivan Show*; Apollo Theater band leader Paul "Hucklebuck"

Williams; Sam Cooke; Jackie Wilson; Lavern Baker; Clyde McPhatter; and the Everly Brothers.

He wrote and recorded the often-covered single "Watch Your Step" in 1961, inspired by Dizzy Gillespie's "Manteca" and Ray Charles's "What'd I Say." The Beatles often performed the song in their early shows, and its guitar riff inspired both the introduction to their "I Feel Fine" and, according to John Lennon, "Day Tripper."

Bobby Parker landed in the Washington, DC, area and performed locally and nationally. He made some really great records, produced by my pal Hammond Scott for the Blacktop label in the 1990s.

I saw some chilling and thrilling shows during those years, with Bobby always well coiffed and dressed to the nines.

"Champion" Jack Dupree

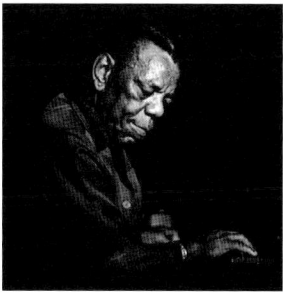

Born in 1910, give or take a year or two, William Thomas "Champion Jack" Dupree was a blues and boogie pianist from New Orleans who had an amazing life and a big influence on piano players to come.

Orphaned at the age of eight, he taught himself to play piano, apprenticed with Tuts Washington and others, and soon was playing in the rough-and-tumble joints of New Orleans. He was also a "spy boy" for the Yellow Pocahontas Mardi Gras Indians. He traveled north to Chicago, Indianapolis, and New York, meeting and playing with blues stars Georgia Tom, Scrapper Blackwell, and Leroy Carr. In 1940, he recorded "Junker Blues," which became his trademark song and later the basis for Fats Domino's "The Fat Man," Lloyd Price's "Lawdy Miss Clawdy," and Professor Longhair's "Tipitina."

He also became a boxer, fighting in over a hundred fights in the Golden Gloves and elsewhere and winning many championships. Thus, he became Champion Jack and carried that name for the rest of his life.

During World War II he was a Navy cook and became a prisoner of war. He composed and recorded the topical "FDR Blues" upon the death of Franklin Roosevelt. He was also one of the first blues artists to relocate to Europe, where he played both with rising stars of the early blues scene there as well as with other expatriate artists. Known for his clever storytelling and sly humor, he left a great recorded legacy from the 1940s to the 1990s, including some fine latter-day albums on Bullseye Blues produced by my pal Ron Levy.

Henry Townsend

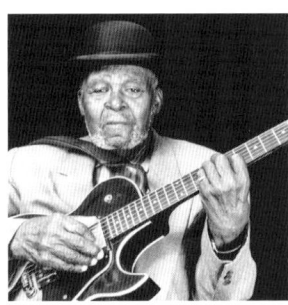

Henry Townsend was born October 27, 1909, in Selby, Mississippi. He grew up in Cairo, Illinois, and left home at the age of nine fleeing an abusive father and hoboed his way to St. Louis. By the late 1920s he had begun touring and recording with pianist Walter Davis. He acquired the nickname "Mule" because he was sturdy in both physique and character. Townsend was one of the only artists known to have recorded in nine consecutive decades. Articulate and self-aware with an excellent memory, Townsend gave many invaluable interviews to blues enthusiasts and scholars. In 1985 he received the National Heritage Fellowship in recognition of being a master artist. His birthday has been declared Henry Townsend Day in St. Louis. I treasure the time I got to spend with him while on assignment for Blues Access magazine making this and other photos. He was something special.

David "Honeyboy" Edwards

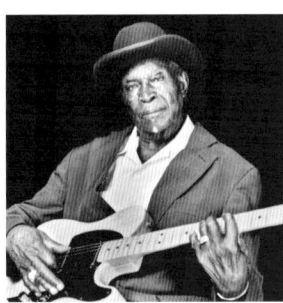

David "Honeyboy" Edwards connected rural Mississippi Delta blues to the modern era. A rambling man for much of his ninety-six years, first as an itinerant street musician and later touring almost to the end of his long life, he was born in Mississippi and died in Chicago.

As a young man he was exposed to the deep blues of Tommy Johnson and Charlie Patton. He went on to travel and perform with many Delta artists, most notably the legendary Robert Johnson. While still in the South, he performed with Muddy Waters, Howlin' Wolf, Big Joe Williams, and Sonny Boy Williamson.

Along with them, he migrated north and was present at the inception of modern electric blues.

I'm glad I got to see and photograph him many times and spend good-quality time with him. The photos in this book are from a portrait session in 2000 and the Juke Joint Festival, Clarksdale, Mississippi, in 2011, at what turned out to be his last public performance, at age ninety-six. At that show, though I had not spoken with him for almost a decade, he was sharp as a tack remembering details of our past encounters and catching up on mutual friends. He was a very special man.

"Homesick" James Williamson

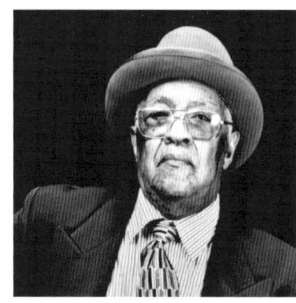

Homesick James Williamson, a master of the slide guitar, has been reported to have been born in 1905, 1910, 1914, or 1924, under three different names. No one really knows.

Homesick James acquired his nickname from a 1952 recording with that title. He worked with many early electric Chicago blues artists, including Baby Face Leroy Foster, Snooky Pryor, Floyd Jones, Lazy Bill Lucas, and Sonny Boy Williamson 2.

He is perhaps best known for his work with his cousin Elmore James. He was Elmore's bandmate and recorded classics including "Dust My Broom," "Sky Is Crying," and "Rollin' and Tumblin'"—recordings that changed my life.

Homesick James also made many great solo records and was a colorful raconteur. As my friend Bill Steber said in a tribute to Homesick, "He never let the truth get in the way of a good story."

The photo is from a portrait session I did in 2000 for *Blues Access* magazine, when he was touring with Honeyboy Edwards, Henry Townsend, and Robert Lockwood as the Delta Blues Cartel. The times I spent with those gents are among my most cherished blues memories.

Homesick died in 2006, age ninety-six, more or less.

Johnny Shines

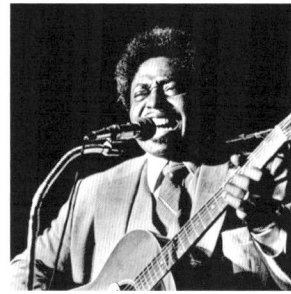

One of the last original Delta bluesmen to carry it on, Johnny Shines (1915–92) was a traveling companion and accompanist in the mid-1930s to the legendary Robert Johnson, who was a major influence on his sound. Shines dropped out of music several times, only to be brought back by new generations of blues lovers entranced by his piercing, haunting slide guitar.

He left the South for Chicago in 1941 and was there at the beginning of modern electric blues, though in 1969 he left for Alabama.

His recordings, especially the sides with harmonica player Walter Horton, have a wonderful, at times ethereal sound. I am very grateful that I got to hear, see, and photograph him. The night I made these photos, Robert Lockwood Jr.—Johnson's stepson, with whom Shines had also toured—shared the bill, and Louisiana Red sat in. Deep blues at its best. Unforgettable.

Memphis Slim

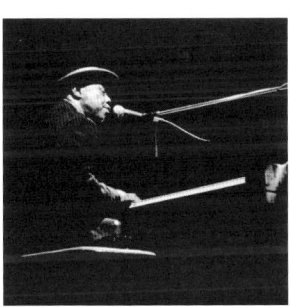

Singer, pianist, bandleader, and songwriter John Chatman, whose first records listed him as Peter Chatman (his father's name), in 1947 reworked an old song to create the first modern version, released in 1949, of the standard "Every Day I Have the Blues," which has since been covered by dozens of artists.

From 1940 on, he performed and recorded prolifically until his passing in 1988. In 1962 he became one of the many African American artists to settle abroad, living in Paris to enjoy a better racial environment, with greater recognition and respect for his art.

His long partnership with Matt "Guitar" Murphy, a studio player for Chess Records, yielded amazing music. In addition, he was a touring and recording partner of Willie Dixon; they enjoyed a great deal of success during the folk revival in the 1960s.

He died in Paris but is buried in the city of his birth, Memphis.

Joe Willie "Pinetop" Perkins

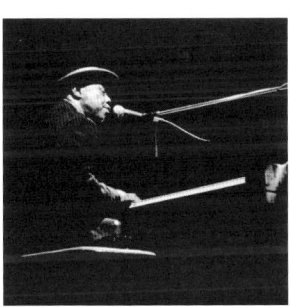

Blues piano player Joe Willie "Pinetop" Perkins, with a career that started in the 1920s and stretched well into the twenty-first century, was one of the last surviving Mississippi Delta blues men and became a beloved elder statesman in the blues community.

He taught Ike Turner piano. He held down the piano chair in the Muddy Waters band for more than a decade. And after that, he continued his career both as a solo player and with various all-star bands.

Along with Willie "Big Eyes" Smith, Pinetop Perkins won a Grammy in 2011 for the *Joined at the Hip* CD, which made him the oldest ever Grammy winner! He died that year, age ninety-seven.

Pinetop Perkins was at the piano in 1976 at the Muddy Waters gig that started my personal blues photography adventure. I am grateful that I got to cross paths with him and thankful for all he gave us. Also, thanks and gratitude to Patricia Morgan, Bob Margolin, Onnie Heaney, and the many others who helped make 'Top's later years healthy, happy, and safe.

Robert Lockwood Jr.

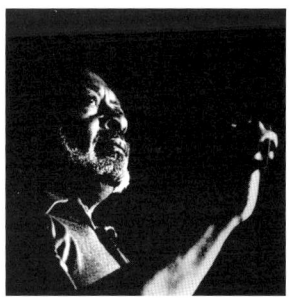

The stepson and student of the blues legend Robert Johnson, Robert Lockwood Jr. while still in the Mississippi Delta played with Sonny Boy Williamson (Rice Miller) on the legendary King Biscuit Time, as well as with Johnny Shines, Howlin' Wolf, Elmore James, and more. He mentored a young B.B. King. After moving to Chicago, he made solo sides in the 1940s and 1950s with some success, then worked as a session guitarist on oh so many classic Chess recordings, with legends such as Little Walter, Willie Dixon, Otis Spann, and more.

In his later years, Robert Lockwood Jr. performed and recorded as a bandleader and festival favorite. He always brought the music with taste and talent—a guitar player's guitar player. And he was a great singer to boot.

He had an undeserved reputation for being gruff, but if you were polite and didn't start a conversation by asking him about Robert Johnson, he was very easygoing, with a wry sense of humor. I found him to be a real gentleman.

One of my favorite memories is of spending an afternoon in a dingy motel room near Newark Airport with him, Honeyboy Edwards, Homesick James, and Henry Townsend. They were relaxing, reminiscing, and telling tales. I had photographed them the night before and had my cameras with me, but I decided not to bring them out. It would have altered the mood, and I chose simply to be present and take in this very special moment with these special men.

Sunnyland Slim

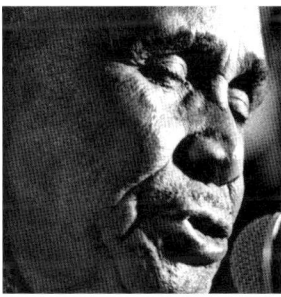

Pianist and singer Sunnyland Slim (1906–95) brought chops honed in the jukes and lumber camps of the Deep South to the city and helped invent modern blues.

Born Albert Luandrew in Mississippi, he moved to Memphis at nineteen and settled in Chicago in 1942, playing with the likes of Muddy Waters, Howlin' Wolf, Robert Lockwood Jr., Little Walter, and more. In fact, it was Slim who first brought Muddy to Chess (then Aristocrat) Records.

Always real and unaffected, Sunnyland Slim went on to a long recording and performing career, mentoring many as a father figure and gaining recognition as a National Heritage Fellow.

Aretha Franklin

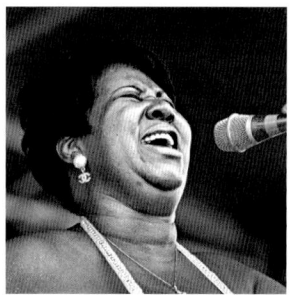

Aretha Franklin (1942–2018) was a prodigy, playing piano at age five, singing solos in her church choir at nine, and recording her first album, *Songs of Faith*, at fifteen. Her father, born in Sunflower County, Mississippi, was the Memphis-trained and eventually Detroit-based Rev. C. L. Franklin, who was a powerful singing and whooping preacher who rose to fame and influence with his gospel caravans and must-hear national radio programs. From her preteen years, she sang in his traveling extravaganzas and got to know her father's famous friends from the gospel world—Mahalia Jackson and Clara Ward were like second mothers to her in the absence of C. L.'s estranged wife—including James Cleveland and the Staples Singers, and from the wider world of Black celebrity. Many of these were also involved in the civil rights movement, and Dr. Martin Luther King Jr. was a fixture in Aretha's life.

Like another friend, Sam Cooke, Aretha wanted to cross over from gospel to more mainstream music, and in 1960 she signed with Columbia Records and had some success, singing in a variety of genres, including a tribute to Dinah Washington. But it was not until she moved to Atlantic Records in 1966 and released *I Never Loved a Man (the Way I Love You)* that she made her mark with chart-topping singles such as the title track, "Do Right Woman, Do Right Man," and, above all others, "Respect," which became a signature song and an anthem of empowerment both for women and for African Americans. (The song's author and original singer, Otis Redding, joked that "this girl just took this song" away from him.)

A long string of hits followed: "Baby, I Love You," "(You Make Me Feel Like) a Natural Woman," "Chain of Fools," "Ain't No Way," "Think," "I Say a Little Prayer," "Spanish Harlem," and so many more.

The awards she received were far too numerous and varied to list here, but it is safe to say she was one of the most recognized and honored artists ever.

Nothing I could say would add to her legacy, so I will quote President Obama after her performance of "Natural Woman" at the 2015 Kennedy Center Honors: "Nobody embodies more fully the connection between the African American spiritual, the blues, R&B, and rock and roll—the way that hardship and sorrow were transformed into something full of beauty and vitality and hope. American history wells up when Aretha sings."

Ray Charles

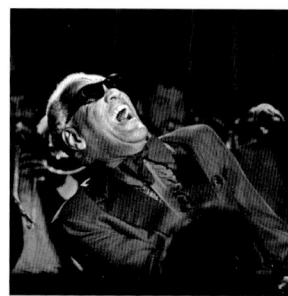

The genre-busting, definition-defying national treasure Ray Charles was born in southern Georgia and raised in northern Florida in dire poverty. Ray Charles Robinson knew nothing but hard times. His little brother George drowned, and Ray was blind by the age of seven. His overwhelmed mother, Aretha, placed Ray in the Florida School for the Deaf and Blind, where he learned braille and studied music. After his mother died, Ray, age fifteen, left school and began performing around Florida.

Only a few years later, the fearless blind teenager uprooted to the far corner of the country, Seattle (where he became friends with an even younger prodigy, Quincy Jones), and began recording for small labels in the style of Nat King Cole and Charles Brown. After some minor hits, Ray joined Atlantic Records in 1952, and 1954's "I've Got a Woman" shot him to stardom—and changed American popular music forever. Its new blend of gospel fervor, bluesy lyrics, and a danceable beat laid a foundation for the soul, rhythm and blues, and rock and roll to follow. Charles's biggest Atlantic hit was the funky, sexy, pop crossover "What'd I Say" (1959), his first gold record. Riding high, Charles left Atlantic that year for ABC-Paramount and the best contract—money and, especially, control—any US recording artist had ever had. For ABC, Charles crossed state lines and timelines with the geographically themed *The Genius Hits the Road* (1960), turning the thirty-year-old standard "Georgia on My Mind" into a timeless classic; scored again with the humorous "Hit the Road Jack" (1961); and crossed more cultural barriers with *Modern Sounds in Country and Western Music* (1962), which spawned four big singles, including the lush "countrypolitan" monster hit "I Can't Stop Loving You." Many more labels and hits followed over a long, improbable life that ran from "Busted" to the most soulful "America the Beautiful" ever.

Wilson Pickett

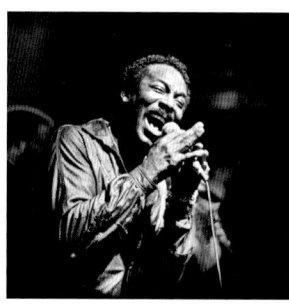

Singer and songwriter Wilson Pickett (1941–2006) developed a gritty, fiery, passionate vocal style out of gospel and rhythm and blues that helped him define soul music and force his way into the rock-and-roll conversation of the 1960s and 1970s.

Born in Alabama and raised in Detroit from his early teens, he started in gospel with the Violinaires, then in 1959 joined the Falcons, an influential rhythm-and-blues group that produced such future stars as Eddie Floyd and Sir Mack Rice. Pickett sang the powerful lead vocal over an almost doo-wop bass and harmonies vocal arrangement on their hit "I Found a Love."

But Pickett hit it bigger, much bigger, in 1965 as a solo with the iconic soul and crossover hit "In the Midnight Hour," which he cowrote with guitarist Steve Cropper and recorded at Stax Studios in Memphis with Cropper's usual Stax session mates, though it was recorded for Atlantic Records.

Pickett went on to make many more hits, among them "634-5789," "Ninety-Nine and a Half (Won't Do)," "Land of 1,000 Dances," "Funky Broadway," and "Mustang Sally," and including reverse crossovers (pop to soul) with covers of songs such as the Beatles' "Hey Jude" and the bubblegum tune "Sugar, Sugar."

His career took a downturn in the 1980s and 1990s, a victim both of changing musical tastes and his erratic behavior due to drug addiction and alcoholism. He made a brief return with an album on Rounder and some touring and festival appearances but never regained his former prominence.

This photo is from the original Lone Star Café in the early 1980s. My old friend Billy Price with his Keystone Rhythm Band was the opening act that night.

Al Green

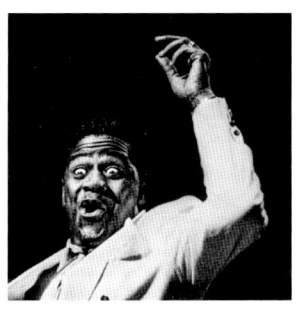

He became the Reverend Al Green, but before that, he was the king of sexy Southern soul in the 1960s and 1970s with huge hits on the Hi Records label. His collaboration with trumpeter / bandleader / record producer Willie Mitchell and the Hi Rhythm Section yielded a long string of sublime soul hits including "Tired of Being Alone," "Let's Stay Together," "I'm Still in Love with You," "Take Me to the River," and "Love and Happiness." After troubles in his personal life and a "reckoning," Green gave it all up to open a church and ministry in his hometown of Memphis. For many years he sang only his unique version of gospel music. He later returned to singing secular music in addition to gospel. A great documentary film by my friend Robert Mugge, *The Gospel According to Al Green*, is both enlightening and entertaining.

Ben E. King

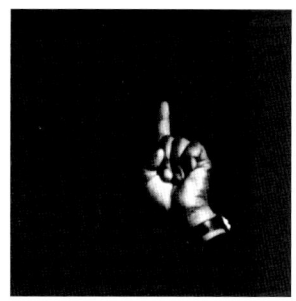

Benjamin Earl Nelson early in his career sang in the Five Crowns, a doo-wop group. In 1958, after lead singer Clyde McPhatter left the original Drifters, their manager, who owned the name, fired them en masse and replaced them with the Five Crowns, with Ben E. as the lead singer. The new Drifters group had a string of classic hit songs, including "This Magic Moment" and "Save the Last Dance for Me," both written by Doc Pomus and Mort Shuman, and "There Goes My Baby," one of the first R&B songs to use a full-blown string accompaniment. As a solo artist, Ben E. King, as he now was calling himself, had hits including "Don't Play That Song," "Spanish Harlem," and the timeless classic "Stand by Me." His voice was part of my generation's musical coming of age and is deep in the fabric of American culture. To quote my friend Sharyn Felder, Doc Pomus's daughter, he was "a gentleman's gentleman and a singer's singer."

Bettye LaVette

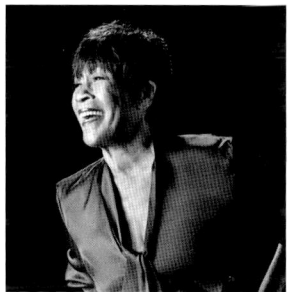

From her first hit at age sixteen, "My Man—He's a Lovin' Man," to ups and downs in the music business, intermittent chart success, and a long run on Broadway in *Bubbling Brown Sugar*, to her present-day success with awards, recognition, and even opening for the Rolling Stones, she has remained true to herself. She is a true song stylist and an emotional and honest singer. She owns every song she sings and takes it to a special, elevated place. No one puts more emotion, more humanity, and more of themselves into a song than Bettye, and her audiences feel that. It's not always been an easy path for her, with deals gone bad, great records going unreleased, hard times a plenty, but she is a survivor and a now enjoys success. She does not disappoint. I'm happy and proud to call her a friend.

Booker T. & the M.G.s

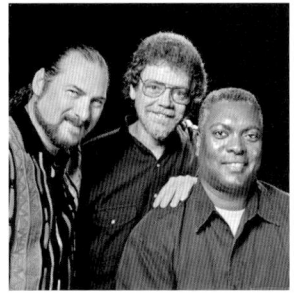

At the core of Stax Records' shifting house bands, Booker T. Jones, Steve Cropper, and Donald "Duck" Dunn helped make stars of Otis Redding, Sam & Dave, Rufus Thomas, Carla Thomas, Eddie Floyd, Johnnie Taylor, Albert King, and many more; not only playing on the singers' records, they often also served as producer, arranger, or songwriter (or a combination of these). And along with drummer Al Jackson Jr., Booker T. & the M.G.s had a long string of their own instrumental hits.

Booker T. Jones, leader of the band and best known for his work on Hammond B-3 organ, was a multi-instrument child prodigy. He began his session-player career as a teenager—on saxophone. Steve Cropper, on anyone's list of top guitarists, produced Otis Redding's only number one hit, "(Sittin' on) the Dock of the Bay," released after Redding's death.

Dunn, not an original member of the band, became one of the most distinctive bass players in soul music.

The classic M.G.s lineup was formed when Dunn replaced original bassist Lewis Steinberg, who with Jones, Cropper, and Jackson had already scored a huge, influential hit with "Green Onions" in 1962.

Carla Thomas

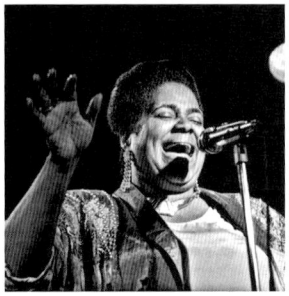

The daughter of Memphis music legend Rufus Thomas, Carla at the age of ten became an underaged member of the Teen Town Singers (Isaac Hayes was another Teen Town denizen), performing on WDIA, where her dad was a popular DJ. Her first hit—"Gee Whiz"—helped cement a relationship between Atlantic and Stax Records and keep Stax afloat. She recorded a string of hits for Stax, including "B-A-B-Y," "Tramp," and "Knock on Wood"—the last two, duets with Otis Redding, with whom she recorded the album "King and Queen." She appeared in the film *Wattstax* and in 1993 received the prestigious Pioneer Award from the Rhythm & Blues Foundation.

Chuck Jackson

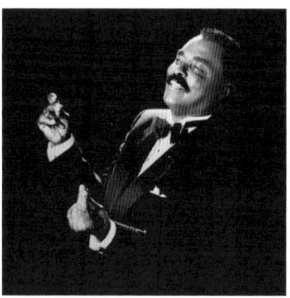

R&B and soul pioneer Chuck Jackson was Uptown Soul elegance, and always a favorite of the ladies.

He was a member of the Del-Vikings, one of the few racially integrated musical groups to achieve success in the 1950s. He went on to a solo career with hits such as "Any Day Now" (written by Burt Bacharach and lyricist Bob Hilliard) and "I Don't Want to Cry" (which he cowrote with Luther Dixon) and then a successful series of duets with Maxine Brown. In 1992 he was awarded the Rhythm & Blues Foundation's Pioneer Award and continued to perform until shortly before his passing in 2023. My pix of both Chuck Jackson and Maxine Brown were taken in a studio for the Rhythm & Blues Foundation, and I like to think that the elegance of the setting and drama of the lighting befitted their style.

Darlene Love

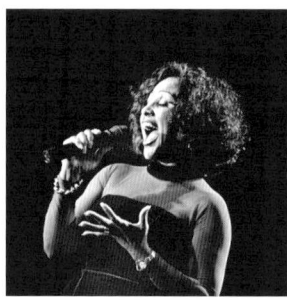

Texas-born (1941), California-raised singer Darlene Wright was invited to join a girl group called the Blossoms while still in high school. The Blossoms began working with producer Phil Spector, and she was renamed by Spector. She was the lead vocalist in the Blossoms—but also, uncredited, was the voice you hear on the Crystals' 1962 hit record "He's a Rebel." She went on to work with top names ranging from Elvis Presley to Sonny and Cher, Sam Cooke, the Beach Boys, and many more—the ultimate backup singer just *20 Feet from Stardom*, as featured in the Oscar-winning documentary of that name, for which she won a Grammy. As an actress, she performed on Broadway and television and was Danny Glover's wife in the *Lethal Weapon* movies. In addition, she is a member of the Rock & Roll Hall of Fame and a recipient of the Rhythm & Blues Foundations Pioneer Award.

I was lucky enough to see her at a free outdoor concert at Lincoln Center to celebrate her seventy-fifth birthday; she commanded the stage like a star one-third her age.

Etta James

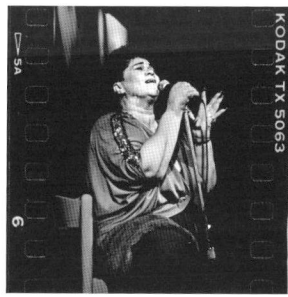

Singer Jamesetta Hawkins—Etta James—was a seminal American artist bridging blues, rhythm and blues, soul, rock and roll, jazz, and gospel.

Born in Los Angeles in 1938, she grew up in California with a frequently absent mother and an unknown father—she said he may have been legendary pool player Minnesota Fats. She met musician and talent scout Johnny Otis when she was just fourteen, and it was he who renamed her and got her going in the music business with "The Wallflower" (a change from "Roll with Me, Henry" due to the sexual suggestiveness of the original title of Otis's "answer song" to Hank Ballard's "Work with Me, Annie").

She signed with the Chess Records group in 1960. Her first LP, *At Last*, a mix of hard-edged soul and string-laden ballads, featured the title tune as well as "Tell Mama," "Something's Got a Hold on Me," and "I'd Rather Go Blind" (for which she wrote the lyrics)—all of which have become standards.

Her LP *Etta James Rocks the House* (1963) is, to my mind, one of the greatest live records ever made.

Her biography by David Ritz, *Rage to Survive: The Etta James Story*, is a great if sometimes harrowing account of a life filled with personal ordeals including poverty, drug addiction, incarceration, and hospitalizations. But in the end, her contributions to America were remembered in a message from President Barack Obama and in-person musical tributes from Stevie Wonder and Christine Aguilera at a funeral attended by hundreds of people in Gardena, California, in 2012.

James Brown

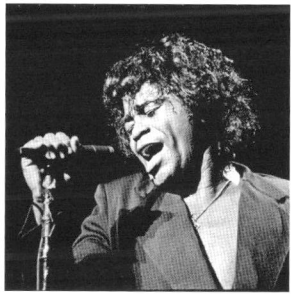

From poverty and youthful experience in gospel, to early R&B hits with the Famous Flames, to genre-defining soul and funk hits, through ups and downs in life, James Brown was always an astonishing singer and dancer, an exacting bandleader, a businessman, and a social activist. His live performances were legendary for their energy and showmanship, as revealed in the movie of the 1964 T.A.M.I. (Teenage Awards Music International or Teen Age Music International) Show, where he upstaged the Rolling Stones. His 1963 LP *Live at the Apollo*, which Brown

bankrolled himself when his label refused to, spent sixty-six weeks on the charts and has been called the greatest thirty-one minutes of live music ever recorded. It also established Brown as an R&B and soul superstar and an economic force. His popularity and social impact were such that his televised concert is credited with quelling riots in Boston while other cities burned after Martin Luther King was killed. He also dabbled in politics, endorsing Hubert Humphrey and befriending Richard Nixon. He was genuinely larger than life. I'm glad I got to photograph him performing when he had all his powers.

James Carr

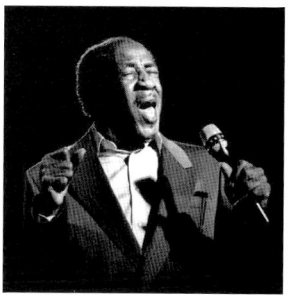

Not one of the most well-known deep soul singers, James Carr (1942–2001) was definitely one of the best. He was a man with a complex and often-troubled personal life, but his music was SUBLIME.

Born in Mississippi and raised in Memphis, he sang in gospel groups before venturing into secular music. He was turned down by Stax Records and went to the smaller Goldwax label. He had some success there with "You've Got My Mind Messed Up" and "Pouring Water on a Drowning Man," but it was 1967's "Dark End of the Street," written by Dan Penn and Chips Moman, that made him a soul superstar. This tale of hidden and forbidden love became an instant soul classic and has been covered by dozens of artists. No matter how many versions have been made, the James Carr rendition is the definitive one and will never be topped. I still get chills whenever I hear it.

He suffered from bipolar disorder, which disrupted his ability to tour and perform and required several hospitalizations. Despite periodic returns to performing, he was never able to really restart his career.

This photo was taken in 1992 at Tramps in New York City during one of those comeback attempts. He was booked for two nights, the first of which I attended. It was a joy, just wonderful, with searing, emotional vocals and a great backing band. Carla Thomas was also on the bill, and they did a duet of, what else, the soul classic "Tramp." Everyone was ecstatic. The *New York Times* gave the show a rave review, and the second night was PACKED in anticipation. But James faltered and did not perform.

I like to think that this photo captures some of the complexity of the man, one side bathed in light and power and the other side on "the dark end of the street."

Jerry Butler

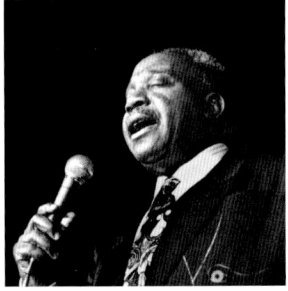

Born in Sunflower, Mississippi, smooth soul singer / songwriter / Cook County board commissioner Jerry Butler grew up in Chicago, and the church. He met future fellow Impression Curtis Mayfield in a church choir. Jerry cowrote the Impressions' first hit, "For Your Precious Love" (1958), a gold record and a soul standard, and had many more hits with the Impressions and as a solo artist, among them "He Will Break Your Heart," "Only the Strong Survive," "Make It Easy on Yourself," and "Let It Be Me" (with Betty Everett). With Otis Redding, he cowrote another soul classic, "I've Been Loving You Too Long." In 1991 he was inducted into the Rock & Roll Hall of Fame as a member of the Impressions, and many believe he deserves to go in as a solo artist too. I'm one of them.

Sadly he passed at the age of 82, in February 2025.

Mable John

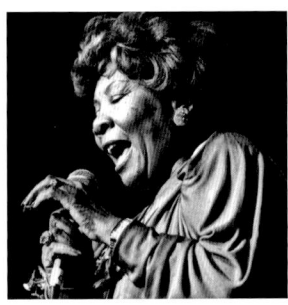

Born in 1930, the eldest of nine (including R&B singer Little Willie John of "Fever" fame), Mable was the first female signed by Berry Gordy to Motown's Tamla label but had little success there.

She wrapped two stints as a Raelette, singing on many Ray Charles hits, around a solo career with Stax Records, though later releases—such as "Stay Out of the Kitchen," "Leftover Love," and "Able Mable"—did not score as big as her debut in 1966, "Your Good Thing Is About to End."

In 1973 she began managing gospel groups, and in 1986 she founded Joy Community Outreach, a charity to feed the homeless in Los Angeles. In 1993, she earned a doctorate of divinity degree.

But the music world had not forgotten her. In 1994, now Dr. Mable John, she received a Pioneer Award from the Rhythm and Blues Foundation, and she was featured in two movies: John Sayles's 2007 musical drama *Honeydripper* and the 2014 documentary *20 Feet from Stardom*.

The last time I last saw her, performing in her mid-eighties at the 2015 Ponderosa Stomp, she was somewhat frail compared to the artist I saw in the 1990s, but she was still wonderful, and warmly received.

Mable John passed in 2022 at the age of ninety-one.

Mavis Staples

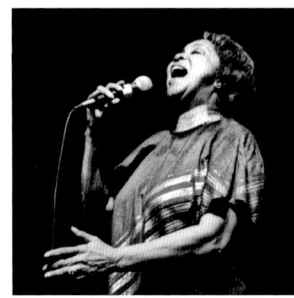

As part of the Staples Singers, a family affair formed by Roebuck "Pops" Staples, Mavis sang what some have called the soundtrack of the civil rights movement, working closely with the Rev. Dr. Martin Luther King Jr. The Staples also had a long string of secular soul hits, including "Respect Yourself," "I'll Take You There," and "Let's Do It Again." These photos are from a show Mavis performed with her sisters, Yvonne and Cleotha, and their Pops at the Bottom Line in New York City in 1992. I'm grateful I got to see her many times and occasionally breathe the same air!

Maxine Brown

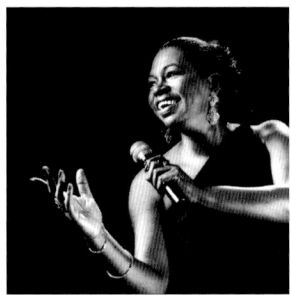

The beautiful and seemingly ageless New York–based singer Maxine Brown had early roots in gospel, then hits such as "All in My Mind" and "Oh No, Not My Baby," and added a series of successful duets with Chuck Jackson. Recording for a series of labels, she had more solo hits, often with backing vocals by Cissy Houston (Whitney's mom), and the Sweet Inspirations. In 1991, Maxine Brown, the personification of soulful elegance, was awarded the Rhythm & Blues Foundation's Pioneer Award.

My photos of both Maxine Brown and Chuck Jackson were taken in a studio for the Rhythm & Blues Foundation, and I like to think that the elegance of the setting and drama of the lighting befitted their style.

Otis Clay

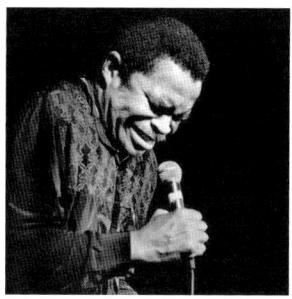

Deep soul singer Otis Lee Clay (1942–2016) was born in Mississippi, but his family, like so many other African Americans, migrated north, in his case to Indiana. He sang with gospel groups before making his first secular recordings in 1962. He had some chart success with One-derful Records in Chicago, but it was Atlantic Records' Cotillion label's debut release, his version of the Sir Douglas Quintet's "She's About a Mover," that gave him his biggest yet hit.

His most successful record, however, would come on Willie Mitchell's Hi label in 1972 with "Trying to Live My Life Without You," a soul blues classic later covered by Bob Seger and others.

Otis Clay continued to have popularity domestically and internationally—his *Live in Japan* CD is especially wonderful—and he had a string of releases leading up to duo CDs with Johnny Rawls (*Soul Brothers*, 2014) and with his (and my) longtime friend Billy Price (*This Time for Real*), which won the Blues Music Award for Best Soul Blues Record in 2015. Sad to say, but shortly after its release, he passed suddenly.

He was a sweet, genuine, affable man. I remember once when he was on a panel on a Legendary R&B Cruise discussing life on the road back in the day. He recounted playing shows where a rope down the middle of the venue separated Black and white audiences; he shook his head, started laughing, and said simply, "Racism is so silly."

A true gentleman. He is deeply missed.

Percy Sledge

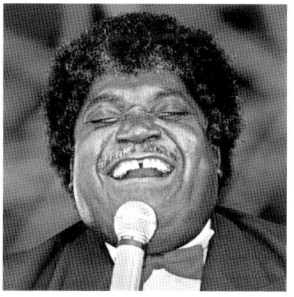

What can you say about the man who gave us "When a Man Loves a Woman?" He was an emotional and sentimental singer sometimes called the "King of Slow Soul." After recording the first version of that song, Jerry Wexler, producer at Atlantic Records, said the horns were out of tune and asked Sledge for a do-over. They got different horn players and gave it another go. In the end, though, the two tapes were somehow mixed up, and Atlantic put out the first version. It didn't affect its success, since it was one of the first soul records released by Atlantic Records to achieve Gold Record status. He followed up with "Warm and

Tender Love," "It Tears Me Up," "Take Time to Know Her," "Out of Left Field," and more—all soul classics. His voice and spirit are part of the fabric of American culture.

Roebuck "Pops" Staples

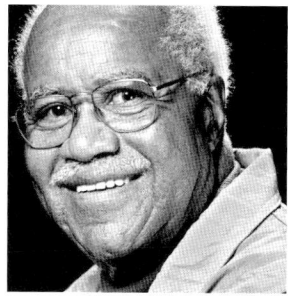

Pops Staples (1914–2000) was a very special man. He glowed.

From blues roots in Mississippi to gospel out of Chicago to soul and beyond out of Memphis, his warm, down-home voice and vibrato-soaked "slinky" electric guitar moved and motivated people.

Born the youngest of fourteen children in Mississippi, he heard and learned from legendary deep Delta bluesmen Charlie Patton, Son House, and Robert Johnson. He moved to Chicago in 1935, and in 1948 he and his wife, Oceola Staples, formed the Staple Singers with their children Cleotha, Mavis, Pervis, and Yvonne.

The Staple Singers first recorded for the United and VeeJay labels, moving on to Epic, and then to Memphis's Stax.

While their earlier output was gospel, they began to make more secular records, yet still inspirational and motivational, reflecting the civil rights and antiwar movements of the time. Their Stax recordings "Respect Yourself" and "I'll Take You There" were huge hits with a strong message.

The Staple Singers worked closely with Dr. Martin Luther King Jr., and their music was often called the soundtrack of the civil rights movement.

I feel blessed that I got to see, photograph, and occasionally breathe some of the same air as Mr. Staples. Studio portrait for the Rhythm & Blues Foundation, New York City, 1995.

Rufus Thomas

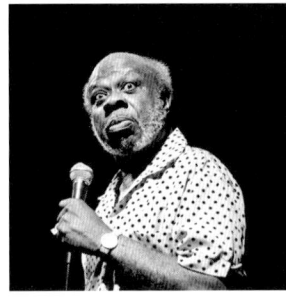

Singer, dancer, and comic showman Rufus Thomas (1917–2001) started in minstrel shows and vaudeville and was a pioneering DJ on Memphis's WDIA, then referred to as the "Mother Station of the Negroes" because it was the first radio station in the United States programmed entirely for African Americans.

From early records on Sun Records such as "Bear Cat," an answer song to "Hound Dog," to hits on Stax Records such as "Walking the Dog" and "Funky Chicken," he always brought the JOY! Harking back to his vaudeville roots, his shows were laced with athletic dancing and sly humor, and he was known for his flamboyant costumes.

He was also the dad of Stax Records recording star Carla Thomas; R&B, jazz, and soul blues singer Vaneese Thomas; and keyboardist/producer Marvell Thomas.

He was one of a kind, and I'm glad I got to see him perform several times.

This photo was from the Lone Star Roadhouse, New York City, 1991.

Solomon Burke

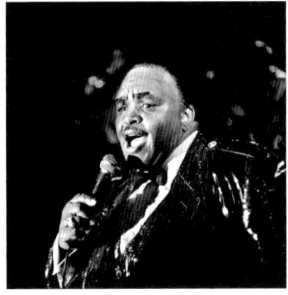

Singer Solomon Burke—one of the first artists, if not the first, to be called a "soul" singer and also one of the first to bring a country feel to soul and to rhythm and blues—was a larger-than-life performer, presence, and personality. His spirit filled any room he was in.

Born in Philadelphia, he was preaching by the age of seven, known as the "Boy Wonder Preacher." He turned to secular music and had some success on Apollo Records and other labels, but it was when he reached a handshake deal with Atlantic Records that his star really began to rise. His early hits helped Atlantic carry on after losing its biggest stars, Ray Charles and Bobby Darin, to other labels.

Many of his songs have become standards: "Cry to Me," "Everybody Needs Someone to Love," "Just Out of Reach," "Got to Get You Off My Mind," "Tonight's the Night," and more.

This photo was taken at Tramps in New York City on a night he shared the bill with Ruth Brown—and Charles Brown was playing in the adjacent piano room. It was a joyful reunion. It was also one of the last shows I saw where he performed standing; he soon began performing seated in a regal throne. Unforgettable!

This photo wound up on the cover of the Rounder CD *A Change Is Gonna Come.*

William Bell

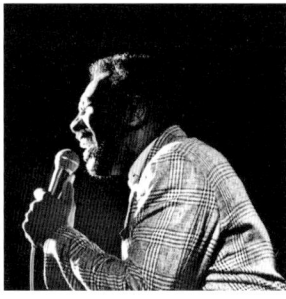

Singer and songwriter William Bell, born William Yarborough in 1939 in Memphis, helped establish his hometown's fledgling Stax Records with its first hit, his 1961 song "You Don't Miss Your Water." He went on to have a string of hits on the label, including "I Forgot to Be Your Lover." Bell also coauthored the Chuck Jackson hit "Any Other Way" and the blues classic "Born Under a Bad Sign," popularized by both Albert King and Cream.

Since his early successes, he has constantly stayed active and creative. In 2014 he was featured in the documentary film *Take Me to the River,* which delved deeply in the music and artists of Memphis.

Three years later he was awarded a Grammy for *This Is Where I Live,* as Best Americana album. The year 2019 found him nominated for Best Soul Blues Male Artist by the Blues Foundation. Just months later, in 2020, he was named a Fellow of the National Endowment for the Arts, the nation's highest honor in the folk and traditional arts. In 2024 the Recording Academy inducted "You Don't Miss Your Water" into the Grammy Hall of Fame and in 2025 Mr. Bell was also inducted into the Blues Foundation's Hall of Fame.

Dizzy Gillespie

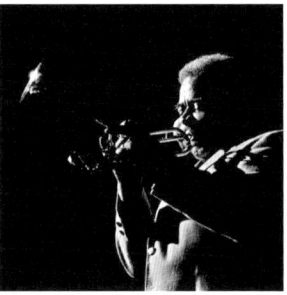

The contribution that trumpet player John Birks Gillespie made to our music and culture cannot be overstated. The musicianship and intellectual complexity he and a handful of other players, Charlie Parker foremost among them, brought in inventing bebop marked a deep change in jazz—and society.

Born in 1917, Gillespie influenced generations of trumpet players, including Miles Davis, Clifford Brown, and Freddie Hubbard, as well as players of all other instruments of jazz. In addition, Dizzy was a showman, an entertainer, and a scat singer, whose outgoing personality and mischievous sense of humor invited audiences into a new music and a hip world that did not always seem so inviting to the uninitiated.

This is a photo from a Saturday afternoon show at the Apollo around 1986. I went uptown with my pal Ted Fox, who wrote *Showtime at the Apollo*, the definitive history of the historic Harlem showplace. I think the cover for the show was $6. Ray Barretto sat in on percussion, and Bill Cosby sang a number. Not an afternoon I'll ever forget.

George Benson

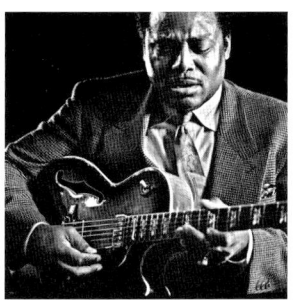

Guitarist George Benson was a child prodigy from my former hometown, Pittsburgh, Pennsylvania. By the age of nine he had two sides released on RCA subsidiary Groove Records. He played locally doing straight-ahead instrumental jazz and by age twenty-one had his first album as leader, *The New Boss Guitar*, featuring organist Jack McDuff. More jazz albums followed, mostly in the B-3 organ trio format, and he also was a sideman on Miles Davis's *Miles in the Sky* album from 1968.

Benson had a great solo career into the 1970s with wonderful stuff on Prestige, Verve, and CTI. The CTI LPs where he played with the likes of Freddie Hubbard and Stanley Turrentine are especially great.

Benson then went to Warner Brothers and had major crossover success with *Breezin'*, which was certified triple platinum and made number one on the Billboard albums chart. *Breezin'* also broke Benson as a singer with the song "This Masquerade," a pop hit that won the Grammy for Record of the Year.

Since then, Benson has won multiple Grammys and even has a star on the Hollywood Walk of Fame.

Also of note are his albums *Inspiration* (2013), a tribute to Nat King Cole, and *Walking to New Orleans* (2019), a tribute to Fats Domino and Chuck Berry.

This photo is from the Newark Jazz Festival, ca. 1993.

Dexter Gordon

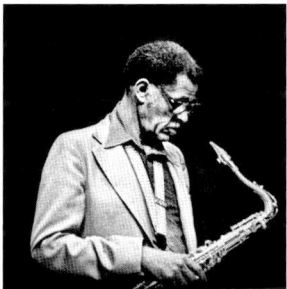

One of tenor saxophonist Dexter Gordon's nicknames, "Long Tall Dexter," was obviously based on his 6-foot-6 height, but another,

"Sophisticated Giant," said much more about the well-traveled jazz innovator.

Born in Los Angeles to an accomplished family—his father was a doctor who counted Duke Ellington and Lionel Hampton among his patients—Gordon was one of the inventors and shapers of the revolutionary new form of jazz known as bebop, along with the likes of Charlie Parker, Dizzy Gillespie, and Bud Powell.

Bicoastal during his US years and a longtime resident of Europe, mainly Paris and Copenhagen, Dexter Gordon had a prolific studio and live-performance career spanning over forty years.

Like too many of his era, he also was a heroin addict, and he did multiyear stints in California's Chino and Folsom Prisons in the 1950s.

His commanding presence and good looks made him a favorite of moviemakers and photographers, and Gordon was nominated for an Academy Award for best actor in a leading role for his performance in the Bertrand Tavernier film *Round Midnight* in 1986. He won a Grammy for the soundtrack album.

Gordon was also a close friend of my friend and mentor, the photographer Herman Leonard, whose photo of Gordon, enveloped in a cloud of cigarette smoke, is perhaps the most iconic jazz photo ever.

This photo was taken in Pittsburgh on his celebratory US homecoming tour in 1977. A few decades back, I actually won a prize for this one!

Les Paul

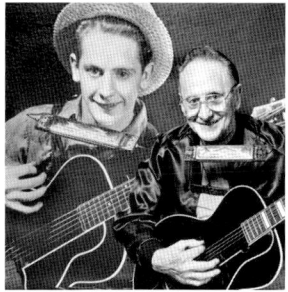

Lester William Polsfuss was a genius—a great guitar player, an innovator, an inventor, a genuinely nice guy, and a true legend.

From early success as a jazz musician to later mass popularity with his then wife, the singer Mary Ford, and from creating innovations such as sound-on-sound recording to refining the design of the electric guitar, Les Paul never missed a beat.

I won't attempt to list all his accomplishments, but he changed all music for everyone with his talent and vision. We should all be very grateful.

This photo was taken for the *New York Times* on the occasion of his eightieth birthday. Many people think it is a montage created in Photoshop; it is not. It is a straight, unmanipulated photograph. Les had a larger-than-life-sized photo of himself at age fifteen in his home lab/ studio in New Jersey. He graciously agreed to pose in front of it for this portrait. He also had the same guitar (with a new neck) and the same harmonica and rack sixty-five years later! The photo ran half a page on the cover of the arts-and-leisure section of the Sunday *New York Times*.

Les Paul died in 2009 at the age of ninety-four. So, with gratitude, love and respect, rest in peace, Mr. Paul.

Betty Carter

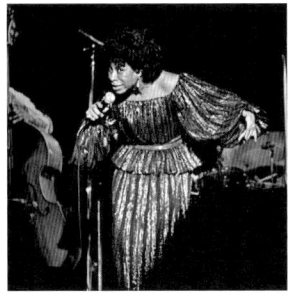

Betty Carter (1929–98; born Lillie Mae Jones) was a jazz singer and more, a musician's musician and a singer's singer.

A trained pianist and a songwriter, Betty Carter brought a jazz musician's perfectionism and creativity to every note she sang, to her part in a piece's arrangement and to her solo improvisations.

And she sang the meaning of a song's words and went beyond words at times, but not as often as her reputation might suggest, to scat "words" and syllables not in any spoken language. Aching ballads, lighthearted novelty tunes, virtuoso showpieces; she made them all her own.

She was right there at the birth of bebop with Dizzy Gillespie and Charlie Parker. She joined Lionel Hampton's band, which meant she also sang with Charles Mingus and Wes Montgomery. At the recommendation of Miles Davis, Ray Charles recorded an album of duets with her. "Baby It's Cold Outside" from this LP is probably her best-known mainstream success, but the other duets are also SUBLIME. Seek them out.

Always a strong, independent woman, she formed her own record label—Bet-Car—in 1969, a bold move for any musician, but especially for a woman of color. It became the sole source for her music for almost twenty years.

Betty Carter continued to record and perform until she left us at age sixty-nine.

This photo is from the Bottom Line in New York City, 1981.

Grover Washington Jr.

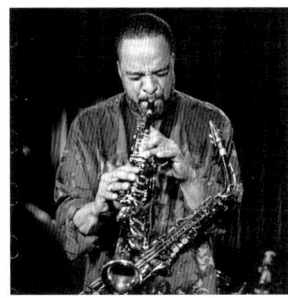

Grover Washington Jr. was a working soul, jazz, and funk saxophone player before he joined the US Army, where he met drummer Billy Cobham, who introduced him to the New York City jazz scene. Washington freelanced there, mostly in organ-based soul jazz bands. A big break came when he substituted for Hank Crawford on a date for CTI subsidiary Kudu Records, which led to the hit "Mr. Magic" and a series of highly successful albums in both the R&B and pop realms.

His career took a major leap forward with his self-produced LP *Winelight* in 1981, which featured singer Bill Withers on "Just the Two of Us." The album went platinum and won the Grammy for Best Jazz Fusion Performance, and the song was Best R&B Song. This LP and George Benson's *Breezin'* are considered cornerstones of the smooth jazz genre that found a mass audience in the 1980s.

Grover Washington died of a heart attack in 1999 at the far-too-young age of fifty-six.

Cab Calloway

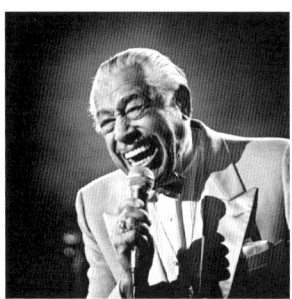

The "Hi-De-Ho" man, a national treasure born on Christmas Day in 1907, got that name from his rendition of "Minnie the Moocher," believed to be the first song by an African American to sell a million copies.

In raucous performances and on hit records in the 1930s and 1940s, Cab Calloway was a jazz singer, with an active, improvising, "scat" style. He was also an athletic, trend-setting dancer. His bands often included some of the jazz greats of the eras, including such giants as Dizzy Gillespie and Ben Webster at different times. Cab Calloway and His Orchestra had a long run at the Cotton Club in Harlem, following and then equaling or exceeding the Duke Ellington band in popularity.

Calloway made many movie appearances from the 1930s forward, including in the *Blues Brothers* film (1980), which brought him a new generation of fans. He was also a character and voiceover in cartoons.

This photo was taken at the Ritz, in New York City, ca. 1986. Roomful of Blues was the opening act.

Al Hibbler

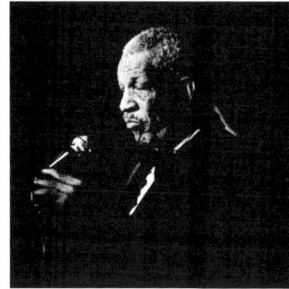

Singer Albert George Hibbler was blind from birth. He attended the Arkansas School for the Blind, where he sang in the choir. He then worked as a blues singer early in his career. He sang with Duke Ellington's orchestra from 1943 to 1951, and many consider him Duke's premier male vocalist. He went on to have several pop hits as a solo artist. Some classified his singing as rhythm and blues, some as jazz, some as pop. Regardless, he was an exceptional interpreter of popular songs who worked with some of the best jazz musicians ever.

He was also a civil rights activist, marching often and getting arrested more than once. His activism discouraged major record labels from signing him, but Frank Sinatra supported him and signed him to his label, Reprise Records.

Hibbler sang two songs at Louis Armstrong's funeral.

His hits "Do Nothin' till You Hear from Me," "I'm Just a Lucky So-and-So," and "Unchained Melody" have become standards and are true gems.

Chet Baker

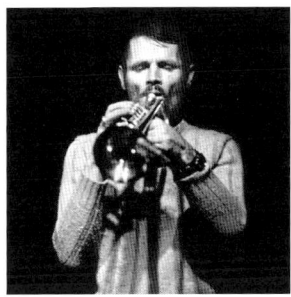

Jazz trumpeter and vocalist Chesney Henry Baker Jr.'s immense talent and movie-star good looks earned him much attention and critical praise through the 1950s, particularly for albums featuring his vocals (*Chet Baker Sings*, *It Could Happen to You*). Jazz historian Dave Gelly described the promise of Baker's early career as "James Dean, Sinatra, and Bix (Beiderbecke), rolled into one."

But his fame—or notoriety –was also driven by his well-publicized drug habit. He was in and out of jail frequently and suffered beatings before enjoying a career resurgence in the late 1970s and 1980s.

There is an Academy Award–nominated 1988 documentary about Baker, *Let's Get Lost*, directed by fashion photographer Bruce Weber.

His story is amazing, if not easy, and his music is classic and timeless.

David "Fathead" Newman

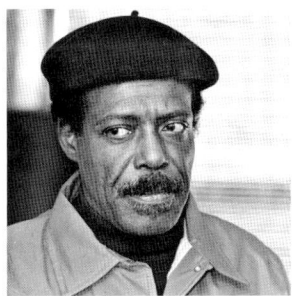

A prolific jazz and R&B saxophonist who made numerous recordings under his own name, David Newman is probably best known for his work with Ray Charles.

A so-called Texas Tenor (like Illinois Jacquet, King Curtis, and others) with a big bluesy sound, Newman studied music in college but left to play in the bands of saxophonist Buster Smith, pianist Lloyd Glenn, and guitarists Lowell Fulson and T-Bone Walker. It was in Fulson's band that he met Ray Charles in 1951. In 1954 he joined Charles's band and stayed until the 1970s, soloing on many of the definitive, classic Charles sides

from that era. Producer Jerry Wexler called Newman Charles's "alter ego on tenor," and Charles himself said that Newman "could make his sax sing the song like no one else."

After leaving Charles, Newman performed and record both as a leader and session and sideman with the likes of Aretha Franklin, B.B. King, Joe Cocker, Dr. John, Art Blakey, Stanley Turrentine, Natalie Cole, Jimmy Scott, Lou Rawls, Herbie Mann, the Average White Band, Jimmy McGriff, Eric Clapton, Hank Crawford, Aaron Neville, Queen Latifah, Richard Tee, Gregg Allman, and Doug Sahm. He also scored films, notably Robert Altman's *Kansas City*. To say that he was versatile would be a serious understatement.

He was a thoughtful and kind man, and I'm glad I got to spend a few heartbeats with him.

Hank Crawford

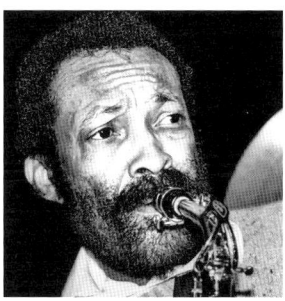

Bennie Ross "Hank" Crawford Jr. was an R&B, hard bop, jazz funk, soul jazz alto saxophonist, pianist, arranger, and songwriter. He appeared on an early 1952 Memphis recording for B.B. King. He later joined the classic Ray Charles band, where he worked with David "Fathead" Newman in the sax section on many of Ray's classic hits. He became musical director for Charles from 1959 to 1963. He also had a solo career, releasing many well-regarded albums on Atlantic, CTI, and Milestone. In 1981, he reunited with B.B. King on *There Must Be a Better World Somewhere*. In 1986, Crawford began working with blues-jazz organ master Jimmy McGriff. They recorded five coleader dates for Milestone Records, often produced by Bob Porter. He continued to tour and record until he left us in 2009.

I had the honor of photographing him for the 1991 CD *Portrait*, produced by Bob Porter.

Illinois Jacquet

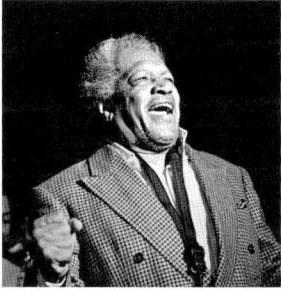

Jean-Baptiste Illinois Jacquet is perhaps best known for his tenor solo on Lionel Hampton's "Flying Home," which pretty much invented and defined the honk and wail of R&B and rock-and-roll saxophone. That said, he was also a sophisticated jazz player and skilled improviser who had a long career in big bands, both as a sideman and as a leader. He played with everyone from Count Basie, Cab Calloway, Nat King Cole, and Lena Horne to Bill Clinton and more.

Jacquet became the first jazz musician to be an artist in residence at Harvard University.

And man, could he swing! In the 1980s and 1990s he played regular swing dance concerts at Roseland Ballroom in New York City that had the whole room jumping. I'm glad I got to see and photograph him more than once.

Jay McShann

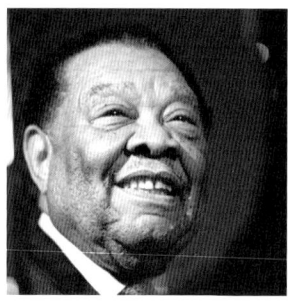

Originally from Oklahoma, bandleader, pianist, songwriter, and singer Jay McShann will always be associated with Kansas City jump blues, jazz, and swing. Born in 1916, he moved to Kansas City in 1936 and formed a big band that spawned some of America's greatest musicians, featuring at various times saxophonists Charlie Parker, Ben Webster, and Paul Quinichette, and vocalists Al Hibbler, Walter Brown, and Jimmy Witherspoon. Parker, who went on to lead the bebop movement and revolutionize jazz, made his first recordings with McShann in 1940.

After World War II, McShann performed with smaller bands fronted by vocalists, scoring R&B hits including Jimmy Witherspoon's classic "Ain't Nobody's Business," a reworking of an old blues standard; "Hands Off," sung by Priscilla Bowman; and "Confessin' the Blues," sung by McShann's cowriter Walter Brown and later covered by Little Walter, whose version in turn was covered by the Rolling Stones.

In the late 1960s, McShann became popular as a singer as well as a pianist, often performing with violinist Claude Williams. He continued recording and touring through the 1990s.

In 1979, he appeared prominently in the documentary movie *The Last of the Blue Devils: The Kansas City Jazz Story*.

This photo is from Tramps, in New York City, ca. 1994

Jimmy McGriff

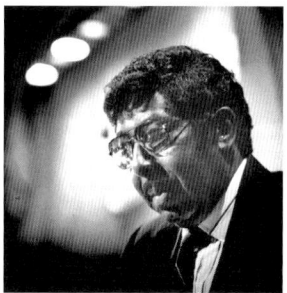

Jimmy McGriff was a soul-jazz and bop organist with a sound at the intersection of blues and jazz.

Hailing from the Philadelphia area, his early influences were Jimmy Smith and Groove Holmes, with whom he studied. He also attended the Juilliard School of Music. His band backed artists such as Arthur Prysock, Carmen McRae, Candido, and Don Gardner when they toured in the Philadelphia area.

In 1961, McGriff had a chart hit with a cover of Ray Charles's "I've Got a Woman" and a follow-up hit with "All About My Girl." He continued to record his blues-based sound on a variety of labels and with a variety of collaborators such as saxophonists Hank Crawford and David Newman; drummer Bernard Purdie; Bob Porter, who produced many of the great Prestige organ trio records; and legendary recording engineer Rudy Van Gelder, whose Englewood, New Jersey, studio was where Prestige, Blue Note, and Impulse recorded many legendary LPs by Coltrane, Rollins, Jimmy Smith, and on and on.

Jimmy McGriff continued to perform and record into the first decade of the 2000s and died in 2008 due to complications of multiple sclerosis.

If you like jazz, soul, blues, funk, and Hammond B-3 organ, you'll like Mr. McGriff.

Jimmy Witherspoon

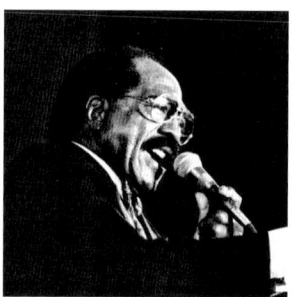

"Spoon" was a great jump blues shouter with a jazz flavor to his sound. He made his first records with Jay McShann's band in 1945. In 1949, also with the McShann band, he had his first hit, "Ain't Nobody's Business," originally recorded by Bessie Smith. It became his signature tune.

In 1950 he had a double-sided hit with "No Rollin' Blues" and "Big Fine Girl." He went on to a long solo career, recording with jazz, blues, and rock greats.

Way back when, when I was a blues DJ, I accompanied him to a show he put on for the inmates at Western Penitentiary outside Pittsburgh (no photos allowed!). Spoon had barely slept and didn't get a nickel, but he put on a great show, and the inmates were absolutely thrilled. I always respected him for doing that.

These photos are from the Chicago Blues Festival, ca. 1991, and with Doc Pomus and Dr. John at the recording session for "Midnight Lady Called the Blues," ca. 1986.

Joe Pass

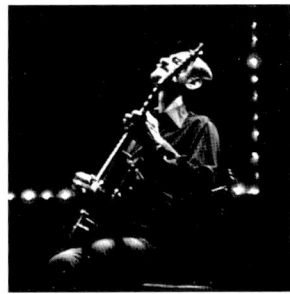

Virtuoso jazz guitarist Joseph Anthony Jacobi Passalaqua (born in 1929) began touring in his teens but within a few years on the road became addicted to heroin and spent much of the 1950s in prison. He made his debut on record while in rehab in 1962, gaining critical notice as a star to watch. *Sounds of Synanon* is a great album, rare and sought after, that I am proud to have in my collection.

He recorded many more albums and was a sideman either in the studio or on tour with Les McCann, George Shearing, Louie Bellson, Frank Sinatra, Sarah Vaughan, Joe Williams, Della Reese, Johnny Mathis, and many others. He also worked on the *The Tonight Show*, *The Merv Griffin Show*, and *The Steve Allen Show*.

In the early 1970s, he and guitarist Herb Ellis regularly collaborated live and on record, and he often worked with pianist Oscar Peterson and vocalist Ella Fitzgerald.

In 1994, Joe Pass died from liver cancer at the age of sixty-five.

This photo from the Top of the Gate in New York City, ca. 1981.

Little Jimmy Scott

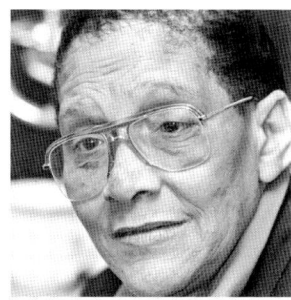

I was honored to spend some time in the orbit of Jimmy Scott along with Doc Pomus, Dr. John, and the Felder family. Those moments are among my most treasured memories. He was a special soul. Jimmy had a unique, high-pitched voice (his voice never changed due to a genetic condition) and the most AMAZING phrasing.

Once, at a rehearsal at Doc's apartment, everyone was chatting, and Jimmy was quietly reading a lyric sheet aloud. He slipped into his singing voice, and soon everyone fell silent in awe listening to the beauty of his voice.

Scott's career spanned sixty-five years. He performed with jazz giants Charlie Parker, Sarah Vaughan, Lester Young, Lionel Hampton, Charles Mingus, Fats Navarro, Quincy Jones, Bud Powell, Ray Charles, and Wynton Marsalis. He also performed with musicians from other genres, such as David Byrne, Lou Reed, Flea, and Michael Stipe. His biography, *Faith in Time*, written by David Ritz, is a great read. He was, as Dr. John once described him to me, a "Prince of the Planet."

If you are not familiar with Jimmy, take the time to get acquainted.

Joe Williams

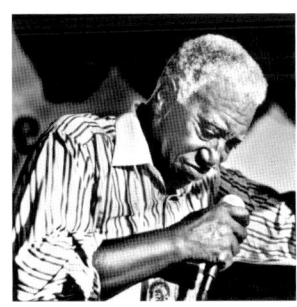

One of the bluesiest of the big-band singers, Joe Williams is best known for his work with the Count Basie Orchestra. During the Basie era he had hits with "Every Day I Have the Blues" and "Alright, Okay, You Win."

But he also sang with other greats of the big-band era—Lionel Hampton, Andy Kirk, Les Hite—as well as smaller jazz ensembles, led by Harry "Sweets" Edison, Junior Mance, George Shearing, Cannonball Adderley, Clark Terry, and Thad Jones.

Even after leaving Basie for a solo career, he maintained good relations and continued to appear with him on occasion.

Williams was also an actor, appearing in films and the television shows *Lou Grant*, *The Cosby Show*, and *Sesame Street*.

Later in life he worked at festivals and on cruise ships and established a residency in the clubs and showrooms in Las Vegas, where he passed at the age of eighty in 1999.

David "Panama" Francis

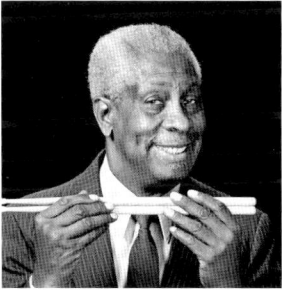

Born David Albert Francis in Miami in 1918, Panama Francis—nicknamed for his trademark hat—had one of the longest and most varied careers of any drummer ever, from Harlem to Hollywood, from swing jazz to rock and roll, from Cab Calloway to Dinah Shore.

Just shy of twenty years old, he moved to New York City, where he worked with Tab Smith, the Roy Eldridge Orchestra, and, for six years, Lucky Millinder's Orchestra at Harlem's Savoy Ballroom. He then spent five years recording and touring with Calloway. He also played with Duke Ellington, Tommy Dorsey, Ray Conniff, and Sy Oliver and became a highly successful studio drummer. He recorded with John Lee Hooker, Eubie Blake, Ella Fitzgerald, Illinois Jacquet, Mahalia Jackson, and Big Joe Turner. He drummed on the Elvis Presley demos and hits by the Four Seasons, the Platters, Bobby Darin, Neil Sedaka, Dion, James Brown, Dinah Washington, Ray Charles, LaVern Baker, and dozens more.

In 1979, Panama Francis reestablished the Savoy Sultans band he had admired at the Savoy Ballroom decades earlier, leading it on tour and recording several Grammy-nominated albums.

I photographed him around 1995 for the R&B Foundation. His stories were so fascinating that I kept shooting well after I knew I had everything I needed for the job.

Pat Martino

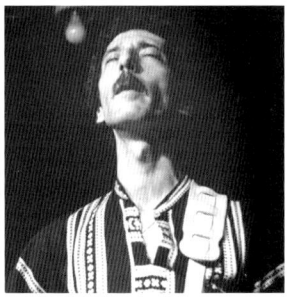

The story of jazz guitar star Pat Martino, born Patrick Carmen Azzara in 1944, was truly amazing. He had to do it twice.

First time around, as a sixteen-year-old from Philadelphia, he jumped straight into the top of the jazz guitar world in New York City, living for a while (by his parents' arrangement) with guitar master and innovator Les Paul in New Jersey. He quickly built a sparkling career both as a sideman, most notably with many of the greats of the Hammond organ, and as a solo artist. He was a mainstay of the Prestige label in the mid-1960s.

But then in 1980 he had a near-fatal seizure and brain operation that left him with amnesia. He could not remember his career or how to operate the tools of his highly successful trade. He had to relearn everything. And he did.

He built a second career both as a venerated performer and as an inspirational person, with numerous recordings, awards, and accolades.

This photo is from the late 1970s, just before his seizure. He came through Pittsburgh, touring behind his recent Warner Bros. release, which had just started to bring him to a much-broader audience and popularity.

Sonny Stitt

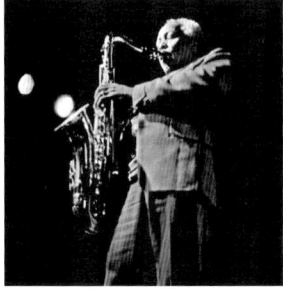

Edward Hammond Boatner Jr., better known as Sonny Stitt, was a jazz saxophonist right there at the founding of bebop. He played in the big bands of Billy Eckstine and Dizzy Gillespie in a style similar to Charlie "Yardbird" Parker—but his peers recognized that he was no mere imitator. "Even if there had not been a Bird, there would have been a Sonny Stitt," said drummer Kenny Clarke.

Stitt started recording as a solo artist in the mid-1940s and performed in various groupings with a who's who of jazz: Dexter Gordon, Gene Ammons, Bud Powell, Eddie "Lockjaw" Davis, Miles Davis, Wynton Kelly, Jimmy Cobb, Paul Chambers, Zoot Sims and Al Cohn, Johnny Griffin, Art Blakey, Dizzy Gillespie, Thelonious Monk, Red Holloway, and more. He continued to tour and record until his passing in 1982, though hampered by ill health and alcoholism.

This photo was taken in Pittsburgh, Pennsylvania, ca. 1978.

Stanley Turrentine

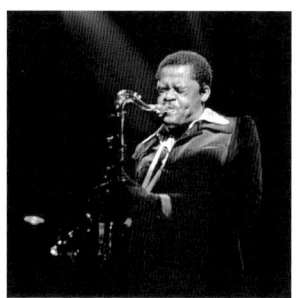

Stanley Turrentine, aka "Mr. T," was a very bluesy, soulful jazz tenor saxophonist. For me he stands at the intersection of blues and jazz. His earlier Blue Note recordings and especially his CTI recordings of the 1970s "Sugar," "Cherry," "Salt Song," and "Don't Mess with Mr. T." opened my eyes very wide. With all-star accompaniment such as George Benson, Freddie Hubbard and more, these records affected me the same way as Muddy Waters and Elmore James did. They had deep soul and emotion. This photo holds a special place for me, as it was the first time I photographed a star, a hero of mine. At the height of his popularity Turrentine came to Pittsburgh, Pennsylvania, his home town, where I lived at the time. I knew I had to overcome my shyness and photograph. The fans came out, his friends from the 'hood came out, and it was COOL! I was at every show. I gave the band prints and got autographs and never looked back. I've been shooting my musical heroes ever since. For that and more, I thank Mr. T. Photo from Pittsburgh, 1974.

Tito Puente

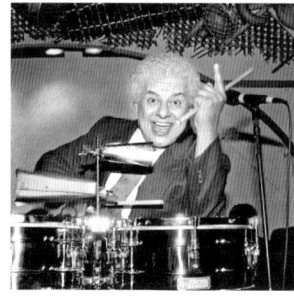

Ernesto Antonio Puente Jr. was a multi-instrumentalist, songwriter, record producer, and bandleader who melded jazz with his Puerto Rican roots. As his first of many nicknames, "Ernestito," became "Tito," Puente (born 1923) grew up in New York City's Spanish Harlem, dabbling in song and dance before joining the Navy, where he played alto saxophone and clarinet in his ship's band and was the ship's bugler. But he also saw combat in World War II, as a machine gunner. After the war, the GI Bill allowed him to study music at the Julliard School of Music, where he studied conducting, orchestration, and theory.

During the 1950s, Puente, the timbales now his main instrument, was at the height of his popularity and helped bring Cuban and Caribbean sounds such as mambo—"King of Mambo" was another of his nicknames—and cha-cha-cha to mainstream audiences. His song "Oye Como Va" was a big hit for Mexican American rocker Carlos Santana in 1970.

Puente was also variously known as "the Musical Pope," "El Rey de los Timbales" (the King of the Timbales), and "the King of Latin Music."

When his band played, if you had any sort of a pulse, you were moving in a minute! His musical legacy is carried on by his son Tito Puente Jr.

Aaron Neville

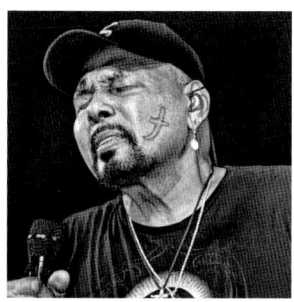

Aaron Neville possesses one of the sweetest voices ever heard. He's also a very physically imposing man, his body hinting at the longshoreman, weight lifter, and street fighter that he once was. And, with a striking facial tattoo, his appearance sometimes seems at odds with or perhaps enhancing the sweetness of his voice.

In his autobiography, *Tell It Like It Is* (2023), he tells openly and movingly of his redemption—of a life journey through crime and prison, addiction and despair—through his faith. That title is also the title of his first national hit, released in 1966 and an instant soul classic.

Before that, in 1960, he had his first regional hit, "Over You," and he sprinkled a few other solo hits, notably "Everybody Plays the Fool" in the 1990s—while joined with his brothers as the iconic family band that personified New Orleans soul and funk for decades. Aaron, Art, Cyril, and Charles—the Neville Brothers—held the status of closing act at the New Orleans Jazz & Heritage Festival.

Aaron was also known for his appearances in the Fest's Gospel Tent. A devout Catholic, Aaron Neville credits his success and survival to St. Jude, the patron saint of hopeless cases and lost causes, and wears a St. Jude medal as an earring.

He found more mainstream success with his duets with Linda Ronstadt, including "Don't Know Much" and "All My Life"; they sold millions of copies, their album was certified Triple Platinum, and they won a 1990 pop Grammy.

In 2021, the eighty-year-old singer announced his retirement from touring, but not necessarily from making more music or performing on special occasions. I'm grateful for all he gave us.

Irma Thomas

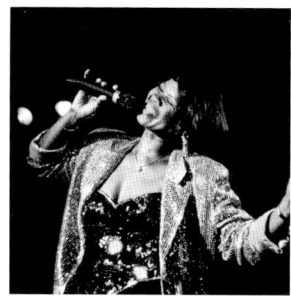

Irma Thomas's amazing voice, ageless beauty, and warm personality have been bringing us joy, soul, emotion, and humor since she sang "You Can Have My Husband, But Please Don't Mess with My Man" in 1959. She had many follow-up hits, including "It's Raining" (1962) and the first vocal recording of "Time Is on My Side," which the Rolling Stones also recorded, in two versions, also in 1964—knocking her version off the charts. Justifiably not pleased with that, and with people assuming it was a Stones song, she refused to sing the song for years, but at a New Year's Eve show in New Orleans, Bonnie Raitt urged her to sing it, and it came back into her repertoire, in 1992. It all came full circle when she sang it with the Stones at the 2024 New Orleans Jazz Fest.

I can't count the times I've seen her, but I'm grateful for every one. I like to think that this photo reflects both her musical and personal warmth.

Henry Butler

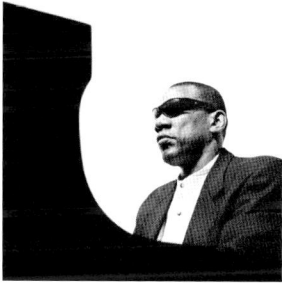

Jazz and blues virtuoso pianist Henry Butler was born in New Orleans in 1948 and grew up in the Calliope housing projects there.

Fellow New Orleans piano player Dr. John said of him, "He is the pride of New Orleans and a visionistical down-home cat and a hellified piano plunker to boot."

Blinded by glaucoma in infancy, Henry Butler attended the Louisiana State School for the Blind, where he studied piano, drums, and trombone and learned to read classical music in braille notation. He carried on the deep tradition of New Orleans piano from his youth until his passing in 2018.

Although blind, he became a noted photographer in addition to his musical accomplishments. My photo here is from an opening in New Orleans of one of his photography shows, which I attended with my friend and mentor, the legendary photographer Herman Leonard, in 1997.

Clifton Chenier

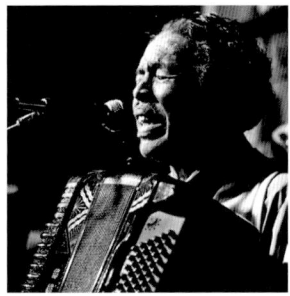

Kermit Ruffins

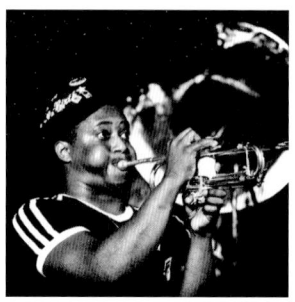

Accordionist and singer Clifton Chenier (1925–87) practically invented zydeco, the music of French-speaking African Americans in Southwest Louisiana, and brought it to a wider world.

He started out playing outside the Port Arthur, Texas, oil refinery where he worked, with his brother and future longtime band partner Cleveland on washboard; Clifton is credited with designing Cleveland's "vest frottoir" (rubboard vest), which became the classic zydeco percussion instrument.

After some early regional success on smaller labels, Clifton Chenier signed with Los Angeles–based Specialty Records in 1955 and started to get some national exposure and tours with the likes of Ray Charles, Chuck Berry, Little Richard, and Etta James. He moved on to Chess Records, the legendary Chicago Blues label, and then in the early 1960s to Arhoolie Records, which gave him new exposure to white folk and rock audiences.

As zydeco spread, he toured nationally and internationally but through it all maintained his core audience, playing legendary dances in his home state and other areas where many Louisianans had relocated, including Texas and California's Bay Area (also the stomping grounds of Queen Ida, who won zydeco's first Grammy, ahead of Chenier, who got the second, in 1983).

He was a National Heritage Fellow, a member of the Blues Hall of Fame and the Louisiana Music Hall of Fame, and, in 2014, a recipient of a Grammy Lifetime Achievement Award. His music inspired generations of Louisiana musicians, and his son C. J. Chenier and many others have carried on the zydeco tradition.

This photo was taken at the Lone Star Café, New York City. I saw his gigs there toward the end of his life. He was very weak, playing an electric accordion, which did not require the effort of a traditional instrument. The band was fierce and driving, keeping the patrons jumping. But then things would quiet down when he would sing an older song, "I'm Coming Home (to See My Mother)." It was so heartfelt, and I sensed that here was a man who knew his time wasn't very long. It was a touching moment that I'll never forget.

While still in high school, jazz trumpeter, singer, composer, and all-around entertainer Kermit Ruffins was a cofounder of the Rebirth Brass Band, a new-generation continuation of second-line parade music fused with more-contemporary genres.

But after touring with the increasingly successful Rebirth, the former French Quarter busker decided he didn't want to be on the road so much, and so in 1992 he parted ways to form the Barbecue Swingers and play regular local gigs—and cook barbecue—for his hometown folks.

In 2014, he reopened the historic Mother-in-Law Lounge (founded by Ernie K-Doe and continued by the Emperor of the Universe's widow, Antoinette, until her death in 2009), and Kermit's Treme Mother-in-Law Lounge became another regular venue for the Barbecue Swingers.

A charmer often compared to his hero Louis Armstrong as much for his engaging personality as his music, Kermit appears in the HBO series *Treme*—as himself; accused of lacking ambition, Kermit is asked if "all you want to do is get high, play some trumpet, and barbecue in New Orleans your whole damn life?" "That'll work," Kermit replies.

Rockin' Dopsie

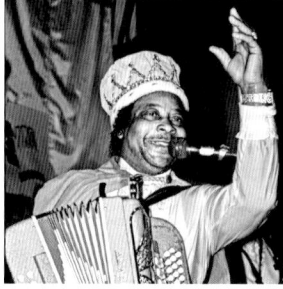

One of the earliest purveyors of the idiosyncratic Southwest Louisiana Creole music called zydeco, accordionist, singer, and bandleader Rockin' Dopsie got people dancing in clubs and festivals near and far, was nominated for a Grammy (for *Louisiana Music*, 1991), and played on albums by Bob Dylan, Paul Simon, and Cyndi Lauper.

Born Alton Rubin in 1932 in Carencro, Louisiana, he started playing accordion at age fourteen, teaching himself to play the instrument upside down since he was left-handed. He became a regular crowd-pleaser around Louisiana, but recognition outside the region came slowly.

After a 1976 performance at the New Orleans Jazz & Heritage Festival, he was signed to a Swedish record label, Sonet. This led to touring and popularity in Europe—which then spread back to the United States.

He always had a wonderful, fiercely driving, Deep South band of seasoned pros with a varied repertoire. You might hear blues, traditional waltzes, two-steps, stompers, soul, and all the mix that makes zydeco so infectious.

He was the father of two keepers of the zydeco flame, Rockin' Dopsie Jr. (David Rubin) and Dwayne Dopsie. Rockin' Dopsie Sr. died at age sixty-one in 1993.

This photo was taken at the original Lone Star in New York City in the mid-1980s. I remember looking around the club at one point, and EVERYONE was dancing—the customers, the wait staff, the bartenders, the bouncers, even the roaches. It is something I'll never forget.

Allen Toussaint

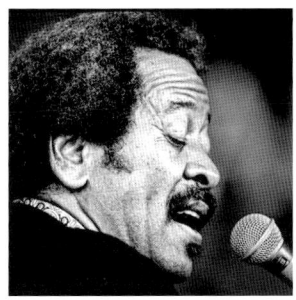

Legendary producer, songwriter, piano player, and arranger Allen Toussaint created much of the music now recognized as classic New Orleans R&B, and reshaped American popular music.

Born in New Orleans in 1938, he soaked up all the pulsating rhythms and sonic colors of his city from childhood, teaching himself the wild, idiosyncratic piano stylings of Professor Longhair and playing with another NOLA genius, guitarist Snooks Eaglin ("the Human Jukebox").

The Toussaint family home in the Gert Town neighborhood was a hangout and rehearsal space for young musicians, many of whom went on to great recognition and success. The young Toussaint became a regular performer at the historic Dew Drop Inn and played some of the piano parts on Fats Domino records.

In 1959 he recorded an album of instrumentals, *The Wild Sounds of New Orleans*, which included the tune "Java," which became a national hit for trumpeter Al Hirt. Another of his instrumentals, "Whipped Cream," written under the pseudonym Naomi Neville (his mother), would be a huge pop hit for Herb Alpert & the Tijuana Brass in 1965.

In the 1960s, Toussaint became an A&R man and producer. He produced a string of hits by Ernie K-Doe ("Mother-in-Law"), Chris Kenner ("I Like It Like That"), Irma Thomas ("It's Raining"), Lee Dorsey ("Working in a Coal Mine"), Benny Spellman ("Fortune Teller"), and others that became hits and standards of the New Orleans repertoire—and beyond.

Throughout the 1970s and 1980s, he continued to produce with great success, working with New Orleans artists such as the Meters and Dr. John and with national acts such as Labelle. He also had success as a solo artist but always said his true calling was as a producer and songwriter. "I never thought of myself as a performer," he said in a 2014 interview with *The Guardian*. "My comfort zone is behind the scenes."

He continued to write, produce, and arrange with a vast range of artists in different genres beyond his New Orleans roots. He collaborated with artists as varied as Paul McCartney, Glen Campbell, Elvis Costello, Twyla Tharp, and more. He appeared in numerous documentary films, and there was even a Broadway show based on his music.

In addition, Allen Toussaint and Dr. John were awarded honorary degrees together by Tulane University in 2013.

Toussaint died of a heart attack in Spain in 2015, at age seventy-seven. I am very grateful to have seen and photographed him many times.

Earl King

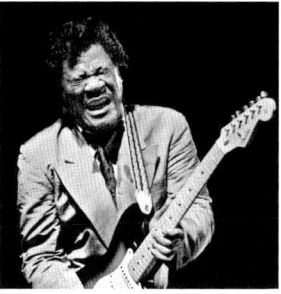

Earl Silas Johnson IV, the songwriter, guitarist, and singer better known as Earl King, was a New Orleans legend. As a composer he wrote blues and R&B standards such as "Those Lonely, Lonely Nights," "Come On" (covered by Jimi Hendrix and Stevie Ray Vaughan), "Trick Bag," and Professor Longhair's "Big Chief."

He developed his own guitar style, but early in his career he was heavily influenced by Guitar Slim (Eddie Jones of "The Things That I Used to Do" fame); in fact, when Slim was injured and could not complete a tour, King finished the tour AS Slim.

For years it was known that Earl King kept office hours at the Tastee Donut on Louisiana Avenue and Prytania Street, where he could be reached on the pay phone. The cover photo of his 1986 LP *Glazed*, on which he was backed by Roomful of Blues, was taken there. *Glazed* was just one of a series of great albums on New Orleans' own Blacktop label in the 1980s and 1990s.

This photo is from a BlackTop Blues-a-Rama show at Tipitina's in New Orleans, 1992.

Art Neville

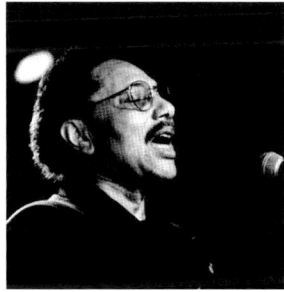

Bandleader and keyboard player Art Neville had the first hit of his long career at the age of sixteen as a member of the Hawkettes, singing *Mardi Gras Mambo* (1954)—a New Orleans standard to this day. He had a string of great singles on his own for the Specialty label—check out "Cha Dooky-Do" and "Zing Zing"—and starting in the late 1960s helped set the template for New Orleans funk with the Meters, who backed other musicians and released their own instrumental albums, offering such classic cuts as "Cissy Strut."

Then in 1976, Art and his younger brothers Aaron, Charles, and Cyril AND the Meters all worked on the brilliant Mardi Gras Indians album

The Wild Tchoupitoulas. The brothers soon formalized their status as a performing and recording band, the Neville Brothers, even as Art continued to play with the slightly renamed and slightly reconstituted Funky Meters (and occasionally also with the Original Meters) into the twenty-first century. Art Neville died in 2019 at age eighty-one.

Boozoo Chavis

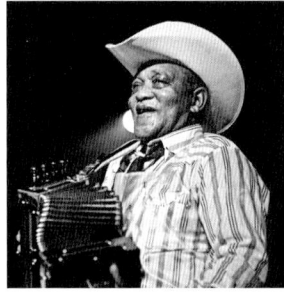

Wilson Anthony "Boozoo" Chavis was a founder of modern zydeco, the music of his Southwest Louisiana Creole heritage. He made some of the earliest recordings of the genre and was active from the 1950s until his death in 2001. Mostly performing regionally at dances, Chavis also worked as a farmer, jockey, and horse trainer. Chavis was also a prolific writer of songs, many of which became standards of the zydeco repertoire.

I will never forget his mock battles of the bands against Beau Jocque at the old Rock 'n' Bowl in New Orleans: Boozoo being carried in triumph like royalty aloft in a sedan chair. But the "battles" (the two musicians were actually friends despite some public trash talk and even a song, "Boozoo's Payback," fanning the flames) were also a showcase of traditional zydeco vs. the younger Beau Jocque's modern take on the genre, and BIG FUN for all. It was very sweet to see Boozoo getting his accolades while bringing joy to so many.

Buckwheat Zydeco

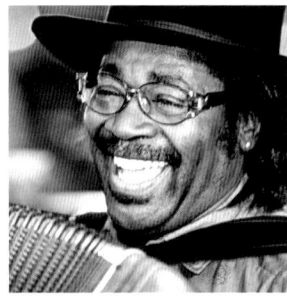

Stanley Dural Jr., better known around the globe as Buckwheat Zydeco, was a special man—a friend to me for over thirty years, as well as to everyone he met and for whom he performed.

He was a worldwide ambassador for the Creole culture of Southwest Louisiana and its music, zydeco. He began his career as a keyboardist playing blues, soul, and funk on his and backing touring artists. Clifton Chenier, the original "King of Zydeco," hired him to play Hammond organ and tour with his band. When they opened for Bob Marley, he saw how Marley honored and promoted Jamaican culture. It was then that he fully embraced the Creole musical idiom, working hard to master the accordion and adapting his childhood nickname to emerge as Buckwheat Zydeco. He became the first zydeco artist signed to a major label, Island Records, in 1987.

This led to touring and performing with major acts such as Eric Clapton, U2, and even the Boston Pops. Buckwheat Zydeco and Ils Sont Partis Band performed at the 1996 Summer Olympics to an audience of three billion people. They performed at both of President Clinton's inaugurals and made dozens of national television appearances.

"Buck," as friends knew him, died in his native Lafayette, Louisiana, at the age of sixty-eight. His spirit enhanced us all, and we are better for having had him in our lives. He is both deeply loved and deeply missed. Love, peace, and happiness.

Carol Fran

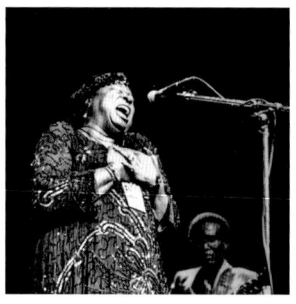

A beloved figure in the Louisiana-Texas blues world, Lafayette native Carol Fran always sang from the heart, and her shows were a joy.

Early on, she sang with the legendary Guitar Slim and had some regional success with a series of records in the 1950s and 1960s, but none more than her first, "Emmett Lee" (1957).

In 1983, she married Houston-born blues, jazz, and R&B guitarist Clarence Hollimon. They recorded some really great albums, produced by my pals Hammond Scott (Black Top) and Jimmy Morello (JSP).

In 2013, Carol Fran received the National Heritage Fellowship Award, the highest honor in the folk and traditional arts.

She continued to perform regionally and in Europe until shortly before her passing in 2021 at the age of eighty-seven. She was a beautiful and sweet lady, loved and deeply missed.

This photo is from a Black Top revue ca. 1992, with her husband, Clarence Hollimon, in the background.

Dave Bartholomew

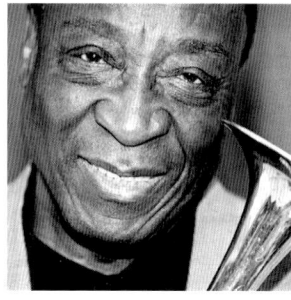

The contributions that Dave Bartholomew made to our music and our culture are beyond measure. He was one of our most influential record producers, songwriters, bandleaders, arrangers, and talent scouts. Ever.

Bartholomew was at the heart of the New Orleans sound from the 1940s onward as it evolved from jump blues and big-band swing to rhythm and blues and rock and roll.

He was best known for his work with Fats Domino, helping the easygoing R&B artist cross over to pop audiences with a string of massive hits to become one of the first stars of rock and roll. Bartholomew, who also played trumpet and tuba, cowrote and produced "Ain't That a Shame," "I'm in Love Again," and "Blue Monday," among many others, and produced Domino's biggest hit, "Blueberry Hill."

But Bartholomew also produced records by such classic New Orleans musicians as Earl King, Robert Parker, Frankie Ford, Chris Kenner, Smiley Lewis, Shirley & Lee, and many more. In addition, Chuck Berry's biggest hit was a cover of Bartholomew's novelty song "My Ding-a-Ling," one of many recordings he made as a leader.

Dave Bartholomew is a member of the Songwriters Hall of Fame, the Rock & Roll Hall of Fame, and the Louisiana Music Hall of Fame. He died in June 2019 at the age of one hundred.

These photos were made while the Rhythm & Blues Foundation was recording a New Orleans oral history, ca. 1995. The smiling image was pirated and used illegally by at least one New Orleans television station and one newspaper when he passed. Glad to help Mr. Bartholomew get his due, I guess, and thievery can be a form of flattery, I suppose.

Mac "Dr. John" Rebennack

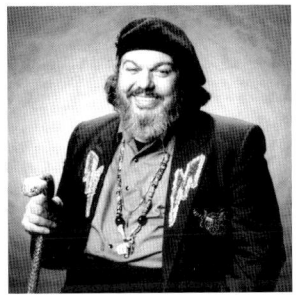

Piano player, singer, songwriter, and record producer Malcolm John Rebennack was an integral part of the New Orleans music and piano tradition from his early teens, when he met the legendary piano genius Professor Longhair and began playing with him—on guitar. But a gunshot wound a few years later would force him to switch to piano.

Deeply involved in most aspects of the New Orleans music scene of the 1950s, he moved to Los Angeles after a two-year prison stint for drugs and was a staple of studio sessions there in the 1960s and 1970s before creating the hitmaking voodoo persona that became Dr. John the Night Tripper.

Plus, he was a sweet and genuine guy. We didn't spend tons of time together, but he was a friend and always had a kind word for me. He once described Little Jimmy Scott to me as a "Prince of the Planet"; I figure it took one to know one.

The photo with Kiki Anderson (dancer) and Flash Fearless (snake) was taken at the Municipal Auditorium, New Orleans, in 1992. The others are from a 1992 portrait session when Mac was signed to Warner Bros.

Earl Palmer

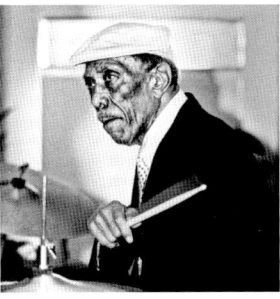

One of those "underneath it all" artists, Earl Palmer was the drummer on countless recordings that helped define rock and roll, rhythm and blues, and, really, all popular American music.

Not content with one unparalleled hitmaking career in New Orleans, he added another in Los Angeles.

It all started with his connection with the Dave Bartholomew Band in the late 1940s. First, there were the Fats Domino hits: "The Fat Man," "I'm Walkin'," "Blue Monday," and more. Also, "Tutti Frutti" and most of the rest of Little Richard's hits. "Tipitina" by Professor Longhair. "Lawdy Miss Clawdy" by Lloyd Price. "I Hear You Knocking" by Smiley Lewis. All classics. And many more, too numerous to list.

Palmer left New Orleans for Hollywood in 1957 and soon started working with the "Wrecking Crew," L.A.'s first-call studio session players. For thirty-plus years he played on thousands of sessions, including for movies and television. He worked with Frank Sinatra, Phil Spector, Ricky Nelson, Bobby Vee, Ray Charles, Sam Cooke, Eddie Cochran, Ritchie Valens, Bobby Day, Don and Dewey, Jan and Dean, the Beach Boys, Larry Williams, Gene McDaniels, Bobby Darin, Neil Young, the Pets, and B. Bumble and the Stingers, among many others.

He also played on jazz sessions with Dizzy Gillespie, Earl Bostic, David Axelrod, Onzy Matthews, and Count Basie, and on blues recordings by B.B. King and T-Bone Walker. He's also a member of the Rock & Roll Hall of Fame.

Earl Palmer died in 2008 at the age of eighty-three, but he's still playing on the radio and in American homes every day.

Ernie K-Doe

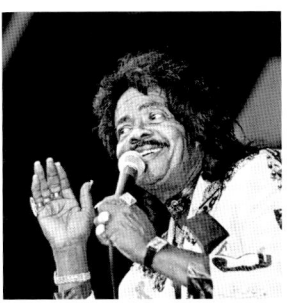

Ernest Kador Jr. built a life and a legend on one huge hit: "Mother-in-Law." That song, written and produced by Allen Toussaint in 1961 for the Minit label, sustained Ernie K-Doe's career for decades, though he continued to record, scoring a few minor hits.

He was a colorful, self-promoting radio personality with many catch phrases: "Burn, K-Doe, Burn," "I'm a Charity Hospital Baby," and "You just good, that's all" (talking to himself).

But it wasn't until the 1990s that he began calling himself "Emperor of the Universe," appearing around town in flamboyant cape and crown. New Orleanians love to swap stories about this true eccentric, his elaborate shows, and absurd incidents from his daily life. There is a wonderful, award-winning book by my friend Ben Sandmel, titled *Ernie K-Doe: The R&B Emperor of New Orleans*, that tells his story in full.

When in New Orleans, you can visit his Mother-in-Law Lounge, operated after his death in 2001 by his widow, Antoinette, until her death on Mardi Gras Day 2009 and reopened five years later by trumpeter Kermit Ruffins. You will not will be disappointed.

Burn, K-Doe, burn!

Paul "Lil Buck" Sinegal

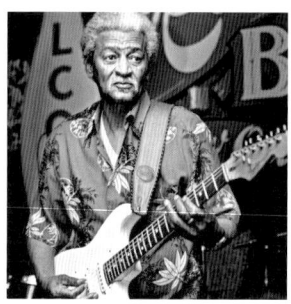

Guitarist Lil Buck Sinegal along with "podners" Buckwheat Zydeco and my dear friend Lee Allen Zeno, a bass player, were anchors of the Lafayette and Louisiana blues and zydeco world, playing together for decades. I first met him in the mid-1980s at a Buckwheat Zydeco recording session, and he was a friend of mine for thirty-plus years.

Paul Alton Senegal was born in 1944 in Lafayette. He started playing guitar around the age of ten and never stopped until he died in 2019 at the age of seventy-five.

He had regional hits on his own and played with virtually every star of zydeco, including Clifton Chenier, Rockin' Dopsie, C. J. Chenier, and, of course, Buckwheat Zydeco. In addition, he backed Gulf Coast and swamp pop artists such as Barbara Lynn, Slim Harpo, Lazy Lester, Katie Webster, and Warren Storm.

He was a regular at the New Orleans Jazz Fest and the Ponderosa Stomp, both as a sideman and bandleader. Stomp organizer Ira "Dr. Ike" Padnos called him his secret weapon for his ability to back a wide range of artists and make them all sound great.

Lil Buck Sinegal was one of the purest and truest blues musicians ever. I'm proud to have known him.

Lloyd Price

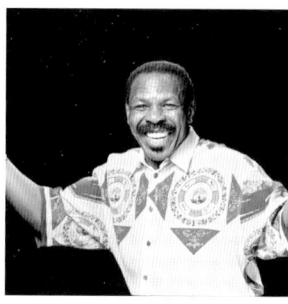

Nineteen-year-old Lloyd Price had his first giant hit record—"Lawdy Miss Clawdy"—in 1952 thanks to local producer Dave Bartholomew and a Los Angeles record company looking to cash in on the popularity of records that rival companies were making in New Orleans. Lloyd was backed on the Specialty Records cut by the Dave Bartholomew Band—with Fats Domino on piano and Earl Palmer on drums!

But after a stint in the US Army, the ever-enterprising Price had his biggest success when he connected with ABC-Paramount and from 1957 to 1959 recorded national hits including "Stagger Lee" and "Personality," adapting the New Orleans sound for a mainstream pop audience.

He always had an interest in business, both in the music world and elsewhere, including boxing and a Times Square nightclub. He formed two labels, "Double L" and "Turntable," which recorded Wilson Pickett and Howard Tate among others. In 2010 he appeared as himself in HBO's *Treme* and was inducted into both the Louisiana and the Rock & Roll Halls of Fame. Lloyd Price died in 2021 at eighty-eight.

This photo was taken for the R&B Foundation in Los Angeles, 1995.

Fird "Snooks" Eaglin

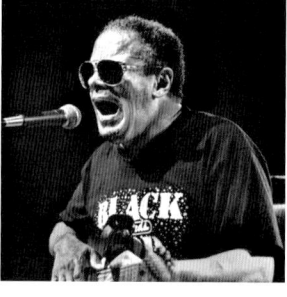

Fird Eaglin Jr., better known as "Snooks" Eaglin, was a New Orleans icon. Blinded at age one by glaucoma, he was a self-taught guitarist with an unusual thumb-and-fingers style and a repertoire of thousands of songs. He played everything—blues, rock and roll, jazz, country, funk, Latin, and more, but it all came out in his own sound and style. His singing was flexible and expressive, and his onstage asides as unpredictable as his way with a song.

His early recordings are both historic in importance and still great to listen to. From the late 1980s though the late 1990s, he recorded a series of wonderful albums for the Scott brothers of Black Top Records and appeared as a sideman for other artists on the label.

I'm glad I got to see him and hear him and photograph him many times. I forget who said it, but it's true: "There is nothing more New Orleans than Snooks at the Rock & Bowl."

Snooks died in 2019 at seventy-three.
These photos were taken in New Orleans, 1990.

Terrance Simien

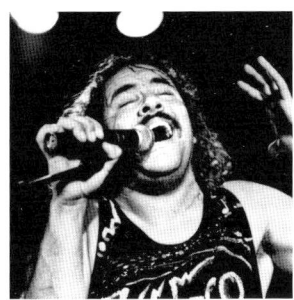

Terrance Simien, hailing from Mallet, Louisiana, is a Grammy-winning singer, accordion player, advocate, educator, and ambassador for zydeco Music and Creole culture.

He and his wife, Cynthia, created the "Creole for Kidz & the History of Zydeco" performing-arts program for school-age children. They have also collaborated with the Disney organization on the film *The Princess & The Frog* and the theme park ride **Tiana's Bayou Adventure.**

Simien tours nationally and internationally, and his shows with his band, the Zydeco Experience, are BIG FUN and should not be missed. His daughter Marcella is also a musician, carrying on the family tradition.

This photo is from original Tramps in New York City, 1983.

Walter "Wolfman" Washington

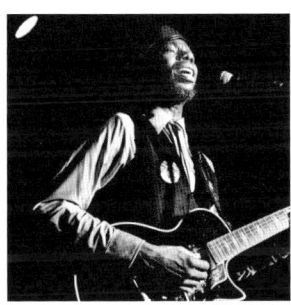

NOLA icon Walter "Wolfman" Washington, born Edward Joseph Washington Jr., was the last word in sophisticated blues, soul, funk, and R&B, New Orleans style, as a guitarist, singer, and bandleader.

As a teenager, he started touring with Lee Dorsey, playing "Working in the Coal Mine" and "Ride Your Pony" (he joked that those were the only songs they played for two years), then worked with other top singers on the New Orleans scene from Irma Thomas to his mentor Johnny Adams (for twenty-plus years), while also going solo and forming his own band, the Roadmasters, who featured horns and his longtime rhythm section of Wilbert "Junkyard Dog" Arnold on drums and bassist Jack Cruz.

Walter Washington had a way of finding all the harmonic changes and emotional possibilities of a song both as a player and a vocalist: playful, sorrowful, celebratory, or stark. And sometimes he howled, a trademark wolf howl. It was especially wonderful to catch him at home at the Maple Leaf Bar.

The Wolfman died in 2022 at age seventy-nine.

Charles Brown

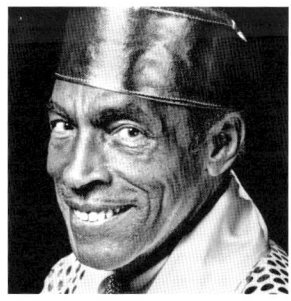

Hailing from Texas before landing in Los Angeles, Tony Russell "Charles" Brown brought a softer, slower, smoother style to the blues with hit records in the 1940s and 1950s such as "Driftin' Blues," "Merry Christmas Baby," "Get Yourself Another Fool," "Black Night," "Hard Times," and "Trouble Blues." Both as a singer and piano player, he was a major influence on a generation of musicians including a young Ray Charles, whose earliest recording are very much in Brown's style. His songs have become standards covered by dozens of artists.

His 1989 album *One More for the Road* revived his visibility and he began touring again, often with Bonnie Raitt. I got to see him a lot in the 1980s at Tramps in New York City. He was an elegant, soft-spoken gentleman—and an inveterate horse player.

Charles Brown is a member of the Rock & Roll Hall of Fame and the Blues Hall of Fame. He received a National Heritage Fellowship from the National Endowment for the Arts, the W. C. Handy Award, and the R&B Foundation's Pioneer Award.

Bill Doggett

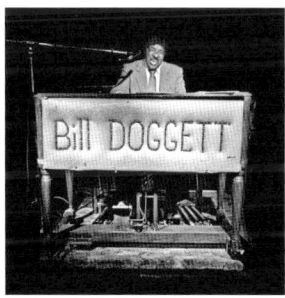

Best known for the classic 1956 recording "Honky Tonk (Part 1 & 2)," keyboardist, arranger and bandleader Bill Doggett (1916–1996) was one of those "underneath it all" artists who made the music happen.

"Honky Tonk" was an absolute standard. The song started as a jam and quotes popular songs of the day. It features Billy Butler on the seminal opening guitar riff and elegant A-side soloing, tenor saxophonist Clifford Scott soloing on both sides, putting the "honk" in "Honky Tonk" on the more raucous B-side, with drummer Shep Shepherd setting a mostly relaxed groove—and no organ solo from Doggett, whose name was on the 45! Every Blues and R&B band from the '50s through the '60s HAD to have it in their set list. Licks and riffs from the Doggett's songs such as "Hold It," "Big Boy," "True Blue," "Quaker City" were a part of the vocabulary of pretty much every working blues guitarist.

Doggett had a string of through the '50s, '60s and beyond which were hugely popular. Previous to all his R&B success he played with or arranged for Louis Armstrong, Count Basie, Ella Fitzgerald, Lionel

Hampton, the Ink Spots, Johnny Otis, Wynonie Harris, Louis Jordan, Lucky Millinder, and more.

And "Honky Tonk" was the opening song of my radio program way back when on WYEP, Pittsburgh, Pennsylvania. Photo from the Westend Café, NYC, 1986.

LaVern Baker

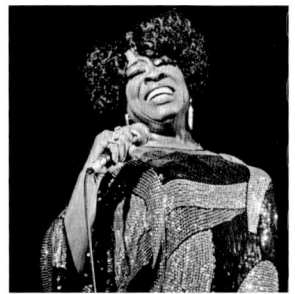

LaVern Baker (1929–97) was a hero to me, and not just for her singing.

A powerful, charming rhythm and blues belter who could put a suggestive burr in her voice at will, she hit the pop charts in the 1950s and early 1960s with such hits as "Tweedle Dee" (1955), "Jim Dandy" (1956), and "I Cried a Tear" (1958).

Often billed as Little Miss Sharecropper as a teenager, she began singing in Chicago clubs in the mid-1940s. In 1953 she signed with Atlantic Records and released the R&B ballad "Soul on Fire." Two years later, the breezier, whimsical "Tweedle Dee" was a million-seller high on the US R&B and pop charts, so, in those days of racial segregation, the white pop and jazz singer Georgia Gibbs copied the tune, scoring a number one hit in the process. Baker considered this stealing and sued for copyright violation, failing to win compensation but sparking a congressional investigation into the issue in the music industry.

More hits led to more fame, and international tours, and on one of those she accepted a job running the entertainment, and performing herself, at the Subic Bay military base in the Philippines—and kept the job for twenty-plus years, until the base closed. But her career was far from ending there.

In 1990, she replaced Ruth Brown as star of the Broadway hit musical *Black and Blue*; that same year, she received one of the first eight Pioneer Awards from the Rhythm and Blues Foundation. In 1991, she became the second female solo artist inducted into the Rock & Roll Hall of Fame (Aretha Franklin was first, in 1987).

The last time I saw her was at the Newport R&B Festival in 1996. She performed from a wheelchair, since she had lost both legs below the knee to diabetes. She joked that one leg was called "Stump" and the other "Stumpy." "Stump and Stumpy" were a popular Black tap dance and comedy duo of the 1930s, 1940s, and 1950s; the reference was lost on most of the audience, and I was a bit stunned, but filled with admiration for her pluck, humor, and fortitude. She passed a few months later.

Roy "Good Rockin'" Brown

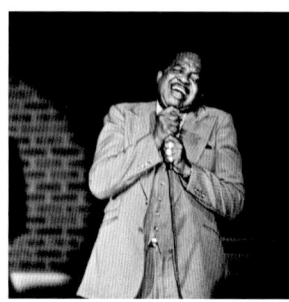

Roy Brown's early recordings are arguably proto rock and roll and are definitely great R&B. He wrote and recorded the original version of "Good Rocking Tonight," which has been covered by Wynonie Harris, Elvis Presley, Jerry Lee Lewis, Bruce Springsteen, Paul McCartney, Ricky Nelson, James Brown, and more.

His gospel-drenched vocals had a HUGE influence on B.B. King, Bobby Bland, Elvis Presley, Jackie Wilson, James Brown, and Little Richard.

I was lucky enough to see a string of shows he did with Roomful of Blues in 1981. Seeing a vocalist of his power with that superb band was truly unforgettable, and he was set to join Roomful as lead vocalist, but just months after those shows, he passed suddenly—truly a great loss to music and the world at large.

Nappy Brown

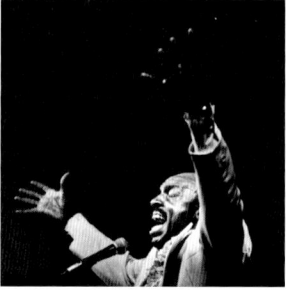

Napoleon Brown Goodson Culp was a blues shouter of the first order with roots—like so many of his peers of their classic era, the 1950s—in gospel. Among his Savoy Records releases were "Don't Be Angry," "Pitter Patter," "It Don't Hurt No More," and "The Right Time" (1957), which served as the template for Ray Charles's hit version, "(Night Time Is) the Right Time."

Nappy Brown was one of the biggest R&B stars of his day, frequently touring with rock-and-roll popularizer Alan Freed's revues. Along with Little Richard, Chuck Berry, and Fats Domino, he was part of the first wave of African American artists to cross over to young whites.

His performances were electrifying, sometimes bawdy, and he was a true wild man onstage, rolling on the floor, jumping into the crowd. With the help of Tinsley Ellis, Bob Margolin, Black Top Records, Blind Pig Records, and others, his career was revived in the 1980s and beyond.

Andre Williams

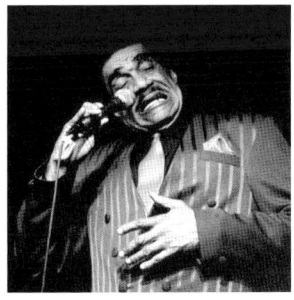

Nicknamed Mr. Rhythm, songwriter/producer Andre Williams, a vocalist who admitted he wasn't that great a singer but knew how to talk-sing a song like his hero Cab Calloway, was a behind-the-scenes force in pre-Motown Detroit and beyond in R&B, doo-wop, rock and roll, and soul from the 1950s to his passing in 2019. He worked with Parliament Funkadelic, Ike Turner, Edwin Starr, Bobby "Blue" Bland, and tons of small labels.

Originally from Alabama, he landed in Detroit, where he had a string of earthy R&B hits: "Jail Bait," "Greasy Chicken," and "Bacon Fat." In the early 1960s Williams cowrote Stevie Wonder's first song, "Thank You for Loving Me." And his song "Twine Time" became a big hit for Alvin Cash and the Crawlers. Williams also cowrote "Shake a Tail Feather," which became a hit for the Five Du-Tones and later for Ike & Tina Turner and James and Bobby Purify; the tune was in a great scene in the Blues Brothers movie, featuring Ray Charles.

He continued to write, record, and produce throughout the 1970s and 1980s. Later in his life, he battled addiction and homelessness but returned to an active performing career with many new and younger fans.

He was truly a larger-than-life personality, funny, raunchy, and outspoken.

Esther Phillips

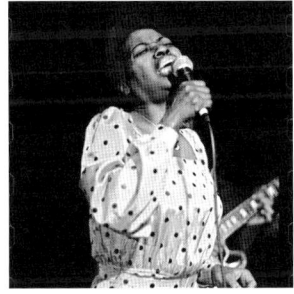

From her early days with Johnny Otis as a teenaged "Little Esther" to country/soul hits such as "Release Me" to the Gil Scott Heron composition "Home Is Where the Hatred Is" to a discofied version of Dinah Washington's "What a Difference a Day Makes," Esther Phillips was a singer's singer.

She was nominated for a Grammy in 1973 for "Home is Where the Hatred Is." When Aretha Franklin won for "Young Gifted and Black," she gave the award to Esther, saying she deserved it more. She had a hard life with addiction and many relapses and left us far too soon at age forty-eight, but her INCREDIBLE voice and talent are with us in her recordings. While she never made a bad record, her Atlantic sides and

especially her live album "Burnin'" are personal favorites of mine and never far from my player. I'm glad I was able to hear her live back in the early 1980s.

Jimmy McCracklin

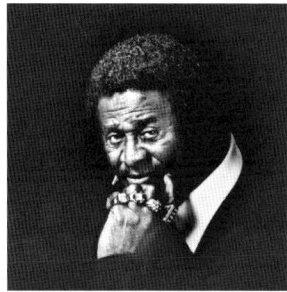

In a career that spanned almost seventy years, Jimmy McCracklin made consistently great music in the blues, R&B, rock and roll, and soul genres. One of the most important artists to come out of the San Francisco Bay area in the post–World War II era, McCracklin made his first records in 1945 and stayed current all the way into the twenty-first century as a vocalist, pianist, songwriter, and sometime club owner.

He recorded for numerous labels, including Swing Time, Checker, Imperial, Peacock, Trilon, Modern, Rounder, Stax, Minit, and Hi.

It was his hit on Checker, "The Walk" (follow-up: "The Wobble"), that led to a breakthrough appearance on *American Bandstand*. The California rock-and-roll/roots band the Blasters adapted their name from McCracklin's band the Blues Blasters. Los Lobos covered his "Georgia Slop." It was a photo of his bejeweled hand that was the impetus for me to expand on that theme, which led to my book *Blues Hands*.

This photo was made for the Rhythm & Blues Foundation in a lounge at JFK International Airport when he was on his way to Europe.

Paul Williams

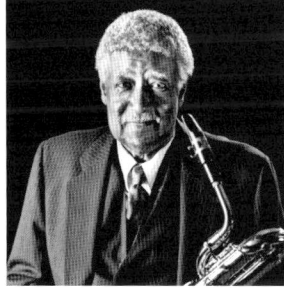

Saxophonist, songwriter, and bandleader Paul "Hucklebuck" Williams was one of the first to employ the honking tenor sax solo that became a hallmark of rhythm and blues and early rock and roll. He was best known for his 1949 hit "The Hucklebuck," a twelve-bar blues that spawned a dance craze. The single went to number one on the US Billboard R&B chart and was covered by Tommy Dorsey, Frank Sinatra, Roy Milton, Lionel Hampton, and others. And who could ever forget Art Carney and Jackie Gleason dancing the Hucklebuck in an absolutely hilarious *Honeymooners* episode? Williams coheadlined the first Moondog Coronation Ball, promoted by Alan Freed in Cleveland in 1952, often claimed as the first rock-and-roll concert—and the first rock-and-roll riot! His orchestra was regularly featured at the Apollo

Theater and was the backing band for touring artists and regulars such as Big Joe Turner, Dinah Washington, Amos Milburn, Ruth Brown, and dozens more, many of whom are featured in *Rhythm and Blues Revue* (1955), filmed at the Apollo Theater. Clips from the film can be seen on YouTube. Paul Williams was also musical director for Lloyd Price and James Brown.

These photos are from a portrait session in the late 1980s, where my friend Bob Porter also conducted an extensive interview.

Ruth Brown

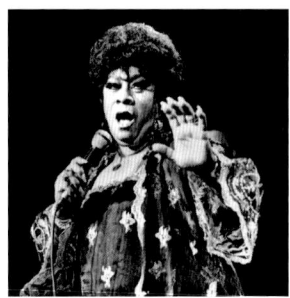

Singer, songwriter, actress, and activist Ruth Brown had R&B hits with a bit of a pop feel in the 1950s with "So Long," "Teardrops from My Eyes," "(Mama) He Treats Your Daughter Mean" and others. Their success made then-fledgling Atlantic Records "The House That Ruth Built" (a play on Yankee Stadium having been built on the success of another Ruth—Babe Ruth).

Brown's long advocacy for musicians too often abused by the industry led to the founding in 1987 of the Rhythm and Blues Foundation, which helped many artists gain at least some portion of what was due them in royalties. She received the foundation's Pioneer Award in 1987.

She also performed on Broadway and in films and received a Grammy Lifetime Achievement Award, a Tony Award for *Black and Blue* on Broadway, and another Grammy for the soundtrack album.

Ruth Brown had recurring roles in several television programs and gave a wonderful performance as Motormouth Maybelle Stubbs in the John Waters cult classic *Hairspray*. More than once in her later years, backstage, I saw how hard it was for her to get to the stage—but once she made it and the spotlight hit and the audience saw her, she was alive and animated, the show was ON, and she OWNED the room, class and heart personified.

Buddy Guy

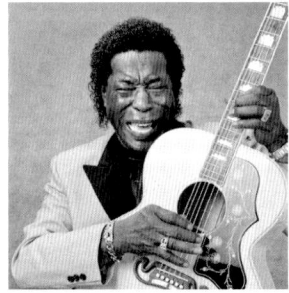

I can't count the times I have seen blues master Buddy Guy perform.

Born in Louisiana in 1936, he began playing gigs in Baton Rouge in the mid-1950s before moving to Chicago in 1957. From his classic sides for the Chess label during its heyday, to a long association with harmonica player Junior Wells, to a storied solo career of well over half a century, to elder statesman status and owner and performer at his Chicago club, Buddy Guy's Legends, he has always been a fierce and passionate guitarist and singer.

Much of his life has been documented in his book, *When I Left Home*, as well as in an American Masters documentary on PBS.

The studio portrait here, part of a cover shoot for *Blues Revue Magazine*, was done in a very small hotel suite. I was told I had an hour for the shoot. I said, "I'll do it in forty-five minutes." In those forty-five minutes, I managed to shoot fifteen rolls of color and black-and-white film with three different backgrounds; after all, this man had been part of my blues life since the 1960s. The space was so cramped that I was either standing on furniture or backed against a wall. At one point, Buddy spontaneously started singing. I slammed a roll of film into the camera and managed to capture what has become one of my all-time favorite studio portraits. And everyone left happy.

Junior Wells

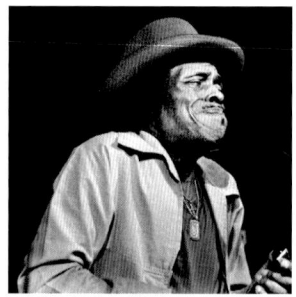

Amos Blakemore Jr.—Junior Wells (1934–98)—was one of those Chicago kids who were born in the South but grew up in the North and played the deep blues. There was a generation of them—including Buddy Guy, Junior's touring partner for twenty years—who followed in the migrating footsteps of the originators of Chicago blues, epitomized by Muddy Waters.

There is a story that Wells told—on the cover of his classic album *Hoodoo Man Blues*—that as a young boy he was caught snatching a harmonica he "had to have" from a pawn shop and leaving less than the full price on the counter. At his trial, Junior reported, the judge asked him to play the instrument; he complied and played it so well the judge paid the balance due—fifty cents—and dismissed the case!

In 1952, still a teen, Junior Wells replaced Little Walter in the Muddy Waters band and recorded sessions with Muddy for Chess Records.

As a bandleader, Junior Wells had a string of hits on local labels, including the classics "Little by Little" and "Messin' with the Kid," which have become blues standards.

But it was his 1965 release "Hoodoo Man Blues" on Delmark Records that altered the course of his career and of blues in general. It featured Buddy Guy, who was credited as "Friendly Chap" for contractual reasons. This was the first blues album to be recorded AS an album, not a compilation of singles, capturing the sound of his band as they played in the clubs. It was a game changer. It is a GREAT album and brought Wells and other contemporary blues artists greater recognition and the consequent touring and recording opportunities.

I got to photograph him many times, on many gigs. One night that stands out was when he and Buddy Guy were the headliners, and Luther "Guitar Junior" Johnson, who had recently left the Muddy Waters band, was the opening act. Guitar Junior and his band, the Magic Rockers, came out just smoking! They threw down a very hot set, but Buddy Guy and Junior Wells were not to be outdone. There was some old-school Chicago head cutting that night! Not one I will soon forget.

John Hammond

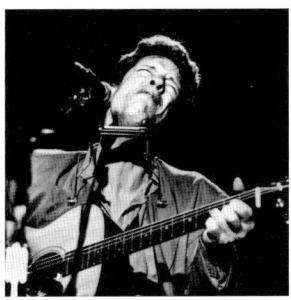

John P. Hammond has been part of my blues life—and many others—since his first recordings in 1964.

A fellow New Yorker, he was there at the beginning of the blues and folk boom of the 1960s in Greenwich Village. At one point he had both Eric Clapton and Jimi Hendrix in his band, playing for a week at the Gaslight Cafe! Regrettably, no recordings were made. He did record with members of the Band (then known as the Hawks) in 1965 and brought them to the attention of Bob Dylan, and they soon became Dylan's backing band. (While he was the son of the legendary talent scout and record producer credited with signing Dylan and many others, the younger John Hammond was not especially close to his father, and the relationship had little influence on his career.)

Equally adept as an acoustic solo performer, often playing a National Steel Reso-Phonic guitar and rack harmonica, or in a band playing electric, he has had a long career that included providing the soundtrack for the 1970 film *Little Big Man*, hosting the 1991 UK television documentary *Searching for Robert Johnson*, winning Blues Music and Grammy awards, and in 2011 being inducted into the Blues Foundation's Blues Hall of Fame.

In addition, he has always been a real gentleman and a down-to-earth, all-around good guy. I am proud to call him a friend.

Albert Collins

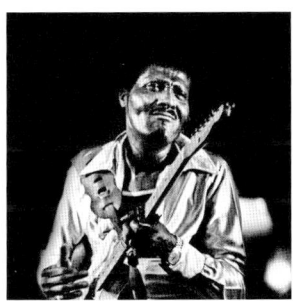

Albert Collins's first record was titled "The Freeze," and his debut album *The Cool Sound of Albert Collins*. Some of the titles that followed: "Defrost," "Frosty," "Thaw-out," "Sno-Cone," and "Don't Lose Your Cool." Also known as "the Ice Man," Albert Collins (1932–93) had an icy, brittle sound that just cut, thanks to a wholly original style using an unusual tuning with a capo.

He and his band just floored me. From the first note, it was OVER. He was such a great entertainer and showman, often leaving the stage, still playing, trailing an ultralong guitar cord, to walk among the audience—sometimes right out the door.

There was a night when a friend of mine, renowned guitarist Ronnie Earl, and I walked up to the original Lone Star Café in New York City, and Albert was sitting on top of a limo parked on the street, playing. The first thing he said to Ronnie was "You're going to play with me?" They jammed the rest of the set.

He was a sweet and funny guy. I miss him.

Collins was photographed here at Mancini's Club in McKees Rocks, Pennsylvania, 1979.

Johnny Copeland

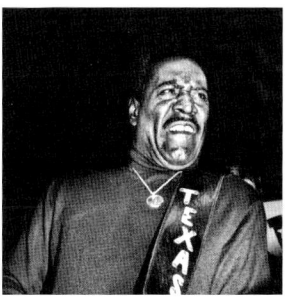

John Clyde Copeland (1937–1997), born in Louisiana and transplanted to Houston, was a Texas Bluesman of the first order, influenced by guitarist T-Bone Walker and R&B shouter Nappy Brown as well as the Soul and Rock & Roll of his time.

He enjoyed regional success, touring and recording singles for Duke, Mercury, Kent and smaller mostly local imprints. In 1976 he moved to New York and connected with Rounder Records, for whom he made a series of award-winning albums. His growing recognition led to his being recruited for the Grammy-winning album Showdown! on Alligator Records, teamed with Albert Collins and Robert Cray, and to opportunities to record and tour extensively in the United States, Europe, and Africa.

He suffered ill health due to a congenital heart condition. At age 60, he died from complications of heart transplant surgery he had undergone six months earlier.

My dear friend Shemekia Copeland, daughter of Johnny and his wife Sandra, has carried on his legacy, dubbed the new Queen of the Blues at the 2011 Chicago Blues Festival and receiving multiple Grammy nominations.

Johnny Copeland was deservedly inducted into the Blues Foundation's Blues Hall of Fame in 2017, posthumously.

Otis Rush

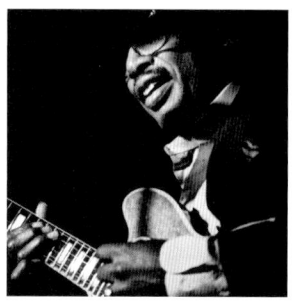

At his peak, no one could touch Otis Rush (1934–2018) for emotion and intensity, both vocally and on guitar. He was one of the Chicago musicians who took the music of first-generation electric-blues artists, such as Muddy Waters, building on it and taking it into a more modern realm, along with Magic Sam, Buddy Guy, and others.

He was also one of the absolute GREATS, but the record business was not always kind to him, with limited and delayed releases and distribution, and he never gained the material success and recognition he deserved. With his giant talent, had he gotten "the breaks," who knows what might have been.

Artistically, his songs and recordings are peak achievements at the very core of modern blues, and many have become standards and touchstones, including "I Can't Quit You Baby" (written by Willie Dixon, released in 1956 as Cobra Records' debut) and his own compositions "Double Trouble" and "All Your Love," both released in 1958 by Cobra.

Dave Van Ronk

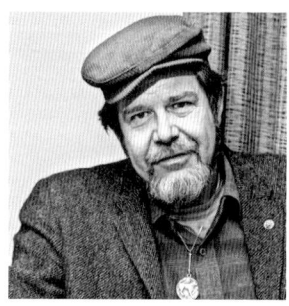

Dave Van Ronk, born in 1936, was a folk and blues singer and guitarist at the heart of the folk scene in New York City's Greenwich Village.

Grounded in traditional jazz and folk blues, especially the acoustic guitar work of the Reverend Gary Davis, he was a big man with a big personality, and a friend and mentor to many artists. He inspired, taught, and promoted Bob Dylan, Joni Mitchell, Tom Paxton, Phil Ochs, Ramblin' Jack Elliott, and many more.

The Animals based their 1964 hit "House of the Rising Sun" on his arrangement of the old song; Dylan also had copied it, for his first album.

He has a great memoir written with Elijah Wald titled with his mayoral nickname, and the main character of the Coen brothers' film *Inside Llewyn Davis* is VERY loosely based on Van Ronk.

Dave was a regular at my favorite New York City bar, the Kettle of Fish, and often attended our softball games.

Among the many singer/songwriters he boosted in his later years was my dear friend Frank Christian (RIP).

Dave Van Ronk died in 2002 at the age of sixty-five, leaving us a deep history both in and outside the music world.

Johnny Winter

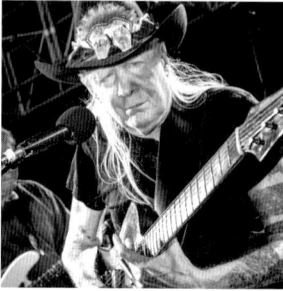

Guitar hero, singer, and record producer John Dawson Winter III (1944–2014) brought me and many of my era into the deep waters of the blues. In an up-and-down career as a high-energy blues rocker, he found international fame and unprecedented fortune but also fell prey to drugs and alcohol and exploitation, needing medical and financial rescues.

He hailed from Beaumont, Texas, where he was steeped in the sounds of blues growing up; both he and his brother Edgar, also a musician in the making, were born with albinism.

Johnny recorded for regional labels before his big break came when he sat in with Mike Bloomfield and Al Kooper at the Fillmore East. This brought him to the attention of Columbia Records, which famously signed him to a record advance of $600,000.

In the late 1970s he produced four albums for Muddy Waters, playing slide guitar with members of Muddy's bands past and present. This led to three Grammys for Waters and one for Winter (for *Nothing but the Blues*). These recordings captured the feel, intensity, and energy of Muddy's classic sides and were largely responsible for reviving and elevating his career. They are great recordings.

In the 1980s, Johnny Winter returned to more straight-ahead blues with a series of highly acclaimed albums on Alligator Records produced by Bruce Iglauer and Dick Shurman, regaining his lost health and abilities to tour and record with renewed vigor. But just a few months after celebrating his seventieth birthday at B.B. King's Blues Club in New York City, he left us.

Eric Clapton

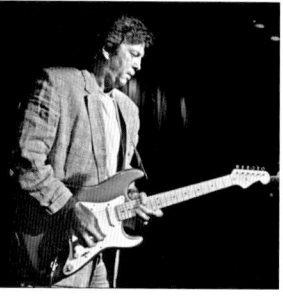

Eric Clapton is a gifted guitarist with an affinity for and love of the blues. His long history, beginning with the Yardbirds, a band he left when they turned in a more pop, less blues direction, to his work with John Mayall and the Bluesbreakers, Cream, Blind Faith, Derek and the Dominoes, and as a solo artist, has always been infused with the blues.

In the 1960s his prowess on guitar led to a deification of sorts, with graffiti in London stating, "Clapton Is God." His extreme notoriety, visibility, and success have brought generations into the blues orbit. Many people would not be aware of the blues if it were not for Eric Clapton. He has recorded albums with B.B. King and a tribute to Robert Johnson.

His 2021 antivaccine/antimasking songs "Stand and Deliver" and "This Has Got to Stop" with Van Morrison led many to rethink their fondness for and relations with him.

Eric Clapton is not God. He is a complex individual who has lived a life in the spotlight. He had a complicated family life growing up and experienced tragedy, the loss of a young son in an accident. He struggled with addiction and then went on to found the Crossroads Rehabilitation Centre, which helps fund the rehabilitation center he also founded and always features top blues artists. Prior to rehab, he made a notorious, inebriated, anti-immigration rant in the 1970s but has always professed his love of Black blues and the artists who created it.

Photo from S.O.B.s Club in NYC, 1986, where he sat in with Buckwheat Zydeco.

Jesse Stone, a.k.a. Charles Calhoun

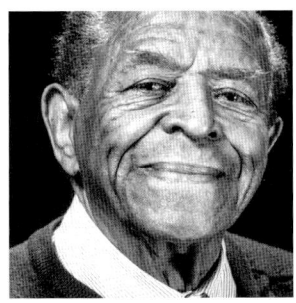

Jesse Stone was a rhythm-and-blues musician and songwriter who wrote under the pseudonym Charles Calhoun. He is one of the underneath-it-all, founding fathers of rock and roll.

His best-known composition as Calhoun was "Shake Rattle & Roll," which many believe to be the first rock-and-roll song, made famous by Big Joe Turner and later by Bill Haley. He was the first Black staffer at Atlantic Records. Ahmet Ertegun, one of the founders of that seminal label, said, "Jesse Stone did more to develop the basic rock-and-roll sound than anybody else." Among the many classics he penned are "Money Honey," "Don't Let Go," "Flip, Flop, Fly," and "Your Cash Ain't Nothing but Trash."

Born in 1901 and originally from Kansas, he made his first records in 1927 with his band the Blue Serenaders. He formed a larger band and also worked as an arranger before Duke Ellington got Stone's orchestra booked at the Cotton Club in 1936. He worked with Chick Webb's and Jimmie Lunceford's bands and then became a bandleader at the Apollo Theater and continued recording under his own name. In 1941, Stone became musical director for the all-female jazz band the International Sweethearts of Rhythm. In 1953, he wrote Ray Charles's hit "Losing Hand" and also penned "Money Honey," the first of many hits for the Drifters. His songs were recorded by a wide range of artists, everyone from Guy Lombardo and Benny Goodman to Louis Jordan.

Stone was honored by the Rhythm and Blues Foundation with their Pioneer Award and inducted into the Rhythm and Blues Hall of Fame in 1992. In 2010 he was inducted into both the Rock & Roll and the Songwriters Halls of Fame.

I took this photo at a Rhythm and Blues Foundation Pioneer Awards event in 1994. The foundation was founded to help artists who were not fairly compensated for their recordings by recouping lost royalties and providing recognition of their achievements. At these events there was a general feeling of achievement, warmth, gratitude, camaraderie, relief, satisfaction, and more that something was finally being done to address the inequities of the past. He was well into his nineties here, and I like to think that some of that can be seen in this portrait.

Louisiana Red

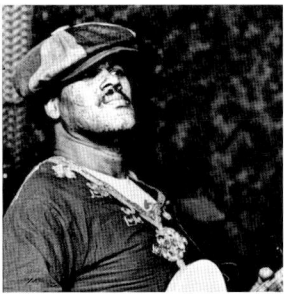

Iverson Minter was raised in an orphanage and then by relatives, orphaned after his mother died and his father was lynched. He recorded as a very young man in the late 1940s for Chess Records as Rocky Fuller—a name that was both a play on "Rockefeller" and his habit of rocking back and forth when he played. He did a stint in the Army and returned to music, performing and recording continuously as Louisiana Red until he passed in 2012, age seventy-nine. He had a two-sided hit with great topical lyrics in 1962: "Ride on Red" about Freedom Riders and escaping the South, and "Red's Dream" about the Cuban Missile Crisis. In "Red's Dream," he sets Castro and Khrushchev straight with a razor and a baseball bat and ends the crisis; in gratitude, the president lets him run the Senate, so Red says:

Ray Charles and Lightnin' Hopkins
And a guy like Jimmy Reed
Bo Diddley and Big Mabelle
Be all I need!
It was a dream, a dream I had last night
I dreamed I went to the UN
And set the whole nation right.

Married three times, Louisiana Red was a longtime companion of singer and activist Odetta. I got to know Red when he lived in Pittsburgh in the 1970s and performed locally—occasionally even on my radio program. When he played, especially acoustic, he seemed transported, trancelike, to another, deeper place. I am grateful our life paths crossed. Photo from WYEP studio, Pittsburgh, Pennsylvania, 1978. Ride on Red!

Robert Cray

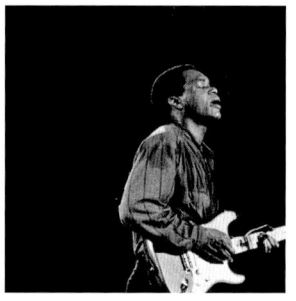

Robert Cray emerged from the Pacific Northwest, where as a young man he saw musical heroes such as Muddy Waters, Freddie King, and Albert Collins. Robert often backed Collins in the 1970s and shared a 1987 Grammy with him and Johnny Copeland for the *Showdown* album. He formed his own band and collaborated with vocalist Curtis Salgado, playing clubs and colleges in the region. Robert played bass in Otis Day & the Knights in *National Lampoon's Animal House*, which was filmed in the region. In 1977 he signed with Hightone Records and began an illustrious career.

It was Robert along with the Fabulous Thunderbirds and Stevie Ray Vaughan who brought blues to MTV and the masses in the 1980s. He is a triple-threat talent as a singer, guitarist, and songwriter.

Success with his national hit *Strong Persuader* album brought him to great prominence, performing at large venues and festivals and sharing the stage and recordings with the likes of Eric Clapton, B.B. King, Buddy Guy, John Lee Hooker, and other "guitar heroes," notably at the Crossroads Guitar Festival. He played with Clapton, Guy, Jimmie Vaughan, and Stevie Ray Vaughan at the 1990 concert that was to be Stevie Ray's last; Stevie died in a tragic helicopter crash later that night.

It is interesting to note that Robert pulled out of Clapton's 2022 tour over Clapton's support and participation in the antivaxing/antimasking song "Stand and Deliver" by Van Morrison. This ended their friendship.

Robert continues to perform his soulful blues and record with his supertight band.

Benny Latimore

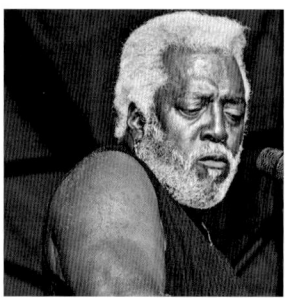

Keyboard player Benjamin William Latimore, who performs simply as LATIMORE, had a jazzy version of T-Bone Walker's "Stormy Monday" that was an R&B hit in 1973. He followed up with "If You Were My Woman," a gender-reversed take on Gladys Knight's "If I Were Your Woman." His biggest hit came in 1974 with "Let's Straighten It Out," a heartfelt plea from a man to his lady to work out their domestic discord; this adult-themed record reached number one on the R&B charts and has become a standard of the genre. There were follow-up hits including

"Keep the Home Fire Burnin'" and "Somethin' 'Bout 'Cha," but with the rise of disco, the national hits ceased.

He moved to the Malaco label, the home of Southern soul, and had a long string of albums and ongoing popularity on the Chitlin' Circuit. He continued to make records and record as a session musician and in 2017 was inducted into the Blues Foundation's Hall of Fame.

He has crossed over to broader and whiter audiences at clubs and festivals and on cruises while maintaining a strong following with his original, mostly Southern Black audience.

Carey Bell

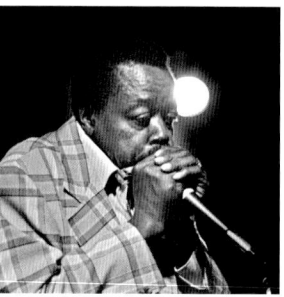

Carey Bell Harrington (1936–2007), performing as Carey Bell, was a first-line Chicago harmonica master by way of Mississippi. As a youth in Mississippi, he was taken by the music of saxophonist Louis Jordan, but his family could not afford that instrument, so he took up the harmonica—often referred to as the "Mississippi saxophone." After moving to Chicago, he played in local clubs with the likes of Hound Dog Taylor and Robert Nighthawk. He also learned bass guitar to further his employment opportunities. He was mentored on harmonica by both Big and Little Walter, originators and geniuses of the genre. He played in the bands of a who's who of blues masters, including Muddy Waters and Willie Dixon, and played and recorded extensively as a leader and sideman. His Alligator CD with Big Walter Horton is blues harmonica at its purest, no-frills best. In addition, his sons—guitarist Lurrie Bell, harp player Steve Bell, bassist Tyson Bell, and drummer James Bell—have carried on his blues heritage and legacy.

This photo is from the original Lone Star Café, New York City, 1981, with Willie Dixon's Blues All-Stars.

Charlie Musselwhite

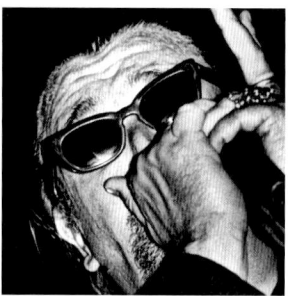

A Tennessee teen steeped in the musical mix of Memphis, Charlie Musselwhite left the South in the late 1950s, seeking better economic opportunities. A blues lover and harmonica player, he worked at the legendary Jazz Record Mart and various blue-collar jobs while immersing himself in Chicago's thriving blues world. He was befriended by many of the masters, including Big Joe Williams, Muddy Waters, Sonny Boy Williamson, Big and Little Walter, Buddy Guy, Junior Wells, and Howlin' Wolf. It was after sitting in with Muddy Waters that he gained some recognition and began gigging around town as a sideman and leader and began a lifelong friendship with John Lee Hooker.

He came to the attention of Sam Charters of Vanguard Records, which led to his inclusion in the eye-opening, game-changing three-record set *Chicago / The Blues / Today!* as part of Big Walter Horton's Blues Harp Band. These LPs brought real Chicago-style blues to a broader audience and led to Charlie's first solo record, *Stand Back! Here Comes Charley Musselwhite's South Side Band* (1967). This LP and the early Paul Butterfield Blues Band's LPs created a sea change both because they were great and because the bandleaders were white; the blues became more accessible to many of my generation of young white folk.

Charlie has been part of my life ever since. Through his years of touring clubs, festivals, and cruises, to playing at the White House and winning multiple Grammy and Blues Music awards, he has always been a brilliant player and singer as well as a sweet, soft-spoken, funny guy. I'm proud to count him and his lovely wife, Henrietta, as friends. It's nice to see a good guy like Mr. Musselwhite enjoy well-deserved success and recognition.

These photos are from Tramps in New York City, and Nyack, New York, 1985.

Hubert Sumlin

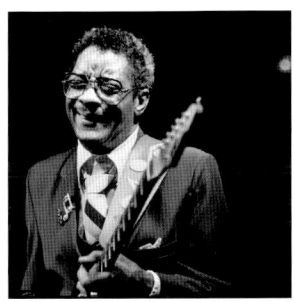

All modern electric guitar players owe Hubert Sumlin (1931–2011) a great debt. He was a genuine genius of the guitar, a true gentleman, and a friend.

Hubert spent twenty-plus years as lead guitarist with Howlin' Wolf and appears on many of the classic Wolf recordings that are the very foundation of electric blues. Among the many guitar stars who have paid tribute to his artistry and influence were Eric Clapton, Stevie Ray Vaughan, and Jimi Hendrix.

My friends Ronnie Earl and Hammond Scott helped revive his career and bring it to new levels with two well-produced LPs on the Black Top label; I did the photography for one of them, *Healing Feeling*.

Also, I must pay my respect to Toni Ann Mamary, his manager. Her guidance and love made his later life and career so happy and productive. He died at the age of eighty, and, according to Toni Ann, Mick Jagger and Keith Richards covered the cost of his funeral.

Hubert Sumlin was well loved and is deeply missed.

Johnny Rawls

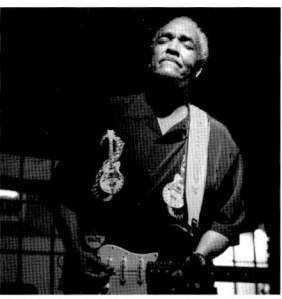

Mixing blues and soul, guitarist Johnny Rawls started at a young age backing soul artists such as Joe Tex and ZZ Hill when their tours swung through his native Mississippi.

While still a teenager, he joined the band of one of the deepest of deep soul singers, O. V. Wright, eventually becoming his bandleader. After Wright's death in 1980, the band continued as the Ace of Spades Band, named after one of O. V.'s signature tunes. They toured and performed with the likes of B.B. King, Bobby Bland, Little Milton, and Little Johnny Taylor, usually in the Deep South.

Along the way, Rawls became a producer and songwriter while also recording prolifically and touring constantly, often teaming with my pals Dave Keller (guitarist) and Billy Price (singer).

Johnny mixes blues and soul like a master and can work a room and rouse an audience like no one else, like the seasoned veteran that he is.

This photo from the Juke Joint Festival preshow, Oxford, Mississippi, 2011.

Little Milton Campbell

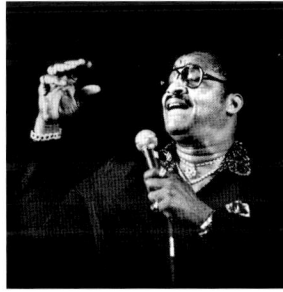

Singer and guitarist James "Little" Milton Campbell Jr. (1934–2005) was deeply rooted in the blues and also crossed over into soul music.

He began his career in the Mississippi Delta, where Ike Turner, acting as a talent scout, brought him to Sam Phillips at Sun Records. He made his first records there, then went to Bobbin Records in St. Louis, where he recorded "Lonely Man" and "That Will Never Do," but it wasn't until he moved to Checker Records that he had the hits—"We're Gonna Make It," "Who's Cheatin' Who," "Grits Ain't Groceries," and more—that made him a blues superstar.

He had continued success at Stax, Malaco, and others and became a popular mainstay of the Southern Soul Chitlin' Circuit. My dear friend Frank "Scrap Iron" Robinson was his road manager for thirty years. Scrap watched the door, the money, and Milton's back, providing occasional muscle when required, and oh man, did he have stories!

Little Milton is in the Blues Hall of Fame of the Blues Foundation, in Memphis, and a statue of him adorns the front of their headquarters.

Lonnie Brooks

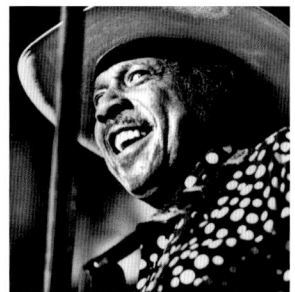

Lee Baker Jr.—Guitar Jr., then Lonnie Brooks—was the patriarch of the Brooks family dynasty of the blues, with sons Ronnie and Wayne.

He began his career in Louisiana as "Guitar Jr.," with recordings including "The Crawl" and "Family Rules," regional hits that remain in the swamp pop canon to this day.

He then moved on to Chicago, where he adopted the stage name of Lonnie Brooks since they already had a Guitar Junior: Luther Johnson, who would go on to play with the Muddy Waters band.

Lonnie played locally on his own and backed other artists, including Jimmy Reed. After a brief stay at Capitol Records, he came to the attention of Bruce Iglauer, who signed him to Alligator Records. A string of successful albums led to his becoming a club and festival favorite with a worldwide audience. He was inducted into the Blues Foundation's Hall of Fame in 2010. His blues heritage and tradition are lovingly carried on by his sons. Much love and respect.

This photo is from the Chicago Blues Fest in 1991.

Luther Allison

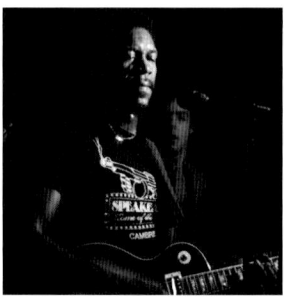

Part of the younger generation of Chicago artists such as Otis Rush, Magic Sam, and Buddy Guy who took the electric blues of Muddy Waters and brought it forward, guitarist/singer/songwriter Luther Allison has a recorded legacy stretching from the 1960s to the 1990s.

He had his debut LP on Delmark, three on Motown, and a long, fruitful relationship with RUF Records. His career really took off in the 1990s, when he signed with Alligator Records, where he had a string of successful records.

He moved to Paris in the 1970s becoming a club and festival favorite on both sides of the Atlantic. His live shows were legendary for their quality, energy, and duration—he would play for hours, leaving the crowds ecstatic and exhausted.

Cancer took him way too soon, in 1997: he was just fifty-eight and at the top of his game. I was all set to photograph him on his last tour when he fell ill and canceled his remaining shows. I do have some earlier black-and-white photos from 1979 and 1988.

He left us with lots of great music and a son, Bernard, to carry on his legacy. He also left us with this thought: "Leave your ego, play the music, love the people."

Son Seals

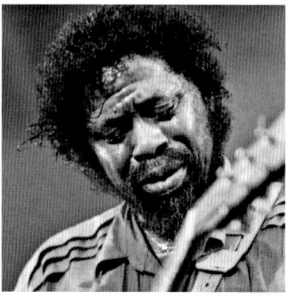

Frank "Son" Seals, known for his intense blues vocals and fierce guitar work, was born in Arkansas, where his father owned a small juke joint. He began performing at a young age and played with many musicians, including Robert Nighthawk, Albert King, Rufus Thomas, Bobby Bland, Junior Parker, and Rosco Gordon, first as a drummer and later as a guitarist.

In 1971, Seals moved to Chicago and his career took off after he was recorded by Bruce Iglauer of Alligator Records. His debut album, *The Son Seals Blues Band*, was released in 1973, starting him on a long, successful recording and touring career, despite a hard life—he was shot by his wife, his guitars were destroyed in a major house fire, and he suffered the partial loss of a leg due to diabetes.

The Holmes Brothers

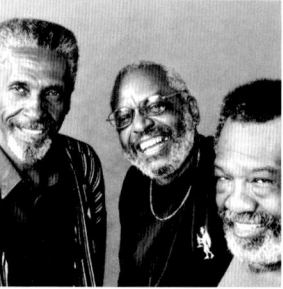

Birth brothers Sherman and Wendell Holmes and honorary brother Popsy Dixon were the Holmes Brothers. The three Virginians had played together in a variety of combinations in the late 1960s before forming the band in 1979. Popsy's soaring, multi-octave voice and solid in-the-pocket drumming combined with Sherman's bass and Wendell's guitar, both adding sibling vocal harmonies, to create a soulful, bluesy, gospel-drenched sound.

They made many LPs and CDs on Rounder, Alligator, and more and never made a bad one. Their live shows were always great, and they were a joy to be around, just very nice people.

The Holmes Brothers were a mainstay of the New York City blues scene in the 1980s and 1990s, especially at the legendary Dan Lynch's Bar, where they were the quasi house band.

I had the pleasure of working with them on several occasions, including a studio session for *Blues Revue* magazine, where this photo was taken. They were friends, a joy to work with, and true gentlemen.

Othar Turner

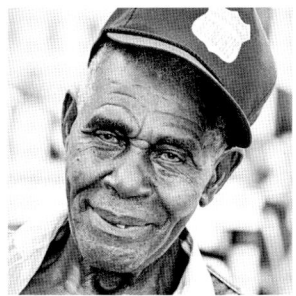

A Mississippi farmer all his long life (1907–2003), playing fifes he fashioned himself out of sugar cane, Othar Turner carried the African American fife-and-drum Hill Country blues tradition into a new century for younger generations to carry on.

Though well recorded and documented, his Rising Star Fife and Drum Band played mostly only at farm parties. His Labor Day picnics near Como, Mississippi, were known around the world.

His granddaughter Shardé Thomas has kept the tradition alive locally, nationally, and worldwide—as well as at the picnic.

Once, at a photo exhibition of mine, a man stood staring at this picture for a very long time. Eventually, I went over to him (he did not know I was the photographer) and asked what he thought of the photo. "Man, that is a face and a half," he said. I could not disagree.

The photo is from Clarksdale, Mississippi, 1998

George Brock

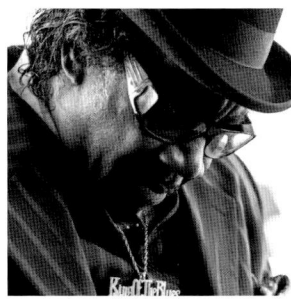

Often introduced as "the Heavyweight Champion of the Blues," singer and harmonica player George Brock set aside a possible career in boxing—he was big enough and tough enough to knock out Sonny Liston in a sparring match at a gym shortly after the future world heavyweight champion got out of prison—for an amazing life in the blues.

He grew up in Mississippi, where he became friends and performed with future blues legends Muddy Waters and Howlin' Wolf. He went on to become a nightclub owner in St. Louis (when not yet twenty-one years old). Muddy, Wolf, Albert King (who had played in Brock's band in St. Louis), Jimmy Reed, and many other blues stars would perform at his Club Caravan, where Big George also led his own band—and was the club bouncer.

His musical style was rough-hewn, idiosyncratic, and timeless. Seeing and hearing him was like being transported to East St. Louis in 1964. A documentary called *Hard Times* (2006) showed him visiting the cotton plantations of his childhood.

As my friend Roger Stolle said of his dear friend Big George, "There's a lot of blues players, but only a few bluesmen." Big George died in St. Louis in 2020, age eighty-seven.

Christone "Kingfish" Ingram

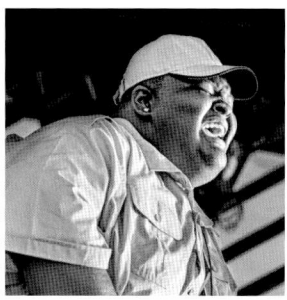

I've lost count of the times I've seen blues prodigy Christone "Kingfish" Ingram play since I first saw him performing as an eleven-year-old in an education program of the Delta Blues Museum in his hometown, Clarksdale, Mississippi. I appreciated then and appreciate now that he is from the Mississippi *culture* that spawned the blues.

He's not a kid and not a novelty anymore. He has matured into an articulate, confident, highly skilled guitar player, singer, and entertainer. He has a modern style, but it's always deeply rooted in the blues. He has risen to great heights, touring and recording with Buddy Guy and Keb Mo as well as headlining his own shows; he has won a Grammy and was even featured in an interview on *60 Minutes*; his CDs and LPs on Alligator Records have received great acclaim.

Kingfish is a bright light in the blues sphere, and we can expect lots more great things from him.

These photos are from the 2010 Juke Joint Festival and six years later on the same stage for the Sunflower River Festival in 2016.

Frank Frost

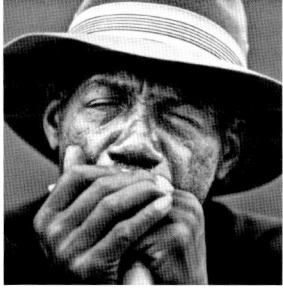

Delta blues singer and multi-instrumentalist (piano, organ, guitar, harmonica) Frank Frost lived a life that began and ended in Arkansas, but he got around in between. He started on piano in church, later switching to guitar. As a teenager he toured with drummer Sam Carr and slide guitar legend Robert Nighthawk (Carr's father). After that, he toured with Sonny Boy Williamson 2, who taught him harmonica, the instrument he became best known for. Later, Frost recorded "Hey Boss Man" and "My Back Scratcher" for the legendary producer Sam Phillips. Another record followed on Jewel, and Frost, Carr, and Big Jack Johnson gigged regionally throughout the 1970s. Late in the decade, Michael Frank recorded the trio as the Jelly Roll Kings on his Earwig Label, leading to broader exposure, with festival and international gigs. Frost continued to play until just days before he passed in 1999, age sixty-three.

L. C. Ulmer

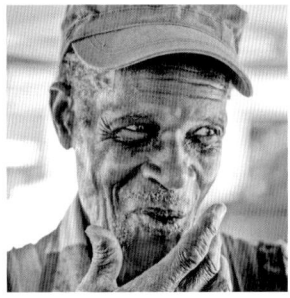

Mississippi-born one-man-band Lee Chester "L. C." Ulmer (1928–2016) traveled all around the country, working various manual-labor jobs but always playing the blues in clubs and festivals—mostly picking the guitar and singing, though he learned to play many instruments. He met a surprising number of famous people, and sat in or worked with Muddy Waters, Elmore James, Howlin' Wolf, Buddy Guy, Hound Dog Taylor, Jimmy Reed, and Sonny Thompson.

He returned to Mississippi in 2001, performing mostly locally but also in other states and even abroad.

You can't see it here, but he wore three or four wristwatches and had lengthy explanations of why he needed each one.

This photo also appears in my book *Blues Hands*. Even though he is obviously old and weathered, there's a youthful, impish, mischievous quality about him that I hope I caught here. L. C. died at his home in Ellisville, age eighty-seven.

This photo is form the Juke Joint Festival in Clarksdale, Mississippi, April 2010.

Delta Blues Cartel

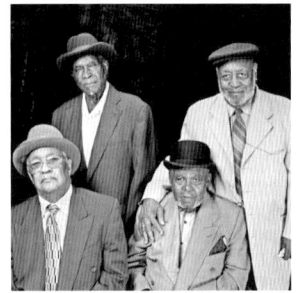

I chose this image of the Delta Blues Cartel consisting of David "Honeyboy" Edwards, Robert Lockwood Jr., "Homesick" James Williamson, and Henry Townsend to close the Mississippi chapter of this book. They were all born in the deep south and were, along with Joe Willie "Pinetop" Perkins and Sunnyland Slim, among the last surviving Delta blues men of note to have made the transition from rural Mississippi blues to urban modern blues. When I look back on this, it was an honor to have met and spent time with them, let alone to have photographed them. They are history. They are the blues.

Big Jack Johnson

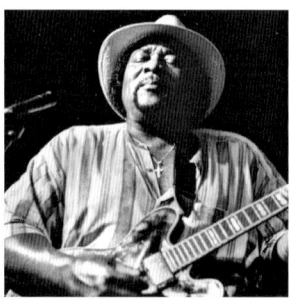

One of my favorite blues memories was seeing Big Jack Johnson—a mainstay of the Mississippi Delta electric-blues scene—in Red's Juke Joint in Clarksdale one Saturday night after Thanksgiving. The audience was mostly Jack's family and other locals. He was playing electric mandolin. His cousin James "Super Chikan" Johnson showed up, plugged in a homemade diddly-bow guitar, and played it with a slide—and the wheels left the pavement! An amazing evening.

From his time with the Jelly Roll Kings (with Frank Frost and Sam Carr) to a great solo career, Mr. Johnson kept it real with deep Delta blues feeling and often-heartfelt topical lyrics. He was nicknamed "the Oil Man" after his day job driving a fuel delivery truck; that became the title of his first album, in 1987. Big Jack died in 2011, age seventy.

Roosevelt "Booba" Barnes

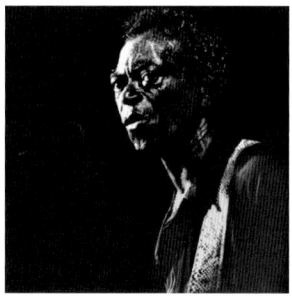

Blues vocalist, harmonica player, and electric guitarist Roosevelt Melvin "Booba" Barnes was born in Longwood, Mississippi, in 1936. He got his start in music in 1960 in the Swinging Gold Coasters, a local outfit. He relocated to Chicago in 1964, where he played in bars and clubs, but returned to Mississippi in 1971 and performed locally into the early 1980s. In 1984, Barnes and teenage electric guitarist and singer Lil' Dave Thompson began playing as a duo on Mississippi's juke joint circuit.

Barnes—an over-the-top onstage showman—opened the Playboy Club in Greenville in 1985 and played there with a backing group called the Playboys, who soon recorded for Rooster Blues Records.

I spent a great afternoon with him and the late John Campbell the day this photo was taken.

R. L. Boyce

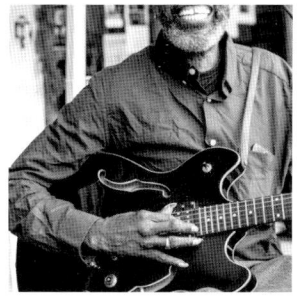

Robert L. Boyce was a Grammy nominated singer, songwriter, and guitarist from Como, Mississippi. He was from the Hill Country school and style of blues. He played with and was mentored by many of the originators of the genre including R. L. Burnside and Mississippi Fred McDowell. He got his start in the 1960s playing drums for his uncle, the master of Mississippi fife and drum music Othar Turner. Later he was the drummer for another Hill Country legend, Jessie Mae Hemphill. He was named a NEA National Heritage Fellow in 2023. R. L. held an annual picnic in Como which was always a blast and a destination for blues lovers from the world over. He is featured is in several documentaries and has a deep recorded legacy. His music was real, unaffected, deep blues. This photo is from Clarksdale, Mississippi, 2019. It is cropped to a square from the left to right, but uncropped top to bottom. Sadly, he passed in 2023.

Cedell Davis

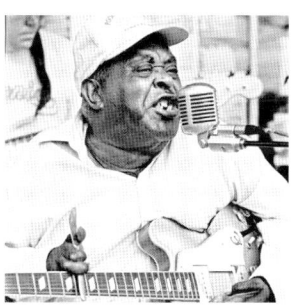

From a far end of the guitar spectrum, raw and real, comes the Delta blues artist Cedell Davis, a true blues SURVIVOR. Polio had left him with a deformed hand, and a nightclub accident—a police raid caused a stampede in which his legs were broken—left him in a wheelchair, so he taught himself to use a kitchen knife as a slide, developed a unique guitar style, and carried on.

Part of Delta legend Robert Nighthawk's band in the 1950s and 1960s, he gained greater exposure and recognition with the 1994 album *Feel Like Doin' Something Wrong*, produced by *New York Times* music critic Robert Palmer. He continued to perform until shortly before he passed in 2017, though a stroke limited him to singing.

In this photo, that's Lightnin Malcolm backing Cedell at a juke joint festival in Clarksdale, Mississippi.

Leo "Bud" Welch

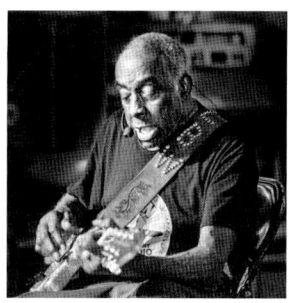

Born in Sabougla, Mississippi, in 1932, Leo "Bud" Welch learned guitar, fiddle, and harmonica while working in a sawmill. After a long stint playing gospel locally and regionally, his second musical career—in the blues—began when he was in his eighties with the album *Sabougla Voices*, released in 2014. That led to touring nationally and internationally and a new celebrity in his home state. There is a great documentary that tells his story, *Late Blossom Blues: The Journey of Leo "Bud" Welch*.

His music was deep and genuine. This is one of my favorite blues photos, taken of Mr. Welch at Red's Lounge, Clarksdale, Mississippi. To quote my friend and Mr. Welch's friend, Roger Stolle, "There's nothing more blues than Bud Welch at Red's."

Welch died in 2017, age eighty-five, at his home in Bruce, less than 25 miles up the road from his birthplace in Sabougla.

R. L. Burnside

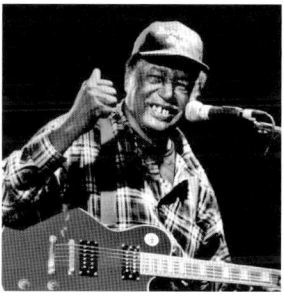

Mississippi isn't all delta, and neither is the Mississippi blues. Hailing from the Hill Country in the north of the state, singer, songwriter, and guitarist R. L. Burnside (1926–2005) took the regional music he learned from his neighbor, slide guitar master Fred McDowell, to the whole wide world.

Early in his career, he stayed close to home in Holly Springs, playing locally and recording mostly for field recordings and European labels. But his appearance in *Deep Blues* (1992), from filmmaker Robert Mugge and music writer/critic Robert Palmer, gave him wider exposure and recognition and led to better gigs and touring opportunities.

His live shows were a joy, keeping the dancers moving with the highly rhythmic almost hypnotic groove of the Hill Country.

The Burnside clan has continued his legacy representing Hill Country Mississippi, most notably his grandson Cedric Burnside.

Sam Carr

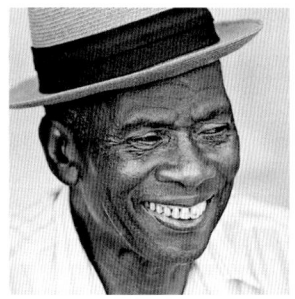

Known for the simplicity of his drum kit—snare drum, bass drum, and high-hat cymbal—Sam Carr was the heartbeat of the Mississippi Delta.

The son of Delta blues legend Robert Nighthawk, with whom he performed and toured, Carr also kept the beat for the Jelly Roll Kings (with Frank Frost and Big Jack Johnson), Sonnyboy Williamson 2, and many more. Born in Arkansas and raised in Mississippi, he did leave for Chicago and then St. Louis, but the Delta was his home and his sound. He returned to Mississippi in 1962. In later years, he lived in Lula, Mississippi, and became a beloved elder statesman, recording with Buddy Guy (*Sweet Tea*, 2001) and being featured in Martin Scorsese's documentary *The Blues: Feel Like Going Home* (2003). Sam Carr died in 2009 at age eighty-three.

T-Model Ford

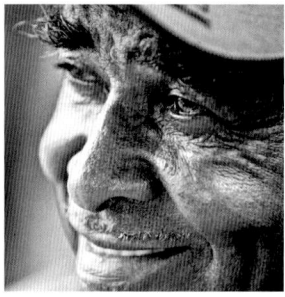

James Lewis Carter Ford, a.k.a. T-Model Ford, was a true Delta blues character and a real-deal bluesman. Unschooled, illiterate, entirely self-taught, he developed his own raw, hypnotic style: singing, hollering, joking, and playing his electric guitar so idiosyncratically, he was said to be "in the key of T," the *New York Times* obituary reported.

He took up music late in life, though his exact age was always in doubt, as were other aspects of his life. He had worked as a lumberman and other blue-collar jobs and served time on a chain gang for murder. That was all before he taught himself to play a gift electric guitar well enough to get gigs in the most basic of local juke joints. But he started to attract wider attention and eventually made a series of recordings that are as rough and raw as he was, starting with "Pee-Wee Get My Gun" in 1997.

A self-professed ladies' man with a fondness for Jack Daniels, he could be friendly or cantankerous as his moods shifted, people who traveled with him said, but I always had a good time with him. I'm glad our paths crossed. He was one of a kind.

Little Richard

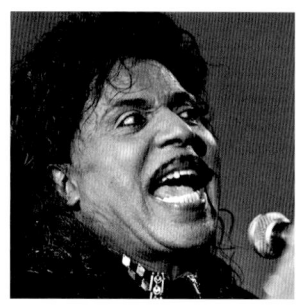

Richard Wayne Penniman (1932–2020), better known as Little Richard, was the "Architect of Rock & Roll." There never was and never will be anyone like him. He changed the world.

Little Richard was inspired to make music his career after his idol Sister Rosetta Tharpe—the guitar-slinging gospel star who would become known as the "Godmother of Rock and Roll"—heard the fourteen-year-old boy singing (he had a part-time job selling Coca-Cola at the Macon, Georgia, auditorium where she was appearing), invited him to open for her, and, afterward, paid him!

Two years later, he left home and a disapproving, abusive father. He toured with traveling minstrel shows, often appearing in drag, and on the road he saw and heard and was influenced by many performers; among the most influential were Billy Wright and Esquerita (Eskew Reeder Jr.), whose frenetic style, outrageous looks—heavy makeup and a towering pompadours—and overall flamboyance were a precursor to Richard's act and persona.

He made records for RCA and Duke, but his career didn't really take off until, at the suggestion of singer Lloyd Price, he sent a demo to Specialty Records. The L.A. label signed him and got him to record in New Orleans with producer Bumps Blackwell, who hired a songwriter to clean up some of the risqué, sexual lyrics that Little Richard sang in one of his "dirty blues" tunes—and the rest is, as they say, history: "Tutti Frutti" (1955) took off in both the R&B and pop realms.

This led to a long string of hits including "Long Tall Sally," "Slippin' and Slidin'," "Rip It Up," "Ready Teddy," "Lucille," and more. His success was huge and led to constant domestic and international touring. It was during a 1957 tour of Australia that Richard shocked the world by giving up rock and roll and saying he would sing only gospel, in the service of the Lord. He entered a Seventh Day Adventist college to study theology. He released several gospel LPs, which had some success, but nothing like his secular music.

It was at a 1962 London show that Little Richard returned to rock and roll. Opener Sam Cooke, who had left gospel to find great pop success, was thrilling the audience, and Richard, not to be outdone, sang "Long Tall Sally" and brought down the house—fans rushed the stage and forced an early closing.

He returned to secular music, and as time passed, his career regained momentum and he began to be recognized as the star and creative force that he was, an influence on generations of rock-and-roll singers—Paul McCartney, for one—and showmen—Prince, for another.

He was, like fellow rock-and-roll titan Chuck Berry and too many other artists, embittered over his financial treatment by the music industry; he sued Specialty Records and eventually received a major settlement.

Similarly, he rightfully felt that his world-changing talents were not recognized properly. There is a 2023 PBS documentary titled *I Am*

Everything that explores his place in history, his music, and his sexuality. It is highly recommended.

Antoine "Fats" Domino

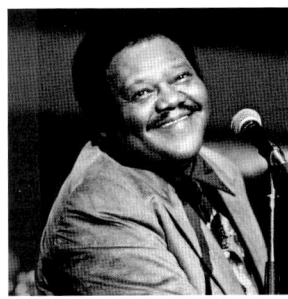

Born and raised in the lower Ninth Ward of New Orleans, with Creole French his first language, Antoine Domino by his early teens was already playing in local bars—solo and with bands. He eventually came to the attention of Imperial Records, and, beginning in 1949, Fats had a long string of hits, produced by the great Dave Bartholomew.

One of the first artists to cross over from rhythm and blues to pop in a big way, Domino's songs such as "Blueberry Hill" and "Ain't That a Shame" became part of the fabric of American music and culture, finding success with white and Black audiences alike. Elvis Presley considered him the real king of rock and roll and said that Domino was a huge influence on him when he started out.

Domino eventually had thirty-seven Top 40 singles, though none made it to number one on the pop charts—Pat Boone's watered-down cover of "Ain't That a Shame" beat him out to the top of the charts.

Domino's easygoing, warm, nonthreatening personality was reflected in his music. Always heavily infused with the spirit of New Orleans, it could be hard-rocking or mellow, but there was always a certain sweetness that I hope I captured in this photograph.

This photo is from 1991 at the Municipal Auditorium, New Orleans, Louisiana.

Chuck Berry

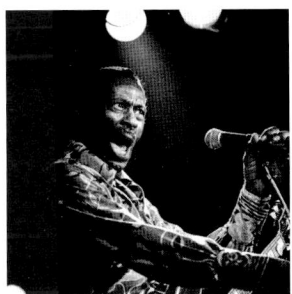

For me, Charles Edward Anderson Berry—Chuck Berry—was and always will be the king of rock and roll.

His first hit in 1955 was "Maybellene," based on a Western swing song by Bob Wills, "Ida Red." It was a blend of blues and hillbilly sounds, with insightful, youth-oriented lyrics, an infectious beat, and great guitar. It hit number one on the rhythm-and-blues chart and number five on the pop chart. "Maybellene" was fresh and different, and not easily categorized. There was often confusion among radio programmers and concert promoters about where to slot the music—and the man. Was it

R&B—was he Black? Was it hillbilly—was he white? But whatever it was, people loved it, and Chuck followed with a long string of hits: "Johnny B. Goode," "No Money Down," "Carol," Sweet Little Sixteen," "Rock & Roll Music," No Particular Place to Go," "Memphis, Tennessee," Nadine," "Brown Eyed Handsome Man," and so many more.

Jerry Lee Lewis quoted his mother as saying, "Now you and Elvis are pretty good, but you ain't Chuck Berry." John Lennon said, "If you tried to give rock and roll another name, you might call it 'Chuck Berry.'" And Bob Dylan called him "the Shakespeare of rock & roll."

He was an intelligent and highly complex man, and along with his hits and successes, his life was fraught with legal and personal troubles. The rewards he received were never equal to his talent and contributions. He was a poet of the people, and his music changed the world.

Jerry Lee Lewis

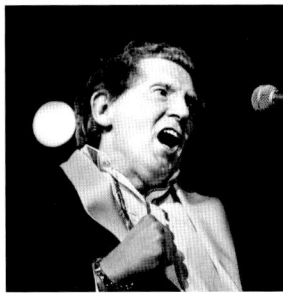

Jerry Lee Lewis, rock and roll's original wild man, started out in music with gospel, even attending a bible institute briefly. But he could not NOT play "sinful" music, tormenting though it was to him at times.

His first hit was a cover of a country song, "Crazy Arms," which he recorded at Sun Studios in Memphis in 1956; "Crazy Arms" sold 300,000 copies, mostly in the South.

But it was a frenzied remake of an R&B tune recorded by Big Maybelle—"Whole Lotta Shakin' Going On"—that brought Lewis fame and a young rock-and-roll audience. Sometimes billed as "Jerry Lee Lewis and His Pumping Piano," he went on to record a string of hits such as the suggestive "Great Balls of Fire," "Breathless," "High School Confidential," and more.

His live performances were energetic and outrageous: He would toss his long hair around, kick aside his piano bench, pound the keys, sit and stand on the piano.

His career looked like it might be over in 1958, when it came to light that the twenty-two-year-old had married his thirteen-year-old cousin, his third marriage already (there would be four more), but after some struggles he managed to put together a long second act in country music until he had to cancel all his scheduled shows due to a stroke in 2019. He left us in 2022, age eighty-seven.

Jerry Lee Lewis thus was the longest-surviving member of Sun Records' "Million Dollar Quartet," outliving Elvis Presley, Johnny Cash, and Carl Perkins.

Big Joe Turner

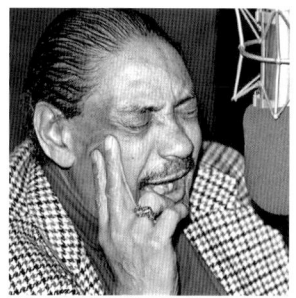

Big Joe Turner (1911–85) was a GIANT of American music. It's hard to categorize an artist of his scope and longevity, from boogie-woogie and jump blues (and Kansas City jazz and rhythm and blues) to the birth of rock and roll.

Joseph Vernon Turner Jr. was born in Kansas City and was singing in the streets and nightclubs there by his early teens. But it was in New York City that he started to gain a wider audience a decade later, and in the 1940s he helped lay the groundwork for R&B (along with Louis Jordan and a few others), and in the 1950s he did the same for rock and roll with his early Atlantic sides such as "Honey Hush," "Shake Rattle and Roll," and "Flip, Flop, Fly."

In the early 1980s, Big Joe did a few extended gigs at the original Tramps nightclub in New York City. Doc Pomus, who wrote many of Joe's hits and was his dear friend, was always there. Ahmet Ertegun, a founder of Atlantic Records, would drop by; always a special occasion.

I had the honor and pleasure of shooting the photos for the *Blues Train* album that Big Joe and Roomful of Blues made, with Dr. John guesting, produced by Doc Pomus and Bob Porter.

Even though the session lasted only a few hours, being there and hearing the tunes come together in the hands of these pros was a highlight of my musical adventure. At one point, after his vocals were recorded, Joe was asked if he wanted to leave the studio. He replied, "No, I'll stay here and listen to these guys play."

Later, outside the studio on the street, Big Joe was leaning against a large planter. Ronnie Earl of Roomful and I approached to say goodbye, and Joe pitched forward and started to fall. Ronnie broke his fall and was momentarily pinned under his weight. Joe had passed out. 911 was called, the police arrived, and once they realized he was ill, not drunk, they were great. Joe was taken to the hospital, where he was rehydrated and stabilized. Doc Pomus, who was waiting in the room, told me that when Joe awoke and saw him, he said from his bed, "Doc, let's get some chicken!"

Bo Diddley

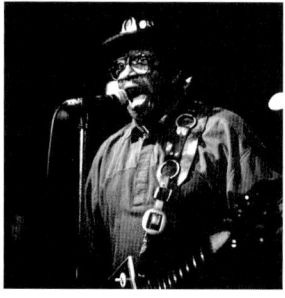

Guitarist, singer, songwriter, and bandleader Bo Diddley—Ellas Otha Bates (1928–2008)—was one of the inventors of electric-guitar-based rock and roll.

Mississippi born and Chicago raised, as a teen he and his friends livened their street corner performances with jokes and insults that would later make their way into his live performances and records, often with longtime pal and maracas player Jerome Green.

At the forefront of the transition of electric guitar blues and R&B into rock and roll in the 1950s and early 1960s, he had a string of hits on Chess/Checker records, driven by his signature Bo Diddley beat—basically a five-note Latin/Caribbean/African rhythm—including "Bo Diddley," a number one R&B hit; "I'm a Man"; "Pretty Thing"; "Who Do You Love"; "Say Man"; "Mona"; and "You Can't Judge a Book by the Cover." Albums included *Bo Diddley Is a Gunslinger* and *Have Guitar, Will Travel*.

Bo also designed and built electronic gear and guitars, often with unusual boxy shapes, and experimented with heavy tremolo and distortion in his performances and recordings.

He featured talented female players in his later bands, with great stage names such as the Duchess, Lady Bo, and Cookie V.

The number of artists who have covered or were influenced by his music is beyond counting but includes the Beatles, the Rolling Stones, Buddy Holly, Jimi Hendrix, the Who, Parliament Funkadelic, the Velvet Underground, and the Clash, and his influence extended into such genres as reggae and rap.

This photo was taken at Tramps in New York City, 1992.

Hank Ballard

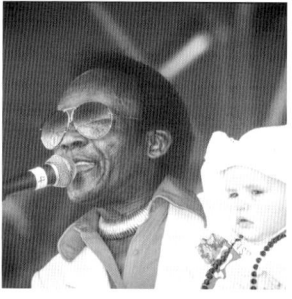

Rock and rollers and twist dancers everywhere owe a lot to seminal R&B artist Hank Ballard. His music is at the foundation of Black rock and roll.

Born John Henry Kendricks (1927–2003), Hank Ballard, like many of his contemporaries, first sang gospel, then transitioned to doo-wop and R&B. He and his group the Midnighters became a mainstay of Federal/King Records of Cincinnati (home of James Brown, Freddie King, Little Willie John, the 5 Royales, Wynonie Harris, and so many more). Their first hit came in 1954 with "Work with Me, Annie," considered very risqué at the time—but nothing compared to the follow-up, "Annie Had a Baby." That song was too scandalous for a lot of radio stations, and they refused to play it, but it spawned several answer songs (notably "The Wallflower" by Etta James). Plus, the notoriety of the "Annie" songs helped a new audience among white teens find the sexy, rebellious new music that was starting to form.

At the 1996 Newport R&B Festival, when Hank did the tune, he left the stage briefly and reappeared with, what else, a BABY! The crowd went nuts.

Ballard also had the original version of "The Twist," in 1959. Chubby Checker covered it a year later and had the big hit (twice!), but Hank, as the writer, did reap some of the financial benefits of the dance craze the tune spawned.

Johnny Otis

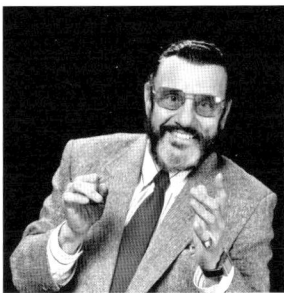

The singer, drummer, songwriter, arranger, bandleader, talent scout, disc jockey, record producer, television host, artist, author, journalist, minister, organic farmer, politician, and impresario Ioannis Alexandres Veliotes was born Greek American but chose to live and work as a Black American.

Among the stars he discovered or helped early in their careers were Etta James, Esther Phillips, Big Mama Thornton, Jackie Wilson, Little Willie John, Hank Ballard, and more, not to mention his son Shuggie.

His tune "Willie and the Hand Jive" was a huge hit. Would-be censors believed that the song was about masturbation, but Otis always insisted that it was based on a rhythm he heard sung by men on a chain gang and was about a man named Willie who danced using his hands.

I had the pleasure of spending a few heartbeats with him while he did his radio program at the Pacifica station in Berkeley, California, and at a lunch afterward while he was interviewed. He was gracious and absolutely hilarious—at one point commenting about a notorious music entrepreneur (some have said gangster), "You are supposed to say good things about the dead. GOOD! HE'S DEAD." A very fond memory. He is in both the Rock & Roll Hall of Fame and Blues Hall of Fame, and his contribution to American music and culture is vast. Photo for the Rhythm & Blues Foundation, ca. 1995.

Otis Blackwell

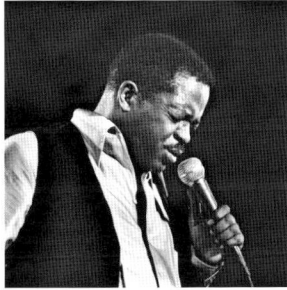

Brooklyn-born songwriter Otis Blackwell's contribution to rock and roll and American music in general was huge, and not just because he wrote for Elvis. Along with such Presley classics as "All Shook Up," "Don't Be Cruel," and "Return to Sender," he wrote "Fever" (under a pseudonym), recorded by Little Willie John, Peggy Lee, and countless others; Jerry

Lee Lewis's "Great Balls of Fire" and "Breathless," "Handy Man," done by (cowriter) Jimmy Jones, Del Shannon, James Taylor; and more.

Blackwell sang on many of the demos of his songs that were presented to Presley, so there is some debate as to whether Presley adopted Blackwell's sound or Blackwell attuned his performance to Presley's style. At this point, who can say?

The photos are from the Bottom Line, New York City, in the early 1980s. That night I found myself at a table with three songwriting giants of the blues, R&B and rock and roll: Otis Blackwell, Doc Pomus, and producer / Harlem record store owner Bobby Robinson. As they swapped jokes and stories about their music and old times, I kept my ears open and my mouth shut. An unforgettable brush with casual, hip, but unpretentious greatness.

Willie Dixon

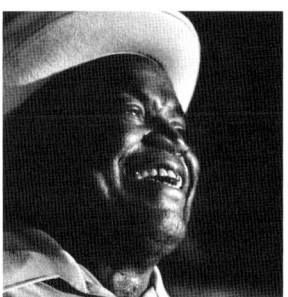

Willie Dixon was a big man, an upright bassist, vocalist, songwriter, arranger, and record producer. He flirted with a boxing career, and it has been reported that he refused military service and served jail time as an objector because he would not fight for a country with institutionalized racism.

He played with various groups including the Big Three Trio before he settled into his best-known role as an in-house songwriter, producer, session musician for Chess Records. He and Muddy Waters are the two men most responsible for shaping modern, electric blues, especially in the Chicago style.

He wrote many classic blues songs including "Hoochie Coochie Man," "I Just Want to Make Love to You," "Little Red Rooster" (the Rolling Stones first #1 hit), "My Babe," "Spoonful," and "You Can't Judge a Book by the Cover" for artists such as Muddy Waters, Howlin' Wolf, Little Walter, Bo Diddley, and more. He also produced or played on classic recordings by those artists as well as Chuck Berry, Otis Rush, Sonny Boy Williamson, Koko Taylor, Little Milton, Jimmy Witherspoon, Memphis Slim, Jimmy Rogers, and dozens more.

His catalog is vast, and his songs have been covered by hundreds of artists. In a well-known case he won a large cash settlement from Led Zeppelin over their appropriating and mis-crediting his music. He titled a song, an album and his book, *I Am The Blues*. He also coined the phrase "the Blues is the roots, everything else is the fruits." I cannot argue with either statement.

ACKNOWLEDGMENTS

Making this book was genuinely a team effort. There so many people who have helped make this book possible whom I wish to acknowledge.

First, I must thank two old friends, David Aschkenas and Gary Hill, both of whom were incredibly generous of their time, expertise, and patience: David for his invaluable effort in preparing the digital files for reproduction, and Gary for his editing and coauthoring of the biographical content of the book. I must also mention Ryan Speth, who created the initial scans of many film negatives for use in the book. This book could not have happened without them.

I am grateful to all the good folks at Schiffer Publishing, especially Peter Schiffer, Bob Biondi, and Jesse Marth, for their support, guidance, and faith in this project.

A huge vote of thanks must go to Jenny Bagert and Amanda Malone of Jenny Bagert Consulting, who guided me through both the fund raising as well as the preparation of the materials for submission to the publisher.

I must thank all the authors who wrote the appreciations and the chapter introductions. In alphabetical order, they are Scott Barretta, Steve Berkowitz, Douglas Curry, Bill Dahl, Tony Outhwaite, Lamont Jack Pearly, Billy Price, Ben Sandmel, Dick Shurman, Mark Thompson, and William Wirths. They each made individual and personal contributions that have enhanced this effort.

My deep gratitude goes to Roger Naber, CEO of the Legendary R&B Cruise, whose friendship and support through the years has helped advance both my career and this book. Thank you, captain.

There are so many others, such as Scott Burnett and Deb Lubin, who helped with the graphics and editing; Zakiya Hooker, Barbara Morgan, and Mike Kappus, who helped in making the cover possible; and Laura Carbone and Rodd Bland, who helped with photos and permissions.

Many, many others stepped up and gave of themselves. I must mention, in no particular order, Holly and Barry Walter, Donna Flaggs, Steve Wilcox, John Price, Janie Soong, Jeff Hirsch, Doug Langdon, Harry Burnett, Geoff Alexander, Shirley Mae Owens and Gimme Five, Lisa and Marc Biales, Debbie Blanchard, John Dooley, Anne and Michael Cloeren, Dale VanDerBogart, Barbara House, Tim Synan, Mona MacDonald and Jimmy McCurley Barbara Gordon, Jamie Archer, my brothers Steve and Rick, and dozens of other folks who contributed in ways big and small to create this book .

I know I will miss many names that should be included, and I hope I am forgiven for that. I am truly grateful to all.

INDEX

Allison, Luther, 138, 204

Baker, Chet, 74, 189
Baker, LaVern, 116, 200
Ballard, Hank, 170, 214
Barnes, Roosevelt "Booba," 157, 200
Bartholomew, Dave, 96, 196
Bell, Carey, 137, 206
Bell, William, 58, 186
Benson, George, 62, 187
Berry, Chuck, 168, 213
Blackwell, Otis, 172, 215
Bland, Bobby "Blue," 26, 177
Booker T. & the M.G.s, 48, 53, 182
Boyce, R. L., 158, 211
Brock, George, 150, 209
Brooks, Lonnie, 139, 208
Brown, Charles, 113, 199
Brown, Clarence "Gatemouth," 39, 175
Brown, James, 46, 183
Brown, Nappy, 125, 200
Brown, Roy "Good Rockin," 120, 200
Brown, Ruth, 122, 202
Burke, Solomon, 59, 186
Burnside, R. L.,
Butler, Henry,
Butler, Jerry,

Calloway, Cab, 70, 188
Campbell, Little Milton, 135, 207
Carr, Sam, 159, 212

Carter, Betty, 67, 188
Cedell, Davis, 154, 211
Charles, Ray, 45, 180
Chavis, Boozoo, 100, 196
Chenier, Clifton, 93, 194
Clapton, Eric, 145, 204
Collins, Albert, 132, 203
Copeland, Johnny, 133, 203
Crawford, Hank, 77, 189
Cray, Robert, 146, 206

Delta Blues Cartel, 163, 210
Diddley, Bo, 168, 214
Dixon, Willie, 40, 215
Doggett, Bill, 114, 199
Domino, Antoine "Fats," 166, 213
Dopsie, Rockin', 108, 194
Dupree, "Champion" Jack, 37, 177

Eaglin, Fird "Snooks," 99, 198
Edwards, David "Honeyboy," 29, 178, 210

Ford, T-Model, 161, 212
Fran, Carol, 104, 196
Francis, David "Panama," 76, 191
Franklin, Aretha, 43, 180
Frost, Frank, 160, 209

Gillespie, Dizzy, 61, 186
Gordon, Dexter, 64, 287
Green, Al, 52, 181
Guy, Buddy, 127, 128, 202

Hammond, John Jr., 130, 203
Hibbler, Al, 73, 188
Holmes Brothers, The, 138, 208
Hooker, John Lee, 17, 174
Hopkins, Lightnin', 23, 175

Ingram, Christone "Kingfish," 152, 209

Jackson, Chuck, 49, 182
Jacquet, Illinois, 78, 189
James, Etta, 56, 183
Johnson, Big Jack, 153, 210

K-Doe, Ernie, 104, 197
King, Albert, 18, 174
King, B.B., 24, 176
King, Ben E., 47, 181
King, Earl, 110, 195

Latimore, Benny, 139, 206
LaVette, Bettye, 51, 181
Lewis, Jerry Lee,
Little Richard, 169, 213
Lockwood Jr., Robert, 34, 179
Louisiana Red, 35, 205
Love, Darlene, 55, 182

Martino, Pat, 82, 192
McCracklin, Jimmy, 123, 201
McGriff, Jimmy, 80, 190
McShann, Jay, 79, 190
Memphis Slim, 33, 179
Musselwhite, Charlie, 136, 206

Neville, Aaron, 88, 193
Neville, Art, 103, 195
Newman, David "Fathead," 75, 189

Otis, Johnny, 171, 215

Palmer, Earl, 98, 197
Parker, Bobby, 27, 177
Pass, Joe, 81, 191
Paul, Les, 66, 187
Perkins, Joe Willie "Pinetop," 30, 179
Phillips, Esther, 117, 201
Pickett, Wilson, 58, 180
Price, Lloyd, 105, 198
Puente, Tito, 68, 192

Rawls, Johnny, 140, 207
Rebennack, Mac "Dr. John," 72, 92, 111, 197
Ruffins, Kermit, 94, 194
Rush, Otis, 42, 204

Scott, Little Jimmy, 71, 191
Seals, Son, 141, 208
Shines, Johnny, 35, 178
Simien, Terrance, 107, 199
Sinegal, Paul "Lil Buck," 106, 198
Staples, Roebuck "Pops," 50, 185
Stitt, Sonny, 83, 192
Stone, Jess (a.k.a. Charles Calhoun), 173, 205

Sumlin, Hubert, 138, 207
Sunnyland Slim, 36, 179

Taylor, Koko, 40, 175
Thomas, Carla, 54, 182
Thomas, Irma, 87, 193
Thornton, Willie Mae "Big Mama," 38, 176
Toussaint, Allen, 109, 195
Townsend, Henry, 28, 178
Turner, Big Joe, 171, 214
Turner, Ike, 41, 176
Turner, Othar, 149, 209
Turrentine, Stanley, 84, 192

Ulmer, L. C., 149, 210

Van Ronk, Dave, 143, 204

Washington Jr., Grover, 69, 188
Washington, Walter "Wolfman," 101, 199
Waters, Muddy, 20, 174
Welch, Leo "Bud," 155, 211
Wells, Junior, 131, 202
Williams, Andre, 120, 201
Williams, Joe, 85, 191
Williams, Paul, 121, 201
Williamson, "Homesick" James, 28, 178
Winter, Johnny, 144, 204
Witherspoon, Jimmy, 72, 190

Zydeco, Buckwheat, 97, 196